The
KNIGHTS ERRANT
OF
ANARCHY

London and the Italian Anarchist Diaspora (1880–1917)

PIETRO DI PAOLA

This edition of *The Knights Errant of Anarchy* is published by arrangement with Liverpool University Press, publisher of the 2013 hardback edition, and the author.

This edition © 2017 AK Press (Chico, Oakland, Edinburgh, Baltimore)

ISBN: 978-1-84935-298-7
Library of Congress Control Number: 2017936245

AK Press	AK Press
370 Ryan Ave. #100	33 Tower St.
Chico, CA 95973	Edinburgh EH6 7BN
USA	Scotland
www.akpress.org	www.akuk.com
akpress@akpress.org	ak@akedin.demon.co.uk

The above addresses would be delighted to provide you with the latest AK Press distribution catalog, which features books, pamphlets, zines, and stylish apparel published and/or distributed by AK Press. Alternatively, visit our websites for the complete catalog, latest news, and secure ordering.

Printed in the USA on acid-free, recycled paper

Cover art by Flavio Costantini
Errico Malatesta and Michele Angiolillo. London, July 1896, 1971
Courtesy Archivio Flavio Costantini, Genova

Typeset by Carnegie Book Production, Lancaster

Contents

List of Abbreviations

ACS	Archivio Centrale dello Stato, Rome
AL	Ambasciata di Londra
Asdmae	Archivio Storico e Diplomatico Ministero degli Affari Esteri, Rome
b.	Box
CPC	Ministero degli Interni, Casellario Politico Centrale
CRIM	Criminal Court of Justice
f.	Folder
NA	National Archive, London
HO	Home Office
Pol. Int.	Polizia Internazionale
PS	Ministero degli Interni, Divisione Generale di Pubblica Sicurezza
IISH	International Institute of Social History, Amsterdam

List of Illustrations

Acknowledgments

I would like to thank a number of people for having contributed in various ways to the preparation of this work. Carl Levy, for his indispensable advice throughout my research. Piero Brunello and Claudia Baldoli for their continuous encouragement, intellectual stimulation, and precious suggestions. Special thanks to Megan Trudell for her invaluable helpfulness and promptness in the proofreading of the manuscript. Stimulating discussions with Constance Bantman, Richard Jensen, and Davide Turcato enriched my views on various aspects of the anarchist diaspora. Valentina Scolari kindly provided me with valuable materials; Bruno Manfroni Lampo gave me useful information on a number of anarchists. I would like to thanks my colleagues at the School of Humanities, University of Lincoln for their support and help; Mieke Ijzermans and all the staff at the International Institute of Social History for their help during my research in Amsterdam. I am very grateful to Anna Costantini and the Archivio Flavio Costantini for allowing the use of Costantini's painting on the cover. Thanks to Elisabetta Farioli and the Musei di Reggio Emilia for the permission of including Luigi Parmeggiani's picture in the text. Thanks to Peter Eade, Sebastian Lexer and all 97 St Asaph Road for their support and friendship. Finally, special thanks to my family in Italy: Costantino, Velica, Ruggero, Davide, Niccolò, Chiara and Bruno.

Introduction to the Second Edition

Since the first edition of this book in 2013, the United Kingdom has gone through dramatic changes. Brexit has completely transformed the social and political landscape of the country. Petty nationalism has re-emerged as a ruling force; there has been an upsurge in racial and hate crimes. Frontiers and borders have reinforced their power, both real and symbolic. Even the reception of a few hundred vulnerable lone-child refugees has sparked political controversy. In such a discouraging panorama this book, if nothing else, can be a reminder that this has not always been the case, that things have been and can be different.

The right to asylum for economic and political migrants was a core value in nineteenth-century Britain. Thanks to an indiscriminate policy of free entry into the country, thousands of anarchist militants were able to find refuge from persecution and continue their struggles for equality and social justice. Among them there were many Italians, who are the subject of this study. The book reconstructs their daily lives and their social, cultural and political activities. One of the difficulties encountered during the research for this book was the impossibility of following the innumerable threads (militants, organisations, ideas) that converged on London and/or departed from there. The resultant frustration was the most immediate and almost physical perception of the fact that, in the late nineteenth century, London was one of the main nodes of a network of anarchist communities that spread across continents, connected by an uninterrupted flow of individuals and ideas. In recent years this network has been the focus of many works that have adopted a transnational approach in the study of the history of the anarchist movement. Some of these have reconstructed the experiences of anarchist exiles in specific locations: the United States, South America, the Middle East. I have found information in these works that has made it possible to retire some of the threads that had to be cut during my research.

One of the positive effects of the challenges in studying anarchism as a transnational movement is that it encourages collaboration and the sharing of information among scholars.

These studies have provided an opportunity for fruitful comparisons that are indispensable for understanding the complex dynamics of the history of anarchist exiles and the anarchist movement more generally. There are significant similarities and differences in the ways in which anarchist communities developed; for example, the level of discrimination that migrant communities experienced in host countries and the degree of assimilation into the domestic labour movement or the success in recruiting new affiliates.

Other works have raised methodological and conceptual questions about the problematic relationships in these studies between local, national and transnational scales of analyses. Some of these reflections stem from the analysis of relations between the various anarchist centres, between political militants and economic migrants and between political exiles and the labour and radical movements in the host countries. These reflections are linked to the challenges that have been posed to a dominant Western-centric perspective on the study of anarchism. These challenges have underlined the importance of expanding the horizon of anarchist studies to the colonial and post-colonial world. The anarchist and syndicalist movements made significant contributions to anti-imperial and anti-colonial struggles. However, the studies of anarchist communities in exile also raise the question of the extent to which anarchist militants were able to escape from internalised racial stereotypes. For example, in the Italian case, some of these stereotypes emerge in the motivations to oppose the invasion of Libya in 1911, or in anarchist militants' attitudes toward native workers in Egypt.

One of the main activities that Italian anarchists involved themselves in was the publication of newspapers and other propaganda materials, which kept their voices heard abroad as well as in their motherland. Newspapers were one of the main instruments through which anarchist exiles shared information, disseminated a radical culture, debated ideas, shaped identities, and reinforced organisational ties. They provide vital information for the reconstruction of the anarchist networks and the development and discussion of anarchist ideas. As a consequence, they are attracting increasing attention from researchers crossing disciplinary boundaries between historical and media studies. This is another potentially positive aspect of the 'transnational turn' in anarchist studies. The broad range of themes and aspects that can be considered when dealing with the transnational history of anarchism induces engagement with other disciplines (migration studies, colonial and post-colonial studies, cultural studies, media studies) with mutual benefits. On the one hand, applying other disciplines' methodologies to the history of the anarchist movement will enrich it by bringing new approaches and perspectives; on the other, it will make anarchism, its history and its significance more present in other fields of research.

This book was born as an academic publication. Higher education and the university system are also going through dramatic changes. The rise of tuition fees in England, now the highest in Europe, and the consequent competition between institutions to attract students for financial survival – the implementation of consumer law in higher education, which has sanctioned the logic that universities are not promoting knowledge but selling a product – has transformed the role and daily life of academics. There is no doubt that the transmission of knowledge from academia to the outside world has always been difficult and is becoming even more problematic. To comply with increasing expectations and to secure their positions, most academics must be strategic regarding what and where to publish their research, aiming for highly rated publishers. A common outcome is that the high cost of hardback books makes the distribution of these works quite limited. It is, therefore, a pleasure for me to have a new paperback edition of my work produced by AK Press, a publisher that is continuing the struggle for 'the sharing of knowledge, history and information' and 'the long tradition of getting the word out by any means necessary' – just as the Italian anarchists did during their long years of exile in London.

Pietro Di Paola, June 2017

Introduction

Amsterdam, 5 July 1895

My dearest,

[...] I did not want to talk about it, but this rebellious nostalgia for cherished friends from whom I am separated by so much uncertainty and, soon, by the widening vastness of the sea jumps from my pen. I did not wish to describe, my dear Edoardo, my deep feelings when I parted from you and the affectionate Razzia. At the moment of boarding, you represented the unforgettable Italian camaraderie to me. Because it is easy to consider yourself cosmopolitan by principle, but feeling has its own imperious laws [...] It is not easy to leave the loyal comrades of the first struggles, those with whom I cheerfully shared the harshness of an Odyssey, without a storm of memories and sadness pouring into the heart. [...] Send my best wishes and my friendship to the good and kind comrades Rossetti, to the good Razzia, to Baracchi, Pacini, Malatesta, Cini, Cambi, Borghesani, Bonometti, Petraroia, Protti and finally to all, all without exclusion, the good and true comrades: Italian, English and from other countries who keep some memory of me. [...] Consider this letter addressed to you as written to everybody. Two more people to whom you will give my dearest regards: Kropotkin and Nettlau. Now I have truly finished.

With love,

Yours, Pietro Gori[1]

Gori, 'the knight of the Ideal', wrote this letter shortly after his departure from London where he lived for several months following his expulsion from Switzerland. He worked as a sailor on a steamer and a number of fortuitous

---

[1] Pietro Gori to Edoardo Milano, Amsterdam, 5 July 1895, IISH, Nettlau archive, f.2793.

circumstances (a storm forced the captain to change course) allowed him to secretly disembark with his inseparable guitar in New York.[2] From there he conducted a propaganda tour across the United States in which he delivered more than 400 lectures in a year; it was through these tours that radicals 'could bring their message to even the most remote immigrant outposts.'[3] In summer 1896 he returned to London where he attended the International Socialist Workers and Trade Union Congress. Stricken by tuberculosis, after two months in hospital he managed to return to Italy where he continued his militancy.[4]

Gori was just one of the many Italian anarchists who conducted their political activity in exile, wandering throughout Europe and overseas.

These peregrinations were part of the long tradition of political exile that characterised the history of Italian socialism from its beginning until the fall of Fascism and the end of the Second World War. Since the *Risorgimento*, the most charismatic exponents of Italian socialism spent long periods of their lives in foreign countries. Giuseppe Mazzini, who was forced to live in exile for about thirty years, embodies the figure of the Italian political refugee. However, almost all the principal leaders of Italian socialism and a myriad of lesser-known activists shared the same lot. According to Gabaccia's analysis of 411 biographies collected in Franco Andreucci and Tommaso Detti's *Il movimento operaio*: 'Over a third of Italy's most prominent pre-war labour activists fled into exile one or more times. Except for a handful, all were men. Anarchist exiles made up 57 percent of these in the 1870s, 63 percent in the 1880s, and 21 percent in the 1890s. During the 1890s and early 1900s, socialist exiles increased rapidly to 74 percent.'[5] In 1911, of the 17,728 subversives recorded by the police (the centralised recording service began in 1894) 1,854 (about 10 percent) were living abroad. Some 590 could not be found; it is not unlikely that a good number of those had also left Italy.[6]

Nineteenth-century exile had a remarkable influence on the development of socialist ideas in Italy and in other countries; one of its most important consequences was the dissemination of revolutionary ideas in Europe and overseas.[7] Indeed, the socialism of various schools was forged mostly in the world of expatriates following the migration routes, first in Europe and

---

[2] Pietro Gori to Edoardo Milano, Paterson, 6 August 1895, IISH, Nettlau archive, f. 2793.

[3] Marcella Bencivenni, *Italian Immigrant Radical Culture: The Idealism of the* Sovversivi *in the United States, 1890–1940* (New York: New York University Press, 2011), p. 54.

[4] Maurizio Antonioli and Franco Bertolucci, 'Pietro Gori. Una vita per l'ideale', in M. Antonioli and F. Bertolucci (eds), *Pietro Gori, La miseria e i delitti* (Pisa: BFS, 2011), pp. 83–87.

[5] Donna Gabaccia, *Italy's Many Diasporas* (London: UCL Press, 2000), p. 109.

[6] Francesco Fantini, 'Origine e scopo del servizio schedario', 8 July 1911, in ACS, *PS*, 'Massime', f. 1.

[7] George Haupt, 'Il ruolo degli emigrati e dei rifugiati nella diffusione delle idee socialiste

then to the Americas.[8] This process, combined with economic migration, was pivotal to the development of anarchism as a political organisation, indeed, 'only mass migration and a dense circulation of working-class people could diffuse anarchism not as a set of ideas but as a mass social movement with dedicated structures.'[9] Exile continued to affect profoundly the Italian Socialist and Communist parties and the libertarian movement in the first half of the twentieth century; many leaders of left-wing organisations matured politically during the anti-Fascist emigration, and this experience influenced their activity after the war.[10]

Italian anarchists played a central role in this process. By the early twentieth century they were, together with Spaniards and Jews, the main vector of dissemination of diasporic anarchism around the world.[11]

Italian anarchists spread their activities over most European countries, as well as in the United States, in Argentina, in Brazil, in Egypt, in Tunisia and in the Balkans.[12] Giuseppe Fanelli introduced Bakuninism to Spain where he organised the first section of the International Working Men's Association in 1864.[13] Between 1885 and 1889 Errico Malatesta and Gori played a significant role on the development of anarchism in Argentina, and Italian anarchist communists and syndicalists initiated labour movements in Brazil and Peru.[14] Giovanni Rossi, one of the last representatives of Italian utopian

---

all'epoca della Seconda Internazionale', in *Anna Kuliscioff e l'età del Riformismo* (Rome: Mondo Operaio, Edizioni Avanti!, 1978), pp. 59–68.

[8] Maurizio Degl'Innocenti, *L'esilio nella storia contemporanea*, in Maurizio Degl'Innocenti (ed.), *L'esilio nella storia del movimento operaio e l'emigrazione economica* (Manduria: Pietro Lacaita editore, 1992), p. 26.

[9] Jose Moya, 'Anarchism', *The Palgrave Dictionary of Transnational History* (Basingstoke: Palgrave, 2009), p. 40.

[10] Fedele Santi, *L'esilio nella storia del movimento operaio e l'emigrazione economica*, in Degl'Innocenti (ed.), *L'esilio nella storia del movimento operaio*, pp. 185–203.

[11] Moya, 'Anarchism', p. 40.

[12] See: Carl Levy, 'Malatesta in exile', in *Annali della Fondazione Luigi Einaudi*, 15 (1981), p. 246; Carl Levy, 'The Rooted Cosmopolitan: Errico Malatesta, Syndicalism, Transnationalism and the International Labour Movement', in David Berry and Constance Bantman, *New Perspectives on Anarchism, Labour and Syndicalism: The Individual, the National and the Transnational* (Newcastle: Cambridge Scholars, 2010), pp. 74–76.

[13] Anselmo Lorenzo, *El proletariado militante* (Mexico: ed. Vertice, 1926), pp. 19–20. Max Nettlau, *La Première Internationale en Espagne (1868–1888)* (Dordrecht: D. Reide, 1969). A recollection of Fanelli by Malatesta in: 'Giuseppe Fanelli', *Pensiero e Volontà*, no. 11, 16 September 1925.

[14] Osvaldo Bajer, 'L'influenza dell'immigrazione italiana nel movimento anarchico argentino', in *Gli italiani fuori d' Italia: gli emigrati italiani nei movimenti operai dei paesi d'adozione 1880–1940* (Milan: Franco Angeli, 1983), pp. 531–48; Zaragoza Ruvira, 'Anarchism et mouvement ouvrier en Argentine à la fin du siècle', in *Le mouvement social*, 103.3 (1978), pp. 14–17.

anarchism, founded the *Colônia Cecilia* in Brazil in 1890.[15] Gigi Damiani lived and was politically engaged there from 1899 until his deportation to Italy in 1919.[16] Giuseppe Ciancabilla, Luigi Galleani and Carlo Tresca were active in the United States, from 1898, 1901 and 1905 respectively.[17] Italian anarchists in the United States were influential in the large immigrant centres, and many were involved in the formation and development of the IWW.[18] Nicola Sacco and Bartolomeo Vanzetti are the dramatic symbols of this story. Italian anarchists also established an influential community in Switzerland.[19] Luigi Bertoni was the director of *Il Risveglio/Le Reveille*, one of the most significant and long lasting organs of international anarchism; it was published for forty years between 1900 and 1940.[20] Exiles also reached the Middle East. The Internationalist Niccolò Converti went to Tunisia to avoid twenty months' imprisonment for collaboration with Malatesta's newspaper *La Questione Sociale* in 1887; there he founded and directed *L'Operaio: Organo degli anarchici di Tunisi e della Sicilia*. Italian anarchist refugees were the first to bring anarchism to Alexandria and other Egyptian towns.[21] The advent of Fascism produced a significant wave of exiles, among

[15] See Giovanni Rossi, *Appello per la fondazione di colonie socialiste sperimentali*, in Pier Carlo Masini, *Storia degli anarchici italiani da Bakunin a Malatesta. 1862–1892* (Milan: Rizzoli, 1972), pp. 337–41; Rosellina Gosi, R. *Il socialismo utopistico. Giovanni Rossi e la colonia anarchica Cecilia* (Milan: Maiozzi, 1977). Isabelle Felici, *La Cecilia. Histoire d'une communauté anarchiste et de son fondateur Giovanni Rossi* (Lyon: ACL, 2000).

[16] Edgar Rodrigues, *Os anarquistas: trabalhadores italianos no Brasil* (Sãn Paulo: Global Editora, 1984). Isabelle Felici, *Poésie d'un rebelle. Poète, anarchiste, émigré (1876–1953)* (Lyon: Atelier de creation libertaire, 2009).

[17] Nunzio Pernicone, *Carlo Tresca. Portrait of a Rebel* (New York: Palgrave Macmillan, 2005); Ugo Fedeli, *Luigi Galleani: quarant'anni di lotte rivoluzionarie 1891–1931* (Cesena: Edizioni L'Antistato, 1956); Ugo Fedeli, *Giuseppe Ciancabilla* (Imola: Galeati, 1965).

[18] Levy, 'The Rooted Cosmopolitan', p. 74.

[19] For the political emigration in Switzerland see Maurizio Binaghi, *Addio Lugano Bella. Gli Esuli Politici nella Svizzera italiana di fine Ottocento* (Locarno: Dadò Editore, 2002); Stefania Ruggeri, *L'emigrazione politica attraverso le carte della polizia internazionale conservate presso l'Archivio Storico Diplomatico del Ministero degli Affari Esteri*, in Carlo Brusa and Robertino Ghiringhelli (eds), *Varese: emigrazione e territorio: tra bisogno e ideale. Convegno internazionale. Varese 18–20 maggio 1994* (Varese: Edizioni Latina, 1994) and Marc Vuilleumier, *Les exilés en Suisse et le mouvement ouvrier socialiste (1871–1914)*, in Degl'Innocenti (ed.), *L'esilio*, pp. 61–80. On Bertoni see: Giampiero Bottinelli, *Luigi Bertoni: la coerenza di un anarchico* (Lugano: La baronata, 1997).

[20] Leonardo Bettini, *Bibliografia dell'anarchismo. Periodici e numeri unici anarchici in lingua italiana pubblicati all'estero (1872–1971)*, vol. I, tome 2 (Florence: CP, 1976), p. 245.

[21] Ilham Khuri-Makdisi, *The Eastern Mediterranean and the Making of Global Radicalism, 1860–1914* (Berkeley, CA; London: University of California Press, 2010), pp. 114–34. Anthony Gorman, 'Diverse in race, religion and nationality… but united in aspirations of civil progress', the Anarchist Movement in Egypt, 1860–1940', in S. Hirsch and L. van der

them Luigi Fabbri who emigrated to Montevideo in Uruguay where he published the influential periodical *Studi Sociali*.[22] Camillo Berneri escaped Fascist persecution, moved to France and later fought in the Spanish Civil War where he was murdered by the Stalinists in 1937. His young daughter Marie Louise settled in London where she played a crucial, albeit brief, role in the revitalisation of the British anarchist movement.

Therefore, among the many diasporas that characterised the history of Italian migration, the anarchists 'formed their own distinctive diasporas', which allows us 'to speak of Italian anarchism as a transnational ideology unbound by migration and spreading wherever Italy's anarchists went'.[23]

Since 'the seductiveness of the use of the term diaspora is that it forces us to look simultaneously at the many places to which migrants travelled, and the connections among them';[24] this monograph intends to contribute to the historiography of diasporic anarchism by exploring practical and ideological aspects of the Italian anarchists – their everyday lives as well as their ideological thought and its development – in London, one of the most significant nodes of the transnational anarchist network.[25]

The study of Italian anarchist diaspora emphasises the advantages and the challenges inherent in a transnational approach to research into anarchism. In recent years, new perspectives have developed in labour history that stem from 'the acknowledgement that historiography has been overwhelmingly written within a national framework and needs to be reconsidered with greater attention for the international context which constitutes, explains, determines or contradicts national developments'.[26] Several works have been published or are due to appear providing new views on anarchism and anarcho-revolutionary syndicalism which take under consideration the transnational and transatlantic networks and informal links that underpinned those organisations and 'have been ignored by classical studies of labour internationalism'.[27] This transnational approach is challenging a number

---

Walt, *Anarchism and Syndicalism in the Colonial and Postcolonial World, 1870–1940: the Praxis of National Liberation, Internationalism, and Social Revolution* (Leiden; Boston: Brill, 2010), pp. 5–31.

[22] Luce Fabbri, *Luigi Fabbri: storia d'un uomo libero* (Pisa: BFS, 1996).

[23] Gabaccia, *Italy's Many Diasporas*, p. 107.

[24] Gabaccia, *Italy's Many Diasporas*, p. 9.

[25] On French anarchists in London see: Constance Bantman, *The French Anarchists in London, 1880–1914. Exile and Transnationalism in the First Globalization.* (Liverpool: Liverpool University Press, 2013).

[26] David Berry and Constance Bantman (eds), *New Perspectives on Anarchism, Labour and Syndicalism* (Newcastle upon Tyne: Cambridge Scholars Publishing, 2010), p. 2.

[27] Berry and Bantman (eds), *New Perspectives on Anarchism*, pp. 2–3. On the network see: Constance Bantman, 'Internationalism without an International? Cross-Channel Anarchist

of established views – for example, that of anarchism as a West European doctrine that diffused outwards to a passive 'periphery'; and it emphasises the need for more studies on the relationships between anarchism and issues such as race, nation, imperialism, national liberation and anti-colonialism.[28]

The investigation of the anarchist exile permits the review of some unsatisfactory interpretations deriving from the predominant national scope in studies of Italian anarchism. As underlined by Davide Turcato, a national framework fails to explain the cyclical patterns of advance and retreat of the anarchist movement, and fosters an image of discontinuity, spontaneity and ineffectiveness leading to the definition of anarchism as a millenarian movement. A transnational perspective reveals, rather, anarchism's continuity, and shows how activity abroad compensated for the lack of initiative in Italy due to repression, and that Italian anarchism was indeed 'a transnational movement stretching around the Atlantic Ocean and the Mediterranean Sea'.[29] In their migrations, Italian anarchists brought 'the outside international world with them. If and when they returned to Europe [...] they brought that extra-Europe experience back home. The main thing was that they did not only work, but they constantly crossed state borders'.[30]

When Italian anarchists began to arrive in London at the end of the 1870s, Britain already had a long tradition of hospitality to Italian political refugees, dating from the beginning of the *Risorgimento* during the 1820s.[31] Although major ideological and social differences distinguished the groups of London expatriates during those years, on arrival anarchists found an extant network of relationships and organisations among political exiles.

The liberal asylum regime that characterised British policy during the Victorian age facilitated the settlement of anarchists in the United Kingdom. Anarchists of all nationalities developed a polyglot community that lasted without interruption up to the First World War. Together with a large

---

Networks, 1880–1914', *Revue Belge de Philologie et d'histoire, 84.4* (2006), pp. 961–81; Ralph Darlington, *Syndicalism and the Transition to Communism: An International Comparative Study* (Aldershot: Ashgate, 2008), pp. 49–93; Carl Levy, 'Social Histories of Anarchism', *Journal for the Study of Radicalism*, 4. 2 (2010) pp. 1–44; Carl Levy, 'Anarchism and Cosmopolitanism', *Journal of Political Ideologies*, 16. 3 (2011), pp. 265–78; Benedict Anderson, *Under Three Flags. Anarchism and the Anti-Colonial Imagination* (London: Verso, 2005); Christian G. De Vito (ed.), *Global Labour History* (Verona: Ombre Corte, 2012).

[28] Hirsch and van der Walt, *Anarchism and Syndicalism*, p. liv.

[29] Davide Turcato, 'Italian Anarchism as a Transnational Movement 1885–1915', *International Review of Social History*, 52 (2005), pp. 407–44.

[30] Benedict Anderson, preface to Hirsch and van der Walt, *Anarchism and Syndicalism*, p. xv.

[31] Maurizio Isabella, *Risorgimento in Exile: Italian Émigrés and the Liberal International in the post-Napoleonic Era* (Oxford: Oxford University Press, 2009); Christine Lattek, *Revolutionary Refugees: German Socialism in Britain, 1840–1860* (London: Routledge, 2006).

number of lesser-known rank and files militants, Peter Kropotkin, Sergej Mikhailovich Kravchinsky Stepniak, Varlaam Cherkezov, and Chaikovsky arrived from Russia; Johann Most and Rudolf Rocker from Germany; Charles Malato, Louise Michel and Emile Pouget from France; Ricardo Mella, Tárrida del Mármol, Pedro Vallina from Spain; Errico Malatesta, Francesco Saverio Merlino and Pietro Gori from Italy; the historian and intellectual Max Nettlau from Austria. Thus, for a long period, London received 'the most qualified congregation of anarchists of all nationalities' who had a remarkable influence on the development and elaboration of anarchist theories, thought, and ideology.[32] The metropolis became 'a focal point of global solidarity and an international exchange of ideas and forms of organisation'.[33]

The relationship between Italian anarchists and other foreign anarchists and anti-parliamentary socialist groups brought significant mutual theoretical influences. In London the major leaders of the movement organised several meetings or circles to discuss and debate their ideas:

> After the deportation of leading anarchists from Spain in 1897 Ricardo Mella and Tárrida del Mármol joined Malatesta, Cherkezov, Kropotkin, Max Nettlau, Rudolf Rocker, John Turner and the occasional London labour leader in a free floating *conversazione*. Little documented, these informal discussions modified the participants' anarchist ideas and introduced British trade unionists to anti-statist socialism.[34]

These contacts were not merely restricted to meetings or circle discussions. Italian anarchists 'were active in the Social Democratic Federation, the Socialist League, the Anarchist groups and even the "first" Fabians'.[35] Merlino collaborated with Kropotkin in the first group around *Freedom*, edited by Charlotte Wilson from 1886. 'His role in the *Freedom* group discussions of anarchist-communism and the organisation of labour in 1887 and 1888 shows that he was then still a committed anarchist'.[36] While living in London Merlino held discussions with George Bernard Shaw, William Morris and Eduard Bernstein.[37]

---

[32] Pier Carlo Masini, *Storia degli anarchici italiani nell'epoca degli attentati* (Milan: Rizzoli, 1981), p. 74.

[33] Levy, *The Rooted Cosmopolitan*, p. 77.

[34] Carl Levy, 'Malatesta in London: the Era of Dynamite', in Lucio Sponza, Arturo Tosi (eds), *A Century of Italian Emigration to Britain 1880–1980s. Five essays*, Supplement to *The Italianist*, 13, (1993), p. 28.

[35] Levy, 'Malatesta in London', p. 25.

[36] Hermia Oliver, *The International Anarchist Movement in Late Victorian London* (New York: St Martin's Press, 1983), p. 45.

[37] Pier Carlo Masini, *Storia degli anarchici italiani da Bakunin*, p. 220.

Silvio Corio was another Italian anarchist with close contacts in the British political world. For several years he was Sylvia Pankhurst's companion, and with her published the *Workers' Dreadnought* and the *New Times and Ethiopia News*. He also knew the journalist Guy Bowman, leader of the British Syndicalist Educational League. Corio maintained his relationships with British political circles and within them promoted anti-Fascist campaigns during the 1920s. The importance of Italian anarchists' links with other socialist organisations in Britain was proved by the massive demonstrations organised in opposition to Malatesta's deportation in 1912, when anarchists were joined by figures from the British left and British trade unions leaders including Tom Mann, James MacDonald and Guy Bowman.

Italian anarchists arrived in London at different periods, following waves of repression in their own country. Many did not stay in the United Kingdom permanently, but managed to return to Italy when conditions allowed or moved to other centres of exile, particularly the United States.[38] In some cases, they escaped to Britain several times, as did Malatesta, although some of them – Emidio Recchioni is an example – took up permanent residence in England and even obtained citizenship.

In spite of this frequent coming and going, the Italian anarchist movement in London maintained a constant active presence until the 1930s. As for economic migrants, expatriates' survival depended greatly on an informal international network that assured them some logistical support. Awareness of the precarious condition of exile led anarchists to set up an extremely flexible form of organisation. Indeed, while militants moved from one country to another, the organisation and network of relationships continued. The identification of the precise periods in which activists were in the United Kingdom, the reconstruction of their social and professional lives, the examination of their political initiatives and the web of their relationships assists an understanding of how the transnational network of the Italian anarchists worked, and what facilitated the continuity of this centre of the anarchist diaspora that began in the late 1870s, a few years after the fall of the Paris Commune.

The events of the Commune were crucial for the growth of anarchism in Italy, as Carlo Cafiero, Andrea Costa and Errico Malatesta – the most prominent figures in the rising anarchist movement together with Bakunin – often remembered in their writings. Indeed, especially for young people, the Commune represented the ideological passage from *Risorgimento* nationalism to the socialism of the First International. Mazzini was one of the firmest opponents of both the Commune and the First International and

---

[38] 'Like the exiles of the *Risorgimento*, almost 90 percent of Italy's exiles eventually returned home' (Gabaccia, *Italy's Many Diasporas*, p. 109).

his struggle with Bakunin to achieve political hegemony over the working class in Italy was based on different interpretations of the significance of the Commune. Mazzini was living in London at the time, and this dispute reverberated in the Italian exile community among whom, only few years later, the anarchists were to find refuge.

Italian anarchists in London were not politically homogenous. In England as well as in Italy, especially during the 1890s, there was a clear-cut distinction between 'anti-organisationalist', and 'organisationalist anarchists', of which Malatesta was the most prominent exponent. The rivalry between these two groups was significant, even if they occasionally collaborated and relationships between militants varied according to external circumstances.

The reconstruction of the political activities of these groups reveals not only the level of influence they had on the wider Italian community and their relationships with the colony of economic migrants, but also the difficulties and limits of anarchists' work in the host country. Indeed, Italian anarchist exiles' political horizons remained predominantly focused on events at home, illustrating the persistence of a practical and conceptual nationalist framework, even when abroad. As Constance Bantman contends, this issue raises a number of questions regarding the effectiveness of the anarchist movement in achieving its internationalist ideals, and on the relationships between the militant elite and the grassroots level.[39]

However, if the anarchists failed to develop an 'institutional internationalism', they definitely created a distinctive subversive culture and self-conscious ideology which helped them to feel part of an imagined transnational community. This radical subculture not only reinforced ties among expatriates in London, but it forged and nurtured a spiritual connection with other centres of the anarchist diaspora. The study of the cultural forms through which exiles expressed their ideals is attracting increasing interest. This work can lead to a better understanding of the ways in which these subcultures were transmitted between centres of the anarchist diaspora through the use of myths (the Paris Commune), martyrology (Chicago Martyrs, Sante Caserio, Ravachol), iconography, songs (the anarchist repertoire is immense), theatrical plays and also through education, with the establishment of Free Schools and Universities – all of which were common features in the centres of anarchist exile.[40] This radical subculture bound together anarchist exiles of different nationalities in London possibly even more than did their political initiatives. The clubs were the main centres

[39] Bantman, 'Internationalism', pp. 961–81.
[40] Tom Goyens, *Beer and Revolution: the German Anarchist Movement in New York City, 1880–1914* (Urbana, Ill.: University of Illinois Press, 2007); Bencivenni, *Italian Immigrant Radical Culture*.

of the production and transmission of this counterculture, particularly through the organisation of social events, but also through the provision of libraries and reading rooms for members. For exiled anarchists, as for all refugees, social and political clubs were the main places of organisation and sociability. The older *German Communist Workers' Educational Union*, (the Kabv) in Rose Street was the model for clubs in most subsequent exiles' circles, such as the *Autonomie Club*, founded in 1878, that became a meeting point for the London anarchist community. Clubs and other societies offered mutual aid, political discussion and social life for fellow countrymen. Club soirées combined fundraising with propaganda and fulfilled the needs of the expatriates and the wider community. It was through these activities that the anarchists collected funds to finance political campaigns and newspapers. The cultural production for these events was particularly rich: poetry, music, speeches, choruses, dancing and theatrical performances; they all played a significative part in the reinforcement of a collective identity among the refugees.

Despite Lord Sainsbury's sarcastic comment that propaganda wishing to achieve revolution by dancing was not really a threat, the anarchist clubs were generally regarded as hotbeds of the most terrifying conspiracies.[41]

The Italian Ministry of the Interior, assisted by the embassy, kept the anarchists under continuous surveillance. The British police collaborated at times, though never officially because such collaboration contradicted the British concept of 'individual freedom'. A considerable number of infiltrators worked for the Italian embassy and the Minister of the Interior. The large volume of reports from these informers is an important source for the study of the Italian anarchists in London and their relations with anarchists in other colonies. Knowledge of the mechanisms of this intelligence service is therefore essential for the evaluation of these controversial and fascinating documents, as it will be discussed in chapter 5. In addition, the international surveillance of anarchists, still regarded as the prototype of international terrorists, can also be considered as an integral part of the anarchist diaspora.[42]

Surveillance of the London anarchists underlined the problematic relations between the Italian and British authorities regarding the controversial use of *agents provocateurs* and informers. For example, the British authorities were greatly annoyed by the outcome of the Rubino affair (Gennaro Rubino,

---

[41] Tornielli to Minister of Foreign Affairs, 21 April 1891, Asdmae, *Pol. Int.*, b. 39, f. 1891.

[42] Michael Collyer, 'Secret agents: Anarchists, Islamists, and Responses to Politically Active Refugees in London' *Ethnic and Racial Studies* 28.2 (2005), pp. 278–303. See also the replies to James Gelvin's article 'Al-Qaeda and Anarchism: a Historian Reply to Terrorology' in *Terrorism and Political Violence*, 20.4 (2008).

unmasked informer of the Italian embassy, attempted to assassinate the King of Belgium as a redemptive act), yet they were certainly involved in framing Malatesta when he was accused of libel by the spy Bellelli.

The anarchists always sent their publications to Italy and the Italian authorities persistently tried to intercept and seize them, often successfully.[43] The surveillance and monitoring of the socialist and anarchist press in Italy was intense, especially during the last twenty years of the nineteenth century. Local police were charged with the systematic collection of copies of the entire 'subversive' press which were mailed to the Minister of the Interior. Unfortunately, the entire press collection, kept at the *Archivio di Stato* in Rome, was lost during the Second World War.[44]

Anarchist newspapers in Italian represent the most visible sign of the widespread experience of Italian anarchist political exile; anarchist expatriates published them all over the world.[45] Therefore, an analysis of these newspapers reveals much about the history of exile and the international relationships Italian anarchists established with the motherland and with other centres of exile.

Newspapers served several functions: they were a means of organisation and transmission of political debate, propaganda, and of the construction of identity. They usually had an international circulation: newspapers published in the United States or in South America were sent by mail to Europe and vice versa. Moreover, they were also a system of exchanging information, through coded messages, and of maintaining contact between anarchist colonies around the world and reinforcing the anarchist network. Articles were frequently written by anarchists who lived in a different country. Newspapers sent home by expatriates were essential in providing an anarchist press in Italy during the most intense periods of government repression. However, the fact that those newspapers were published abroad heavily influenced their content, as they were often disconnected from Italian realities. It has been argued that this was the case with *La Rivoluzione Sociale* published by the London anarchists in 1902–1903. However, on other

[43] See: V. Castronovo and N. Tranfaglia, *La stampa italiana nell'età liberale* (Bari: Laterza, 1979); Patrizia Audenino, *Cinquant'anni di stampa operaia dall'Unità alla guerra di Libia* (Parma: Guanda, 1976); Mariella Nejrotti, 'La stampa operaia e socialista 1848–1914', in Aldo Agosti and Gian Mario Bravo (eds), *Storia del movimento operaio e del socialismo e delle lotte sociali in Piemonte* (Bari: De Donato, 1979), pp. 375–445.

[44] See: Antonio Fiori, 'Introduction' in *Direzione Generale della Pubblica Sicurezza. La stampa italiana nella serie F1. 1894–1926* (Rome: Ministero per i Beni Culturali e Ambientali. Ufficio Centrale per i Beni Archivistici, 1995).

[45] See: Leonardo Bettini, *Bibliografia dell'anarchismo. Periodici e numeri unici anarchici in lingua italiana pubblicati all'estero (1872–1971)*, Vol. 1, (Florence: Crescita Politica Editrice, 1976).

occasions, as in the aftermath of Bresci's assassination of the King of Italy and the single issue *Cause ed Effetti*, these publications were crucial in providing the political line to the anarchist movement in Italy.

It was through newspapers that major issues were debated. This was particularly the case with the outbreak of the First World War, which had a crucial impact on the experience of the exile. The deep ideological schism caused by contrasting attitudes towards the war within the anarchist community destroyed the international solidarity that was at the basis of the refugees' political activities. London was a central point in this dispute, and *Freedom* was the main vector of the debate. On its pages Kropotkin announced his support of the Entente forces, and was promptly rebuked by Malatesta. The controversy reached its highest point in February 1916 when Kropotkin and other eminent anarchists published the 'Manifeste des Seize' in which they publicly supported the war and the *Entente* against German imperialism.[46] This ideological rupture also affected the Italian anarchist community in London and its leaders. Moreover, the special provisions of the Defence of the Realm Act, the censorship and the internment of enemy aliens, brought anarchist activity almost to a standstill.

Following the end of the war in 1919, Malatesta concluded his long history of exile and returned to Italy, where he received a triumphal welcome.[47] However, another chapter in the history of London's colony began. In 1921, a section of the Italian *Fasci* Abroad, one of the first created outside Italy, opened in London.[48] Soon a dramatic conflict was to begin within the Italian community when anarchist expatriates joined socialists and communists in the fight against Fascism.[49]

This monograph unveils the intriguing world of anarchist refugees in London from the second half of the nineteenth century to the outbreak of the First World War. It combines an investigation of anarchist political organisations and activities with a study of the everyday life of militants through identifying the hitherto largely anonymous Italian anarchist exiles who settled in London. Central to the book is an examination of the processes and associations through which anarchist exiles created an international revolutionary network which governments and police forces esteemed to be an extremely dangerous threat. The monograph investigates political,

---

[46] This manifesto was published in *La Bataille* in Paris, on 14 March 1916.

[47] Carl Levy, 'Charisma and Social Movements: Errico Malatesta and Italian Anarchism', *Modern Italy*, III.2 (1998), pp. 205–17.

[48] On the exportation of fascism to the Italian colony in London: Claudia Baldoli, *Exporting Fascism. Italian Fascists and Britain's Italians in the 1930s* (Oxford and New York: Berg, 2003).

[49] Alfio Bernabei, *Esuli ed emigrati nel Regno Unito,1920–1940* (Milan: Mursia, 1997).

social and cultural aspects of the colony of Italian anarchist refugees in London in order to understand the nature of the transnational anarchist diaspora and its relevance in the history of the anarchist movement.

The first two chapters of the monograph reconstruct the settlement of the colony of anarchist refugees in London and their relationship with the colony of Italian emigrants. Chapters three and four deal with the activities that the Italian anarchists organised in London, such as demonstrations, conferences, and meetings. They likewise examine the ideological differences that characterised the two main groups in which the anarchists were divided: organisationalists and anti-organisationalists. Italian authorities were extremely concerned about the danger represented by the anarchists. The fifth chapter provides a detailed investigation of the surveillance of the anarchists that the Italian embassy and the Italian Minster of Interior organised in London by using spies and informers. At the same time, it describes the contradictory attitude held by British police forces toward political refugees. Chapter six reconstructs the anarchists' social life and the political and cultural activities that they organised in their clubs. Chapter seven examines the impact that the outbreak of the First World Word had on the anarchist movement, particularly in dividing it between interventionists and anti-interventionists; a split that destroyed the network of international solidarity that had been hitherto the core of the experience of political exile.

1

The Fugitives:
Anarchist Pathways Toward London

> ...The Knight-errants
> dragged northwards
> depart singing
> with hope in their hearts[1]

Repression and exile

For the anarchist diaspora, London was an essential landmark. Anarchists from all European countries took refuge in the United Kingdom from the late 1870s onwards and their presence grew as a result of the increase in persecution in their home countries and internationally. The anarchist movement in Italy in particular was heavily affected by governmental persecution aimed at eradicating the activities of militants.

To this end several special measures were enforced during the last decades of the nineteenth century including preventive detention, which compelled dozens of anarchists to spend many months in jail before being tried, laws restricting the anarchist press, police surveillance, curfews and, most damagingly, impositions of restrictions on freedom of movement and on the activities of individuals (*ammonizione*) and internal exile (*domicilio coatto*).[2]

Originally, the laws concerning *ammonizione* and internal exile were

---

[1] Pietro Gori, 'Addio Lugano Bella'. *Addio Lugano Bella, antologia della canzone anarchica in Italia* (I dischi del sole: Edizioni del Gallo).

[2] See: John Davis, *Conflict and Control: Law and Order in Nineteenth-Century Italy* (Basingstoke: Macmillan, 1988); Daniela Fozzi, *Tra prevenzione e repressione. Il domicilio coatto nell'Italia liberale* (Rome: Carocci, 2010); Nunzio Pernicone, *Italian Anarchism. 1864–1892* (Princeton, N. J.; Chichester: Princeton University Press, 1993), pp. 130–33; Vittorio Lollini, *L'Ammonizione e il domicilio coatto* (Bologna: Fratelli Treves, 1882); Ambra Boldetti, 'La repressione in Italia: il caso del 1894', *Rivista di storia contemporanea*, VI. 4, (October 1977), pp. 481–515; Giorgio Sacchetti, 'Controllo sociale e domicilio coatto nell'Italia crispina', *Rivista storica*

aimed at common criminals, in particular at fighting banditry in south and central Italy immediately after unification, but they were increasingly used against anarchist Internationalists, especially after the Left came to office in 1876.

Ammonizione was an administrative procedure based solely on police statements; there was no trial and it was impossible for the accused to defend him or herself before a magistrate. People under *ammonizione* suffered significant restrictions on their movements and their personal freedom; punishments for violating *ammonizione* were severe, including long terms of imprisonment. Those suffering such supervision, and their families, were often driven to despair. As leading anarchist Armando Borghi recalled in his memoirs, the life of a man under *ammonizione* was that of a prisoner on bail: 'He cannot find a job, his life is dominated by dangers and fears; he and his relatives live at the discretion of the police'.[3]

Moreover, the Minister of the Interior could decide at any time to convert *ammonizione* to forced domicile and 'on any given night, a family is awakened from their sleep, the father is taken away from his sons, the spouse from his wife, the unfortunate is taken to prison and from there to an island'.[4]

The institution of forced internal exile also was based on a highly arbitrary system that did not allow for a proper defence. Deportation to small islands or remote villages in the interior for a period of up to five years was imposed by commissions of governmental bureaucrats and police officers, presided over by the local prefect.[5] Internal exile proved over time to be an effective system for maintaining social control through 'preventive repression'. It was used against individuals who were considered 'socially dangerous elements' and this category was systematically broadened to include different sections of the population according to the repressive needs of the dominant class.[6]

Following the attempted insurrection in spring 1877 in the Matese mountains in south-central Italy, and a series of violent deeds for which anarchists were held responsible the following year, 'thousands of anarchists were condemned to prison and internal exile not for illegal acts or even for the intent to commit them, but solely for the ideas they professed'.[7]

dell'anarchismo, III.1 (1996), pp. 93–104; Ouida, 'The legislation of fear', *Fortnightly Review*, 56 (1894), pp. 552–61.

[3] Armando Borghi, *Mezzo secolo di anarchia 1898–1945* (Naples: E.S.I., 1954), p. 32.

[4] Francesco Saverio Merlino, *L'Italia qual'è* (Milan: Feltrinelli, 1974), p. 140. (1st edition 1890).

[5] Richard Bach Jensen, 'Italy's Peculiar Institution: Internal Police Exile, 1861–1914', in J. K. Burton (ed.) *Essays in European History: Selected from the Annual Meetings of the Southern Historical Association, 1986–1987* (Lanham: University Press of America, 1989), pp. 99–114.

[6] Boldetti, 'La repressione in Italia', p. 485.

[7] Pernicone, *Italian Anarchism*, p. 155. On the Matese expedition see: Pier Carlo Masini, *Gli internazionalisti. La banda del Matese, 1876–1878* (Milan, Rome: Edizioni Avanti!, 1958).

Ammonizione and internal exile were strengthened and widely used by Francesco Crispi's government, under which another wave of violent repression was unleashed on Italian society. 'In the 1890s repression of opposition groups in Italy reached dimensions unmatched in any other major European country except Russia'.[8] Compared with the previous decade, the number of indicted crimes in the 1890s increased by a third and reached peaks unequalled even under Fascism.[9]

In the early 1890s food riots, strikes and demonstrations grew in frequency and intensity. In 1893, protests organised in Sicily by worker and peasant associations, the *Fasci dei lavoratori*, erupted into a full-scale uprising. Crispi placed the island under martial law; press freedom and freedom of association were suspended. Some 40,000 troops were despatched to savagely suppress the rebellion. Thousands of the protesters were convicted to several years' imprisonment and 2,000 sent into internal exile. Repression also hit harshly those workers who rebelled in solidarity with the uprising in Lunigiana and Massa-Carrara – a traditional anarchist stronghold in Central Italy. Alongside these events, the failed attempt on Crispi's life by Paolo Lega on 16 June 1894 and the assassination a week later of the French President Sadi Carnot by Italian anarchist Sante Caserio generated a climate of fear that allowed Crispi – 'the Mussolini of his time'[10] – to introduce emergency legislation against suspected anarchists.

Explaining the new measures to the Chambers, the spokesman stressed that: 'exceptional measures are needed to fight exceptional evils that escape ordinary means of prevention and repression'.[11] These measures consisted of three distinct laws. The first was directed against criminal offences committed with explosives or intent to use them. Severe sentences were introduced for possession of explosive materials or the chemicals to concoct them. The second law was aimed at the control and suppression of the subversive press, in particular the prevention of anarchist political organising among soldiers which incurred heavy penalties for 'incitement to class hatred'. The third, most controversial, law was called the '*Provvedimenti eccezionali di pubblica sicurezza*'. It restricted freedom of association and expression, facilitating the practice of sending political activists into

---

[8] Robert Goldstein, *Political Repression in 19th Century Europe* (London: Croom Helm, 1983), p. 316.

[9] Sacchetti, 'Controllo sociale e domicilio coatto', p. 99.

[10] Emidio Recchioni to Max Nettlau, 26 09 1931, IISH, Nettlau archive, Correspondence, microfilm no. 60–61.

[11] Report by Costa to the Chamber, 15 July 1894, in Raffaele Majetti, *L'anarchia e le leggi che la reprimono in Italia* (Caserta: Stabilimento Tipografico Elzeviriano, Domenico Fabiano Editore, 1894), p. 41.

internal exile.[12] Police were empowered to impose internal exile not only on individuals considered dangerous to public order but also on those convicted, or acquitted for want of evidence, for public order offences and those who made manifest their intention of committing such crimes.[13] Introducing the novelty of associative crime, the provision could also be applied to members of organisations aiming at subverting the social order. As 'social order' was an extremely broad term, this article was open to a wide range of interpretations allowing for a great deal of arbitrariness.[14] The approval of the '*Provvedimenti eccezionali di pubblica sicurezza*' was the first step toward the suspension of political liberties under Crispi's government. In the subsequent two years more than 3,000 anarchists were detained on islands such as Favignana, Lampedusa, Pantelleria, Ustica, Lipari, Ponza, Ventotene and the so-called 'Italian Spielberg', the fortress of Porto Ercole.[15] Taking advantage of its vagueness, the authorities also used the law against socialists and republicans and hundreds of them joined anarchists in internal exile, to isolated locations. In October 1894 the government dissolved the Socialist Party and hundreds of trade unions and workers' associations; the number of *coatti* (forced exiles) increased so sharply that the government was compelled to find more space in which to segregate them. A penal colony was opened at Assab in Eritrea. The government was hoping that 'the harshness of the climate and the severity of the discipline will act as a deterrent to other *coatti* in Italy and will break the ranks of their criminal associations'. However, the unhealthy climate – extremely dangerous for warders and prisoners alike – and the heavy cost of prisoner transportation forced the Italian government to close the colony only a few months after it opened.[16]

Several revolts broke out in these ghettoised locations in protest at the appalling living conditions. One particularly violent took place on the Tremiti Islands in March 1896; during the disorders the anarchist Argante Salucci was killed by police.[17] On other occasions some of the detainees succeeded in audacious breakouts. In 1899, Errico Malatesta, Giorgio Vivoli and Edoardo Epifani escaped from the island of Lampedusa and reached Tunis; the following year Luigi Galleani fled the island of Pantelleria. Those who succeeded in escaping often joined their comrades in exile. For instance,

[12] Pier Carlo Masini, *Storia degli anarchici italiani nell'epoca degli attentati* (Milan: Rizzoli, 1981), pp. 53–66.

[13] Fozzi, *Tra prevenzione e repressione*, p. 188.

[14] Report by Costa to the Chamber, 15 July 1894, Majetti, *L'anarchia e le leggi che la reprimono*, p. 53.

[15] Pernicone, *Italian Anarchism*, p. 288.

[16] Boldetti, 'La repressione in Italia', pp. 512–13.

[17] Valerio Bartoloni, *I fatti delle Tremiti. Una rivolta di coatti anarchici nell'Italia umbertiana*, (Foggia: Bastogi Editrice Italiana, 1996).

Galleani reached the United States and Malatesta moved to London where he joined the Defendi family in their house in Islington.

Thus, following the establishment of the First International, the anarchist movement was hit by waves of severe repression that left militants with few alternatives: 'The only way to escape [...] was to go underground or flee into exile.'[18]

The countries where most Italian anarchists found refuge were France, Switzerland and Belgium, but some of them emigrated to the United States while others established small communities in the Balkans, in the Levant and in South America.[19] However, the nations where the anarchists expatriated varied according to political events, change of governments and to the international pressures that were imposed on their hosts. This happened especially after the acts of violence and attempts on the lives of sovereigns and heads of government committed by anarchist militants throughout Europe in the 1890s. Countries with a remarkably long traditions of granting asylum began to expel the anarchists.[20] One of these was Switzerland, which had since the time of the First International provided hospitality to a large number of anarchist refugees, among the most prominent of whom were Cafiero, Bakunin and Kropotkin. Following Sadi Carnot's assassination in 1894, the Federal Swiss Council issued a decree for the capture and subsequent expulsion of Italian refugees. Pietro Gori and sixteen other Italian anarchists were arrested and expelled from the Confederation.[21]

During his days in prison awaiting expulsion Gori wrote the song that became the anthem of Italian anarchism: 'Addio Lugano Bella'. Gori and his comrades, after expulsion from Switzerland and seeking refuge elsewhere in Europe, eventually landed in the United Kingdom – at that time the only country where a refugee could feel relatively safe.

Unlike other European countries, England consistently allowed free entry to religious and political refugees and consequently became one of the most prominent centres of political emigration in Europe. The tradition of free access was deeply rooted in British culture, being tightly linked with the idea of free trade and based on an understanding of the advantages of utilising foreigner's skills. This differed in the case of political refugees who did not provide any economic return to British industry. There were many

[18] Pernicone, *Italian Anarchism*, p. 134.

[19] Carl Levy, 'Malatesta in Exile', *Annali della Fondazione Luigi Einaudi*, XV (1981), pp. 245–80.

[20] On Switzerland's tradition of asylum towards political refugees see: M. Binaghi, *Addio Lugano bella. Gli esuli politici nella Svizzera italiana di fine Ottocento* (Locarno: Casa Editrice Dadò, 2002).

[21] Pietro Gori (1865–1911), lawyer and poet, was a leading figure in the Italian and international anarchist movement.

disadvantages in accepting political refugees: most of them were poor, they did not have special skills, they could create domestic problems if they joined domestic left-wing movements (the Chartists, for example), and they caused diplomatic difficulties with other countries. In the case of political refugees acceptance therefore was based on 'principle'.[22]

However, in the absence of substantial problems, the British government did not pass any legislation to regulate immigration, except under very specific circumstances. Therefore all immigrants, whether refugees or not, enjoyed complete free access to the United Kingdom between 1826 and 1905 – apart from a gap as a result of the revolutions of 1848-50.[23]

An additional element that made England safer than other countries was its policy on extradition. British law did not authorise extradition for the discussion of political ideas or holding of unorthodox opinions; as the English delegate explained at the International conference to fight anarchism held in Rome in 1898:

> This law does not recognise either native or aliens' expulsion, and opinions that do not reach the stage of incitement to commit crimes will not constitute a ground for prosecution [...]. The principle that it is not possible to extradite for a crime that is undoubtedly political needs equally to be maintained.[24]

Since the law was based on the presumption of innocence, there was no possibility for legal intervention before a crime was committed. As the same conference delegate explained: 'We do not persecute opinions. The only question with us is, is there crime or not?'[25]

Therefore, foreign governments could only obtain the extradition of political opponents from the United Kingdom by requesting it for common crimes. In spite of urgent appeals from other European countries, England never accepted the idea of enacting laws dealing specifically with political refugees to prevent their entrance to the country or to allow for their expulsion. Reasons for this position were varied, but in particular one of the

[22] Bernard Porter, *The Refugee Question in Mid-Victorian Politics* (Cambridge: Cambridge University Press, 1979), pp. 6–9.

[23] 'England once possessed an Alien Act passed as measures of national defence during the war with revolutionary France. After the restoration of peace their provision had been steadily eroded, until nothing more was required than the production of a passport by the immigrants and a declaration by the captain of the ship of their presence on board. Finally the requirement of the passport had been removed, and the captain's declaration had been allowed to fall into abeyance'; Elie Halévy, *A History of the English People in the Nineteenth Century* (London: Benn, 1951), vol. 5, p. 373.

[24] Sir P. Curie to the Marquess of Salisbury, 23 December 1898, NA, HO 45/10254/X36450/9.

[25] Sir P. Curie to the Marquess of Salisbury, 6 December 1898, NA, HO 45/10254/ X36450/19.

unquestionable principles of British legislation was the general application of any law. Moreover, the British government refused to pass laws under pressure from other countries since this was understood to be an unacceptable interference in British domestic affairs. As a consequence, until the Aliens' Bill of 1905, 'no foreigner was ever [...] expelled, whatever his or her status or political opinion'.[26]

Thus the liberal asylum regime that characterised British policy in the Victorian age facilitated the settlement of anarchists in the British capital where they established a cosmopolitan community that lasted without interruption up to the First World War.

Nevertheless, the opportunity for anarchists to reach British shores undetected, coupled with foreign governments' practice of expelling undesirable refugees to England, was cause for domestic concern. In 1892, following news of the possible expulsion of forty or more reputed anarchists from France, Colonel Howard Vincent, former Director of Criminal Investigations at Scotland Yard, asked whether the Home Secretary was aware that

> as the frontiers of Germany, Italy, Spain, Switzerland, and Belgium are closed to them by the administrative laws of those nations, and also, to a great extent, the ports of the United States [...] the United Kingdom is practically the only refuge for the rejected of Europe [...] and whether having regard to their increasing numbers, he proposes to take any step for the legislative reinforcement of the powers of the Executive in the matter'. The Home Secretary replied that he had no reason to believe the French government had expelled or was about 'to expel members of the criminal classes'.[27]

Yet, a couple of weeks later, a confidential report informed the Home Secretary that the French government had deported one Austrian and two Italian anarchists to Belgium without alerting the local authorities, despite a previous request from the Belgian government for the French to conduct only Belgian subjects to their frontiers and for advanced notification in any such case.[28] The Assistant Commissioner of Police was therefore instructed to update the Under Secretary of State on the arrival of any anarchists into the country, and controls at the harbours were consequently strengthened.[29] On

---

[26] John Saville, '1848 – Britain and Europe', in Sabine Freitag (ed.), *Exile from European Revolutions. Refugees in Mid-Victorian England* (New York, Oxford: Berghahn Books, 2003), p. 24.

[27] Parliamentary debates, 'Continental Anarchists', House of Commons, Hansard, 5 April 1892.

[28] Report by the Secretary of the Legation at Brussels M. Gosselin, 12 April 1892, NA, HO144/587/B2840C/2.

[29] 'Expulsion of two Belgian anarchists from France', 29 April 1892, NA, HO144/587/

19 May 1892, the Home Office was notified of the arrival of Antonio Agresti, who had been arrested in Brussels, expelled from Belgium and directed to London. On disembarkation from the steamer 'Norwich', Agresti was promptly questioned by the officer on duty at the port of Harwich and on his arrival in London 'he was again put under observation and followed to no. 112 High Street Islington, the residence of Malatesta, the notorious anarchist'.[30] In the British capital Agresti met and later married Olivia Rossetti, niece of the poets Christine and Dante Gabriel Rossetti, and co-editor with her sister Helen and her brother Arthur of the anarchist newspaper *The Torch*.[31]

The efficacy of border controls was nevertheless limited. The Police Commissioner, reporting on the arrival of one Polish and three French anarchists to Britain, underlined that he could obtain definitive information only in the case of anarchists officially expelled from foreign countries. In fact, 'Many Foreign Anarchists anxious to avoid a decree of expulsion, which would make them liable to penalties if they returned, or to escape criminal process in their own countries, have quietly crossed the channel without attracting notice, and are found in the usual haunts frequented by their confederates in London; but at present they act with great caution and it is a matter of difficulty to ascertain even their names.'[32]

The deportation of anarchists to England was another cause of diplomatic controversies. At times remonstrations were made to the representatives of foreign governments against the sending of 'dangerous characters' to Britain. The correspondence between the Belgian *Ministre des Affaires-Étrangères* and the Foreign Office during the last months of 1893 provides, in this sense, a typical example. In October 1893 Sir Francis Plunkett, British Minister in Brussels, made a protest to the Belgian foreign minister against the deportation to England of Henry Dupont, a French individualist anarchist who had in previous years published one of the most inflammatory and violent anarchist journals, *L'International*, in collaboration with the Italian anarchist Luigi Parmeggiani and the French anarchist Auguste Bordes. In his complaint, Sir Plunkett objected that 'H. M. could not calmly look on and tolerate the unlimited deportation to England of the refuse of the continent'.[33] The *Ministre des Affaires-Étrangères*, after providing assurance

B2840C/3.

[30] Assistant Commissioner of Police to the Under Secretary of State, Home Office, 19 May 1892. NA, HO144/587/B2840C/7.

[31] See Agresti, Olivia Rossetti, *The Anectodage of an Interpreter. Reminiscences, Rome 1958, Columbia University in New York*, Manuscript Collection.

[32] Assistant Commissioner of Police to the Under Secretary of State, Home Office, 24 May 1892. NA, HO144/587/B2840C/8.

[33] Her Majesty's Minister at Brussels to Foreign Secretary, 1 December 1894, NA, HO144/587/B2840C/52.

that Belgian authorities always made every effort to safeguard the interests of their neighbours when dealing with expulsions, expressed his regret that the British authorities believed the Belgian government 'had not behaved properly' and that they 'appear to think that the Belgian authorities habitually discharge into England the dangerous foreigners who they may wish to get rid of [...] and were in the habit of using England as a "dumping ground" for undesirable foreigners'.[34] In fact, Belgian law allowed the deportee to choose his final destination. However, the British protest caused some anxiety in the Belgian government 'as to what can now be done with foreigner anarchists and other undesirable characters. France, Germany, Holland and even the Grand Duchy of Luxembourg refuse to receive all such of foreign nationality, and if England also now refuses to admit them it is not easy to see how they are to be got rid of in the future'.[35]

A similar event took place a few years later in July 1897 when the Spanish authorities, without alerting the British government, expelled and embarked twenty eight anarchists on the steamship 'Isla de Luzon' bound for Liverpool.[36] These were some of the 400 militants arrested in the aftermath of an explosion that killed six people at a Corpus Christi procession in Barcelona in June 1896. Some prominent figures such as Teresa Claramunt Creus, 'the Spanish Louise Michel', and Jaime Torrens Ros, 'regarded as one of the most dangerous anarchists of Barcelona', were among the anarchists deported.[37] Also on board was Juan Montseny, author of many of the letters smuggled to the republican press denouncing the systematic torture and inhuman treatment of detainees at Montjuic prison.[38]

This shipment greatly annoyed the British authorities. Not only had the Spanish government sent twenty eight destitute Spaniards of anarchist opinion to Britain without any previous intimation of their intention to do so, but they had even deceived the British consul by denying their action.[39]

---

[34] Note from Mérode Westerloo, Ministre des Affaires-Étrangères Belgique, to the Foreign Office, 30 November 1894, NA, HO144/587/B2840C/52.

[35] Her Majesty's Minister at Brussels to Foreign Secretary, 1 December 1894, NA, HO144/587/B2840C/52.

[36] Consul in Barcelona William Wyndham to Foreign Office, 12 July 1897, NA, HO144/587/B2840C/68.

[37] Consul Willam Wyndham to Foreign Office. 12 July 1897, NA, HO144/587/B2840C/68.

[38] Following the bombing, martial law was declared and hundreds of people of 'advanced ideas' were arrested and detained at Montjuic prison. Rumors of systematic torture soon emerged and an international protest campaign was organised in several European countries. Notwithstanding the clear irregularities, five of the detainees were executed in May 1897. Jose Alvarez-Junco, *The Emergence of Mass Politics in Spain* (Portland Oreg.: Sussex Academic Press, 2002), pp. 55–66.

[39] Foreign Office to the Under Secretary of State, Home Office, 28 July 1897, NA, HO144/587/B2840C/68.

Moreover, the Spanish authorities had yielded to the objections of the French Government to the passage of other fifty anarchist prisoners through their frontiers and resolved to send them to England instead, as soon as the detainees could pay the cost of passage.[40]

Upon being informed of these events, the Home Secretary, Viscount Ridley, urged the Prime Minister, the Marquess of Salisbury, to address 'an immediate and strong protest to the Spanish government against their action' and, to prevent the shipment of the fifty anarchists, to inform it that such action would be considered 'an act of international discourtesy to a Friendly Power'.[41]

The news of the shipment of the twenty eight prisoners also prompted the Foreign Office to enquire whether there were any legal grounds on which to prevent the landing of those migrants; however, there was no statutory power which could do so.[42]

On 28 July the Spanish refugees landed at Liverpool, and the following day arrived at Euston station where they were greeted by Louise Michel and a large group of sympathisers.[43] The newcomers were driven to the German Club in Tottenham Street and secured places of residence in Soho.[44] A few weeks later, on 22 August, the refugees participated at a mass meeting held in Trafalgar Square to protest against the cruelties and tortures inflicted by the Spanish Government on the prisoners at Montjuic prison. The arrival of the twenty eight anarchists was widely reported by the press, provoking some harsh comments by Howard Vincent who remarked in a letter to *The Times*:

> That the English law should in such times stand by impotent while Spanish anarchists land defiantly at Liverpool, while activity is reported by sensational prints in Anarchist clubs in London is nothing less than an international scandal [...] Alone among civilized nations have we no power to expel foreigners holding, proclaiming, acting upon, doctrines the entire nation views with abhorrence. Small wonder, then, that the evil is increasing.[45]

British policy toward immigration changed drastically with the introduction of the 1905 Aliens Act. During the last years of the nineteenth

---

[40] Consul Wyndham to Lord Salisbury, 17 July 1897, NA, HO144/587/B2840C/70.

[41] Draft of Ridley's letter to Sailsbury , 21 July 1897, NA, HO144/587/B2840C/70.

[42] Foreign Office minutes, 17 July 1897, NA, HO144/587/B2840C/70.

[43] 'The exiled Spanish Anarchists. Arrival in Liverpool', *Liverpool Mercury*, 29th July 1897, p. 6.

[44] 'The Spanish Anarchists', *The Times*, 31 July 1897, p. 11.

[45] C. E. Howard Vincent, 'Letters to the editor. Aliens and the Anarchists', *The Times*, 18 August 1897, p. 10.

century British public opinion supported the passage of an act to prohibit the immigration of destitute aliens – especially after a large wave of Jewish immigrants from Russia arrived in the UK and settled in London's East End in the wake of government-backed pogroms beginning in 1903. Moreover, because the supporters of an Aliens Bill believed the increase in socialist and anarchist activities in London to be a direct consequence of immigration, this legislation was meant to 'raise the material position of the poor, and to ward off the revolution'.[46] The myth of London as the secret centre for international anarchist plots played a role in increasing support for the bill, together with stereotypes of Italians and Jews as dangerous and violent people who, in the common imagination, were seen as 'criminal and anarchists'.[47] Although attempts to introduce laws regulating immigration were twice rejected by Parliament in 1894 and 1903, eventually the Aliens Act came into force on 1 January 1906. With the introduction of the Act, the poor were no longer granted leave to enter the country unless they could demonstrate an ability to provide for their own means of subsistence. This was not applicable to those who could prove they were refugees fleeing political or religious persecution. In this way, even though the right of asylum had been partially safeguarded, it lost its most important characteristic: no longer automatic, it became discretionary since the victims of political or religious persecution had to prove their status. Moreover, a new power established by the Act allowed the Home Office, with the permission of the court, to expel immigrants convicted of a common crime and this endangered exiled anarchists. The threat of expulsion caused considerable apprehension and, apparently, to counter this eventuality the Italian anarchists living in England and France constituted a secret group prepared to help comrades issued with deportation orders and organise public campaigns in their support.[48]

The community of anarchists in London were soon faced with the consequences of the Act. As early as August 1905, the British police arrested two Italians, Adolfo Antonelli and Francesco Barberi, for publishing and distributing the newspaper *L'Insurrezione* on 29 July which celebrated the anniversary of King Umberto I's assassination by Gaetano Bresci.[49] According to the prosecutor this paper justified the crimes of assassination

[46] Bernard Gainer, *The Alien Invasion. The Origins of the Aliens Act of 1905* (London: Heinemann Educational Books, 1972), p. 102.

[47] On Jewish immigration to England see: J. Garrard, *The English and the Immigration 1880–1910* (London, New York,Toronto: Oxford University Press, 1971). For the radical Jewish in London: W. Fishman, *East End Jewish Radicals. 1875–1914* (Nottingham: Five Leaves, 2004).

[48] Inspector Frosali's report to Ministry of Interior, October 1905, ACS, *PS*, 1905, b.22.

[49] On Antonelli and Barberi see: ACS, *CPC*, b. 154 and b. 320; P. Di Paola, *Dizionario Biografico degli anarchici italiani*, I, (Pisa: BFS 2003), *ad nomen*.

and incitement to murder of the sovereign heads of Europe. The two were sentenced respectively to nine and ten months of hard labour.[50] In his monthly report, the Italian inspector in charge of the surveillance of anarchists in London informed the Ministry of the Interior that some anxiety existed in the anarchist community regarding the fate of their comrades. Many feared that Antonelli and Barberi were going to be deported at the end of their sentences because they had been convicted of a common crime and the ruling made no mention of the political context of their illegal act. However, the anarchists were not only intentioned to protest against a possible deportation, but also to oppose and legally challenge the implications of the bill. If Barberi and Antonelli were to receive an expulsion order, Malatesta was determined to dispute it and to transform the affair into a 'test case'.[51]

Several years later, in 1912, Malatesta himself was nearly extradited to Italy when he was sentenced to five months' imprisonment after a spy for the Italian government, Ennio Bellelli, had accused him of criminal libel.[52] The British government was forced to reconsider this decision as a result of international pressure and the mass demonstrations held in London to support Malatesta.

These cases marked a break with previous tradition; from the second half of the nineteenth century until the beginning of the twentieth, the sojourn of Italian anarchists in London continued a long history of hospitality towards Italian political refugees.

The roots of Italian political emigration to England date back to the very beginning of the *Risorgimento*. The first significant groups of Italian refugees moved to London during the 1820s to escape the repression that followed the failure of the revolutions in Naples and Piedmont in 1820–21 and in central Italy in 1832. During that period Italians refugees made up, together with Poles, the largest community of exiles in the British capital. To help overcome the great difficulties that characterised the lives of all refugees, Italian exiles benefited from the widespread Italophilia prevalent among the educated middle and upper classes in Britain during the Romantic era in which a capital of mutual interest and liking was accumulated.[53] Because the Italian language was considered an essential part of education for the professional and upper classes, many exiles easily found work as language teachers, which provided them with the opportunity of forging links with

---

[50] NA, HO144/795/131464; CRIM1/98/8, *Antonelli Adolfo, Barberi Francesco. Charge: Inciting to murder the Sovereigns of Europe.*

[51] Inspector Frosali's report to Ministry of Interior, December 1905, ACS, *PS*, 1905, b. 22.

[52] E. Malatesta, 'Alla Colonia Italiana di Londra',1912, IISH, Nettlau archive, f. 2781.

[53] Franco Venturi, 'L'Italia fuori d'Italia', in *Storia d'Italia. Dal primo settecento all' unità* (Turin: Einaudi, 1973), vol. III, p. 1195.

the British cultural élite and political circles and to defend the Italian cause within these *milieux*. As a result of their contacts with the British establishment, Italian exiles 'contributed at a very early stage to shaping British politicians' understanding of the Italian question'. At the same time, 'the exiles' direct observation of British political institutions, society and its economy stimulated debates about the features of the Italian nation'. Thus, *Risorgimento* exiles 'played a primary role in discussing foreign political models, in assimilating and spreading progressive ideas which were thus absorbed into Italian culture'.[54] As a consequence, by the 1830s, the community of Italian refugees in the United Kingdom became one of the most active and influential centres of Italian emigration in Europe.[55] Some of these expatriates eventually integrated themselves into English life, and gained important positions in society. Antonio Panizzi became director of the British Museum; Antonio Gallenga was professor at the University College and, a few years later, foreign correspondent of *The Times*; Gabriele Rossetti, whose grandchildren were to publish the anarchist newspaper *The Torch*, worked as professor of Italian at King's College.[56]

In January 1837, Giuseppe Mazzini, the refugee who had the greatest impact on the Italian community during the first half of the nineteenth century, arrived in London. For thirty years he played a crucial role in the exiles' world and became the most prominent personality among both Italian and foreign political refugees. Mazzini used the network of political exiles as a base for his agitation for Italian national independence. He expended great efforts to create a network of relationships with British politicians and intellectuals to win support for the unification of Italy. He also established contacts with British Chartism, the New Model trade unionists, secularists and other reformers in the labour and co-operative movements.

Plotting forays to Italy with other exiles and British supporters of his cause, Mazzini also worked actively within the Italian community in London, which suffered from great poverty. In 1840, he organised the self-help society *Unione degli operai italiani* as a section of the *Giovine Italia*, probably also in opposition to the explicitly German socialist *Arbeiterbildungsverein*.[57] The *Unione* marked an important point in the history of the Italian labour movement; it was the first artisan and workers' association that went beyond mutual aid and

[54] Maurizio Isabella, 'Italian Exiles and British Politics' , in Sabine Freitag (ed.), *Exiles from Euopean Revolutions* (Oxford–New York: Berghahn Books, 2003), pp. 60–61.

[55] Galante Garrone, 'L'emigrazione politica italiana del Risorgimento', in *Rassegna Storica del Risorgimento*, XLI, 1954, pp. 223–42.

[56] On exiles in London during the *Risorgimento* see: Enrico Verdecchia, *Londra dei cospiratori. L'esilio londinese dei padri del Risorgimento* (Milan: Tropea, 2010).

[57] Enrico Verdecchia, 'Tedeschi e italiani: rapporti e contrasti tra due comunità nell'esilio londinese', *Bollettino della Domus Mazziniana*, 1996, p. 181.

had political activity as one of its central tenets – preceding the lines of development of sections of the labour movement between 1860 and 1871.[58] Indeed, these experiments in workers' education and self-help outside Italy 'formed an important foundation for Italy's emerging labour movement'.[59] The association's newspaper, *L'Apostolato popolare*, which served as an instrument of education and propaganda, explicitly espoused Mazzini's views regarding the *'education'* of workers and the necessity of collaboration between social classes. During the same period Mazzini organised a free school for the children in the Italian community, most of whom were employed as organ-grinders and worked up to twelve hours a day.[60] According to Gabaccia, Mazzini's attempt to link Italian nationalism with migrants' economic concerns was successful; over a third of the Mazzinian supporters were labour migrants who became republicans and nationalists while living outside Italy.[61] Mazzini's activities were interrupted when he left for Italy to take part in the revolutions of 1848 in which he played a leading role in the constitution of the Roman Republic. Following the failure of the revolutionary attempts, the number of political refugees who escaped to the United Kingdom from the European reaction probably reached its apogee. It has been alleged that, during the Victorian age, 100,000 Italians became exiles from Italy.[62] Among them was Mazzini, who was forced to return to his refuge in London in 1851. His participation in the Roman Republic made him a charismatic figure and a political symbol among radical circles, and his fame reached the most politicised sections of the British working class. During this second exile, Mazzini had a hegemonic influence among Italian exiles and he mobilised support for the Italian cause among a wide section of the British public.[63]

Mazzini continued his activities among the workers in the colony, and founded the 'Italian Working Men's Association of Mutual Progress' which in 1864 claimed 350 members. On 13 December 1865, this association joined the 'International Workers' Association' (the First International) with great

[58] Franco Della Peruta, *Mazzini e i rivoluzionari* (Milan: Feltrinelli, 1974), p. 357.

[59] Donna R. Gabaccia, 'Class, Exile and Nationalism at Home and Abroad: the Italian Risorgimento', in Donna R. Gabaccia, Fraser Ottanelli (eds), *Italian Workers of the World: Labour Migration and the Formation of the Multiethnic States*(Urbana: University of Illinois Press, 2001), p. 31.

[60] On the organ-grinders, see: R. Paulucci di Calboli, *I girovaghi italiani in Inghilterra ed i suonatori ambulanti* (Città di Castello: Lapi tipografo editore, 1893).

[61] Gabaccia, *Italy's Many Diasporas*, p. 47.

[62] Gabaccia, 'Class, Exile and Nationalism', p. 27.

[63] However, there were also dissenting voices that focused more on the social injustices, for example Luigi Pianciani whose activity 'represents an interesting example of the dissemination of socialist ideas among Italians in England', Isabella, 'Italian Exiles and British Politics', pp. 67–76.

enthusiasm.[64] At this time Mazzini believed that he could influence the new radical internationalist organisation.[65]

Mazzini's role in the constitution of the I.W.A. is well known.[66] On 28 September 1864, his delegates Domenico Lama and Major Louis Wolf, members of the Italian Working Men's Association, attended the inaugural meeting of the I.W.A. held in St Martin's Hall. Wolf was elected to the sub-committee that wrote the draft of the I.W.A. constitution. This draft was later rewritten and significantly altered by Karl Marx. Lama, the president of the Italian Working Men's Association, was named secretary of the I.W.A. council. Fontana, who had requested membership of the International, was elected a member of the committee. Eight Italian Londoners were present at the General Council in December 1864, among them Setacci and Aldovrandi, respectively vice-president and councillor of the Mazzinian organisation. Mazzini and the other Italians withdrew from the I.W.A. after Marx and other currents overshadowed them. In the last years of his life, Mazzini's activities focused on the fight against Michael Bakunin and the influence of the First International in Italy that had developed and grown as a result of the initiative and powerful charisma of the Russian conspirators.[67] Bakunin was able to intercept the widespread dissatisfaction among the younger generation provoked by the persistence of social inequalities in the country, notwithstanding national unification, and by the inadequacy demonstrated by the two principal leaders of the democratic movement in engaging with the new political situation.

> Mazzini and Garibaldi continued to be idolised by the most advanced youth who wanted to have them as leaders and guides, but found it increasingly difficult to follow them. Mazzini became more rigid in his political and theological dogmatism in response to the upsurge of new tendencies and excommunicated those who did not believe in God; while Garibaldi, who wanted to persuade himself and others that he was always at the head of

---

[64] A declaration was read by G. P. Fontana, vice-president of the 'Italian Working Men's Association of Mutual Progress', at the central council meeting of the International on 3 January 1865. Members of the council of the Italian Working Men's Association of Mutual Progress were: D. Lama (president), G. P. Fontana and C. Setacci (vice-presidents), A. Vaccansi (treasurer), G. Geninazzi, F. Fenilli, F. Solustri, Gintini, Biloshy, and Velati (councillors), Dr G. Bagnagatti (secretary). See Institute of Marxism-Leninism, *General Council of the First International 1864–1866* (London: Lawrence & Wishart, 1962), pp. 1–61.

[65] Richard Hostetter, *The Italian Socialist Movement. Origins (1860–1882)* (Princeton: van Nostrand, 1958), p. 72.

[66] Max Nettlau, *Bakunin e l'Internazionale in Italia dal 1864 al 1872* (Geneva: Edizioni del 'Il Risveglio', 1928); Nello Rosselli, *Mazzini e Bakunin. Dodici anni di movimento operaio in Italia (1860–1872)* (Turin: Einaudi, 1967), (first ed. 1927).

[67] See: Franco Damiani, *Bakunin nell'Italia post unitaria 1864–1867* (Milan: Jaca Book, 1977).

progress, talked nonsense and basically understood nothing. Hence the moral and intellectual discomfort [...] among the best Italian youth. In this dispirited state a man like Bakunin, with the reputation of a great European revolutionary that accompanied him, with his wealth of ideas and modernity, with his passion and the captivating force of his personality, could not fail to make an impression on those who approached him.[68]

The fight within the International between Mazzini and Bakunin was crucial for the rise of Italian socialism and for the transition from *Risorgimento* nationalism to social revolutionary ideology and, concurrently, it marked the decline of Mazzini's political influence in Italy. This became evident after the experience of the Paris Commune, which had an enormous influence among young socialists but which Mazzini vigorously opposed, notably in his newspaper *La Roma del Popolo*. This fight had widespread repercussions within the Italian Left which divided and split Mazzini's group. Indeed, the most important members of Italian internationalism came from Mazzini's ranks: Osvaldo Gnocchi Viani, Errico Malatesta, Vincenzo Caporusso, Saverio Friscia, Celso Ceretti, Carlo Gambuzzi, Francesco Natta, Leoncavallo, Fanelli, Francesco Piccinini, and Vincenzo Pezza. Mazzini's condemnation of the Commune sealed his breach with the emergent socialist left in Italy.

> We were testing, we were wondering, we were seeking when, at last, the Paris Commune [*sic*.] ... it was like the beginning of a new life [...] What until then had been present in us (I speak of us, the generation that grew up after the establishment of the Kingdom of Italy) became idea ... So, starting from the denial of divine authority (the great foundation of Mazzini's theory) we necessarily and gradually arrived at the denial of human authority, that is, anarchy.[69]

It is difficult to say to what extent the divisions within the Italian Workingmen's Society and the socialist world affected the Italian colony in London. On the one hand, Mazzini's presence in London probably limited or retarded the growth of the International within the Italian community. On the other hand, such an important debate, with huge international consequences, could not but have had some sort of influence. Moreover, the Franco-Prussian war and the events of the Commune had already had an impact on the community of Italian political refugees in London, some of whom left the British capital to fight for the defence of Paris.[70] After the

---

[68] Errico Malatesta, 'Foreword', in Nettlau, *Bakunin e l'Internazionale*, p. 20.

[69] Carlo Cafiero, 'Il socialismo in Italia. Altre osservazioni sull'opuscolo di Osvaldo Gnocchi Viani "Le tre Internazionali"', *La Plebe*, 15, 16, 17 January 1876, quoted in Pier Carlo Masini, *Cafiero* (Milan: Rizzoli, 1974), p. 26.

[70] This was the case of G. Carusi, P. Savio and G. Carnevali. Emilia Civolani, 'La parteci-

fall of the Commune, London became the natural place to which radicalised refugees escaped. Among the many Italians there was Federico Ravà who fought with Garibaldi in France and was well known among the community of Italian refugees in the 1880s.

There is some evidence that two of the meeting places for political refugees, the Hotel Venezia and Bendi's public house – respectively described as Garibaldinian and Mazzinian – in subsequent years became meeting points for the anarchists. Bendi's public house also became the headquarters of the radical *Romagna Society*. This did not happen to the *Mazzini and Garibaldi Club* which, on the contrary, lost all its political connotations – to such an extent that it included among its honorary members the King of Italy. The contrast between the earlier *Risorgimento* generation and the young Internationalists inspired a script that Pietro Gori, anarchist poet and organiser, sent to his comrades in London. The play – based on 'an old Garibaldinian patriot and his anarchist son' – was staged in one of the anarchist clubs in London.[71] However the legacies of the earlier nationalist and republican traditions were not completely ignored by the younger generation and neither did the older generation completely shun the causes of the young. In 1881 the Italian anarchists in London arranged collections in favour of Amilcare Cipriani, the prominent leader of the Paris Commune who was on trial in Italy for a murder that had taken place fifteen years earlier in Alexandria in Egypt. They likewise organised parties at *Rose Street Club*. In November 1881, a list of subscribers from London was published in Costa's newspaper *Avanti!* This list included about twenty people: most of them were anarchists; the others were old republicans; Vincenzo Melandri was one of them. The others were Francesco Zoli, Giuseppe Perazzoli, Domenico Lama, the secretary of Mazzini's Working Men's Association, and Bendi, the owner of the public house in Greek Street. In 1882 Melandri, Bendi, Lama and others signed a statement in support of Cipriani's self-defence plea. The three testified that when he arrived in London from Egypt in 1867 and stayed at Melandri's house in Soho Square, his right arm was seriously injured.[72] Melandri, an innkeeper in Laystall Street that held strong anticlerical views, provides a good example of the links between the *Risorgimento* rank and file refugees with the Internationalists. Nicknamed *barilone* 'big barrel', he was native

pazione di emigrati italiani alla Comune di Parigi', *Movimento operaio e socialista*, II. 21 (1979), pp. 174–75.

71   Secret agent Calvo's report, London, 4 June 1894. ACS, *CPC*, b. 1519, f. (Cova Cesare).

72   Reports by the informer DM, Italian Embassy in London to the Italian Foreign Office, 23 February 1882, Asdmae, *Pol. Int.*, b. 4, f. (Divisione Affari Politici, 1 semestre 1882). On Amilcare Cipriani see Vittorio Emiliani, *Libertari di Romagna. Vite di Costa, Cipriani, Borghi* (Ravenna: Longo Angelo Editore, 1995) and Luigi Campolonghi, *Amilcare Cipriani. Una vita di avventure eroiche. Memorie raccolte da Luigi Campolonghi* (Società editoriale italiana, 1912).

of Faenza in central-north Italy.[73] In 1834 Melandri was convicted by the Papal authorities for a murder committed during the revolution of 1831 and in 1837 he was deported to Brasil.[74] In 1854 he was imprisoned in Rome and he was again deported to the United States. However, the following year he returned to Europe. The consul of the Papal State signalled his presence in Marseille to the French authorities that expelled him to England.[75]

Despite the unbridgeable political differences and the struggles with Mazzini and his supporters, the importance of Mazzini's role was always acknowledged by the Internationalists, as Malatesta recalled many years later:

> We who were still young dared to stand up against the Giant and fiercely fought him over his attacks against the International and the Paris Commune; we who are proudly keeping alive the memory of those struggles ... We were opposed to Mazzini for his understanding of the social struggle, for the providential mission which he attributed to Italy and Rome, for his religious dogmatism. There were, as always in the thick of the fight, excesses and misunderstandings on both sides, but in calmer spirits we recognise that in the depths of our souls, in the feeling that inspired us, we were Mazzinians as Mazzini was an internationalist.[76]

As it had been for the refugees from the *Risorgimento* and the European revolutions in the mid-Victorian era, England also for the later anarchists 'was a refugee's last choice rather than his first'.[77] In 1882, after one year spent in exile in London, Kropotkin and his wife resolved to leave and go back to France, in spite of the high degree of risk involved in that decision.

> The year that I then passed in London was a year of real exile. For one who held advanced socialist opinions, there was no atmosphere to breathe in. There was no sign of that animated socialist movement which I found so largely developed on my return in 1886 [...] My wife and I felt so lonely at London, and our efforts to awaken a socialist movement in England seemed so hopeless, that in the autumn of 1882 we decided to remove again to France. We were sure that in France I should be soon be arrested; but often we said to each other, 'Better a French prison than this grave'.[78]

---

[73] Italian consul to Italian ambassador, 4 November and 20 December 1881, Asdmae, *AL*, b. 70.

[74] Elio Lodolini, 'L'esilio in Brasile dei detenuti politici romani 1837', *Rassegna Storica del Risorgimento*, LXV.1 (1978), pp. 142–44

[75] Elio Lodolini, 'Deportazioni negli Stati Uniti d'America di detenuti politici dello Stato pontificio (1854–1858)', *Rassegna Storica del Risorgimento*, LXXXVIII. 2 (2001), p. 335.

[76] Errico Malatesta, 'Giuseppe Mazzini', in *Umanità Nova*, in Malatesta, *Scritti scelti*, vol. I, p. 324.

[77] Porter, *The Refugee Question*, p. 2.

[78] Petr Kropotkin, *Memories of a Revolutionist* (Boston, New York: Houghton Mifflin

The attitude of refugees is also vividly described in the story of the arrival of Gori and Edoardo Milano in London in the autobiographical novel by the Rossetti sisters: *A Girl Among the Anarchists*:

> One day, not long before Christmas, and after I had been nearly a year in the movement, when all London was lost in a heavy fog and the air seemed solid as a brick of wall, there landed at the *Tocsin* a small batch of three Italians fresh from their native country [...] None of these Southerners had ever been in England before, and having heard grim tales of the lack of sunshine and light in London, they took this fog to be the normal condition of the atmosphere [...] They then advanced towards me and avvocato Guglielmo Gnecco [Pietro Gori] held out his hand [...] "I am very glad to meet you at last Comrade," and we all shook hands. "So this is London! I had heard grim enough tales of your climate, but never had I conceived anything like this. It is truly terrible! But how do you get through your work? ... How do you find your way about the streets? [...] Giannoli (Edoardo Milano) here sees badly enough at all times, but today he has only escaped by the skin of his teeth from the most horrid series of deaths. It is not so, Giacomo?" Giannoli (Edoardo Milano) [...] looked up at this. "Oh I've had too much London already," he exclaimed fervently. "We must leave here for some other country tonight or tomorrow at the latest. We should be better off in prison in Italy than at liberty here".[79]

Even so, the Italians formed one of the largest groups in the polyglot community of anarchist expatriates in London. Almost all the Italian anarchists that took refuge in England lived in the capital. In 1909, fifteen consular agents and the Italian consuls in Glasgow, Cardiff and Dublin replied to a request of the Ministry of Interior stating that neither anarchists nor socialists resided in the territory under their jurisdiction. The only positive reply came from the consular agent in Southampton, where five Italian anarchists lived, among them there was Emilia Armetta that put up anarchists either on their way to or on their return from the United States.[80]

Italian anarchists lived in Holborn, Soho and Clerkenwell, the areas where the Italian community traditionally settled. The Italian colony in those years was generally very poor, although this poverty was alleviated by mutual aid due to the existence of a long standing and supportive community. The first Italian immigrants who moved to London for economic reasons, particularly during the period 1840–1870, were mostly unskilled workers and their activities were mainly itinerant: most of them were organ-grinders,

---

Company, 1899), p. 412. Kropotkin was indeed arrested and imprisoned for beeing part of the International from 1883 to 1886.

[79] Isabel Meredith, *A Girl Among the Anarchists* (London: Duckworth & Co., 1903), p. 109.

[80] Frosali's report to Ministry of Interior, 9 September 1909. ACS, *PS*, 1909, b. 4, f. 5075/103.

street pedlars, plaster figure makers or ice-cream sellers. It was to these workers that Tito Zanardelli, one of the first anarchists to arrive in London, addressed his bombastic propaganda in 1878.[81]

Vagrancy was regarded as the main feature of Italian immigration, from a negative perspective, as late as 1893.[82] Indeed, the large number of destitute immigrants in the Italian community raised concerns in part because of their possible links with revolutionary secret societies:

> Many Italians arrive in this country in an absolutely destitute condition, knowing no trade and having neither friends nor money [...] They are ignorant of the country, of its language, of its laws, and being thus unnameable to any good influences which may exist, they quickly fall into bad hands. [...] Professional beggars lay in wait for them, and teach them how to approach with success the different charitable societies, or, worse still, they fall an easy prey to one of the secret socialistic or revolutionary leagues which abound in the metropolis. I am informed upon trustworthy authority that the number of foreign revolutionists in this country has very largely increased during the last three years, and [...] there can be no doubt that in this rapid increase of foreign revolutionary societies lurk the elements of a very grave and serious social danger.[83]

The British authorities and public opinion were also concerned about the condition of the districts where Italians lived, in particular Holborn and Saffron Hill, where houses were overcrowded and unhygienic, as the medical journal *Lancet* reported:

> the colony is very compact and where the Italian lives English rarely reside. [...] the Italians, on fine, dry summer evenings, come out of the wretched houses and sleep on the smooth flag-stones of the court just as they may be seen sleeping on the church steps in Italy. On these occasions the court is so crowded with prostrate Italians that it is impossible to walk down. But a glance at the interior of the houses would suffice to show why the open street on a fine evening is preferable and far healthier [...] The inhabitants were all men who go out with the organs all day long, no one remaining at home to make the smallest pretence at cleaning the place. It was admitted to us that the floors had not even been swept for two years, much less scrubbed or washed. It was not possible to see through the window-panes for the dust that had accumulated upon them [...] The rooms contained as many double beds as could be got into them, and no other furniture whatsoever [...]. There were no washing-stands, no basins, no towels,

---

[81] Zanardelli Tito, *Della utilità e dello scopo di un Circolo italiano di Studj Sociali a Londra* (London: Biblioteca del circolo di studi sociali, 1879), p. 1.

[82] Paulucci di Calboli, *I Girovaghi italiani*, p. 30.

[83] W. H. Wilkins, 'The Italian Aspect', in: Arnold White, *The Destitute Alien in Great Britain* (London: S. Sonnenschein & Co, 1892), pp. 146–47.

nothing – but beds with very scanty, filthy black bedding, swarming with vermin [...] Two, if not three, men sleep in each bed [...] this small area would occasionally shelter as many as twenty persons for the night [...] In Somers Court [...] the drains were so constantly stopped that they overflowed, and the inhabitants had to place planks on stones so as to step from house to house without treading in the sewage matter lying exposed in the open court [...] the overcrowding and the disgraceful intermixing of the sexes continue unchecked.[84]

According to Giuseppe Prato, the social conditions of Holborn's Italian colony in 1900 were not very different. Italians lived 'in the absolute negation of every principle of hygiene and cleanliness, in the most scandalous promiscuity of sex, ages condition, completely lacking in collective organs of improvement and cultivation'.[85]

The anarchists tried several times to organise the workers in the community. At the end of the century, catering became the main sector of employment for Italians that were employed in large numbers as cooks and waiters in the restaurants, particularly in the Soho area.[86] Not surprisingly, the catering sector became one of the centres for organised politics, from the anarchists to the Fascists.[87] In 1890, the Italian Ambassador Count Tornielli wrote to Francesco Crispi that the propaganda in London was directed in particular at the numerous chefs and waiters who were organised into an association numbering several hundred members.[88]

In July 1893, Malatesta, Gori, Merlino and Agresti referred to the establishment of a new workers' association in opposition to the *Circolo Mazzini-Garibaldi* in a letter to the director of the newspaper *Londra-Roma*, Pietro Rava, and raised the issue of poor working conditions in the restaurants.

---

[84] Report of The Lancet Special Commission on the sanitary condition of the Italian quarter, *The Lancet*, 18 October 1879, vol. 2, pp. 590–92.

[85] Giuseppe Prato, 'Gli italiani in Inghilterra', *La Riforma Sociale*, VII, 10, 1899, pp. 680–81.

[86] On Italian emigration to Britain: Lucio Sponza, *Italian Immigrants in Nineteenth-Century Britain. Realities and Images* (Leicester: Leicester University Press, 1988). Prof. Todeas Twattle-Basket, pseud. [i.e. Tommaso de Angelis], *Note di Cronaca, ossia i giornali, gli istituti e gli uomini illustri italiani a Londra durante l'era Vittoriana, 1837–1897* (Bergamo: 1897), p. 85.

[87] For example in August 1932 Dino Grandi, only one month after he became Ambassador to London, wrote to Mussolini that 'his intention was to appear as a 'father' to the Italian community ... In particular he emphasised the absence of an organisation among Italian cooks and waiters, although they numbered many thousands and were spread almost everywhere throughout the city'. (Claudia Baldoli, *Exporting Fascism. Italian Fascists and Britain's Italians in the 1930s* (Oxford, New York: Berg, 2003, p. 19.) Two years later two catering societies were created in London: the Italian Culinary Society, and The Wine and Food Society.

[88] Ambassador Tornielli to Crispi, London 22 October 1890, Asdmae, *Pol. Int.*, b. 36.

In the Italian restaurants the kitchen boys work sometimes sixteen hours a day in a humid and fiery basement ruining their health for a few shillings a week. There are some restaurants where the pay is so paltry that workers, however wretched, remain only a few weeks; and there are others in which the owners, in agreement with the middlemen, sack laborers to allow the middlemen to pocket new tips. Many other serious abuses are committed against us, abuses that the Circolo does not care to suppress.[89]

On 12 January 1901 the newspaper *L'Internazionale* announced the first meeting of the 'Lega di resistenza fra i lavoratori in cucina' set up by the Socialist Anarchist Group.

Italian anarchists also sought to organise schools for workers' education, an initiative reminiscent of Mazzini's. They opened a *Circolo Educativo* for Italian workers, although it did not last very long. In 1905 they rented a room in Euston Street, not far from Soho and the Italian area, where they established the *Università Popolare*. The *Università Popolare* had a cosmopolitan flavour, and was opened by speeches from Tárrida de Mármol and Errico Malatesta on 25 February 1905.[90] In 1910, the 'North London Comunist Group opened the International School Francisco Ferrer in Windmill Street. The school was closed for lack of means. The evening School Francisco Ferrer was reopened at 99 Charlotte Street in 1919, enrolling twenty five children. In the opening speech Malatesta attacked the Church and the Spanish monarchy.[91]

The activities of Italian anarchists, as well those of other political refugees, were directed not only at the local community but also at their homeland, as reported by the police inspector Mandolesi in 1905.

Political activity in London can easily be divided into two categories (and this applies as much to that of the Italians as it does to those of other countries). Propaganda aimed at affecting emigrants who are resident here. Agitation to help financially or morally the movement in the native country or in countries where events are taking place that arouse interest and sympathy. It is thus, according to the situation, that the hidden subversive movement makes itself manifest.[92]

The next chapters will focus on these two categories of political activity that were at the centre of the Italian anarchist exiles in London.

---

[89] 'Voci del pubblico', *Londra–Roma*, 22 August 1893, p. 3. (The letter was signed by Pietraroja, Bianconi, Agresti, Merlino, Malatesta, and Bertani.)

[90] *Relazione sul movimento sovversivo in Londra nel mese di Febbraio*, ACS, *PS*, 1905, b.22.

[91] Inspector Frosali's reports to Minsitry of Interior, 27 November 1910, 31 August and 1 September 1912. ACS, PS, 1912, b. 36.

[92] Inspector Mandolesi to Ministry of Interior, May 1905. ACS, *PS, 1905*, b. 22.

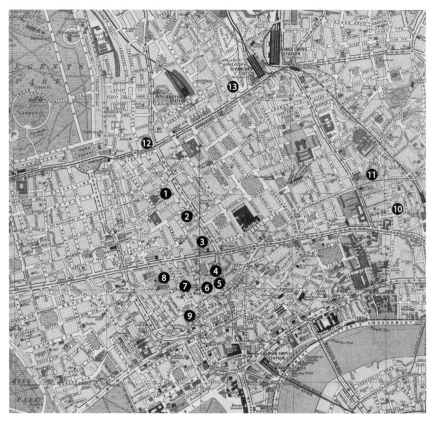

The anarchist milieu in London.

1 Charlotte Street, Fitzroy Square
Communist Club, n. 57 (1897)
Communist Club, n. 107 (1911)
Gruppo di studi sociali di Londra, n. 99 (from 1912)
Evening school Ferrer, n. 99 (from 1912)
International Working Men's Society n. 83 (1901)
2 Windmill Street
Autonomie Club (1890)
White Art, Free House. N. 17. Circolo Italiano di Studj Sociali (1879)
3 Hanway Street 38-40. Circolo Filodrammatico

4 Rose Street (now Manette Street)
German Communist Workers' Educaional Union (1848)
5 Greek Street
Free House owned by Bendi (1870s)
Club cooperativo
6 Frith street
Lega di resistenza dei lavoratori della mensa, n. 55. (1905)
7 Wardour Street
International Working Men's Society, n. 104. (1901)
8 Poland Street,
Università popolare (1904)

9 Archer street,
Defendi's shop, n. 12.
10 Hatton Garden Clerkenwell
Università popolare, n. 58
11 Laystall Street
Melandri's Free House, n. 10 (1870s)
12 Euston road, Università Popolare, no. 4.
13 Ossulston Street, Euston Road,
The Torch offices, no. 127

2

The Making of the Colony

Origins: the late 1870s and Tito Zanardelli

Repression of the social conflicts that erupted across new and old European nation-states during the 1870s and early 1880s led to waves of political refugees who swelled the communities of expatriates already present in London: French, German, and Russian in particular. Following the fall of the Paris Commune and its bloody aftermath in 1871 around 3,500 men, women and children fled to England.[1] A few years later, hundreds of militants fled Germany to escape persecution under Bismarck's anti-socialist law of 1878. In Russia, the killing of Tsar Alexander II in 1881 sparked violent reaction; more than 225,000 Jews left the country, driven by pogroms and repressive regulations. The majority went to the United States but a good number found shelter in the East End of London.[2]

In Italy, Giovanni Passanante's failed attempt on the life of King Umberto I on 17 November 1878 led to a surge in repression against the International. The assassination attempt caused the fall of the Cairoli-Zanardelli government. Agostino Depretis constituted a new cabinet in which he was both Prime Minister and Minister of Interior. Government repression denied the Italian Federation of the First International political importance or legitimacy – it was legally considered to be an 'association of malefactors'. Therefore its associates were considered members of criminal organisations unconnected to politics and, consequently, they were 'persecuted almost at

---

[1] P. K. Martinez, 'A Police Spy and the Exiled Communards, 1871–1873', *The English Historical Review*, 97. 382 (1982), pp. 99–112.

[2] William J. Fishman, *East End Jewish Radicals. 1875–1914*, (Nottingham: Five Leaves, 2004), p. 30; Paul Knepper, 'The other invisible hand: Jews and anarchists in London before the First World War', *Jewish History*, 22.3 (2008), pp. 295–315.

will as criminals and outlaws'.[3] Although the government's judicial offensive did not succeed in its aim of outlawing the International, the repression destroyed the organisation and virtually put paid to the Italian Federation of the I.W.A.[4] Many Italian anarchists chose exile over imprisonment; some of them eventually reached England, often after passing through several countries on the way.

The beginnings of anarchist militancy in London's Italian community emerged with the arrival of Tito Zanardelli in the city following his expulsion from France in 1878.

Born in the northern Italian town of Vittorio Veneto in 1848, Zanardelli began his political life in the Republican Party. Mazzini's ideas, particularly regarding the education of the working classes, had a strong influence on him. Zanardelli oscillated between reformist socialism and anarchism throughout his life; he 'probably never accepted the premises that impelled Costa, Malatesta and Cafiero to argue a dialectical incompatibility between their vision of a future society and that envisaged by a Mazzini or a Garibaldi'.[5]

In 1870 he sojourned in Naples, where he enrolled at the university to study natural sciences and became the leader of the Mazzinian Republican students. He promoted several demonstrations that led to his arrest and a sentence to five months' internal exile.[6] In 1871 Zanardelli joined the Internationalists and, together with Carlo Cafiero, Alberto Tucci and Carlo Gambuzzi, founded the newspaper *La Campana*. Over the course of the following years he participated in several enterprises. He attended the Conference of Rimini, where the Italian Federation of the International Workingmen's Association was established in August 1872; he subsequently opened sections of the I.W.A. in Rome with Gnocchi Viani and in Venice with Pietro Magri; and he presided over the second congress of the Italian Federation of the I.W.A. in Bologna in 1873.[7] During his travels around Italy

---

[3] Pernicone, *Italian Anarchism*, p. 134.

[4] Pier Carlo Masini, *Storia degli anarchici italiani da Bakunin*, pp. 151–68; Pernicone, *Italian Anarchism*, pp. 147–57. For the historiographical debate on the periodisation of the First International in Italy see: Pier Carlo Masini, 'La Prima Internazionale in Italia. Problemi di una revisione storiografica', in *Il Movimento operaio e socialista. Bilancio storiografico e problemi storici. Convegno di Firenze. 18–20 gennaio 1963* (Milan: Edizioni del Gallo, 1965), pp. 85–142.

[5] Richard Hostetter, *The Italian Socialist Movement, I: Origins (1860–1914)*, (Princeton, N.J.: D. Van Nostrand Co., 1958), p. 300.

[6] Misato Toda, *Errico Malatesta da Mazzini a Bakunin: la sua formazione giovanile nell'ambiente napoletano (1868–1873)* (Napoli: Guida, 1988), p. 42.

[7] Francesco Moisio, *Anarchici a Venezia* (Venice: La Tipografica, 1989); Marietta Nejrotti, 'Zanardelli Tito', in F. Andreucci and T. Detti (eds), *Il movimento operaio italiano: Dizionario biografico, 1853–1943* (Rome: Editori Riuniti, 1975–1979), v. 6, pp. 266–71.

Zanardelli worked as an 'itinerant conjurer and hypnotist'; an occupation that also took him to Serbia and the Austro-Hungarian territories.[8]

According to a Ministry of Interior report, Zanardelli was one of the organisers of the uprising in August 1874 in the Romagna that ended in total failure. Following the collapse of the insurrectionary attempt, he left Italy to avoid arrest and took refuge in Switzerland.[9] A year later, together with the Italian Internationalist Ludovico Nabruzzi and the Swiss Joseph Favre, Zanardelli established in Lugano a dissident section of the International Working Men's Association which sided with the reformist wing of the International: the *Sezione del Ceresio*.[10] The section, under Benoît Malon's influence, aimed at winning leadership of the International in Italy by uniting socialist forces around a moderate programme that considered electoral participation and working class education to be the chief means of political struggle.[11] The *Sezione del Ceresio* strongly criticised the Italian anarchists – especially the *Comitato per la Rivoluzione Sociale* led by Malatesta and Cafiero – for their intransigent position towards parliamentary socialist parties and their policy of insurrection that led to the armed rebellion in the Matese massif near Benevento in April 1877.[12] At the World Socialist Congress in Ghent in September of the same year where he represented some of the Italian reformist socialist groups, Zanardelli expressed his criticisms by fiercely attacking Malatesta, Cafiero and the Matese attempt.[13] This political position deeply affected Zanardelli's relationship with the Italian anarchist community in London a few years later.

In March 1878 Zanardelli was arrested in Paris, where he had gone to establish links between the *Sezione del Ceresio* and French sections of the International in an attempt to organise the moderate forces within the IWA.[14] On expulsion from France he departed for London where he

---

[8] Piero Brunello, *Storie di anarchici e di spie* (Donzelli: Rome, 2009), p. 82.

[9] Ministry of Interior to Foreign Ministry, 27 October 1881, Asdmae, *Pol. Int.*, b. 6, f. (Ministero dell'Interno. Corrispondenza ricevuta, 1881).

[10] Franco Della Peruta, 'Il socialismo italiano dal 1875 al 1882', *Annali dell'Istituto G.G. Feltrinelli*, 1, (1958), pp. 15–58.

[11] Romano Broggini, 'Un gruppo internazionalista dissidente: la sezione del Ceresio', in Liliano Faenza (ed), *Anarchismo e socialismo in Italia (1872–1892)* (Rome: Editori Riuniti, 1973), pp. 187–208. Vincent, K. Steven, *Between Marxism and Anarchism. Benoit Malon and French Reformist Socialism* (Berkeley Los Angeles, Oxford: University of California Press, 1992), pp. 52–57; Binaghi, *Addio, Lugano bella*, pp. 247–64.

[12] On the Matese attempt: Masini, *Gli internazionalisti: la banda del Matese, 1876–1878* (Milan: Avanti, 1958).

[13] Leo Valiani, 'Dalla Prima alla Seconda Internazionale (1872–1889)', *Movimento Operaio*, 2, (1954), p. 192.

[14] Alongside Zanardelli, the French police also arrested Ludovico Nabruzzi, Andrea Costa and the Russian Anna Kuliscioff.

joined the community of political refugees, attending the *réunions socialistes* organised by émigrés from the Commune.[15] It was in this milieu that Zanardelli met the Communard refugees Jean-Baptiste Clément and Jules Louise Alexandre Joffrin, with whom he conceived a new undertaking.[16]

In September 1878, a prospectus announced the forthcoming publication of the bilingual *La Guerre Sociale/La Guerra Sociale*, a new socialist organ in French and Italian that intended 'to plead the cause of the hungry against the full, of the workmen who ask for bread and freedom in exchange for their labour against those who lord it over the world seated on a pile of corpses'. Several newspapers in Italy, France, Belgium, and London reported its imminent appearance.[17] Socialists in Cesena sent their encouragement to the editors and wished the newspaper a 'prosperous and long life'.[18]

La Guerra Sociale got off to a promising start: two hundred people subscribed to the newspaper, including Karl Marx.[19] It was composed of two sections, one in French and the other in Italian.[20] In London it was available in all French bookshops and in other stores in the Soho and Euston areas where other French and Italian revolutionary publications were available.[21] *La Guerra Sociale* was also sold in Brussels, Geneva and Liege. The newspaper's chosen title was explained in the first issue. An unsigned Italian article proclaimed that workers needed to subvert the economic bases of society if they wished to insure a dignified life for themselves. Economic and political reforms, universal suffrage and parliamentarism were ineffective means; social war – *la guerra sociale* – was the only way to win social and economic emancipation. The editorial expressed these hopes in bombastic and violent language:

---

[15] P. K. Martinez, *Paris Communard Refugees in Britain, 1871–1880*, Ph.D. thesis, University of Sussex, 1981, p. 463.

[16] Martinez, *Paris Communard Refugees*, p. 271.

[17] 'A New Socialist Organ', *The Graphic*, 7 September 1878. See also: *La Guerre Sociale. Journal Socialiste-Révolutionnaire*, 2 October 1878, no. 1, p. 2.

[18] V. Valducci and Gallo Galli, 'Nostra Corrispondenza', *La Guerre Sociale/La Guerra Sociale. Journal Socialiste-Révolutionnaire*, 2 October 1878, no. 1, p. 4.

[19] Martinez, *Paris Communard Refugees*, p. 271.

[20] *La Guerre Sociale – La Guerra Sociale (1878) Amministrazione e redazione a Robert Warwick, 7 Noel Street, Oxford St, Londres*. In total four issues appeared between October and November 1878.

[21] The selling points were: 'Morel, 36 Charlotte Street (*Le Mirabeu* and *Le Cri du People* from Verviers, *Le Socialism Progressif* from Lugano, *La Jeune Icarie* from Jowa, *La Voix de l'Ouvrier* and *L'Avenir du Travailleur* from Bruxelles, *La Plebe* from Milan, *L'Agitatore* from Siena, and *Il Povero* from Palermo); Victor Richard, 67 Charlotte Street, Fitzroy Square; C. Rossi, 8 Charles Street, Hatton Garden; Louis Doirier 46b Rathbone Place, Oxford Street; W. Kraan 27 Rathbone Place, Oxford Street; Simmon, Greek Street, Soho; S. Nava, Church Street, Soho; Petit-Jean, 3 Old Compton Street, Soho.

We want social war because it is the only means left to the worker to gain his economic emancipation. We want it with its deaths, its violences and its reprisals since it is only too true that those who leave the revolution half made are digging their own graves. We want it driven by despair, provoked by egoism and pressed by necessity that makes even more just a war already just in itself [...] You, bourgeoises, do you really believe that an empty stomach and a poor pocket are not a *Casus Belli*? Those who sow the wind, reap the whirlwind [...] Our time is coming. You have wanted it, you bear entire responsibility for it.[22]

The style of the newspaper and its extremist invectives were a cause for concern among the Communard refugees, some of whom feared it might hinder the granting of an amnesty.[23] Its tone attracted strong criticism from other publications like the republican newspaper *Fanfulla* published in Rome and the monarchist *Satana*, published in Cesena.[24] *La France*, a French publication, likewise blasted the newspaper for its Socialist theories. *La Guerra Sociale* was also subject to attacks from Charles Bradlaugh who had exposed the newspaper in a meeting, 'to public vengeance as preaching the murder and wishing to put a profane hand on his divinity the capital'.[25]

La Guerra Sociale responded by underlining the gap that separated its detractors from the working class. It condemned the affected and refined language of the two Italian newspapers and the atheist Bradlaugh's rather abstract fight against the powers of heaven through alliance with earthly authorities. However, the fact that *La Guerra Sociale* provoked such responses in Italy, France and England does suggest that it enjoyed a healthy circulation despite its limited print run of 500 copies.

The editors of *La Guerra Sociale* were in close contact with the Internationalists of Emilia-Romagna and most contributions from Italy to the paper came from that region.[26] These included accounts of the persistent repression against the International's activities by the new government of the Left that made it impossible for the militants 'to take any step without being put under *ammonizione*, arrested, or subjected to other arbitrary actions'.[27] *La Guerra*

[22] 'La Guerra Sociale', *La Guerre Sociale/La Guerra Sociale,* 2 October 1878, no. 1, p. 3.

[23] Martinez, *Paris Communard Refugees in Britain*, p. 271.

[24] 'Fanfulla di Roma e Satana di Cesena', *La Guerre Sociale/La Guerra Sociale,* 2 November 1878, no. 4, p. 3; 'Il governo delle manette e la caccia ai socialisti', *La Guerre Sociale/La Guerra Sociale* , no. 3, 25 October 1878, p. 3.

[25] 'Monsieur Bradlaugh et la Guerre Sociale', *La Guerre Sociale/ La Guerra Sociale,* 2 October 1878, no. 3, p. 1.

[26] 'I Socialisti Cesenati a tutti i compagni di Italia', *La Guerre Sociale/La Guerra Sociale,* 9 October 1878, no. 2, p. 3; 'Associazione Internazionale dei lavoratori, regione italiana, sezione riminese. Ai compagni dell'esercito', 25 October 1878, no. 3, pp. 3–4.

[27] 'I socialisti cesenati a tutti i compagni di Italia', *La Guerre Sociale/La Guerra Sociale,* no.

Sociale denounced repression and harassment by the judiciary and the police in other parts of Italy as well. Reporting on the arrest of Anna Kuliscioff, Luisa Pezzi and Francesco Natta in the round-up of Internationalists in Florence on 1 October 1878, on the trials of the editors of several Italian newspapers and the disruption of a congress in Padova by police, one article concluded that:

> Nothing is allowed to the Socialists. Not demonstrations, conferences, congresses, or newspapers. To discuss rights is a crime punished by law … Rights of association, of writing, of speech […] they are all denied to proletarians … This proves that they are precluded from the so celebrated peaceful means. The masters are those forcing the proletariat to take the way of the barricades.[28]

La Guerra Sociale also dealt with issues that would become predominant subjects of debate among anarchist and socialist ranks in the years which followed. The failed assassination attempt against King Alfonso of Spain carried out by Oliva Moncasi was occasion for the newspaper to expound its views on regicide, which it did not support for various reasons.[29] Firstly, because regicide did not remove the causes of exploitation. According to the newspaper, to shake the social structure to its base the socialist struggle must be directed against individual property and against the economic tyrannies that made political tyrannies possible. Moreover, regicide was an individual act, while the socialists aimed at the involvement of the masses in a revolutionary movement.[30] These views did not, however, prevent the newspaper from expressing its full sympathy for the author of the assassination attempt.

Probably prompted by the scale of disruption and violence that had characterised the cotton strikes in Lancashire a few months before, the French section of *La Guerra Sociale* addressed the issue of industrial action in a series of two articles. The paper's position was clear: strikes were the outposts of the social revolution. They deepened solidarity among the workers and strengthened class consciousness. Strikes were positive even when they failed to obtain tangible results:

> When after a strike, the workers return to their workshops or descend into the mines without having achieved any gain, do not believe that nothing

---

2, 9 October 1878, p. 4.

[28] 'Il governo delle manette e la caccia ai socialisti', *La Guerre Sociale/La Guerra Sociale*, no. 3, 25 October 1878, p. 3.

[29] Moncasi shot at the king without hitting him on the 25 October 1878. He was sentenced to death and executed about a month later.

[30] 'Il regicidio', *La Guerre Sociale/La Guerra Sociale*, 2 November 1878, no. 4, p. 3.

has been done. It is not a submissive man who returns to the workshop, but a rebel, an enemy. Rancour and revolt are in his heart.[31]

La Guerra Sociale was shortlived. By the third issue, an appeal urging readers to settle their subscriptions revealed serious financial difficulties that were the likely cause of the newspaper's closure after its fourth issue.

Zanardelli, however, continued his activity among the community of political exiles and also came into contact with the British left. In May 1878 he was co-opted onto the general council of the *International Labour Union*, and a month later was named correspondent secretary for Italy.[32] The *International Labour Union* was established at the end of 1877 in an attempt to revive the First International.[33] Its main objective was 'to combine into one central organisation all the national and local labour organisations throughout the world. The *Union* acknowledges for its basis justice for all men without regard to sex, colour, creed or nationality'.[34] The organisation assembled a broad range of British radicals: members of the old International like Hermann Jung, John Hales, Johann Georg Eccarius, Weston, van der Hout, Tom Mottershead and Harriett Law; the radical free thinkers Charles Bradlaugh, Annie Besant and J. Groutand; the trade unionists G. Shipton and E. Hopes; the Christian socialist Steward Headlam and the Danish Social Democrat Fritz Schumann; political refugees like the French Victor Delahaye and the Russian L. B. Lazar Gol'denberg. The *International Labour Union* sent a letter to the Trades Union Congress at Bristol, stressing the necessity of international organisation and offering its assistance in negotiating with foreign labour societies to restrain the immigration of foreign workers into the country.[35] Zanardelli and Schumann proposed that three delegates attend the International Workmen's congress in Paris at the beginning of September 1878. Schumann was one of the delegates, but was arrested by the police shortly after his arrival in Paris and only released toward the end of the month.[36] During Schumann's detention, members of the *International Labour Union* put pressure on the Foreign Secretary,

---

[31] 'La question des grèves', *La Guerre Sociale/La Guerra Sociale*, 2 November 1878, no. 4, p. 2.

[32] Max Nettlau , 'Ein verschollener Nachklang der Internationale: The International Labour Union (London 1877–1878)', in Carl Grünberg *Archiv für die Geschite des Sozialismus und der Arbeiter bewagung Neunter Jaughang*, 1921, p. 137.

[33] Valiani, 'Dalla prima alla seconda Internazionale, pp. 177–247.

[34] 'Trade News. The International', *The Dundee Courier & Argus and Northern Warder*, 18 January 1878, p. 7.

[35] The letter signed by the Chairman H. Young and the General Secretary J. S. Howell in: 'Trades' Union Congress', *The Bristol Mercury and Daily Post*, 13 September 1878, p. 2.

[36] Nettlau, 'Ein verschollener Nachklang der Internationale', p. 143. Cfr. F. Schumann, 'To the editor of the Standard', *the Standard*, 3 October 1878, p. 5.

the Marquess of Salisbury, to facilitate his release. Zanardelli and Jung apparently also organised a collection to support Schumann's wife and sons.

In November 1879 Zanardelli, Paul Brousse, the Spanish Casanova and Johan Most were among speakers at a meeting organised by a German club in protest at the arrest of the anarchists Just and Kaufmann in Germany for smuggling Most's newspaper *Freiheit*.[37]

Concurrently, in the summer of 1879, Zanardelli, Enrico Vercellino and Giorgio Brogio Boezio promoted a club, the *Circolo Italiano di Studj Sociali*, which aimed at organising and educating workers in the Italian colony. In announcing the constitution of the circle, the executive committee asked other refugees to donate books and newspapers for the formation of a library.[38] Meetings were held every Tuesday evening at the public house *White Hart*, in 17 Windmill Street, off Tottenham Court Road.[39]

The handbill announcing the constitution of the club, and the speeches addressed by Zanardelli to its members in two public houses – *The Bull's Head* and the *Hat and Tun* in Hatton Wall – give an idea of the paternalistic attitude that characterised the club's charter. After describing the misfortunes and hardships that workers faced daily (daughters prostituting themselves to feed their parents, aged people committing suicide to avoid to dying of famine, parents becoming murderers to save their children), Zanardelli proclaimed the aims of the *Circolo di Studj Sociali's* founders. In contrast to the patronising and ineffective character of friendly societies, the circle's main aim was the political education of Italian workers who were incapable of understanding their social position and their rights by themselves.[40] The club was intended to be a school in which workers could understand the causes of their pitiable conditions, become aware of their own strength and find a way to gain their own social and economic emancipation: 'In a word we want to fill the stomach and not allow the brain to languish. To ask and to obtain Bread, Science and Work.'[41]

In establishing our Circle, we had a highly humanitarian belief; we put one hand on our heart, the other on our conscience and we bravely looked ahead and behind you [...] We said: "Let us see if there is a way to open the eyes of these workers, so blind and indolent to reach depravity; to make

[37] Marc Vuilleumier, 'Paul Brousse et son passage de l'anarchisme au socialisme', *Cahiers Vilfredo Pareto*, 3.7/8 (1965), p. 75. Cfr also *Le Révolté*, 15 November 1879. On Kaufmann cfr: Andrew Carlson, *Anarchism in Germany* (Metuchen: The Scarecrow Press, 1972), p. 210.

[38] Handbill, 'Circolo Italiano di Studj Sociali', 3 June 1879. IISH, Jung archive, f. 535.

[39] The secretary's office of the Circle was located at 57 London Street, Tottenham Road. Membership fee amounted to one shilling plus a weekly contribution of six pence.

[40] In 1882 Zanardelli published one of his speeches under the title: *L'operaio in Italia e la sua non coscienza delle proprie forze e dei propri diritti* (Naples: Tipografia di L. Gargiulo, 1882)

[41] 'Circolo Italiano di Studj Sociali', 3 June 1879. IISH, Jung archive, f. 535.

them study the evils that torment them, not for the sake of study, but to suggest and bring about a real, effective, immediate remedy. [...] To reach your emancipation, once again, you must associate with each other [...] Let us establish the League of the poor against the rich." [...] Workers! You are poor, ignorant, you eat little and you dress badly, you sleep even worse. We are offering you a new life![42]

The club published its own bulletin: the *Bollettino Socialista Rivoluzionario*. Four issues appeared between March and May 1879. They all addressed workers and political activists in Italy without discussing any specific concern in the lives of Italian migrants in London.[43] Written in a rhetorical and archaic style, they condemned the capitalist system and its pillars, the State and the Church, and urged workers and peasants to rise up against their exploiters to transform the current social structure and win social and economic emancipation. The bulletins echoed old polemics with the republicans. In particular, the first issue denounced Italian national unification for not achieving either individual or economic freedom, and reiterated criticisms of parliamentary actions –proclaiming the uselessness of fighting for the overthrow of the monarchy and installation of a republican system, and soliciting workers to join the socialist revolutionary camp instead.[44]

We cannot be certain about the number of workers who joined the circle, or the impact it had on the Italian community. According to Giuseppe Prato, the circle was a complete failure. However, his only sources were the consul Minghetti, in charge of the surveillance of the Italian anarchists in London, and Pietro Rava, editor of the newspaper *Londra-Roma* – described by the British police as a 'strong anti-anarchist journal' – and a very popular man in the Italian colony on friendly terms with the Italian Ambassador.[45]

---

[42] Tito Zanardelli, 'Discorso I, tenuto sabato 28 Giugno 1879, at "Hat Tun" Hatton Wall'; 'Discorso II, tenuto domenica 6 luglio 1879, a "The Bull's Head"', in Zanardelli, *Della utilità*, pp. 5–6; 9–11.

[43] The first issue, *Agli operai d' Italia non ancora socialisti*, was an appeal to the Italian workers to leave reformist parties and join socialism. The second issue, which came out on 18 March, celebrated the anniversary of the Paris Commune. The third issue, directed at peasants, sharecroppers and day-labourers, urged them to rebel and to appropriate the land and its produce. The fourth and last issue was a strong attack against the main exponents of the democratic parties in Italy (Minghetti, Sella, Depretis, Cairoli, and Nicotera) who had criticised the Internationalists.

[44] 'Agli operai d'Italia non ancora socialisti', *Bollettino Socialista Rivoluzionario*, no. 1, 6 March 1879.

[45] Giuseppe Prato, 'Gli italiani in Inghilterra', *La Riforma Sociale*, 15 January 1901, XI, p. 17. The editor of the newspaper *Londra-Roma* Pietro Rava, who quarrelled with a group of Italian anarchists (*La Riforma Sociale*, X, 1900, p. 674). A British policeman, after inquiring about the publication of a fake issue of the *Londra-Roma*, (published by the antiorganisa-

A consideration of the funds collected from subscriptions, more than six pounds in May 1880, would seem – in contrast – to indicate a fair number of affiliates.

In 1880, Zanardelli and Schumann promoted the widening of the *Circolo Italiano di Studj Sociali* to refugees of other nationalities and merging with a Spanish circle. This prompted the constitution of the *Club International des Études Sociales, Circolo Studj Sociali* that held as 'its aim the intellectual development of its members and as its means the discussion of social issues, the establishment of a circle – centre of daily relations – the constitution of a library, the organisation of conferences'.[46] The *Club International* met in the same location as the *Circolo Italiano,* in *The White Hart* public house at 17 Windmill Street. The new organisation included French, Russian, Spanish and German exiles, such as the communards J. B. Clément and Ant. Arnaud, the French Paul Brousse and Gustave Brocher, the Spanish Figueras, and the Russian Leo Hartmann, the nihilist who had attempted against the life of the Tsar Alexander II at the end of 1879.[47] Several Italians were involved in the management of the club: Conti was named secretary; Carrosso was a member of the financial committee; Antolini was part of the propaganda committee together with Orlando De Martijs, informant for the Italian consulate in the early 1880s who took also part in the Club's administrative committee.[48]

The *Club International* published its own newspaper, *Le Travail. Bulletin mensuel du Club International des Études Sociales de Londres,* with the support of a dozen collaborators.[49] Brousse acknowledged that Zanardelli played a relevant part in preparing the ground for the bulletin's publication.[50] *Circolo*

---

tionalist group in 1894) reported: 'The *Londra-Roma* is a strong anti-anarchist journal [...] The *Londra-Roma* published a strong appeal to Italians in London to have nothing to do with Anarchism [...] since that time Rava has been the object of attack from Italian anarchists. M. Rava is very indignant about this publication and expressed an opinion that it is the mark of Italian Anarchists and is done to annoy him and ruin his reputation. [...] M. Rava is a very popular man in Italian Society in London and is especially friendly with the Italian Ambassador'. (*Sergeant John Walsh's report to Sir G. Lushinghton K.C.B. Home Office,* 20 August 1894. NA, HO 144/258/A55684).

[46] Club International d'Études Sociales de Londres, *Règlement,* 1880. IISH.

[47] Valiani, 'Dalla Prima alla Seconda Internazionale', p. 239.

[48] 'Communications officielles du club', *Le Travail,* May 1880, no. 7, October 1880.

[49] The collaborators were: Brocher, Conti, Costa, Dardelle, Figueras, Guesde, Hall, Hartmann, Malon, Muller, Lombard, Xavierde Ricard, Verrycken. *Le Travail ,* no. 1, April 1880, p. 1.

[50] 'Zanardelli eut fait pour nous tous absents un excellent cuisinier pour le journal', in Vuilleumier, 'Paul Brousse', p. 72.

Italiano di Studj Sociali funds were deposited with those of *Le Travail* for the publication of a bulletin in Italian which, however, never saw the light.[51]

In mid-1880, Zanardelli's position within the anarchist community in London was weakened by the arrival of other Italian anarchists, most of whom supported the politics of the Italian Federation of the I.W.A and the insurrectional approach and whose number included Malatesta and Solieri. A few days after Malatesta's arrival in London, Zanardelli was summoned before a court of honour.[52] Brousse, Malatesta, Antolini and Defendi were the main witnesses against him. According to two letters and some documents exhibited by Malatesta, Zanardelli jeopardised the very existence of all the anarchist circles he had been involved with during his stay in Italy; together with Nabruzzi he had blackmailed Michael Bakunin, threatening to reveal a revolutionary plot to the police. Finally, Zanardelli had also carried out several frauds in Italy.[53]

This event may be related both to Brousse's resignation from the committee of the *Club International des Études Sociales* and his disengagement from *Le Travail*, and to the dispute between Zanardelli and Malatesta 'which apparently demanded a duel'.[54]

About a month later, in August 1880, Zanardelli sold all his furniture and left London with his wife and mother. He moved to France, apparently with the intention of joining the socialist newspaper edited by Malon, *La Lotta Sociale*, but the polemics followed him.[55] In Paris, Zanardelli joined Cipriani and a project for insurrection in Italy;[56] although Malatesta tried to dissuade Cipriani from involving him in the scheme, Zanardelli went to Milan to pave the way for the enterprise.[57] However, some anarchists were arrested shortly after having contact with him. Moreover, in January 1881 Cipriani was arrested in Rimini during a visit to his ill father. He was charged and subsequent condemned to twenty five years' imprisonment for the murder of an Italian in Alexandria, an action that had previously been judged to be in self-defence. For the following six years anarchists, socialists,

[51] 'Communications officielles du club', *Le Travail*, no. 2, May 1880.

[52] Malatesta arrived from Brussels on the 6th of June 1881. De Martijs report, 6 June 1880, Asdmae, *Pol. Int.*, b. 5, f. (Rapporti Ambasciata di Londra).

[53] Report by DM, (Orlando De Martijs), 9 June 1880. Asdmae, *Pol. Int.*, b. 5, f. (Rapporti Ambasciata di Londra).

[54] David Stafford, *From Anarchism*, p. 311, note 39.

[55] Report by De Martijs, July 1880. Asdmae, *Pol. Int.*, b. 5.

[56] Cipriani, Zanardelli, Nabruzzi, and Zirardini published the 'Manifesto agli oppressi d'Italia' announcing insurrectionary actions. The manifesto was read out at the Chiasso congress. Cfr. Pernicone, *Italian anarchism*, pp. 183–85.

[57] Franco Della Peruta, 'Il socialismo italiano dal 1875 al 1882', *Annali dell'Istituto G. G. Feltrinelli*, I, 1958, pp. 81–84.

democrats, and intellectuals campaigned for his liberation until an amnesty was granted in 1888.[58]

In the autumn of 1881 Zanardelli returned to London with the intention of reopening an Italian circle there.[59] His arrival aroused the fury of Malatesta and other refugees who considered Zanardelli responsible for Cipriani's arrest. Apparently Malatesta revived former suspicions that Zanardelli had disclosed the plans of the 1874 insurrection organised by the Internationalists in the Romagna to the Italian police.[60] Kropotkin made clear his intention of throwing him out if Zanardelli dared to pay him a visit. According to consular reports, Zanardelli was acting so unwisely that he was in danger of being beaten up by Cipriani's friends,[61] and was, therefore, eventually forced to leave London again.[62] In December 1882, the newspaper *Tito Vezio*, prompted by news of Zanardelli's brief arrest in Turin, published letters including one from Paris signed Gaetano Lombardi and one from A. Oldrini, a Communard refugee in London, accusing Zanardelli of being a spy for the French and Italian police and responsible for the arrest of the anarchists in Milan.[63] Other newspapers and militants, including Solieri, confirmed these allegations. As a consequence of these controversies, Zanardelli left the anarchist movement and moved to Brussels where he devoted himself to philological studies.

The 1880s and the International Revolutionary Socialist Congress

It was during the early 1880s that an identifiable colony of Italian anarchist militants began to establish itself in London. Malatesta left Italy in 1878 after having been acquitted at trial for instigating the Benevento uprising. Between 1878 and 1880 he went to Egypt, Romania, Switzerland and France. He stayed briefly in London in the spring of 1880, then went to Brussels where he was arrested and subsequently expelled from Belgium. He reached London again in March 1881.[64] Giovanni Defendi, one of Malatesta's best

---

[58] Vittorio Emiliani, *Gli anarchici* (Milan: Bompiani, 1973), pp. 113–44.

[59] Italian consul to Foreign Ministry, 19 and 21 November 1881, Asdmae, *AL*, b. 70 (Corrispondenza con il consolato).

[60] Ministry of Interior to Foreign Minister, Rome 27 October 1881, Asdmae, *Pol. Int.*, b. 6, f. (Corrispondenza ricevuta 1881).

[61] Italian consul to Foreign Ministry, 29 November and 7 December 1881, Asdmae, *AL*, b. 70.

[62] Italian consul to Foreign Ministry, London 19 December 1881, Asdmae, *AL*, b. 70.

[63] 'Questione Zanardelli', *Tito Vezio*, 30 November 1882, pp. 2–4; 7 December 1882, p. 2; 10 February 1883, p. 3. Nejrotti, 'Zanardelli Tito', p. 271; Masini, *Storia degli anarchici italiani da Bakunin*, p. 199.

[64] Italian consul to Italian ambassador, 29 March 1881, Asdmae, *AL*, b. 70.

friends in Britain, was a Garibaldinian who had fought for the Vosges army in the Franco-Prussian war. He was sentenced to fifteen years for his participation in the Commune and spent eight in jail – apparently his peculiar gait was due to continual walking in a small cell. Defendi arrived in London around 1880 after his sentence was commuted to banishment.[65] On 1 May 1880, he joined Emilia Trunzio Zanardelli, Tito Zanardelli's stepsister, in a *union libre* at the presence of some socialist friends.[66] Emilia Trunzio was native of Cosenza; she had lost her partents during a cholera epidemic and was adopted by the Zanardelli family.[67] Ernesto Antolini, from Naples, arrived in London in the late 1870s. Another Internationalist living in London at the time was Federico Ravà, native of the Italian town of Reggio Emilia. Like Defendi, he had fought with Garibaldi in France before moving to England.

In October 1881, Carlo Cafiero returned to London, where he stayed only a few months until the spring of 1882, when the first symptoms of his mental illness appeared.[68] Solieri, born in 1858 in Frassineto near Imola, was expelled from Switzerland with Malatesta in April 1879 and was in London by the beginning of 1881.[69] The young count Francesco Ginnasi, also from Imola, joined this group of refugees in August 1881. Ginnasi had taken part in the Benevento uprising; after being tried for his participation in the insurrection he moved to Geneva where he shared lodgings with Malatesta for few months. Considered to be the co-author of a manifesto praising Passanante's attempt, Ginnasi was banished from the country and moved to Brussels. A few months later he left for England to avoid an Italian arrest warrant for avoiding conscription. Pietro Cesare Ceccarelli arrived in London at the beginning of January 1882 after a period spent in Romania with Napoleone Papini. They had both also participated in the Benevento

[65] Italian consul to Italian ambassador, 21 February 1881, Asdmae, *AL*, b. 70. Martinez, *Paris Communard refugee in Britain*, p. 498. Cfr: Emilia Civolani, 'La partecipazione di emigrati italiani alla comune di Parigi', *Movimento operaio e socialista*, II, no. 21, 1979, pp. 172–73.

[66] 'Cher Citoyen … Les raisons qui les ont déterminés à se passer du mariage juridique, ainsi que du mariage religieux c'est qu'ils les considèrent comme des institutions bourgeoises creés dans le seul but de régler les questions de propriété et d'héritage; n'offrant aucune garantie sérieuse aux prolétaires des deux sexes; consacrant l' assujettissement de la femme; engageant pour l'avenir les volontés et les consciences, sans tenir compte des caractères; et s'opposant à la dissolubilité qui est a la base de tout contracte.' Handbill Giovanni Defendi, Emilia Tronzi Zanardelli , Londres April 1880. IISH, Jung archive.

[67] ACS, *CPC*, b. 5324, f. (Trunzio Emilia).

[68] Cafiero left London and went to Milan where he was arrested. In prison he tried to commit suicide; because of his mental illness Cafiero was admitted to mental hospital several times. He died in 1892. See: Pier Carlo Masini, *Cafiero* (Milan: Rizzoli, 1974).

[69] Cfr. M. Antonioli, *Dizionario biografico degli anarchici italiani* (Pisa: BFS, 2003), *ad nomen*.

attempt.[70] The two left Romania in April 1881 where they had been engaged in a trading enterprise that ended in bankruptcy with a debt of 100,000 francs. Papini wrote to Malatesta from Belgrade asking him to provide a false passport to enter Italy. Malatesta promptly fulfilled the request from London.[71]

Italian expatriates generally settled in Soho and Clerkenwell: Defendi lived at 17 Charles Street, St Pancras, then moved to 17 Cleveland Street, Fitzroy Square; Solieri lived at 2 Church Street in Soho; Ginnasi resided at 53 Huntley Street off Tottenham Court Road; Cafiero lived at 72 Myddelton Square in Clerkenwell. Often the refugees shared lodgings and recently arrived expatriates would take over the housing of comrades who moved to Europe or the United States. Cafiero, for example, rented the room vacated by Ginnasi when he left for New York and Kropotkin was offered lodgings that had been occupied by Miss Lecompte.[72]

Exiles were employed in a variety of occupations. Ceccarelli started trading with a partner called Leon. At some point they split and Ceccarelli only managed to recover his own merchandise – golden and silver brooches – from Leon's house with the help of Malatesta and Solieri. Shortly thereafter he pawned part of it. Solieri worked as a barber's boy in a shop at 30 Greek Street, near Tottenham Court Road. Malatesta received his mail, addressed to Leopoldo Pelillo, at the same barber's shop. Antolini was employed as a waiter, first at the Hotel de Rome et de Venise and later in a café. Defendi worked as a confectioner, and his companion Emilia was a dressmaker. In a later period they opened an Italian delicatessen at 12 Archer Street. She worked in the shop, while Giovanni Defendi sold their products by cart. However, poverty often affected refugees' everyday life. According to the Italian ambassador in 1882 Ravà, Ceccarelli, and Alvini found themselves in such hardship that they sold a pair of shoes for two shillings to feed themselves. Most of their wardrobe had already been sold for the same reason.[73]

---

[70] In 1879 Ceccarelli was acquitted together with Merlino and other Internationalists at a trial in Lucera. They had been arrested after a riotous demonstration of workers in Naples. See: Masini, *Storia degli anarchici italiani da Bakunin*, pp. 165–66; Giampietro D. Berti, *Francesco Saverio Merlino: dall'anarchismo socialista al socialismo liberale (1856–1930)* (Milan: Franco Angeli, 1993), p. 20.

[71] Italian consul to Italian ambassador, 7 April 1881, Asdmae, *AL*, b. 70. In May 1881, Malatesta received a letter from Ceccarelli and Papini from Trieste. Papini thanked Malatesta for the passport. Ministry of Interior to Foreign Ministry, 10 May 1881, Asdmae, *Pol. Int.*, b. 6, f. (Ministro degli Interni. Corrispondenza ricevuta 1881).

[72] Italian consul to Italian ambassador, 18 October 1881; 19 November 1881, Asdmae, *AL*, b. 70.

[73] Italian embassy to Foreign Ministry, 7 June 1882, Asdmae, *Pol. Int.*, b. 4.

In June 1881, Errico Malatesta rented a workshop in a back yard at 9 Smith Street, Northampton Square, Clerkenwell, for five francs a week, and slept in a curtained-off area in the shop. According to the informer De Martijs, Defendi and Solieri – who earned ten francs a week as a barber – helped Malatesta to pay the rent. Malatesta 'was always very careful so that nobody should look into his workshop, the windows were whitewashed and, at night, a rough curtain made of pack-cloth was drawn across the windows'. Inside there was 'a bed which only contained a mattress and a sheep-skin serving as bed-clothes, all very filthy, the room was strewn over with revolutionary papers: *I Malfattori, la Favilla* – *Le Révolté* etc. and numerous letters, having the Italian post-mark, towards the window stood a small desk work bench, to which a vice was attached and on the sides were ranged files, hammers and screw cutting implements, all new and not used'.[74]

Malatesta worked as a mechanic at Smith Street. In June 1881 he considered participating in a competition organised by the *Esposizione di Milano* for developing a 'shell-peas' machine with a prize of 10,000 *lire*. The Italian consul recommended to the embassy that this opportunity should be taken advantage of by putting Malatesta in contact with a spy posing as engineer to keep a watch on him.[75]

Malatesta's activities in the workshop worried the Italian authorities, as when Malatesta and Hartmann allegedly worked together at 'mechanical or electrical experiments', which led to a good deal of alarm that the two were secretly studying and experimenting with new bombs and other powerful weapons.[76] The British police tried to keep Malatesta's workshop under surveillance as well. A police inspector approached a local woman asking to use a room in her house to spy on Malatesta. The woman played for time and managed to alert Malatesta of the attempt. After putting his papers in a safe place, Malatesta conferred with Young and they decided to let the detective watch the workshop from the facing house.[77]

This anxiety about alleged mysterious weapons reflected the central concerns of the Italian police which were associated with possible assassination attempts against the King of Italy, or anarchist insurrections – in the Romagna and southern Italy in particular. For example, in January 1881 the Italian consul anxiously reported Malatesta and Covelli's intention to take part in an insurrection in the Romagna and other locations in Italy. The two revolutionaries planned to travel to Lugano, one of the most important

[74] Italian ambassador to Foreign Minister, 19 April 1882, Inspector Charles von Tornow's report. Asdmae, *Pol. Int.*, b. 4.

[75] Italian consul to Italian ambassador, 22 June 1881, Asdmae, *AL*, b. 70.

[76] Italian ambassador to Foreign Ministry, 24 May 1882. Asdmae, *Pol. Int.*, b. 4

[77] Italian consul to Italian ambassador, 30 June 1881. Asdmae, *AL*, b. 70.

centre of anarchist exiles, and from there to Geneva where Solieri would join them with weapons and money.[78] A few years later, the embassy sent several warnings to the Minister of Interior regarding consignments or shipments of weapons and explosives hidden in sardine cans or barrels of beer that were allegedly sent to Italy by the anarchists in London.[79]

Malatesta received daily visits in his workshop from Kropotkin, who was in London for the first time in November 1881. Accompanied by the Russian revolutionary and other Italian refugees including Solieri, Defendi and Ceccarelli, Malatesta regularly visited the *Rose Street Club*, in what is now Manette Street in Soho. This club, founded in 1878, was the central meeting point for revolutionary refugees in London and was organised into five sections according to nationality.[80] Here Malatesta and his comrades became acquainted with Franz Kitz, Johann Most – leading figure in the colony of expatriated German Social Democrats – and with the polyglot revolutionary community in London more generally. Malatesta was in close contact with Russian refugees as well; he often paid visit to the nihilists Lazar Gol'denberg, Leo Hartmann and Nicholas Chaikovsky.[81]

This variegated community also met for social events: Malatesta, Nathan Ganz and Cafiero had Christmas dinner at De Martijs's house in 1881. A week later, Cafiero, Malatesta, Solieri, Baldassarre Monti, De Martijs, Kropotkin and Chaikovsky and their families along with Gol'denberg, LeCompte, Hoffmann, and Signoff met to celebrate the New Year.

In May 1881 Solieri, Malatesta and Cafiero published a programmatic circular launching a new anarchist-communist newspaper: *L'Insurrezione*.[82] This programme, in opposition to Costa's turn to parliamentary socialism, still considered insurrection to be the main strategy to demolish the authoritarian institutions that prevented the free development of social progress towards anarchy.

Anything that facilitates and brings the time of the insurrection nearer,

---

[78] Italian consul to Italian ambassador, 24 January 1881, Asdmae, *AL*, b. 70.

[79] Foreign ministry to Italian ambassador, 24 and 28 January 1884, Asdmae, *Pol. Int.*, b. 38.

[80] J. Quail, *The Slow Burning Fuse* (London: Paladin, 1978), p. 8.

[81] Leo Hartmann, a member of the Russian group 'People's Will' took refuge in London after a failed attempt on the life of Tsar Alexander II in November 1879. He was arrested in Paris in February 1880 at the instigation of the Russian government. He was threatened with extradition but a hastily organised press campaign persuaded the French government to expel him from France. On reaching England his mission in London was to propagate the policies of 'People's Will'. Cfr. D. Senese, *S.M. Stepniak-Kravchinskii: the London Years* (Newtonville, Mass.: Oriental Research Partners, 1987).

[82] Italian consul to Italian ambassador, 12 April 1881, Asdmae, *AL*, b. 70.

is good; all that keeps it away, though maintaining the appearance of progress, is bad. This is the principle that will guide us.[83]

Malatesta sent hundreds of copies of this circular to anarchist militants in Italy and in Marseilles, Brussels and Lugano, most of which were seized by the police.[84] Apparently, Malatesta and Solieri prepared a mock-up of the newspaper composed of sixteen pages. However, the newspaper never appeared; the promoters abandoned the scheme, as an English police inspector reported to the Italian consul, 'no doubt for want of funds'.[85]

Indeed, the Italian anarchists' scope for action from England was heavily circumscribed. The persistent scarcity of funds was the main obstacle to the realisation of their projects. The consul and the ambassador underlined this several times in their correspondence, declaring with relief that the best protection against the wicked plans of the anarchists was their lack of means.[86] In the same way, the worries of Italian authorities increased sharply when they believed the anarchists were about to receive some financial support. This happened, for example, when Malatesta was waiting for part of a legacy left to him by an aunt in Marseilles. To receive this legacy Malatesta signed a proxy at the Italian consulate; the spy De Martijs was one of his witnesses.[87]

The anarchists' forced inaction often caused tension and frustration: feelings which commonly affected the lives of all political refugees.[88]

In the first half of 1881 Malatesta and the other anarchists were also engaged in preparations for the International Revolutionary Socialist Congress scheduled in London for 14 July in *The Wheat Sheaf* public house in Charrington Street. The manifesto announcing the congress, 'Au révolutionnaires des deux Mondes', was published in *La Révolution Sociale*, *Le Révolté*, and *L'Intransigeant* in March 1881, shortly after the assassination of Tsar Alexander II. The aim of the congress was the reconstitution of the International.[89] Preparations for the congress, promoted by the Jura

---

[83] *Le Révolté*, Geneva, 6 August 1881; now in Carlo Cafiero, *La Rivoluzione per la rivoluzione*, Gianni Bosio (ed.), (Milan: Edizioni del Gallo, 1968), pp. 117–18. 'Le journal paraîtra tous les huit jours. Prix d'abonnement 2 fr. Par trimestre. Adresse: Vito Solieri, 8, Windmill Street, Tottenham Court road, Londres.'

[84] Minister of Interior to Foreign Minister, 10 May 1881. Asdmae, *Pol. Int.*, b. 6., f. (Ministero dell'Interno Corrispondenza Ricevuta). Another eighty copies were sent in August 1881.

[85] Italian ambassador to Foreign Minister, 19 April 1882, Inspector Charles von Tornow's report. Asdmae, *Pol. Int.*, b. 4.

[86] Italian consul to Italian ambassador, 22 and 24 June 1881, 5 July 1881. Asdmae, *AL*, b. 70.

[87] Italian consul to Italian ambassador, 22 January 1881, Asdmae, *AL*, b. 70.

[88] The consul reported about tensions between Solieri, Cafiero and Malatesta. Italian consul to Italian ambassador, 7 November and 10 December 1881, Asdmae, *AL*, b. 70.

[89] 'Au révolutionnaires des deux Mondes! Travailleurs! Les efforts courageux de nos

Federation, Kropotkin and Malatesta, took several months. An initial organisational committee composed of seven people was established in London at the beginning of February 1881; the informer De Martijs was the Italian representative.[90] A room was rented at 41 Upper Rathbone Street for regular meetings. Malatesta, after his arrival in March 1881, worked on the organisation of the congress with Brocher, who was elected secretary, and the *Rose Street Club* was the organisational headquarters. During that period Malatesta kept up an extensive correspondence with Cafiero, Kropotkin and other anarchist leaders. Malatesta hoped that the date of the 14th of July would become a milestone date 'in the history of the Revolution' for its incentive to the revolutionary movement.[91]

The Italian authorities were seriously concerned about the outcome of the congress. Once the embassy knew the anarchists' intentions, they made preparations for surveillance. Two Italian spies, along with police spies of other nationalities, attended the congress despite the precautions taken by the organisers. De Martijs was one of them. He was already working for the Italian embassy in London and had even assisted in the organisation of the congress. Moreover, Malatesta received his correspondence at De Martijs's address at 51 Stillington Street so the Italian authorities received copies of the letters sent to Malatesta.[92]

De Martijs was named as delegate to the congress by the International Club of Social Studies and, according to the consul's reports, also attended the private meeting as the representative for Naples and Rome.[93] The second informer, Raffaele Moncada, was sent to London from Marseilles. Malatesta received a report from the anarchists in Marseilles that warned him of Moncada's real identity. These suspicions were apparently averted when Moncada arrived in London with a reference from Cafiero. These two spies

frères de Russie viennent enfin d'être couronnés de succès. En présence de la coalition de toutes les forces bourgeoises, il est nécessaire de lui opposer la coalition de toutes les forces révolutionnaires et de rétablir l' Association Internationale des Travailleurs. C'est à cet effet compagnons que nous vous convoquons tous un [*sic*.] Congrès International Socialiste Révolutionnaire qui se tiendra à Londres le 14 Juillet 1881 et dont l'unique ordre du jour sera: "Reconstitution de l'Association International [*sic*.] des Travailleurs'". Consul in Geneva to Ministry of Interior, 29 May 1881, Asdmae, *Pol. Int.*, b. 6. See also: Errico Malatesta, 'Les eléments du congrès de Londres', *Bulletin du Congrès*. IISH, Brousse archive.

90 The other representatives were: Biedermann for Switzerland, Figueras for Spain, Brocher for Alsace and Lorraine, Hartmann for Russia and Magnin for France, C. Hall for London.

91 Malatesta to Brousse, 26 June 1881. IISH, Brousse archive.

92 Italian embassy to Foreign Ministry, 18 August 1881, Asdmae, *Pol. Int.*, b. 3. However, as a result of the British inspector's visit to Malatesta's neighbour, Malatesta asked his comrades to stop sending letters to his usual addresses. Italian consul to Italian ambassador, 8 July 1881, Asdmae, *AL, b.* 70.

93 Italian consul to Italian ambassador, 30 April 1881, Asdmae, *AL*, b. 70.

sent the Italian embassy more than 400 reports describing developments at the congress.[94]

One the last day, a public meeting was held at Cleveland Hall at which the resolution of the congress and a document of protest against Most's conviction were approved.[95]

The results of this congress have been extensively investigated. Its unequivocal support for 'propaganda of the deed', and the lax organisation which characterised the anarchist movement during the following years opened the door to individual terrorism and the spread of anti-organisationalist groups which seriously weakened the anarchist movement. Moreover, the idea of considering themselves a political vanguard (*minoranza agente*) cut off anarchists from the labour movement, leaving the latter to the growing influence of reformist socialism.[96]

Delegates at the congress discussed the use of 'chemical materials' for revolutionary purposes, and the final resolution urged militants to apply themselves to the study of this matter:

> In abandoning the legal ground on which our action has generally been based until now, to take it onto the ground of illegality, which is the only way leading to revolution – it is necessary to resort to methods which are in conformity with this aim [...] Technical and chemical sciences having already rendered services to the revolutionary cause, and being called on to render it still greater ones in the future, the Congress recommends organisations and individuals taking part in the International Workingmen's Association to give great weight to the study and application of these sciences, as methods of defence and attack.[97]

This resolution explains the concerns of the Italian consul when he was informed that Malatesta and Chaikovsky were spending considerable time in the British Library 'reading books on chemistry and mining engineering, probably with criminal intent!'[98]

An information bureau was established at the end of the congress. Its members were Malatesta, Chaikovsky and Trunk, from Germany; Figueras,

---

[94] Berti, *Francesco Saverio Merlino*, p. 51. For detailed information on Moncada see: Peter van der Mark, *Revolutie en Reactie. De Repressie van Italiaanse Anarchisten, 1870–1900*, Ph.D., Rijksuniversiteit Groningen, 1997.

[95] Italian consul to Italian ambassador, 19 July 1881, Asdmae, *AL*, b. 70. Most was arrested and sentenced to eighteen months penal servitude for publishing an article in favour of the attempt on Tsar Aleksander II.

[96] The proceedings of the congress and its consequences have been extensively covered. Berti, *Francesco Saverio Merlino*, p. 53. Caroline Cham, *Kropotkin and the Rise of Revolutionary Anarchism 1872–1886* (Cambridge: Cambridge University Press, 1989), p. 157–58.

[97] Cham, *Kropotkin*, pp. 157–58.

[98] Italian consul to Italian ambassador, 10 September 1881, Asdmae, *AL*, b. 70.

Neve and Gol'denberg were their deputies.[99] Malatesta, as the secretary, kept a complete set of papers from the congress.

On Figueras's suggestion, a section of the International Workingmen's Association was established in London on 30 August 1881. The Frenchman Paul Robin, Ferrand and De Martijs were named as secretaries.[100] This committee was composed of more than twenty members.[101] Weekly meetings were held every Monday in the *Sun Tavern* on Nermon Street, Oxford Street or in private houses: Malatesta's and Chaikovsky's, for example. Cafiero, Malatesta, Ginnasi, Solieri, De Martijs, Figueras, Robin, Hoffman and Chaikovsky were among those who attended. Further meetings and conferences were organised at the *Rose Street Club*.[102] However, no particular enterprise followed from the establishment of the information bureau or the section of the International and, after the congress, the movement in London remained substantially inactive.[103]

At the end of July 1882, Malatesta and Ceccarelli left London for Alexandria to join the Urabi revolt in Egypt. Malatesta's absence from the United Kingdom probably contributed to the decrease in initiatives among Italian expatriates; Italian anarchists in London did not publish any newspaper until Malatesta's return in 1889. Moreover, Solieri, who along with Malatesta and Merlino showed the strongest sense of initiative, also left London for Paris in February 1886 and subsequently moved to the United States.[104] However, the network of political refugees did not completely disappear. In 1884 two Internationalists, Lombardi and Berni, were in contact with the Central Committee of the International in Florence where Malatesta was publishing *La Questione Sociale*. In 1885, an Italian anarchist section still existed, promoted by Defendi, Solieri, and Biagio Poggi.[105] Moreover, in February 1885 Francesco Saverio Merlino, one of the main leaders of Italian anarchism, took refuge in London at 19 Charrington

---

[99] Oliver, *The International Anarchist Movement*, pp. 16–17.

[100] Italian consul to Italian ambassador, 30 August 1881, Asdmae, *AL*, b. 70.

[101] Italian consul to Italian ambassador, 21 August 1881, Asdmae, *AL*, b. 70.

[102] In September 1881 secretary Robin sent a circular asking the editors of English newspapers to publicise a meeting organised by the International Association of Working Men. Malatesta and Brocher gave speeches on anarchist propaganda. Italian consul to Italian ambassador, 26 September and 5 December 1881, Asdmae, *AL*, b. 70.

[103] Giampietro Berti, *Errico Malatesta e il movimento anarchico italiano e internazionale: 1872–1932* (Milano: Franco Angeli, 2003), p. 98.

[104] Foreign Ministry to Ministry of Interior, 24 February 1886 and 14 September 1886, Asdmae, *Pol. Int.*, b. 39, f. (Londra ambasciata 1886–1887). In New York Solieri founded the first anarchist newspaper in Italian: *Il Grido degli Oppressi*.

[105] Letterio Briguglio, *Il partito operaio italiano e gli anarchici* (Rome: Edizioni di Storia e Letteratura, 1969), p. 22.

Street.[106] Until 1888 documentation regarding Merlino's activity is scarce, probably because he dedicated himself principally to theoretical studies, working extensively in the library of the British Museum.[107] In 1886 it was reported that the Spanish and Italian revolutionists met in a private house in Russell Square 'under the leadership of doctor Merlino, who was sentenced last year in Naples to three years' penal servitude for high treason. He is a lawyer of some ability, and with a great talent for organising'.[108] 'In 1887 Merlino organised an Italian revolutionary committee that kept an intense correspondence with Italy, France, and Belgium'.[109] This correspondence may be linked with an anarchist active in London, Attilio Melchiorri, who sent a manifesto entitled *11 Novembre* to Italy in the same period. Concurrently, Merlino published a pamphlet aimed at Italian workers in London: *La nuova religione*.[110] The Italian revolutionary was involved in several initiatives organised by socialists of various tendencies. He joined leaders of other socialist groups in the commemorations of the Paris Commune from 1886 to 1888, always speaking in Italian.[111] The commemoration held in March 1888, also attended by Kropotkin, H. M. Hyndman and William Morris, was reported to have been 'the largest and most enthusiastic which has yet taken place in London [...] The whole character of the speeches was revolutionary, and their tone more decided than in any previous year; and the more thoroughgoing the Socialism, the more enthusiastically it was received.'[112]

When Lucy Parsons, widow of one of the anarchists executed in Chicago in 1887, made a propaganda tour of London and the provinces, Merlino participated in one of the several meetings sponsored by socialists and anarchists in the capital to welcome her. The event was chaired by Morris, the other speakers were Kropotkin, Kitz, J. Blackwell, Trunk, and the MP Cunningham Graham.[113]

Merlino's sojourn in the United Kingdom had considerable relevance to

---

[106] Italian ambassador to Italian consul in London, 2 January 1887. Asdmae, *AL*, b. 122, f. 5 (1887. Corrispondenza al consolato di Londra). In the same letter the ambassador reported Merlino's intention to publish his work *Monopolismo o Socialismo?*. Cfr. Max Nettlau, *Saverio Merlino* (Montevideo: Edizioni Studi Sociali, 1948).

[107] On Merlino in London see: Berti, *Francesco Saverio Merlino*, pp. 109–20.

[108] 'The Revolutionists in England', *The Sheffield and Rotherham Independent*, 1 March 1886, p. 3.

[109] Ministry of Interior to Italian ambassador in London, 12 January 1887, Asdmae, *Pol. Int.*, b. 39, f. (Londra Ambasciata' 1886 –1887).

[110] Berti, *Francesco Saverio Merlino*, p. 85.

[111] 'Notes', *Freedom*, April 1888; H. Seymour, 'The Paris Commune', *The Anarchist*, April 1887; 'This Evening's News' , *The Pall Mall Gazzette*, 19 March 1886.

[112] 'Notes', *Freedom* , April 1888.

[113] 'The Chicago Martyrs and Bloody Sunday', *Raynolds's Newspaper*, 11 November 1888.

the development of his ideological and theoretical thought.[114] Shortly after his arrival he engaged in a debate with Seymour on mutualist, collectivist and communist anarchism and the economic organisation of society after the revolution, out of which emerged some of the themes he developed in his work *Socialismo o monopolismo?*[115] In London Merlino became acquainted with Charlotte Wilson and the anarchist circles around the Fabians that under Kropotkin's leadership founded *Freedom*, one of the most long-lived anarchist newspapers. With Kropotkin, Merlino was 'unquestionably the most important early member of the Freedom Group'.[116] He contributed to the monthly public discussions on anarchist socialism that the Freedom Group organised from February 1888. Dozens of militants from different organisations attended the conferences. At the session in May, Merlino lectured on Communist Anarchism and engaged with a member of the Social Democratic Federation in 'an exceedingly useful debate' that brought to light 'the real differences of opinion between Social Democrats and Communist Anarchists'. These differences were examined in succeeding meetings.[117] The following October, Merlino's paper on the organisation of Labour sparked a lively discussion among his audience.[118] In December Merlino left the United Kingdom, moved to Brussels and shortly thereafter to Paris where he attended the International Workers' Congress in July 1889.

The number of reports regarding Italian anarchist activities sent by the embassy in London to the Ministry of Interior decreased during this time; confined mainly to information regarding the arrival and departure of anarchist militants. This confirms the decline in initiatives organised by the Italian colony, but the drying up of police sources regarding the activities of Italian refugees was also related to the fact that, at the end of 1886, the spy De Martijs was forced to leave the United Kingdom and the Italian embassy did not have informers or spies to replace him until 1889, when Count Giuseppe Tornielli-Brusati di Vergano employed a new informer, known as Calvo, who provided information over the next decade.[119]

---

[114] Berti, *Francesco Saverio Merlino*, p. 80.

[115] S. Merlino. 'Anarchism. Communistic & Mutualistic', *The Anarchist*, 14 March 1886, p. 2.

[116] Oliver, *The International Anarchist Movement*, p. 45.

[117] 'Freedom discussion meeting', *Freedom*, June 1888.

[118] 'Freedom Discussion Meeting', *Freedom*', November 1888. Merlino's paper was published in the same issue under the title 'Work and Organisation'.

[119] When the ambassador sought information about a manifesto published by the Italian anarchist Melchiorri, the Italian consul replied that it was not possible to follow anarchists' intrigues without someone specifically in charge of that task and he returned the manifesto to the sender. In order to solve this problem the consul suggested the ambassador to have De Martijs returned to London. Italian consul to Italian ambassador, 2 December 1887, Asdmae, *AL*, b. 122.

3

The 1890s

Organisationalists and anti-organisationalists

During the 1890s the enclave of Italian anarchists in London grew and the relationships among political expatriates became more complex. The anarchists embedded themselves in the expanding community of Italian economic migrants. On their arrival, new refugees found an established colony and therefore could settle more easily. The arrival from the 1880s of a new wave of expatriates, mainly from France, revitalised the colony. In 1888, the embassy was notified about the transfer to London of five individualist anarchists from Paris: Alessandro Marocco, Vittorio Pini, Luigi Parmeggiani, Giacomo Merlino and Caio Zavoli. They were 'more dangerous as a group of thieves rather than as a political group'. However, their political relations were of some importance and in Paris they had produced several inflammatory publications.[1] In 1889, Malatesta and the members of the editorial committee (Luisa Minguzzi, Emilio Covelli and Francesco Pezzi) moved the printing of *L'Associazione* from Nice to London. At the end of December 1889, the consulate's informant reported that Galileo Palla – 'well-built and with a black thick beard' – had travelled from France to London with the young Venetian cook Vittorio Del Turco and the waiter from Magenta Giuseppe Stoppa.[2] In 1891, a list of the anarchists in London included: Matteo Benassi (nicknamed 'Gobbo') from Carrara, unemployed; Pietro Bianchi, described as a very witty person from Lucca; Cesare Carpanetti, a forty eight year old from Imola; Demetrio Francini; Luigi Parmeggiani, shoemaker; Giacomo Marchello from Turin, a baker; Francesco Prodi, a waiter; Luigi Rosati, plaster figure maker; Ludovico

---

[1] Italian consul to Italian ambassador, 11 January 1888, and De Martijs's report, 10 January 1888. Asdmae, *Pol. Int.*, b. 39, f. 1888.

[2] Calvo's reports, 27 and 30 December 1889, Asdmae, *Serie politica P.*

Scacciati, a famous swindler; and Francesco Vittorio (Ciccio) from Siena, forty year old ice-cream seller.[3] The following October, the ambassador reported that anarchists expelled from Belgium and Switzerland had qualitatively strengthened the local group.[4] In 1892, the Florentine Agresti arrived in London from France where he had been particularly active.[5] In September 1894 Francesco Cini, Germano Polidori, Raffaele Ferlaschi and Pilade Cocci also arrived. Other anarchists in London in 1894 included Giuseppe Verga, a Milanese army deserter and cabinet-maker, and Franco Piccinielli, the owner of a barbershop where anarchists used to meet. Isaia Pacini, a tailor, moved to London in 1895 on expulsion from Switzerland where he had lived for ten years. Pacini was a native of Pistoia and had escaped the city in 1885 after being sentenced to two years' imprisonment for publishing an anarchist manifesto against the monarchy.[6] In March 1895, Pietro Gori, Riccardo Bonometti, Domenico Borghesani, Luigi Radaelli – nicknamed 'Razzia' – and Edoardo Milano, all expelled from Switzerland, went to London where they temporarily lived at the office of *The Torch* newspaper in Euston Road.[7] Years later, Gori gave an affectionate description of the meeting this group had with Kropotkin in the house of the Russian revolutionary.[8]

One Saturday evening, grey and filled with dirty fog, we knocked at Kropotkin's door in Bromley, a solitary town near London. He took in the expedition at one glance. Reclus's snow-white mop lit up the dark group. Luigetto, a printer from Brescia, incorrigible singer of subversive songs, was there, whistling melodies of exile. Next to him, Giosuè from Mantua; a vile dauber of canvas. He was particularly grim in roles of police informer or pimp that he obstinately persisted, like nobody else, in including in his repertoire of revolutionary theatre. The silent Razzia was present as well; the nom de guerre of a Milanese mechanic. His blue eyes in dismaying contrast to his dark conscience that brooded over the most evil attempts against the stray cats of Churchway Street's rooves – cats that he passed off as hares in the cannibalistic orgies organised by survivors from the sweet, small Italian islands to while away foggy evenings in the metropolis. [...] Thus, that evening the coterie was really curious:

[3] Tornielli to Foreign Minister Crispi, 20 January 1891, Asdmae, *Pol. Int.*, b. 39, f. 1891.

[4] Tornielli to Foreign Minister, 3 October 1891, Asdmae, *Pol. Int.*, b. 39, f. 1891.

[5] ACS, *CPC*, b. 31, f.(Agresti Antonio).

[6] ACS, *CPC*, b. 3638, f. (Pacini Isaia); Foreign Office to Secretary of State, 4 July 1895, NA, HO/144/587/B2840C/60.

[7] Assistant Commissione of police to Undersecretary of State, 7 March 1895, NA, HO/144/587/B2840C.

[8] Pietro Gori, *Pagine di vagabondaggio* (Milan: Editrice Moderna, 1948).

Pietro Gori, Edoardo Milano, Olivia and Helen Rossetti on a boat.
14 May 1895 (IISH Call number BG A42/395)

Russian, French, English ... and Milanese dialect mixed frequently over
the cosmopolitan table.[9]

In September 1896, Sante Cenci, a tailor from Rimini, migrated to
London after serving two years of *domicilio coatto* in Porto Ercole.[10]

During this time the Italian anarchists in London were divided into two
main groups: the 'anti-organisationalist' and the 'organisationalists'.[11] One
of the points of divergence between these groups was a contrasting concept
of the relationship between the individual and society. Organisationalists,
Malatesta primarily, considered the individual to be a product of society, and
organisation a prerequisite for the free development of human civilisation.
For the individualists, on the contrary, society was a union of self-governed
individuals who might or might not, according to the potential benefits
expected, associate with one another. Influenced by Kropotkin's theories,
these types of anti-organisationalists believed in the natural inclination of
human beings towards anarchy. Hence, they considered any kind of organi-

---

[9] Pietro Gori, 'Tra i fucinatori di bombe', in *Pagine di Vagabondaggio*, pp. 77–80. On Gori
in London see: P. Di Paola, 'La più forte e qualificata concentrazione di anarchici di tutte
le nazionalità. Pietro Gori a Londra', in M. Antonioli, F. Bertolucci, R. Giulianelli, *Nostra
Patria è il mondo intero. Pietro Gori nel movimento operaio e libertario italiano e internazionale*,
Quaderni della Rivista Storica dell'Anarchismo (Pisa: BFS), no. 5, 2012, pp. 131–42.

[10] ACS, *CPC*, b. 1239, f. (Cenci Sante).

[11] Definitions are always problematic. In London most of the 'anti-organisationalists'
defined themselves also as 'individualists', and the organisationalists as 'anarcho-communists'.
However, in the anarchist movement there were also individualists that supported anarcho-
communism. Distinction between individualists and anarcho-communists is therefore fluid
and debatable.

sation as an artificial and authoritarian 'superstructure', impeding progress. At the beginning of the 1880s some Italian anarchists, such as Carlo Cafiero and Emilio Covelli, advocated the avoidance of stable and formal organisations to make it more difficult for the police to suppress their activities during the government campaign to outlaw the International. While for Cafiero this anti-organisational approach was merely a contingent tactic, for the individualist 'anti-organisers' the tactic became a principled position and they considered all political organisations to be inherently authoritarian.[12]

Moreover, the insurrectionist approach, which in Italy reached an apogee with the Benevento uprising in 1877, was no longer practicable. The policy of propaganda by the deed evolved from demonstrative acts of guerrilla warfare to a series of revenge acts and assassinations which shook the European ruling elite during the 1890s – the so called 'era of attempts'.[13] Sadi Carnot, President of France (1894), Antonio Cánovas del Castillo, Prime Minister of Spain (1897), Empress Elisabeth of Austria (1898), Umberto I, King of Italy (1900), and William McKinley, President of the United States (1901) all fell at the hands of anarchists. Government officials and establishment representatives were equally targeted by individual terrorism: anarchists blew up public buildings, and exploded bombs among crowds.[14] The acts of Michele Angiolillo, Auguste Vaillant, Sante Caserio, François-Claudius Ravachol and Emile Henry had an enormous impact on European society and the widespread stereotype of the bomb-throwing anarchist developed during these years.[15] Indeed, the mystique of dynamite caught on among anarchist groups:

> The knife was merely the expression of the old personal quarrel with a personal tyrant. Dynamite is not only our best tool, but our best symbol. It is as a perfect symbol of us as is incense of the prayers of the Christians.[16]

[12] M. Antonioli, 'L'individualismo anarchico', in M. Antonioli, P. C. Masini (eds), *Il sol dell'avvenire. L'anarchismo in Italia dalle origini alla prima guerra mondiale* (Pisa: BFS, 1999), pp. 55–84.

[13] Masini, *Storia degli anarchici italiani nell'epoca degli attentati* (Milan: Rizzoli, 1981).

[14] A. Butterworth, *The world that never was: a true story of dreamers, schemers, anarchists and secret agents* (London: Vintage, 2011); J. Maitron, *Ravachol et les Anarchistes* (Paris: Gallimard, 1992); J. Joll, *The anarchists* (London: Methuen, 1979); J. M. Merriman, *The Dynamite Club: How a Bombing in fin-de-siècle Paris Ignited the Age of Modern Terror* (London: JR Books, 2009); R. Jensen, 'Daggers, Rifles and Dynamite: Anarchist Terrorism in Nineteenth Century Europe', *Terrorism and Political Violence*, 16.1 (2004).

[15] Haia Shpayer-Makov, 'A Traitor to His Class: the Anarchist in British Fiction', *European Studies*, XXVI (1996): pp. 299–325.

[16] G. K. Chesterton, *The Man Who Was Thursday* (Harmondsworth, Middlesex: Penguin Books Ltd, 1975), 1st ed.: 1908, p. 66.

The antiorganisationalists

The idea of destroying the bourgeois world by using bombs and engaging in 'expropriations' guided the individualists active in London who were, 'besides Paolo Schicchi, the most famous individualists of 1889 to 1897'.[17] Their group was known variously as *I Ribelli di St Denis*, *Gli Intransigenti di Londra e Parigi*, *Gli Straccioni di Parigi*, *Il gruppo degli Introvabili*, *L'Anonimato*, and *La Libera Iniziativa*.[18] The group operated between Paris and London, advocating and practising 'expropriation' as its chief revolutionary activity. Its leading figures were Vittorio Pini and Luigi Parmeggiani. Pini, as a result of several audacious and successful robberies, became such a legendary character that Cesare Lombroso used him as the prototype of 'the born criminal' to illustrate his theory of 'criminality arising from anarchism'.[19] Apparently, the hoard of goods stolen by Pini's gang in Paris was worth between 400,000 and 500,000 francs.[20] Moreover, the members of this group allegedly planned several bomb attempts and murders and stabbed a suspected Italian police agent named Farina.[21] In France they published the newspapers *Il Ciclone*, *Il Pugnale* and several pamphlets and leaflets.[22] Some of their publications provided detailed instruction on manufacturing bombs and explosives, from nitroglycerine to dynamite. *Il Pugnale* did this under the revealing heading: 'Our programme'.[23] Parmeggiani was believed to have taken part in the publication of *L'Indicateur anarchiste*, the most well-known of these 'manuals' that was republished several times under different titles in subsequent years.[24]

In the autumn of 1888, the group began a violent campaign against Cipriani because of his proposal for a *Union of Latin Peoples* to oppose

---

[17] Pernicone, *Italian anarchism, 1864–1892*, p. 270.

[18] Parmeggiani's biographical record, ACS, *CPC*, b. 3740, f. (Parmeggiani Luigi).

[19] Cesare Lombroso, *Gli Anarchici* (Turin: Fratelli Bocca, 1895), pp. 42–43.

[20] Jean Grave, *Quarante ans de propagande anarchiste* (Paris: Flammarion, 1973), p. 429.

[21] Farina was the same name of the informer who revealed the plans of the 'Matese' expedition to police. A list of the activities of the group in: Italian consul to Italian ambassador, 11 January 1888, and De Martijs's report, 10 January 1888. Asdmae, *Pol. Int.*, b. 39, f. 1888.

[22] Among others: *Le procès des anarchist de Chicago/L'Anarchiste Duval devant ses Juges* , *La défense du compagnon Pini, La Verità, Vigliacchi e farabutti alla porta*, and *Manifesto al Popolo d'Italia*.

[23] 'Il Nostro Programma', *Il Pugnale*, 1889. Well known was also Johann Most's *Science of revolutionary warfare*.

[24] Parmeggiani's biographical record, ACS, *CPC*, b. 3740, f. (Parmeggiani Luigi); *L'Indicateur Anarchiste*, IISH, Nettlau archive, mf. 3248. *L'Indicateur* was already a reprint of a series of articles published in 1883 in the anarchist newspaper *La Lutte*. See: Alvan Sanborn, *Paris and the Social Revolution* (Boston: Small Maynard & Co, 1905), p. 86.

Crispi's foreign policy, which seemed to be leading to war against France.[25] In a manifesto they counterposed 'social revolution' to the idea of 'race' and 'fatherland', which was supported by Cipriani, and preached unity between Prussian and Latin workers against the power of capitalism. In addition, they claimed that Cipriani had consistently lied about many aspects of his past revolutionary life.[26]

In response to the attacks on Cipriani, in December 1888 the socialist newspapers *Il Sole dell'avvenire* and *La Giustizia*, published in Mirandola and Reggio Emilia respectively, accused Parmeggiani and Pini of being spies.[27] The two anarchists travelled to Italy to take revenge on the editors of those newspapers, Celso Ceretti and Camillo Prampolini. On 13 February 1889 they stabbed Ceretti in Mirandola.[28] Three days later they were discovered by the police in Reggio Emilia, Prampolini's hometown. Pini and Parmeggiani managed to escape following a shoot-out with the police. However, shortly after his return to Paris, Pini was arrested by the French police –allegedly as a result of the revelation of a confidant, probably Carlo Terzaghi – and sentenced to twenty years' hard labour in Cayenne.[29] At the hearing, Pini proclaimed his robberies had been politically motivated and that he considered the expropriation of the bourgeoisie to be the best revolutionary means.[30] Pini's statements gave rise to a wide-ranging debate among the anarchist groups about the role of 'expropriation'. *L'Associazione* gave considerable significance to Pini's arrest and to the role of 'expropriation' in the revolutionary movement.[31] With its usual coherence and relativism,

[25] I gruppi intransigenti di Londra e Parigi, Gli Straccioni di Parigi, I Ribelli di Saint Denis, *Manifesto degl' anarchici in lingua italiana al popolo d'Italia*, London 11 Novembre 1888, in ACS, *Carte Crispi, DSPP*, b. 136; A. Cipriani, *Appel à l'Union des Races Latines*, IISH, Nettlau archive, b. 369.

[26] Apparently, the section of the manifesto against Cipriani was written by Marocco with the help of other Internationalists from the Romagna region. (Solieri, Zavoli and Scipioni). The group distributed 5,000 copies, and were planning to send 25/30.000 copies to Italy by post. Police Inspector to Ambassador in Paris Menabrea, 9 October 1888. Asdmae, *Pol. Int.* b. 27.

[27] See *La Giustizia*, 22 December 1888, p. 2 .

[28] According to the reconstruction at Pini's trial, after introducing themselves at Ceretti's home they were moved by seeing his small child. To avoid a mortal wound, Pini put a piece of cork on the blade of the knife.

[29] See: La Libera Iniziativa, 'Fra Anarchici Onesti e Disonesti', *Il Comunista*, April 1892. According to Masini Terzaghi played a role in Pini's capture. On Pini see: E. Sernicoli, *L'Anarchia e gli Anarchici, etc. (Gli attentati contro Sovrani, Principi … Note cronologiche, etc.)* Milan: Fratelli Treves, 1894), C. M. Flor O'Squarr, *Les Coulisses de l'Anarchie* (Paris: Albert Savine Éditeur, 1892).

[30] 'La Défence du Compagnon Pini', IISH, Nettlau archive, mf. 3248.

[31] See in *L'Associazione*: Francesco Saverio Merlino, 'Nostra corrispondenza', 30 November

L'Associazione argued that the significance of robbery varied according to the conditions and the ends for which it was committed. There were different kinds of robberies that needed to be judged in different ways. Those who robbed professionally, in the same way in which they might practice any other trade, with the only goal being to get rich at somebody else's expense, were not anarchists; they did not differ from the bourgeoisie, and should be dealt with accordingly. Stealing that was carried out to finance the movement was excusable. Robberies committed by poor people to satisfy their more urgent needs could be equated with acts of rebellion. They could, moreover, in the right political context, be considered positive because they eroded deference for individual property and authority:

> We would like workers, peasants, and the people to understand that everything should belong to those who have produced it, and that the owners are the usurpers, the thieves; and therefore that they got used to taking what they need, not with the guilty conscience of those who have done wrong, but with the tranquillity and intimate satisfaction of those who are exercising a right and doing their duty.[32]

Merlino disagreed with the analysis of *L'Associazione.* He rejected the theory of robbery as an act of protest and propaganda. Political robberies were individual acts that contributed to the atomisation of the anarchist movement; they were committed against other individuals, not against the system itself. The anarchists' duty was, on the contrary, to generalise rebellions.

> Our act of propaganda and initiative must be capable of expanding, diffusing and moving from individual to collective rebellion, from spark to fire. How can robbery do this, when it is compelled by its very nature to cover itself in secrecy?[33]

For Merlino there was also a moral motivation: he refused to elevate stealing to a human principle or duty, any more than violence or homicide; such tactics could only be considered to be temporary necessities in the

---

1889, no. 4, p. 3; 'Il furto' and 'Vittorio Pini', 7 December 1889, no. 5, p. 3; 'Ancora del furto' and Saverio Merlino, 'Contribuzione allo studio della questione del furto', 21 December 1889, no. 6, pp. 1, 3–4; 'Contribuzione allo studio della questione del furto', 23 January 1890, no. 7, p. 4.

[32] 'Contribuzione allo studio della questione del furto', *L'Associazione* 21 December 1889, no. 6, pp. 2–3.

[33] S. Merlino's letter in 'Contribuzione allo studio della questione del furto', *L'Associazione,* 21 December 1889, no. 6, pp. 2–3.

struggle for human emancipation.[34] He developed this point further a couple of years later in his influential pamphlet *Nécéssité et bases d'une entente*.[35]

The debate in the newspaper concluded on a note of ideological relativism. The editorial group (most likely Malatesta) underlined the fact that the newspaper had received several contributions expressing a broad range of views on the issue. While they differed in opinion, all contributions shared a clear opposition to individual property, respect for human dignity and freedom and they all 'were deeply socialist'. In summing up the debate, the newspaper suggested that robbery not be judged in the abstract as a special case, but by adhering to the principles of socialism that guided anarchists, 'because all human actions can be or become either good or bad according to the circumstances and the times'.[36]

After the raid in Italy Parmeggiani avoided arrest and took refuge in London where, however, he was taken into custody for the attempted murder of Ceretti at the request of the Italian authorities in June 1889. Since Ceretti, not wishing to be regarded as an informer, refused to travel to London to identify his attacker, the judge opposed the extradition request and freed Parmeggiani.[37] He was therefore able to remain in London where he assembled a large group of followers. In one of his communications, the Italian consul reported that around eighty people attended a meeting of *La Libera Iniziativa*.[38] Thus, Parmeggiani continued to praise secretiveness above organisation and to propagandise expropriation as 'the most powerful weapon against the capitalist bourgeoisie'.[39] In a polemical leaflet printed in English, French and Italian on the occasion of the celebrations for May Day in 1891, he sarcastically attacked not only the nature of the demonstration, but also its major political aim: the eight-hour working day.[40] *The Comedy*

---

[34] Merlino expressed his solidarity with Prampolini and Ceretti after the attack. For this reason a vitriolic article against him was published in *Il Pugnale*, April 1889.

[35] S. Merlino, *Nécéssité et bases d'une entente* (Brussels, 1892).

[36] 'Contribuzione allo studio della questione del furto', *L'Associazione*, 23 January 1890, no. 7, p. 4.

[37] Ceretti explained his reasons in his own newspaper *Il Sole dell'Avvenire*. *La Giustizia*, in a harsh reply, argued that Parmeggiani was a dangerous lunatic criminal who deserved to be in prison (11 August 1889). *L'Associazione* took inspiration from this to discuss the causes of crimes in society and the relation between the 'police' and the socialists ('Debbono i socialisti fare la spia?' *L'Associazione*, 6 September 1889, p. 2). On Parmeggiani's extradition see: Transcription of Parmeggiani v Sweeney trial, Italian inspector Frosali to Minister of the Interior, 11 November 1905, ACS, *CPC*, b. 3740, f. (Parmeggiani Luigi).

[38] Italian ambassador to Foreign Minister, 22 August 1893, Asdmae, *Pol. Int.*, b. 39, f. 1893.

[39] 'Vive le Vole!!! Manifeste adressé a tous les souffreteux du monde entier', IISH, Nettlau archive, mf. 3457. During the Sweeney-Parmeggiani trial, Bordes declared that Parmeggiani was the author of this leaflet.

[40] According to Calvo, Parmeggiani intended to print 10,000 copies of the manifesto, most

of the 1st of May condemned the 'yearly promenade' as a harmless manifestation in which workers paraded inoffensively and 'triumphantly in their best dresses in sight of their sweaters' that begin to get (now) accustomed' to it. It would be impossible to launch a revolt during the May Day demonstration because it was called months in advance and the police and the army would be well positioned to act if necessary, whereas 'revolutions burst forth by dint of the Individual act'. The only achievement of May Day could be to restore the confidence of the bourgeoisie regarding 'the universal calmness of the slaves'. Moreover, the aim of the eight-hour day was at best reinforcing workers' impression that they were 'born specially to toil whilst others [...] were born to be Bankers, Magistrates, Bosses'.

Instead, while 'perambulating through the streets', workers should be struck 'by the care with which all (our) bourgeois close hermetically their storehouses and shops' as they tremble at the idea that workers could take into their own hands 'the products they have there accumulated'.

> If they do not fear your attempts to revolt, armed as they are for that purpose, what could they do to prevent 20 millions of hands to expropriate collectively or individually, without any more ado all they need, not in one single day of the year but at any hour and everywhere? [...] Therefore we say: Away with your nonsensical talk, and your speeches a thousand time re-echoed and attack individually unceasingly common understanding, property under whatever form you find it according to your strength and capacity. [...] Let us march on to the conquest of the material goods of this earth before anything else!! [...]

> Down with organizations and organizers!
> Long live individualism and positivism!
> Long live expropriation! the strongest of our means in the struggle.[41]

Parmeggiani's ideas about and estimations of May Day also emerged in a long account from the police informer Calvo, whom Parmeggiani visited shortly after the celebration. Parmeggiani hoped to seize control of the leadership of the London anarchists because Malatesta had left London. Chatting with Calvo, he described an improbable revolutionary plan to be carried out in Rome, and made clear his idea of 'expropriation':

> If one hundred police officers or soldiers died, the government surely does not cry because it always has a large number of them at its disposal; but if we touch property, then it has had it! Bosses and governments are thieves;

of which were to be sent to Italy, Milan in particular. Calvo's report, 25 April 1891 ACS, *CPC*, b. 2949, f. (Malatesta Errico).

[41] '*The Comedy of the 1st of May*', leaflet in ACS, *CPC, b.* 2949, f. (Malatesta, Errico).

if you take property off them, their capability of exploiting ends. [...] when people hear that one hundred anarchists are capable of plundering a town, after the terror we will have aroused, they will join us. We will enter their houses, take their money and stay in their beautifully decorated homes. With the money we will help the starving people and so on. Those who do not participate because they are idiots will, by seeing their comrades flourishing so, take up arms and take to the streets with us, too. To be an anarchist, says good buddy Parmeggiani, it is necessary to be brave and a thief. Twenty anarchists are enough to spread terror. Forty bombs well-launched mean something (he has the gift of gab!) says Parmigianello!!! [...] This is the drivel that crazy, wretched Parmeggiani has in his brain and that he wants to communicate to his comrades in London and abroad. And that I faithfully report to you.[42]

In London Parmeggiani put his theories into practice and for several years led a 'gang of anarchists and thieves, refugees of different nationalities, all habitual criminals' and organised robberies and fraud as he had in Paris.[43] On 10 June 1894, Calvo warned the Italian embassy to keep Parmeggiani under surveillance because he was planning to burgle a private house. According to police records, in August 1894 the anarchist Giuseppe Fornara, a key forger, made twelve forged keys for Parmeggiani. However, they did not work properly and Parmeggiani was unable to burgle the house from which he had hoped to steal £10,000. Fornara forged keys for Parmeggiani and the members of *La Libera Iniziativa* many times, with varying results.[44] During these nightly forays Parmeggiani's accomplices were Cesare Firpo, nicknamed 'Venezia', Cesare Carpanetti and Ludovico Scacciati. The Italian Ministry of the Interior wondered if it was necessary to inform the local police about these crimes, but the ambassador in London rejected the idea: a disclosure of information provided by the secret agent could reveal his real identity and endanger his safety.[45]

In contrast to Pini, it is likely that Parmeggiani used most of the stolen goods he acquired for his own benefit rather than for the anarchist cause. To some extent he even attempted to justify this conduct in a polemical leaflet issued against the 'moralistic MM' (probably Malato or Merlino and Malatesta): 'We frankly declare that we are anarchists not to sacrifice ourselves to a pile of idiots and vampires, but to enjoy all the pleasures of life! While awaiting for the masses to rise and destroy the authoritarian

---

[42] Calvo's report, 3 May 1891, ACS, *CPC*, b. 2949, f. (Malatesta, Errico).

[43] Parmeggiani's biographical record, ACS, *CPC*, b. 3740, f. (Parmeggiani Luigi).

[44] Fornara's biographical record, ACS, *CPC*, b. 2121, f. (Fornara, Giuseppe); Ambassador Tornielli to Foreign Ministry, 28 April 1894, Asdmae, *Pol. Int.*, b. 39, f. 1894.

[45] Italian ambassador to Foreign Ministry, 18 January 1891, Asdmae, *Pol. Int.*, b. 39, f. 1891.

system, we want to satisfy our personal needs as much as possible, because we cannot, and do not want to, wait until the arrival of anarchy to do so'.[46]

Despite his illegal nocturnal activities, in public Parmeggiani managed to appear respectable. He used to 'speak quietly, in a very distinctive way. His words are persuasive, and he has a way of speaking as if he were a man of great abilities and experience'.[47] In the pubs around Tottenham Road that he visited regularly, draped in a loose MacFarlane and wearing a large wide-brimmed hat, Parmeggiani was known as the '*beau Louis*'. Between 1894 and 1895 he bought a house near the British Museum, at 1 Bedford Square, where he opened an antique shop, 'thanks to some Escusurra [*sic.*] ladies, Spanish antiquarians living in Paris, and some robberies'.[48] Parmeggiani, known as Mr Louis Marcy, become quite successful in this trade. Indeed, he had 'an outstanding success in the English market',[49] and his gallery became an essential stop for collectors visiting London. Sir Charles Robinson, Surveyor of the Queen's Pictures for Queen Victoria and the first superintendent of the art collections at the Victoria & Albert Museum was acquainted with Parmeggiani and was an affectionate client. Parmeggiani sold Edward III's sword to Robinson for 1,000 guineas and also sold several expensive 'medieval' items to the British Museum. Queen Victoria's daughter, the Empress of Germany, visited his shop in 1898.[50] In fact, most of the objects of medieval or Renaissance style that were sold around Europe by Marcy's gallery were forgeries, and 'the term "Marcy fake" is now a byword'.[51]

However, at the same time Parmeggiani was heavily involved in the activities of *La Libera Iniziativa/L'Anonimato*, particularly in preaching individualism and conducting polemics against the organisationalist anarchists.

The members of *L'Anonimato* considered individual acts to be the most effective method of undermining bourgeois society and of minimising the

[46] *A bas les bourriques!* December 1894/January 1895, IISH, Nettlau archive, mf. 3457. Satisfaction of individual needs was also praised in others of the group's publications.

[47] Calvo's report, 27 December 1890, Asdmae, *Pol. Int.*, b. 39, f. (1890).

[48] Virgilio's report, London, 29 June 1903. ACS, *CPC*, b. 3740, f. (Parmeggiani Luigi). The relationship with the antiquarian Escourras of Paris and his daughter is another fascinating chapter of Parmeggiani's multifaced life. See: C. Blair and M. Campbell, *Louis Marcy: oggetti d'arte della Galleria Parmeggiani di Reggio Emilia* (Turin, London: U. Allemandi, 2008).

[49] M. Jones, P. Craddock and N. Barker (eds), *Fake? the Art of Deception* (London: British Museum Publications Ltd, 1990), p. 185.

[50] Transcription of Parmeggiani v Sweeney trial, p. 48, Italian inspector Frosali to Ministry of the Interior, 11 November 1905, ACS, *CPC*, b. 3740, f. (Parmeggiani Luigi). The authenticity of Edward's III sword is still questioned.

[51] Jones, *Fake?* p. 185.

risks. To leave the political initiative to individual will, without containing it within the boundaries of formal organisations, not only precluded the establishment of hierarchies and authoritarianism inherent in any organisation, but also prevented the arrest of anarchist militants *en masse*, as happened when the police, often with the help of *agent provocateurs*, got their hands on anarchist groups' membership lists.[52] *L'Anonimato* was, therefore, a tactic of war that was indispensable in protecting militants; those who, like Malato, had rejected it in favour of organisation were to blame for the 'absence of the many of us captured by the bourgeois'.[53] Even a temporary agreement between members of the group to contrive a plot could only ever be an exception to this rule:

> The murderer who decides to commit a crime does not trust anybody – he must act from his own will; this is the doctrine of the free thinkers! It is true that plots may happen, but they are rare and the anarchists of the *Libera Iniziativa* do not admit it, because they say: it is better to compromise one than many.[54]

The group enthusiastically honoured the dynamiters as anarchist heroes. Caserio, Ravachol, Pallas, Vaillant and Henry not only struck terror into the heart of the bourgeoisie, they also conducted invaluable acts of propaganda. For this reason, the *Libera Iniziativa* repeatedly published the speeches delivered at the trials.[55] In line with this point of view, the instructions on manufacturing bombs contained in *L'Indicateur Anarchiste* were also republished and circulated in a leaflet that ended with the following incitement:

> To *infallibly* obtain splendid results, either by destroying government buildings or by killing the rich in their palaces, the system we have indicated here must be adopted [...] So comrades, do not pity the enemy because the enemy never pitied us! Come on! Let's get down to work![56]

A copy of this publication in French was found in Henry's lodging after he was arrested for the bomb launched in the hall of the Café Terminus at the Gare Saint-Lazare in Paris.[57] The members of the *Libera Iniziativa*

[52] The article 'Fra Anarchici Onesti e Disonesti' in *Il Comunista* 9 April 1892 reported the cases of the anarchists in Florence betrayed by the spy Magini and in Lyon by Valandier.

[53] 'L'Anonymat aux plumtifs de l'anarchie!!!', IISH, Nettlau archive, mf. 3457. This leaflet was published against Charles Malato who had criticised the group of *L'Anonimato* in his book *De la Commune a l'Anarchie* (Paris, 1894).

[54] Calvo's report, 9 June 1897, ACS, *CPC*, b. 1239, f. (Sante Cenci).

[55] 'La défense du compagnon Pini', 'Dèclaration de Caserio Santo'; 'La presa di Porta Pia XX. Settembre 1870', 'Extraits de la défense de l'anarchiste Salvador Frank'.

[56] *Studio igienico alla portata dei lavoratori* , ACS, *Carte Crispi DSPP*, b. 136, f. 928.

[57] J. C. Maitron, *Ravachol et les anarchistes* (Paris: René Julliard, 1964), p. 92.

probably met Henry during his stay in London at the *Autonomie Club*, the principal meeting point of the anarchists.[58] In March 1894, following Vaillant's execution and Henry's arrest in Paris, *La Libera Iniziativa* issued a leaflet entitled 'Vendetta!!' (Revenge!!) They sent hundreds of copies of this flyer to several Italian cities: Rome, Bologna, Florence, Naples and Turin, and also distributed them among the Italian colony in London.[59] In this leaflet, a typical example of the group's literature, *La Libera Iniziativa* strongly defended the actions of Vaillant and Henry and, at the same time, threatened the bourgeoisie.

> The innumerable revolts, the mass executions, the arrests and the sentences, the siege can only generate revenge! Reprisals demand reprisals; the glow of towns set alight and the bloodbath which will drown your planet will do what reason has been unable to accomplish up to now. [...] Yes, the earth will become an immense brazier, it will, it will! For every one of us whose blood you spill, we are determined to send *ad patres* a thousand of you. Hundreds of cops are needed to assassinate just one of us, one of us is enough to annihilate a thousand of you in a second [...] In our turn let us strike terror, fear, suffering and death to everything that represents an obstacle to the exercise of our freedom. Justice comrades! In the name of those who die in the hardship of starvation, cold and all the other privations. Ah, revenge! Ah, revenge![60]

The article considered everyone who did not support these actions as an enemy to be destroyed; even the apolitical masses were in danger.

> Hey, chameleon people, the bombs will come only for you!? You are blind and deaf who refuse to see or hear anything, you run inescapably toward your end, because: the one in charge and the coward who obeys do not deserve to live.[61]

The leaflet, as with many others issued by the group, did not spare the anarchists and socialists who disagreed with terrorism and individual acts.

> These revolutionary events are anathematized by the eunuchs who reduce the revolution to processions preceded by black and red rags, drums in the lead, etc. [...] and at every bombing one sees these redeemers stop their ears, and with tears in their eyes ask the titans for thunderbolts ... What? Bombs in restaurants, hotels, theaters, in the homes of poor judges

---

[58] J. M. Merriman, *The Dynamite Club: How a Bombing in fin-de-siècle Paris Ignited the Age of Modern Terror* (London: JR Books, 2009), pp. 122–25.

[59] Giuseppe Fornara distributed two hundred copies of this leaflet around the Italian colony. Biographical record, ACS, *CPC*, b. 2121, f. (Fornara Giuseppe).

[60] *Vendetta!!* (Milan: Tip. Della Sera) (but London: 1894); ACS, *Carte Crispi DSPP*, b. 136, f. 928 and ACS, *Min. Giu. Miscellanea*, b. 105, f. 991.

[61] *Vendetta!!*

and, even worse, among the crowd? Yes! Hypocrites with a hundred faces! Await your turn![62]

Indeed, Parmeggiani and the members of *La Libera Iniziativa/Anonimato* engaged in endless quarrels with the organisationalist anarchists and their leaders Merlino and Malatesta, but also with Malato, Pouget, and Grave, and targeted the organisationalists whenever they criticised the authors of bombing attempts or *L'Anonimato*.[63]

Moreover, Parmeggiani and *L'Anonimato* opposed all of Malatesta and Merlino's initiatives to create an anarchist organisation to escape from the impasse the anarchist movement found itself in at the beginning of the 1890s. They circulated a vast amount of hostile leaflets and pamphlets that accused the organisers of authoritarianism ('Papism') and of leaning towards legalitarianism. These allegations even found space in correspondence by one member, Amilcare Pomati, in *La Révolte*, forcing Kropotkin to intervene to refute the allegations. Parmeggiani was also involved in the publication of *L'International*, an extremist individualist periodical written in French that appeared in London in 1890, which reprinted in instalments the *Indicateur anarchiste* at the end of each issue. The editor of *L'International* was Auguste Bordes, a controversial character suspected of being an agent provocateur.[64] Copies were smuggled to France under false titles such as 'Small Treaty on Geography', 'Report on the Submarine Tunnel ', 'Translation of Dickens' Tales', 'Letters by a Priest on the Bible'.[65] The newspaper was almost entirely devoted to celebrating robberies, inciting the use of explosives, and challenging the organisationalist anarchists. It also reported on the debates among London's anarchist colony on organisation and the antiorganisation-alists' attempt to: 'delay, and in this way to hinder the development of ideas that they [the organisationalists] are attempting to indoctrinate'.[66]

Years later Parmeggiani described Malatesta as an authoritarian and intolerant person, incapable of accepting criticism, who wanted to ignite 'the social revolution everywhere at the same time. [...] I occasionally tried to oppose his baroque and sectarian ways [...] This madman, who could not

---

[62] *Vendetta!!*

[63] For example Malato was targeted for his memoirs *De la Commune a l'Anarchie*, Pouget for the articles published in the newspaper *The Evening News*. 'Une infamie' , 28 Decembre 1894, IISH, Nettlau archive, 'In Memoriam. Malatata-ho-ho-ho & le génie Pouget', IIHS, Nettlau archive, b. 3457.

[64] See Bordes' testimony at the Parmeggiani trial in 1905, 'Processo Parmeggiani v Sweeney ed altri' , ACS, *CPC,*b. 3740 (Parmeggiani Luigi).

[65] O'Squarr, *Les Coulisses de l'Anarchie*, p. 103.

[66] 'Aux doctrinaires' *L'International*, 2 June 1890, p. 20. See also: 'Mouvement en Angleterre', *L'International*, August 1890, p. 53.

bear me, hated me mortally when I baptised him "Tartarin Napoletano".[67] Parmeggiani's relationship with Malatesta had begun less uneasily and only gradually deteriorated. In March 1889, according to Calvo, Malatesta together with Parmeggiani and his best friend Pietro Bianchi went outside London to speak to Italian workers who were replacing British labourers on strike in a weapons factory.[68] The Italian authorities were concerned about the dangerous effect of anarchist propaganda among Italian workers. They also feared possible violent reactions against Italians by British workers, instigated by the Italian anarchists. The day after their outing Malatesta and Bianchi met, probably in order to write a manifesto announcing a meeting to celebrate the anniversary of the Paris Commune.

In another report, in an evident case of *captatio benevolentiae*, Calvo wrote that it was much easier for him to gather information when the two groups were united, 'but now that they are divided after what happened, it is hard for me to be a friend to both of them'.[69] However, a year later, the two groups still found practical reasons for collaboration, probably because extradition was an issue of common interest. In July 1892, during a trip to Paris, Parmeggiani was arrested for violation of a former deportation order and sentenced to one year's imprisonment. A few months later it emerged that the Italian authorities intended to request Parmeggiani's extradition for the attempted murder of Ceretti, for which he had been sentenced by default to thirty years of penal servitude. In September 1892, Calvo informed the consulate that Malatesta and another anarchist, Marocco, visited him and discussed sending a letter to the Parisian newspaper *L'Intransigeant* to protest against the extradition request. Malatesta dictated the letter to Marocco in French.[70] The following week an article opposing Parmeggiani's extradition appeared in that newspaper. It included a document allegedly written by 'notable London tradesmen' when the Italian government made the same demand to the British authorities. As had been reported by Calvo, the document published on *L'Intransigeant* stated that the Italian government dealt with political opponents as common criminals, and that the signatories could testify that Parmeggiani was in London at the time of Ceretti's stabbing.[71] Two days later Malatesta, Defendi, Louise Michel,

---

[67] Luigi Parmeggiani, *Ricordi e riflessioni* (Paris: 1914), pp. 17–18.

[68] Calvo's report, 4 March 1890, Asdmae, *Pol. Int.* b. 39, f. 1890.

[69] Calvo's report, 30 April 1891, ACS, b. 2949, f. (Malatesta Errico).

[70] Calvo's report, 11 September 1892, Asdmae, *Pol. Int.*, b. 39.

[71] 'Une extradition impossible', *L'Intransigeant*, 23 September 1892, pp. 1–2. The document was signed by Marocco, Lauria (Calvo), G. Defendi, G. Brocher, Siaccerato, G. Combault, R. Lormier, and Federico Rava.

the informer Calvo, and other anarchists contributed to a collection to help finance Parmeggiani's wife's journey to visit her husband in Paris.[72]

Despite this, after Parmeggiani's return to London the quarrels between the two groups became more frequent and harsh.[73] The quarrels were ignited by the difference in attitude towards individual acts and bombings and attempted bombing taking place in Europe at the time. In the pages of *Der Communist/Il Comunista*, which *L'Anonimato* published between 1892 and 1894, Merlino was repeatedly attacked and accused of being a police spy for the negative remarks he had made about Ravachol in *L'Homme Libre*, and for having distanced himself from terrorist practices.[74] Merlino was also targeted for publishing the pamphlet *Nécessité et bases d'une entente* that aimed at disseminating the programme for the constitution of a Socialist Anarchist party that emerged from the Congress of Capolago.[75] Malatesta also came under attack for his position towards Ravachol's attempts. Malatesta and Merlino were also accused of having planned the killing of two members of the *Libera Iniziativa* at an anarchist club.[76] The vilification perpetrated by *L'Anonimato* against its rivals also took curious forms. A fake copy of *Londra-Roma*, the only newspaper of the Italian colony that had by then suspended publication, appeared in August 1894. This issue, characterised by extremely violent and scurrilous language, attacked the 'arse-licker' and 'syphilitic' Crispi and his law on *domicilio coatto*.[77] Along with the usual death threats directed at the bourgeoisie, the broadsheet also censured Malatesta:

> Whatever the notorious, humble and modest chameleon Punch, Tartarin of ancient repute, may say, he who recently vomited (in an interview published in the newspaper To-day) on Émile Henry and on Salvador, calling their acts stupid and terrible, justifying Caserio's act but adding that it would be idiotic to imitate it against the old queen of England (?!); saying as well that only the Italian anarchists understand true socialism (!?). Beware, fool, we know who you are, oh Menateste![78]

---

72 Calvo's report, 13 September 1892, Asdmae, *Pol. Int.*, b. 39).

73 Report by Virgilio, 1 July 1903, ACS, *CPC*, b. 3740, f. (Parmeggiani Luigi).

74 A series of fourteen issues, a considerable number considering the difficulties that all anarchist groups had to face in order to fund such enterprises. *Der Communist* appeared between 1892 and 1894 and various issues were written in German, French and Italian. 'Un nuovo Terzaghi collaboratore de l'Homme Libre', *Il Comunista*, no. 2, April 1892; 'Biographische Notizen über eine "anarchistiche" viper', *Der Communist*, no. 8, June 1892.

75 'Früchte der Moral', *Der Communist*, no. 8, June 1892.

76 'Vigliacchi e spudorati alla gogna!', *Il Comunista*, no. 14.

77 *Londra-Roma*, 18 August 1894.

78 A report of the investigation carried out by a detective of Scotland Yard into the publication of this issue, together with a copy of it, can be found in NA 144/258/A55684. The detective wrongly attributed the publication of this issue to Malatesta and Merlino as revenge

The informer, Virgilio, dated the beginning of the controversy to 1896. According to his reports Parmeggiani began openly to attack the organisationalists following the decision of an anarchist court of honour concerning the behaviour of the anarchist Francesco Cini. Cini was accused of stealing some of the money he had collected in support of the Spanish militants tortured in the Montjuic fortress in 1896. Emilia and Giovanni Defendi, Pacini and Parmeggiani were the judges. Parmeggiani defended Cini, but the court of honour found him guilty and seemingly expelled him from the movement.[79] From that moment, according to Virgilio, the relationship between these two groups turned hostile.[80] Since the controversies began well before 1896, Virgilio was evidently wrong in his reports, but it is true that between 1896 and 1897 there was a proliferation of publications issued by *L'Anonimato* targeting the leaders of the Italian anarchist movement. These publications were most likely prompted by the International Socialist Workers and Trade Union Congress that took place in London in July and August 1896, and by the publication of the single issue *L'Anarchia* in which Malatesta set out a well-defined political strategy for the anarchist movement prioritising collective action and therefore marking a clear line of demarcation between the organisationalists and individualists. Malatesta continued to advocate this strategy in the pages of *L'Agitazione* in Ancona where several remarks against *L'Anonimato* group were published.[81] The antiorganisationalists replied by attacking with their usual bitterness and colourful, crude sarcasm, the 'Pope' Mal-di-Testa' (headache) and all the 'pontiffs of anarchy': Merlino the snake, Grave the renegade, Pouget the slut, Malato-oh-oh!, Landauer the Jesuit, Agresti the idiot. They even published a false obituary for Malatesta, 'killed by a shot in Candia where he went with Cipriani to defend freedom', in which they announced the speakers at his funeral oration in Islington: Kropotkin was going to speak against organisation, Merlino against parliamentarianism, Pietro Troja (Pietraroja) against robbery, etc.[82]

During the same period, Merlino's turn to parliamentary action was taken by the members of *La Libera Iniziativa* as confirmation of their claims that he, along with all the organisationalists, was not, and had never been, a true anarchist, and that organisation led inevitably to idolatry and authori-

---

for Pietro Rava's opposition to the anarchist attempts to open an Italian workers' circle. The issue is also kept in the *Londra-Roma* collection in Colindale Newspaper Library. Parmeggiani's comments on Malatesta in: Luigi Parmeggiani, *Ricordi e riflessioni* (Paris: 1914).

[79] Dante and Virgilio's report, 24 April 1901, ACS, *CPC*, b. 1350, f. (Cini Francesco).

[80] Virgilio's report, 1 July 1903, ACS, *CPC*, b. 3740, f. (Parmeggiani Luigi).

[81] 'Polemica', *L'Agitazione*, 4 April 1897.

[82] 'Errico Malatesta, 14 Aprile 1897', IISH, Nettlau archive, mf. 3459.

tarianism.[83] Moreover, those who had previously admired and now criticised Merlino were considered hypocritical since they were, as *La Libera Iniziativa* had always claimed, moving in the same direction. The International Workers' Congress held in 1896 inspired the text and images in the satirical *International Socialist, Communist, Anarchist and Papist Congress in London* in which Malatesta (riding a wooden rocking horse), Merlino (pictured as an adder), Malato, Grave, Pouget Landauer, Gori (the pulveriser), Agresti and Most, worried about losing the economic gains made from exploiting the good faith of anarchist militants, confer about how to stop the growing influence of the individualists on the anarchist movement and crush them once and for all. The 'congress' ends abruptly when the attendees panic and flee after hearing street news vendors shouting the title of the bulletin *Why We Are Individualist*.[84] This publication was a reply to the articles on individualism in *L'Agitazione*.[85]

An absence of polemical and virulent statements and a clarity of ideological exposition marks out *Why We Are Individualist* from other *Libera Iniziativa/L'Anonimato* publications. The bulletin endorses the sovereignty of individuality and rejects the despotism of organisation with its dismissal of both majorities and minorities; it insists on the individual as the key force for progress, and emphasises a willingness to fight using all possible means in order to satisfy the needs of the individual. However, hints of frustration emerge amongst the usual criticism of the organisationalists. The bulletin views the present generation as made up of mummified individuals lacking in initiative, accustomed to misery and servitude and unwilling to rebel to win freedom and prosperity. Therefore, nothing could be expected of people who were 'even more conservative and reactionary than the most ferocious bourgeois, full of ignorance and prejudice inculcated by the bourgeoisie and by the 'pontiffs of anarchy'.

> Once, the bourgeoisie was afraid of anarchism. That was after Duval and up to Caserio. But after the pontiffs stifled their enthusiasm by dint of insinuation, slander and denouncements, we have reached the point that anarchy is admitted even into the lounges and the bourgeois can eat peacefully, and digest in comfort. [...] If Emile Henry, Reinsdorf and many other comrades could look back, do you believe they would still sacrifice their lives if they could see the decomposition and putridity of anarchism? For a cause that today has become a sickening farce?[86]

[83] 'L'ultimo passo di Merl…o', IISH, Nettlau archive, mf. 3459.

[84] 'Congresso Internazionale. Socialista, Comunista, Anarchico e Papista di Londra', IISH, Nettlau archive, mf. 3459.

[85] 'Ai babbei dell'Agitazione', IISH, Nettlau archive, mf. 3459.

[86] 'Perché siamo individualisti', IISH, Nettlau archive, mf. 3459.

At the end of the 1890s there were rumours that Parmeggiani was an *agent provocateur*. A handbill was circulated accusing him of being a police spy responsible for the arrest and condemnation of Pietro Bianchi. Parmeggiani issued a long leaflet denying the rumours:

> Snitch, me? A funny snitch who fought the organisation of groups, who is not a partisan of clubs, meetings and conventions; who never wrote to anybody and to whom nobody from anywhere in the world wrote, who receives only some rare and old friends! Snitch, me? For 15 years I have been in the movement; who among my opponents or my enemies can stand up and say that on this or that occasion, for hate or revenge, I have betrayed or abused even one of his secrets?[87]

However, his behaviour, the nature of the pamphlets he published, and his disruptive actions suggest otherwise. The prefect of Reggio Emilia described him as 'an enigmatic individual, a man whose wealth has absolutely mysterious origins. A former anarchist, he is suspected of being linked with international freemasonry and even of being a regular receiver of international stolen goods'.[88] According to Virgilio, Parmeggiani was considered a spy because he was spotted a few times taking Inspector Melville by the arm. Maria Carronis, Parmeggiani's former mistress, alleged that he was a German or French agent and that she was scared of him because of 'his audacity and his close relations with the police'.[89] However, according to archival sources, there is no clear evidence that Parmeggiani worked for the Italian or any other government.

In the second half of the 1890s Parmeggiani gradually became less politically active and concentrated on his business activities. At the end of the 1890s he left London and went to Paris where his shop flourished. However, in 1903 he was arrested in Paris for stealing. He reappeared in London in 1905; John Sweeney, a former police officer, had described Parmeggiani in his memoirs as an anarchist and Parmeggiani sued him for libel.[90] At the trial in London Parmeggiani denied ever have been an anarchist and pretended to having been mistaken for his brother, but he lost his case.[91]

[87] L. Parmeggiani, 'La Décadence des Anarchistes a Londres', (no date) IISH, Nettlau archive, b. 310.

[88] Prefect of Reggio Emilia to the Ministry of the Interior, 12 September 1930, ACS, *CPC*, b. 3740, f. (Parmeggiani Luigi).

[89] From the Italian Consulate to the Ministry of the Interior, 1 July 1903, Virgilio's report 30 June 1903, ACS, *CPC*, b. 3740 f. (Parmeggiani Luigi).

[90] J. Sweeney, *At Scotland Yard* (London: Grant Richards, 1904).

[91] Transcription of Parmeggiani v Sweeney, Italian Inspector Frosali to Ministry of the Interior, 11 November 1905, ACS, *CPC*, b. 3740, f. (Parmeggiani Luigi). See also: Metropolitan Police: Libel action against an ex-police officer (Parmeggiani v. Sweeney), NA, HO144/606/ B31076. Parmeggiani lived in Paris and in the 1920s returned to his native town of Reggio

Luigi Parmeggiani in his art gallery shop in Paris.
(by courtesy of I musei di Reggio Emilia)

Although the groups of *L'Anonimato* ended their activities before the turn of the twentieth century, the presence of antiorganisationalist anarchists in London remained considerable.

The organisationalists

The transfer of the press that printed Malatesta's newspaper, *L'Associazione*, from Nice to London in November 1889 represented an important milestone in the revitalisation of activities among Italian anarchists in London.[92] The general revival of socialism, beginning in 1889 with the two International Workers' Congresses held in Paris, the magnitude of the London dock strike, and the fact that he was in possession of the necessary means, prompted Malatesta to take up this enterprise on his return from Argentina.[93] Malatesta gathered a number of prominent refugees around the newspaper:

Emilia. A few years before his death he donated his entire collection of antiquities to the city council; nowadays it is possible to visit the 'Galleria Comunale d'arte Parmeggiani'.

[92] Levy, 'Malatesta in London: the Era of Dynamite', pp. 25–43.

[93] Max Nettlau, *Errico Malatesta, vita e pensieri* (New York: Casa editrice Il Martello, 1922), p. 126.

Francesco Merlino, Luisa Pezzi, Giuseppe Consorti, Galileo Palla, F. Cucco, and Giuseppe Cioci.[94] Malatesta published three issues in Nice and used it to uncover the activities of the master police spy Carlo Terzaghi (alias Azzati) but, as a result, the police became aware of his presence in France and he was forced to move to London to avoid arrest for violation of an old expulsion decree.[95] Thus, from its fourth issue *L'Associazione* was published from Malatesta's new house, at 4 Hannell Road, Fulham.[96] The newspaper was not intended to be an organ of mass agitation, but rather to serve as an instrument of analysis and debate among militants; in part because it was produced abroad.[97] Its political aims were ambitious: the reorganisation of the anarchist movement and the constitution of an international socialist-anarchist revolutionary party with a common platform; a party whose unity and discipline derived not from leaders or official deliberations but from co-operative action, consciousness and the sharing of means and aims, the fulfilment of one's pledges and a willingness to do everything to promote the cause and nothing to hamper it.[98]

L'Associazione stated four main principles around which the anarchist forces could assemble and unify: anarchy as the rejection of all governments; revolution as the instrument to overthrow a society founded on violence; the refusal of parliamentarianism and anarcho-communism as the solution to the social question – although this last point was left open to debate. Indeed, *L'Associazione* called for an end to anarchist dogmatism. The controversies and contrasting philosophical speculations regarding the social and economic organisation of future society were to be postponed until the final success of the revolution. When that point was reached, various experiments and practices would have indicated how to build a new society through the 'free will of all'. This relativism was the way in which the anarchist movement could disentangle itself from the theoretical controversies and ideological debates that had paralysed action. This approach, for example, could allow common action between collectivist and communist anarchists – two groups that held different opinions regarding the future structure of

[94] *L'Associazione* was important in the development of Malatesta's thought. The attempt to reorganise the anarchist movement and to create a socialist-anarchist revolutionary party reached its culmination at the Capolago congress in 1891.

[95] *L'Associazione*: 'Ultim'ora', 16 October 1889 and 27 October 1889, p. 4; 'Azzati-Terzaghi Una spia smascherata' 30 November 1889, p. 2. On Terzaghi's activities see also: Brunello, *Storie di anarchici e di spie*.

[96] Max Nettlau, *Die erste Blütezeit der Anarchie, 1886–1894* (Vaduz: Topos, 1981), p. 159.

[97] 'Ai nostri corrispondenti', *L'Associazione* , 16 October 1889, p. 4.

[98] 'Programma', *L'Associazione*, 6 September 1889, p. 1.

society, but that shared the same revolutionary programme and agreed on the methods to attain it.[99]

In view of the impending outbreak of revolution, party members' course of action was clearly defined:

Propaganda through writing, through words and deeds against property, governments, religion; to arouse the spirit of revolt in the masses, to fight all parliamentarian methods and to drive everyone away from the ballot boxes; to take advantage of all opportunities, all economic, political and legal events to induce the people to seize things, to offend authority, to disregard and violate the law; to inspire love, solidarity, and a spirit of sacrifice for the poor and oppressed and hatred against the bosses and oppressors.[100]

L'Associazione also called for a revision of old tactics. Malatesta was aware that political conditions had evolved and revolutionary methods needed to conform to the contemporary situation. The small armed bands had become unpractical and anarchists should instead rely on the constant and spontaneous actions of individuals and groups.[101] Chiefly, Malatesta began to emphasise the relevance of the working class, economic struggles and strikes as forms of collective action. L'Associazione represented the starting point for Malatesta's development of a syndicalist strategy that he articulated more comprehensively in successive years, particularly in the publication of L'Agitazione in Ancona. Malatesta was impressed with the London dockworkers' struggle of September 1889 and with the wave of strikes taking place simultaneously in Europe.[102] He found new value in the industrial action that the anarchists, 'perhaps still imbued with the old Jacobin spirit that attached little importance to the action of the masses', had neglected, so leaving the labour movement in the hands of reformist and reactionary parties. Anarchists could re-establish their contacts with the masses through promoting and taking active participation in strikes, their duty was to give strikes a revolutionary character and turn them into attacks against the state and the expropriation of the bourgeoisie:

The masses arrive at great vindications by means of small protests and small revolts. Let us join them and spur them forward. (Spirited men throughout Europe are at this moment disposed toward great strikes of agricultural or industrial workers that encompass vast regions and numerous associations). Therefore, let us provoke and organise as many strikes as possible;

---

99 'I nostri propositi', L'Associazione, 30 November 1889, p. 1.

100 L'Associazione's programme was also translated and published into French and Spanish.

101 'La propaganda a fatti', L'Associazione, 16 October 1889, p. 2.

102 'A proposito di uno sciopero'; 'Un altro sciopero', L'Associazione, 6 September 1889, p. 1; 16 October 1889, p. 3.

let us ensure that strikes become contagious, that when one explodes it extends quickly to ten or a hundred different trades, in ten or a hundred towns. Indeed every strike has its revolutionary characteristic; every strike finds energetic men to punish the bosses and, above all, to attack property and show the strikers that it is easier to take than to ask.[103]

Malatesta promoted this view among the other anarchist circles in London and through his correspondence with other anarchists. In August 1890 he attended a small conference at the *Autonomie Club* organised by the Socialist League to consider united international revolutionary action, with the participation of native, foreign and Jewish groups, at which he 'proposed that the main anarchist sects – communist and collectivist – should unite in a revolution to seize property, and only after that plan for the future'.[104] Malatesta also supported a general strike if it were supplemented with military action, because a 'strike was not the Revolution but only an occasion to make it.'[105]

In the columns of *L'Associazione* Malatesta also developed his concept of association, an idea that became central to his political thought. He regarded association or organisation as fundamental both before and after revolution. He considered it essential that the political forces of anarchism be organised to enable the movement to play a leading role in the struggle for human emancipation. He realised that the anarchist groups had become atomised and lost influence as a result of the collapse of the First International and governmental prosecutions. The rejection of all forms of organisation, which the anarchists had theorised and practised as a form of protection against police repression and infiltration by spies, together with their faith in the efficacy of the 'individual act', had detached the anarchists from the common people. To reverse the decline, Malatesta envisaged the establishment of an anarchist party comprising all members who embraced a common programme. This organisation had to be anarchist, without leading authority and with complete freedom of action for individuals and groups. Members could express any opinion and use any tactic that did not contradict the freely accepted principles and did not interfere with the activities of other members. The degree and nature of co-operation between members could vary according to local situations, personal knowledge, personal temperaments, and the political climate. Thus the very organisational structure of the anarchist 'party' within which individuals were free to join the groups they felt to be most congenial would educate people to take their own

---

[103] 'A proposito di uno sciopero', *L'Associazione*, 6 September 1889, p. 1. Translation in Pernicone, *Italian Anarchism*, p. 249.
[104] Oliver, *The International Anarchist Movement*, p. 68.
[105] Quail, *The Slow Burning Fuse*, p. 92.

initiatives and, consequently, prevent the constitution of renewed authoritarian power after the revolution.

Paradoxically, it was an act of robbery that ended the publication of *L'Associazione*. In December 1889 the administrator, Cioci, stole all the newspaper's funds, 5,000 francs, and escaped to Italy where he was arrested.[106] This financial loss caused the abrupt end of the newspaper.

Despite the closure of *L'Associazione* Malatesta and Consorti persevered in stimulating political and theoretical debate. In August 1890 a circular that assumed the programme of the defunct newspaper announced the publication of a series of pamphlets under the title of *Biblioteca dell' Associazione*.[107] Some of Malatesta's most influential works were published, in particular *Fra contadini* (in a new edition), *In tempo di elezioni* and *L'Anarchia*, which was printed in many thousands of copies.[108]

Although short-lived, *L'Associazione* played a crucial role in revitalising Italian anarchist activities and led to the organisation of the national congress in Capolago in January 1891: 'One of the most original and interesting initiatives of the socialist anarchists at the end of the century'.[109] The congress aimed at the unification of all the revolutionary forces and marked the unbridgeable distance between the Italian anarchists and the legalitarian socialists. At the end of the congress the 'Social Revolutionary Anarchist Party, Italian Federation' was established, following the internationalist tendency 'formulated two years before in *L'Associazione*'.[110]

On 29 March 1891 Malatesta participated at a conference, again at the *Autonomie Club*, called to prepare demonstrations for the following May Day and for 'a nation-wide propaganda organisation'. In the discussion the point

---

[106] Cioci's arrest had a bizarre aftermath. In order to prosecute him, the Minister of the Interior asked the embassy to provide testimony from the editors of *L'Associazione* regarding the stolen money. The ambassador replied that the anarchists were not in the habit of testifying to the Italian authorities. In any case the funds concerned were said to be of dubious origins. Moreover, it was nearly impossible for the editors of *L'Associazione* to travel to Italy to give evidence since most of them had outstanding sentences hanging over their heads. Italian ambassador Tornielli to Foreign Minister Crispi, 20 January 1890, Asdmae, *Pol. Int.*, b. 39, f. (1890).

[107] The pamphlets announced in the circular were: *La politica parlamentare nel movimento socialista*; *Programma e organizzazione di un partito internazionale socialista-anarchico-rivoluzionario*; *Che cos'è il socialismo: sua base fondamentale, sua condizione e tendenza*; *Che cos'è il comunismo anarchico*; *Fra Contadini*. Reported by the Ministry of the Interior to the Italian ambassador, 27 August 1890, Asdmae, *Pol. Int.*, b. 39, f. (1890).

[108] Calvo's report, 25 April 1891, ACS, *CPC*, b. 2949, f. (Malatesta Errico). The others were Malatesta *La Politica parlamentare nel movimento socialista*, and Emilio Sivieri: *Un anarchico ed un repubblicano* (1891).

[109] Enzo Santarelli, *Il Socialismo anarchico in Italia* (Milan: Feltrinelli Editore, 1973), p. 77.

[110] Berti, *Errico Malatesta e il movimento anarchico*, p. 169.

was reiterated, probably by Malatesta, that the anarchists should have done more to 'take advantage of workers' movements such as strikes'.[111]

For the celebration of May Day in 1891 the Italian anarchists organised a meeting at the *Club Nazionale* in Frith Street addressed to Italian workers at which Malatesta was announced as one of the main speakers. In reality, the advertisement was a deception to hide Malatesta's plans for leaving London and returning in secret to Italy, where large demonstrations were expected. In the spring of 1891 the anarchist movement had been preparing for an insurrectionary attempt in Sicily and Tuscany around Labour Day. The demonstrations around Europe were evidently the cause of some concern for the British authorities. Indeed, a few days before May Day, the Metropolitan Police warned the Italian Embassy of Malatesta's intentions:

Information has been received that about a week or 10 days ago Malatesta & a most intimate friend of his named Consorti (another desperado) left this country en route for Italy, and supposedly for Rome, for the purpose of fomenting disturbances on the 1st of May. The few Italians in London, who are aware of Malatesta's departure are very silent respecting it, and with a view to deceiving any person who would give information to the Italian Gov. about it, handbills are being printed announcing that Malatesta will speak in London on 1st of May. From this circumstance it is believed that Malatesta has gone to Italy for very important business.[112]

The ambassador considered this to be an exceptional document, since 'English police do not make investigations into foreigners' political conduct and it is unheard of that they would communicate information in their possession to foreign governments'.[113]

Following the political line defined by *L'Associazione* and the Congress of Capolago, at the beginning of the 1890s Italian anarchists paid increasingly attention to the colony of immigrants and initiated more propaganda activities among their compatriots.

In the autumn of 1891 the anarchists addressed their efforts to the catering sector, one of the most common areas of occupation in the Italian community, using a variety of methods. At the end of August a meeting of chefs and waiters was announced at the *Autonomie Club*.[114] In September

---

[111] Oliver, *The international anarchist movement*, p. 60.

[112] Metropolitan Police Criminal Investigation, Dept. New Scotland Yard, 27 April 1891, Asdmae, *Pol. Int.*, b. 39.

[113] Italian ambassador to the Foreign Ministry, 29 April 1891, Asdmae, *Pol. Int.*, b. 39, f. (1891). Malatesta's hopes for an insurrection in Italy were not realised and he was arrested on his way back to England.

[114] Ambassador Tornielli to Foreign Minister Di Rudinì, 20 August 1891. Asdmae, *Pol. Int.*, b. 39, f. (1891).

the ambassador Tornielli reported that Merlino was conducting active propaganda among Italian waiters and chefs, who numbered a few thousand in London. A month or so later he reported that Italian anarchists, following the English example, had begun holding public meetings in the poorest areas of the Italian colony which were well received after initial suspicion among the population. This activity was a cause of concern for the Italian ambassador who felt it necessary to inform the Foreign Secretary, Lord Salisbury, of the 'dangerous propaganda delivered by the Italian anarchists in the public streets'.[115] At that time Malatesta's group was apparently named the *Circolo dei ribelli rivoluzionari*.[116]

At the beginning of 1893 Malatesta, Pietraroja, Merlino, Bertoja and others formed a group, called *Solidarietà*, with its office in Pietraroja's home at 35 East Street, off Theobald's Road.[117] This group was set up in opposition to the individualist group of *La Libera Iniziativa*, and focused on instigating popular uprising.[118] To this end it produced a number of manifestos that were distributed in many Italian towns for May Day 1893, agitating for a general strike and armed insurrection.[119] Concurrently, initiatives were directed towards the workers of the *Società Italiana*. This institute's management was well aware of the anarchists' activities and was 'doing its best to keep the dangerous element at bay'.[120] A few months later Merlino, Malatesta, Agresti, Pietraroja and Antonio Bertani announced a meeting to establish an association of Italian workers 'for the improvement and emancipation of the workers without president or elected committee but with weekly meetings open to all members to discuss the interests of the association.'[121] Pietro Rava, the editor of *Londra-Roma*, stood against this proposal, praising the common sense of Italian workers in staying away from people who 'could hardly account for the source of their means of subsistence'. Emancipation could be achieved only through industriousness and saving. 'No one feels the need for a bunch preaching anarchy and sowing suspicion among the British population towards Italian workers'. Anarchist theories were simply to be dealt with by police.[122]

[115] Ambassador Tornielli to Foreign Minister Di Rudinì, 6 September and 5 November 1891, Asdmae, *Pol. Int.*, b. 39, f. (1891).

[116] Calvo's report, 5 April 1891, ACS, *CPC*, b. 2949, f. (Malatesta Errico).

[117] Calvo's report, 29 February 1893, ACS, *CPC*, b. 1519, f. (Cova Cesare).

[118] Italian ambassador to the Foreign Minister, 7 May 1893, Asdmae, *Pol. Int.*, b. 39, f. (1893). The group *L'Anonimato* promptly attacked them in 'Zur Solidaritats – Phraserei!', *Der Communist*, June 1892.

[119] Berti, *Francesco Saverio Merlino*, p. 223.

[120] Italian ambassador to Foreign Ministry, 22 March 1893, Asdmae, *Pol. Int.*, b. 39, f. (1893).

[121] 'Ai nostri operai', *Londra-Roma*, 28 July 1893; 'Voci dal pubblico', 22 August 1893.

[122] 'Ai nostri operai', *Londra-Roma*, 28 July 1893.

This position caused a quarrel with the Italian anarchists, several of whom stormed Rava's office in order to have a response published. This led the police to believe that Malatesta and the others were responsible for the publication of the fake issue of *Londra-Roma*.

The *Solidarietà* group also paid attention on the dramatic events in Sicily and issued a leaflet urging the comrades in Italy to organise revolutionary *Fasci* in support of a likely riot in South Italy.[123] Indeed, Malatesta and Merlino expressed great interest in the activities of the Sicilian worker and peasant associations, the *Fasci dei Lavoratori,* which were attracting thousands of members and which the anarchist leaders believed could be transformed into a general armed insurrection on the island.[124] Towards the end of 1893 Malatesta, Merlino and Bertone left London and travelled to Italy to organise this uprising. Merlino was arrested in Naples in January 1894.[125] After Merlino's arrest, while Italian authorities were desperately trying to capture Malatesta, the Ministry of the Interior received a letter from London informing it that Malatesta and Malato were in Massa Carrara. This note was sent by the British *provocateur* Auguste Coulon, who had been at the centre of the Walsall anarchists' case.[126] Despite this, Malatesta managed to get back to London unhindered.

On Malatesta's return to London in March 1894 his group issued another manifesto, apparently written by Pietraroja and corrected by Malatesta, that commented on the bloody repression of the popular revolt in Sicily and the anarchist uprising in Lunigiana and attributed the failure of the insurrection to the lack of support received from other regions of Italy.[127]The manifesto urged Italian workers to revolt to free themselves from government and to establish 'anarchy: that is a society without government, people in freedom'. A secret agent in London informed ambassador Tornielli about the mailing of this publication, and as a result, Italian authorities were able to seize four

---

[123] Gruppo Solidarietà, 'Agli anarchici italiani', leaflet, IISH, Nettalu archive, f. 3311.

[124] Pernicone, *Italian Anarchism*, pp. 282–94.

[125] Berti, *Francesco Saverio Merlino*, pp. 219–30.

[126] Foreign Minister to Italian ambassador, 8 February 1894, Asdmae, *Pol. Int.*, b. 39, f. '1894–1895'. In January 1892 six anarchists were arrested in Walsall and London, and charged with manufacturing bombs. Three of them, among whom was the Italian shoemaker Jean Battolla, received a sentence of ten years' imprisonment. The whole event was the result of a conspiracy organised by Inspector Melville of Scotland Yard through the agent provocateur Auguste Coulon, employed by the British police. See: Quail, *The Slow Burning Fuse*, pp. 103–61; Oliver, *The International Anarchist Movement*, pp. 77–81; David Nicoll, *The Walsall Anarchists* (London: 1894).

[127] *Gruppo Solidarietà*, 'Al popolo d'Italia', London 1 March 1894, ACS, *Min. Giu.*, *Miscellanea*, b. 105, f. 991, 'Stampa straniera sediziosa'. Another appeal for insurrection, launched by the group *Solidarietà*, was reported by Tornielli in his letter of 11 November 1893. Asdmae, *Pol. Int.*, b. 39, f. (1893).

hundred copies of it at the post office in Turin.[128] The police drew up a list of the people in different cities to whom the manifestos were addressed and, using the law against subversive publications, many were arrested and tried. The most incriminating passage in the manifesto was:

> People! It is up to you to be free! Write to your sons in the army and urge them to desert, prevent the others from joining the army. Stop paying taxes. Take up arms and take to the streets determined to fight your exploiters. Break telegraph cables, blow up rail bridges, interrupt all communications between different locations: in this way the government will lose control of information and consequently it will lose control of repression [...] Assault police stations, burn down tribunals, archives, council and county halls, set fire to all documents: title deeds, sentences and convictions that are kept there. Seize all properties. You have produced everything with your labour and you should benefit from everything instead of being naked and starving.[129]

However, since it was not possible to demonstrate either the relationship between the defendants and the publishers or the will to distribute them in Italy, those charged were generally acquitted.[130]

In summer 1896 the International Socialist Workers and Trades Union Congress was scheduled to take place in London. The anarchists were excluded as a result of a motion passed at the previous congress in Zurich that limited membership of the Congress to groups and parties which accepted the use of political rights and legislative machinery to win political power. From September 1895 the London community of anarchists started a campaign to uphold their right to attend the congress as 'a section, and by no means an unimportant section, of the working classes'.[131] Malatesta was part of the Anarchist and Anti-Parliamentary Committee established to create a libertarian front at the Congress and in articles for *The Torch* and *Liberty* he 'rallied the disorganised forces of anarchism [...] Throughout 1895 and 1896 he won over Tom Mann, Keir Hardie, Shaw, Cunningham-Graham, and Morrison Davidson to his position'.[132] Malatesta also published a kind of manifesto in the *Labour Leader* and in the French *Le Parti Ouvrier* (also signed by August Hamon) explaining why the communist and the collective

---

[128] Ambassador Tornielli to Foreign Minister Blanc, 10 March 1894. Asdmae, *Pol. Int.*, b. 39, f. (1894–1895).

[129] *Gruppo Solidarietà*, 'Al popolo d'Italia', London 1 March 1894, ACS, *Min. Giu., Miscellanea*, b. 105, f. 991, 'Stampa straniera sediziosa'.

[130] Various reports in ACS, *Min. Giu. Miscellanea*, b. 105, f. 991 (Stampa Straniera Sediziosa).

[131] 'The International Socialist Workers and Trades-Union Congress of 1896, Shall Politicians Rule it?', London September 1895, IISH, Netllau archive, b. 3294.

[132] Levy, 'Malatesta in London: The Era of Dynamite', p. 34.

anarchists should be considered socialists. Consequently, he pledged to avoid divisions and demanded the right for all workers to fight the bourgeoisie despite political differences and each according to his own methods, yet united in the economic struggle.[133]

Differently from the Zurich Congress, the anarchist-socialists tried to maximise the number of militants entrusted with union mandates, so that 'inclusiveness replaced intransigence'.[134]

The International Socialist Congress was held at Queen's Hall between 26 July and 1 August, and was attended by more than 700 delegates and many of the most prestigious names in international socialism. The congress featured a grandiose debate between socialists and anarchists that for the last time challenged the International from within. The anarchists and the anti-parliamentarian socialists, expelled from the Congress, organised an alternative mass demonstration at Holborn Town Hall and at the Workingmen's Club and Institute with the participation of more than 3,000 people.[135]

In L'Anarchia, Malatesta published a mordant report of the International Congress.[136] Malatesta recalled that the anti-parliamentarians, though conscious that the democratic socialists had a strong majority at the congress, hoped to have the opportunity to debate and discuss fundamental questions like parliamentarianism, the general strike, and workers' economic organisations. In particular, the anti-parliamentarians wanted to discuss their ideas with other trade union delegates. However, at the congress there was neither agreement nor discussion. The anarchists had been mistaken: they had relied on the 'labour spirit', but it was precisely that spirit that was missing. During the Congress preliminaries Malatesta addressed the organising committee secretary, Will Thorne, as 'Dear comrade' and was addressed in return as 'Dear Sir'.[137]

According to Malatesta, the Congress had clearly revealed the social democrats' authoritarianism and parliamentarian policy. Social democrats reduced the solution of the social question to an electoral confrontation and their unique aim was to gain votes 'by whoever and in whatever way'. Meanwhile, the Congress had convinced the anarchists of the need to

---

[133] Malatesta, surprised, complained with Hamon that the French anarchist Pelloutier had defined the article as: 'not anarchist'. Malatesta to Hamon, 11 July 1896, IISH, Hamon archive, b. 109.

[134] Davide Turcato, 'The 1896 London Congress: Epilogue or Prologue?' in Berry, Bantman (eds), New Perspectives, p. 117.

[135] A. Hamon, Le Socialisme et le congrès de Londres, étude historique (Paris: P.-V. Stock, 1897); The Labour Leader, 'Full report of the Proceedings of the International Workers' Congress, London', July and August 1896.

[136] Errico Malatesta, 'Il congresso Internazionale', L'Anarchia, 1896, pp. 2–3.

[137] Malatesta to Hamon, 17 July 1895, IIHS, Hamon archive, b. 109.

address their efforts towards organising the working class. Indeed, the anti-parliamentary opposition at the Congress represented 'a transitional link between an older Bakuninism, and other varieties of populist socialism, and conscious syndicalism'.[138] In its wake the Italian exiles gained much publicity and the organisationalist anarchists, led by Malatesta, sought to revitalise the revolutionary anarchist movement in Italy from exile in London. Concurrently, the fall of Crispi's government facilitated the return of many militants in Italy from forced domicile, and it was thus a propitious time for a revival. However, followers of Malatesta's strain of anarchism had much lost ground to recover in terms of support among the working and peasant classes of Italy as a result of the wave of anarchist terrorism in Europe and the ideological and political confusion generated by individualist anarchists.

The Congress proceedings consolidated the idea that, in order to have an anarchist party capable of engaging with the labour movement and winning political influence, the organisationalists needed to split from the individualists and gather around them only those militants who completely agreed on a common plan of action. Malatesta's previous optimistic vision of a union of all anarchist tendencies, supported in *L'Associazione*, had vanished. In March, he revealed his concerns to Niccolò Converti, arguing that unbridgeable ideological differences and internal conflicts had paralysed the anarchist movement. Moreover, misunderstandings grew not only among anarchists, but also among the people to whom the anarchists addressed their message. Therefore, it was 'necessary first to divide, and then to assemble those who agreed with each other and had a common course of action'.[139]

Thus, in August 1896, shortly after the Congress, a group of socialist-anarchists composed of Malatesta, Pacini, Cini, Agresti and Radaelli, published the single edition of *L'Anarchia* to investigate the crisis of the anarchist movement and to suggest possible solutions. *L'Anarchia* was to exert great influence within the Italian anarchist movement, especially through Malatesta's articles 'Socialismo e Anarchia' and 'Errori e rimedi'.[140]

The editorial group made clear that if their ideas caused a schism which 'in fact had been latent for several years, let it be soon and definitive because nothing is more damaging than confusion and ambiguity'.[141]

---

[138] Levy, 'Malatesta in London', p. 34.

[139] Errico Malatesta to Niccolò Converti, 10 March 1896, in E. Malatesta *Epistolario 1873–1932. Lettere edite ed inedite*, edited by Rosaria Bertolucci (Carrara: Centro Studi Sociali, 1984), p. 74.

[140] Leonardo Bettini, *Bibliografia dell'anarchismo*, vol. 2, *Periodici e numeri unici anarchici in lingua italiana pubblicati all'estero (1872–1971)* (Florence: Crescita Politica Editrice, 1976), p. 154.

[141] Il gruppo editore, 'Avviso', *L'Anarchia*, August 1896, p. 1.

Almost all the articles published in *L'Anarchia* asserted the need to disengage from the antiorganisationalists. According to Luigi Radaelli, detachment from the anti-organisationalists was necessary in order to resume effective political agitation among the lower classes.[142] Agresti shared this belief: 'We are two different groups in the same tight circle. Frankly, separation is best for everybody – place ourselves in two different camps and each of us go his own way'.[143]

L'Anarchia analysed philosophical and political aspects to clarify the profound differences that distinguished organisational anarcho-communists from the other wings of the anarchist movement and to avoid further misunderstandings. Malatesta and Agresti underlined moral questions in their writings. In 'Errori e rimedi', Malatesta criticised the anarchists who denied the existence of morality arguing that they disregarded the fact that, to fight bourgeois morality, it was necessary to oppose it with a superior moral system, both in theory and in practice through the creation of new institutions that would correspond to anarchist ideals of human relationships.[144]

Agresti stated that anarchy was impossible without morality. In an anarchist society where authority was absent only moral principles could ensure people would observe their obligation towards society. The anti-organisationalists were accused of disdain for human solidarity, a disdain that had political as well as ethical consequences. The idea that, in an ideal society, individuals had only to take care of their own interests was an anti-human doctrine.[145] The rejection of organisation had significant political implications; the idea that the fight against the bourgeois world was delegated to individuals had caused the spread of terrorist actions, and the use of violence had degenerated. Some of the anti-organisationalists not only praised, but even theorised, the use of indiscriminate violence: workers who did not rebel were blamed just as much as the bourgeoisie for the existence of exploitation in society. Terrorist acts could be carried out, and were carried out, against the ruling order and common people alike.[146] This method allowed governments and public opinion to come together in condemnation of all anarchist currents. For the publishers of *L'Anarchia*, the supporters of

---

[142] R. Luigi Razzia (Luigi Radaelli), 'Spieghiamoci', *L'Anarchia*, p. 3.

[143] Antonio Agresti, 'L'Individualismo', *L'Anarchia*, pp. 3–4. Only one article, 'Reminiscenze', differed substantially from this position. The author was Isaia Pacini who called for a union of all anarchists.

[144] Errico Malatesta, 'Errori e rimedi', *L'Anarchia*, pp. 1–2.

[145] F. Cini, 'Praticità nell'ideale', *L'Anarchia*, p. 4.

[146] Ciancabilla wrote in *L'Agitazione* that there were not 'innocent people in bourgeois society'. Quoted by Maurizio Antonioli, *Il sole dell'avvenire*, p. 61.

terrorist actions were therefore 'the most loyal allies and the most effective auxiliaries of the dominant bourgeoisie'.[147]

Because bourgeois society was based on violence, Malatesta did not reject the use of force to overthrow it. Gradual and peaceful reforms were ineffective; anarchists and socialists were revolutionary parties because institutions could not be changed other than by revolution. However, violence did not have to be used more than necessary.

> Unfortunately, there is a tendency to confuse means with ends; and for many, violence, which for us is and must remain a harsh necessity, becomes almost the only purpose of the fight. [...] The anarchists must not and cannot be executioners; they are liberators.[148]

Radaelli insisted that, to escape the political stalemate caused by the quarrel with the anti-organisationalists, the anarchists who believed in popular collective action must regain people's confidence that had been lost as a result of their inactivity. Organisation was essential in reaching that goal. Radaelli rejected the anti-organisationalists' claim that a structured organisation led unavoidably to minority authoritarian leadership. The organisationalists were well aware that allocating the direction of a political movement to a minority was a mistake. The anarchists did not tolerate any authority within their organisation; every anarchist knew his own duties and to accomplish them needed companions, not leaders. Neither could the organisationalists be likened to the socialists, who deceived workers with the mirage of electoral victories. Therefore, all the criticisms advanced by the anti-organisationalists were 'nonexistent shadows'.[149] Organisation was also the foundation of the future post-revolutionary society. Malatesta carefully addressed this point in 'Socialismo ed Anarchia' where he explained the inextricable connection between means and ends. Socialism was the end, while 'the free organisation from the bottom up, from simple to complex, through the free associations and federations of producers and consumers that is anarchy is the means that we prefer.'[150]

Agresti, Cini and Malatesta reiterated the argument that the anarchists had made a substantial error in neglecting the working class; they had lost

---

[147] F. Cini, 'Praticità nell'ideale', *L'Anarchia*, p. 4.

[148] Malatesta, 'Errori e rimedi', *L'Anarchia*, p. 1. On Malatesta and the individualists see: Stefano Arcangeli, *Errico Malatesta e il comunismo anarchico italiano*, (Milan: Cooperativa Edizioni Jaca Book, 1972), pp. 157–72; Gino Cerrito, 'Sull' anarchismo contemporaneo', in *Malatesta. Scritti scelti*, Gino Cerrito (ed.), (Rome: Samonà e Savelli, 1970) pp. 15–17; Malatesta, *L'organizzazione degli anarchici*, pp. 123–35; Luigi Fabbri, *Malatesta, l'uomo e il pensiero* (Naples: Edizioni RL, 1951), pp. 171–84.

[149] R. Luigi Razzia, 'Spieghiamoci', *L'Anarchia*, p. 3.

[150] Enrico Malatesta, 'Socialismo e Anarchia', *L'Anarchia*, 1896.

contact with real life and left the socialists an uncontested arena. The rather ineffectual role played by the anarchists within the *Fasci Siciliani* and the failure of the Lunigiana rising demonstrated the crisis of anarchism in Italy. The establishment of an organised anarchist movement that focused its propaganda and actions on workers and their organisations was the proposed solution, a strategy Malatesta had indicated in previous years.[151]

The release of *L'Anarchia* had wide ramifications and succeeded in promoting a debate among the anarchist movement, especially in Italy. *La Questione Sociale* wrote on 30 December 1896 that the alarm raised by the anarchists in London had 'a powerful echo among the comrades in Italy'.[152] This discussion certainly helped Malatesta, once he returned to Italy in early 1897 where his presence was required in the reorganisation of the anarchist movement. Enriched by the experience of exile and by the contacts he had made with foreign anarchist leaders in London, Malatesta went to Ancona where he published *L'Agitazione*, one of the most important Italian anarchist newspapers of the nineteenth century. He continued to emphasise 'the organisation of an anarchist-socialist party, the development of close ties between the movement and the masses, the formation of workers' resistance leagues, and strike action'.[153]

Malatesta returned to London in the new century which began with the murder of Umberto I, the King of Italy, by another anarchist exile, Gaetano Bresci.

---

[151] Francesco Cini, 'Praticità nell'ideale', *L'Anarchia*, p. 4. Malatesta had already launched this proposal with the article E. Malatesta, 'Andiamo tra il popolo', *L'Art 48*, 4 February 1894, and persisted in promoting it in *L'Agitazione*. See for example: 'Organizzatori e antiorganizzatori', *L'Agitazione*, 4 June 1897.

[152] Armando Borghi, *Errico Malatesta* (Milan: Istituto Editoriale Italiano, 1947), p. 116.

[153] Pernicone, *Italian Anarchism*, p. 289.

4

The New Century

Everyone remembers the ferocious and shameful cry with which the vile bourgeoisie of Milan, hiding behind the shutters, incited the soldiers of King Umberto while they murdered the unarmed workers on the streets: Pull hard, aim right!

An avenger has arisen who pulled strong, who aimed right.[1]

The new century opened with a dramatic event that signalled a turning point in Italian history. On the evening of 29 July 1900, the anarchist Gaetano Bresci shot dead Umberto I, nicknamed respectively 'the good King' and 'the machine-gun King' by the bourgeoisie and the anarchists. Bresci's act avenged the bloody repression of the 'bread riot' in Milan when more than eighty civilians were killed by troops under the command of General Bava-Beccaris in 1898. The king had rewarded Beccaris for the successful operation by decorating him and appointing him senator.

Bresci's act provoked violent reactions. The conservatives and liberals attacked all anti-monarchist groups – socialists and republicans included. The socialist and republican press also condemned the deed; socialist lawyer Filippo Turati refused the regicide legal advice.[2] The assassination stirred Tolstoy to express his views on the ineffectiveness of regicide in the article 'Thou Shalt Not Kill'.[3]

The anarchist movement seemed deeply shaken by the event, incapable of reacting effectively or assuming a coherent, homogeneous position. Initially,

---

[1] Amilcare Cipriani, *Bresci e Savoia, il regicidio* (Paterson: Libreria Sociologica, s.d.).

[2] Bresci was defended by Francesco Saverio Merlino; he was found hanged in his cell on 22 May 1900. The official version of suicide was rather unconvincing.

[3] Tolstoy's article appeared in 'Listkì svobodnago slova', no. 17, 1900. See: Piero Brunello's introduction to: L. Tolstoi, *Per l'Uccisione di re Umberto* (Chieti: Centro Studi Libertari, 2003), pp. 7–25.

some anarchists did not openly support the assassination, others dissociated themselves from the deed or, like *L'Agitazione*, strongly condemned it.[4] Anarchist leaders outside Italy enunciated a more thoughtful and articulate analysis of the incident, providing a clear guideline for their comrades. Felice Vezzani in Geneva urged anarchists to break with the lynch-mob and to stop adopting bourgeois arguments.[5] In September, Malatesta and other anarchists in London published a single issue significantly entitled *Cause ed effetti. 1898–1900*.

This publication was designed to defend anarchists from the widespread attacks from both conservative and socialist camps, most importantly by countering allegations that anarchism was inherently violent, and clarifying anarchists' views on the use of force. Although the anarchist movement was comprised of several different tendencies, anarchists shared the belief that physical force was not a permanent feature of human relations and did not regard violence as a progressive factor in the social evolution of the human race. Having eliminated institutional violence from society, people would organise themselves to satisfy general needs without resort to authoritarian measures. Consequently, the anarchists' first aim was to do battle against violence. Yet violence was often the only possible defence against violence: 'But even then, the violent one is not he who defends himself, but he who forces others to defend themselves'.[6]

In his contribution to the publication Malatesta declared, without disowning Bresci, that the anarchists could not be held responsible for the regicide. In Italy, the government and the police forbade workers to associate with each other and to fight peacefully for the improvement of their conditions. Harsh repression of all dissidents, socialists, anarchists, and workers' associations deprived people of hope in peaceful change. The effect of this was the rebellion of the oppressed; it was the lack of freedom that caused outbursts of violence.

By defending their privileges through force and violence the monarchs, oppressors and exploiters coerced the anarchists to employ the same means.

---

[4] On Bresci, see Giuseppe Galzerano, *Gaetano Bresci. La vita, l'attentato, il processo e la morte del regicida anarchico* (Salerno: Galzerano Editore, 1988), Massimo Ortalli, *Gaetano Bresci. Tessitore, anarchico e uccisore di re* (Rome: Nova Delphi, 2011). On anarchist attempts in Italy: C. Levy, 'The Anarchist Assassin and Italian History, 1870s to 1930s', in S. Gundle and L. Rinaldi, *Assassinations and Murder in Modern Italy: Transformations in Society and Culture* (Basingstoke: Palgrave Macmillan, 2007); Erika Diemoz, *A Morte il tiranno. Anarchia e violenza da Crispi a Mussolini* (Turin: Einaudi, 2011).

[5] Felice Vezzani, 'Alto là', *Il Risveglio*, 18 August 1900. See also: Masini, *Storia degli anarchici italiani nell'epoca degli attentati* , pp. 161–73.

[6] 'Che cos'è l'anarchia', *Cause ed Effetti*, September 1900, p. 1.

We would willingly extend our hand to kings, oppressors and exploiters, if only they wished to become men among men, equals among equals. But so long as they insist on profiting from the existing situation and defending it by force, causing martyrdom, wretchedness and the death through hardships of millions of human beings, we are obliged – we have a duty – to oppose force with force.[7]

Yet, the anarchists knew that violence and authority were inherently linked: the more violent a revolution, the more likely the outcome would be authoritarian. For this reason, the anarchists were trying to undermine the principle of authority, to educate people and to acquire the moral and material strength necessary to minimise the use of violence during revolution.

We know that what is essential and undoubtedly useful is to kill not just a king, the man, but to kill all kings – those of the courts, of parliaments and of factories – in the hearts and minds of the people; that is, to uproot faith in the principle of authority to which most people owe allegiance.[8]

In addition to other articles supporting Malatesta's position and some sarcastic comments that the death of the king was a professional hazard, *Cause ed effetti* also carried a note calling for the publication of a newspaper in Italian since repression meant there was no anarchist press in Italy.[9]

Shortly afterward, a circular advertised the forthcoming fortnightly *L'Internazionale: Periodico Socialista Anarchico*. The promoters, though forced to live away from their homeland where their work could have been more effective, did not intend to remain inactive. Consequently, they had resolved 'to publish a new periodical, now that an intense propaganda of anarchist ideals and methods is needed'.[10] Silvio Corio, who arrived from Paris at the beginning of 1901 after serving two months' imprisonment for contravening an expulsion order, was central to *L'Internazionale*.[11] The periodical was to be a platform for the various tendencies of the anarchist movement to hold a constructive debate. Anarchists needed 'to equip themselves with coherent and well-discussed criteria because the time for revolutionary action is approaching'.[12] The contributors to the newspaper were drawn from

---

7 E. Malatesta, 'La tragedia di Monza', *Cause ed Effetti*, September 1900, p. 2.

8 E. Malatesta, 'La tragedia di Monza', *Cause ed Effetti*, September 1900, p. 2.

9 'Un'iniziativa', *Cause ed Effetti*, September 1900, p. 4.

10 Circolare 'L'Internazionale, Periodico Socialista Anarchico', IIHS, Fabbri archive, b. 29. The signatories were Arcelli, Basilico, Bertiboni, Campagnoli, Cappelli, Cazzanigra, Cenci, Cuccioli, Giovanni Defendi, Enrico Defendi, Felici, Ferrari, Galassini, Giorgi, Gualducci, Lanfranchi, Magnoni, Maiolo, Malatesta, Mariani, Musso, Panizza, Pietraroia, Pozzo, Romussi, Rossetti, Rossi Carlo, Rossi Giulio, Rubini, Scolari and Tonzi.

11 Biographical record, C. Silvio, ACS, *CPC*, b.1474.

12 'Crastinus (Silvio Corio), 'Quattro parole ai compagni', *L'Internazionale*, 26 January

the international anarchist colony in London. In addition to pieces written by the Italians – Corio, Malatesta, Bacherini, D'Angiò, Cicognani and Pietraroja – *L'Internazionale* carried articles by Louise Michel, the Russian anarchist Cherkezov and the Spaniard Tárrida del Mármol.[13] The result was a heterogeneous publication. Issues concerning the labour movement and the general strike were dominant; *L'Internazionale* provided information on the labour movement in Europe and the Americas as well on anarchists' attempt to organise the waiters and dishwashers employed in London restaurants.

With the expansion of catering services at the turn of the century the number of Italian cooks and waiters increased steadily. Employees in restaurants and hotels were not organised; they accepted work under any conditions and were subject to a harsh sweating system: 'the German, Swiss or Italian waiter usually did not receive any wages but, on the contrary, he had to pay his employer a percentage of 6*d.* or more in the pound of his gross takings in tips'.[14] Thus, cooks and waiters became a source of potential recruits and, in 1901, the Italian anarchists 'took the initiative to create workers' associations where there were none', and announced the first meeting of the *Lega di Resistenza fra i lavoratori in cucina in Londra* to be held at the headquarters of the *Circolo Filodrammatico*, at 38–40 Hanway Street.[15] The *Circolo Filodrammatico* (called also *Club Italia*) was run by the tailor Isaia Pacini and had been established a few weeks previously when Pacini changed the legal status of the club he formerly ran.[16] According to its promoters, the *Lega di Resistenza* was not intended to be another friendly society but focused on economic struggles: over the reduction of working hours, increase of wages, and the fight against many of the Italian bosses who took advantage of the miserable conditions and adaptability of their compatriots to exploit them.[17]

On 20 January 1901 several orators spoke to a large audience at the *Circolo*

1901, no. 2, p. 1.

[13] Bacherini was born in Livorno in 1863 where he worked as shoemaker. He was arrested several times between 1882 and 1886 and had to seek refuge abroad. In 1890 Bacherini was sentenced to ten months' imprisonment for '*associazione a delinquere*' and escaped to France and Belgium. He arrived in London between 1897 and 1900 and died in the city in March 1921. ACS, *CPC,* b. 231, f. (Bacherini Alfredo).

[14] Sponza, *Italian Immigrants*, pp. 103–04

[15] 'Cronaca', *L'Internazionale*, 12 January 1901, no. 1, p. 2.

[16] Calvo's report, 14 January 1901. ACS, *CPC*, b. 2949, f. (Malatesta Errico). Isaia Pacini from Pistoia had left Italy in 1885, after being sentenced to two years' imprisonment for publishing a subversive manifesto. He subsequently lived in Lugano where he continued his anarchist militancy until 1895 when the confederation expelled all the anarchists in its territory. ACS, *CPC*, b. 3638, f. (Pacini Isaia).

[17] 'Cronaca', *L'Internazionale*, 12 January 1901, p. 2.

Filodrammatico Italiano, and a British worker urged the audience to join the *Amalgamated Waiters' Society*; the meeting ended by endorsing a resolution that urged waiters to fight for 'the abolition of tips and for a fair salary'.[18]

The dynamism of anarchist activities in this period is confirmed by the informer Calvo:

> Yesterday evening the usual meetings at the *Circolo Filodrammatico* and in Wardour. Such energetic propaganda was never seen among the comrades. They believe that, as Michel keeps repeating, the revolution is round the corner.[19]

However, there is a dearth of information regarding the progress of these initiatives because from as early as its second issue *L'Internazionale* began to suffer financial problems and severe delays in its publication. Approximately two months passed before the third issue appeared.

To overcome these difficulties Corio proposed Malatesta as editor of the newspaper, but was refused. Malatesta's motivations highlight the difficulties the anarchist leader was experiencing during that period of exile and the persistence of unresolved conflicts with the individualists.

Moreover, Malatesta disagreed with the general tone of the newspaper and, if in charge, he would edit it differently:

> I believe that if I edited a newspaper I would be able to keep it going. But a newspaper under my editorship would have a precise line in which opinions different from mine would find space only as pieces of information or to be refuted.

Therefore, he judged that his presence was likely to create rather than solve problems because of the strong opposition to which he was subject from a group of anarchists in London:

> What happened with *L'Internazionale* proved it. Those who share my opinions and would support a newspaper of the kind I would like to do, did not find what they expected and cooled off; those who are my determined opponents fought the newspaper more or less secretly because I was involved; and the others, the eclectics or the mediators, were on their guard again because of me, who many like to describe as sectarian and authoritarian.[20]

As it turned out Malatesta did not contribute to the last issue. Lack of time was the main reason, but also because he did not consider it worthwhile to publish a journal that had such long intervals between editions; he would

---

[18] 'Cronaca Londinese', *L'Internazionale*, 26 January 1901, p. 4.

[19] Calvo's report, 18 March 1901. ACS, *CPC*, b. 1992, f. (Felici Felice).

[20] Letter to Silvio Corio, no date. ACS, *CPC*, b. 2949, f. (Malatesta Errico).

have rather used his time to write for newspapers in Italy which suffered a shortage of contributions.[21] The botched layout of the last issue, with pages and articles mixed up, illustrated the difficulties the editorial group was facing. Indeed, *L'Internazionale*'s fourth issue was also its last.

However, the debate on the involvement of anarchists in labour organisations and the relevance of the general strike for the social movement that the entire Left was engaged in, continued.

In Italy, the liberalisation of trade union legislation under Giolitti gave new life to trade unions. Membership increased steadily and general strikes took place in Turin, Rome and Torre Annunziata. This political climate persuaded the anarchists to join labour organisations, as Malatesta had suggested years before in both *L'Associazione* and *L'Agitazione*. Many anarchist militants entered trade unions, chambers of labour, *leghe* (leagues) and federations despite their opposition to the reformist ideas held by the majority of trade union members, especially the leadership.[22]

Discussion and reports on these changes found space in the pages of *Lo Sciopero Generale*, the newspaper that replaced *L' Internazionale* in March 1902 in which Corio, Carlo Frigerio and Arturo Campagnoli were key figures. Newspapers carrying the same title appeared simultaneously in French and in English, a fact that highlights the relevance of the labour movement to the international anarchist colony. As the title suggested, the general strike was considered central to political and social action. However, for the editorial group, the general strike was only the first step toward a popular insurrection aiming at the destruction of government; it would be ineffective if not accompanied by armed insurrection.[23]

The idea of the general strike as a simple abstention from work, which would naturally lead to revolution or to economic and political improvements, was misleading. Nevertheless, according to the newspaper, the anarchists had made a mistake in previously neglecting strikes as a means of struggle. Although strikes with limited aims did not gain effective results, they nurtured the seeds of revolt. Consequently, the anarchists must concentrate their efforts and activism on workers' associations within which they could propagate their views about the inefficiency of reformism and the necessity to expropriate and socialise the means of production. Thus anarchists should retain their anarchist identity to prevent these organisations from becoming

[21] Letter without date and address. ACS, *CPC*, b. 2949, f. (Malatesta Errico).

[22] See: Maurizio Antonioli, *Il sindacalismo italiano. Dalle origini al fascismo, studi e ricerche* (Pisa: BFS, 1997); Gian Biagio Furiozzi, 'Sindacalisti rivoluzionari e anarchici', *Ricerche Storiche*, 2–3 (1982), pp. 495–512. C. Levy, 'Currents of Italian Syndicalism before 1926', *International Review of Social History*, 45. 2 (2000), pp. 209–50.

[23] La redazione, 'Per Incominciare', *Lo Sciopero Generale*, 18 March 1902, no. 1, p. 1.

centres for reformist tendencies.[24] *Lo Sciopero Generale* introduced to Italian anarchist newspapers in London a new element of activism that dominated Italian politics in later years: anti-militarism. The army represented capitalists' ultimate defence against popular claims, and militarism was the 'most powerful and direct impediment to the rise of new, free, egalitarian forms of social relations'.[25] Consequently, *Lo Sciopero Generale* considered political activity among soldiers to be extremely valuable because it could affect the main apparatus used by the bourgeoisie to repress workers' protests.[26] Anti-militarism was closely connected to another recurrent theme in the newspaper: that of anti-colonialism.[27] The newspaper suggested that anarchist militants in Italy should celebrate the May Day in front of barracks to protest against the seemingly imminent Italian military expedition in Libya.[28]

In June 1902 *Lo Sciopero Generale* announced a meeting of Italian associations in London about the proposed constitution of a *Università Popolare,* an initiative the anarchists had been discussing since the beginning of 1901, perhaps prompted by the rapid growth experienced by these educational organisations in Italy.[29] About fifteen societies in the Italian colony joined the project.[30] A series of meetings were organised in the headquarters of these societies to promote the *Università Popolare* which opened at 58 Hatton Garden in Clerkenwell, also the headquarters of *L'Unione Sociale Italiana di Mutuo Soccorso.* The committee was Ennio Bellelli, Antonio Galassini, and Ascanio Santos. The informer Calvo remarked:

> I send you the leaflet on the Università Popolare Italiana! Look at how the good old mates are studying! They believe that by assembling people of

[24] 'Sullo sciopero generale', *Lo Sciopero Generale,* 18 March 1902, no. 1, p. 2.

[25] 'L'ultimo riparo', *Lo Sciopero Generale,* 2 June 1902, no. 3, p. 1.

[26] *Lo Sciopero Generale* reported on demonstrations and mutinies of conscripts in several Italian cities.

[27] 'L'Africa agli africani', *Lo Sciopero Generale,* 18 March 1902, no. 1, p. 2, for example, supported the Boers.

[28] The publication of *Lo Sciopero Generale* happened as Italy and France held diplomatic talks for the recognition of Italian rights in Libya.

[29] Virgilio's report. 7 December 1901, ACS, *CPC,* b. 2949, f. (Malatesta Errico). 'Agli Italiani della colonia di Londra', June 1902. ACS, *PS 1905,* b. 22.

[30] They were: *Società per il Progresso degli Operai italiani in Londra; Circolo Mandolinistico Italiano; Veloce Club Italiano; Circolo Italiano dell'Arte culinaria; Circolo Filodrammatico Italiano; Banca Popolare; Lega di resistenza dei mosaicisti; Gruppo sarti italiani; Lega di resistenza fra camerieri; Lega fra i lavoranti di cucina; Comizio veterani e reduci; Gruppo operaio internazionale; Società di M.S. 'Unione' Circolo Educativo; Unione sociale italiana di M.S.;* and *Società italiana fra cuochi, camerieri ed affini.*

different opinions and social positions they will obtain a great result: that of propagandising their famous ideas![31]

However, the *Sciopero Generale* ceased publication abruptly. It is likely that this was due in part to financial difficulties and in part to the fierce arguments that erupted in the Italian colony following the discovery of the spy Gennaro Rubino. Following the cessation of *Lo Sciopero Generale*, twenty Italian anarchists signed a note written by Malatesta to launch another newspaper, *La Rivoluzione Sociale*.[32] This paper intended to express the change in the anarchists' political tactics.[33] By now, Malatesta had begun to consider the widespread entry of anarchists into workers' organisations in Italy to be a mistake. By joining labour associations, the anarchists had partially succeeded in their effort to break out of their isolation. However, the anarchists had been overconfident about the potential of the working class movement and had sympathised with republican and socialist groups that were ideologically and politically antagonistic to anarchism – factors that were eroding the anarchists' radicalism.[34] Malatesta argued that the anarchists had overestimated the importance of workers' associations: it was an illusion to believe that the labour movement alone, by its very nature, could lead to social revolution. Although it was necessary to take part in the labour movement in his opinion, the trade unions included conservative and reactionary elements which anarchists had to resist by avoiding assimilation into these organisations.[35]

The labour movement was a convenient target for political campaigns and was very useful for assembling forces for the coming revolution. Nevertheless, to achieve structural change in society an armed insurrection was unavoidable. Consequently, the anarchists had to prepare and organise themselves with a view to armed conflict. For Malatesta, preparing the ground for an armed revolution must be the priority for anarchists, both inside and outside workers' associations. In his article 'L'Insurrezione armata' he distinguished between political action that belonged to masses – strikes, protests, and demonstrations – and military action that was only practical for

---

[31] Calvo's report. 1 July 1902, ACS, *PS 1905*, b. 22.

[32] The circular was signed by: Cappelli, Carrara, Cenci, Corio, Cuccioli, Curetti, Defendi Giovanni, Defendi Enrico, Felici, Frigerio, Folli, Galassini, Goldoni, Magnoni, Malatesta, Mariani, Quarantini, Rossi Carlo, Rossi Giulio. Editor was Carlo Frigerio. 'Agli Anarchici di Lingua Italiana', London, September 1902, IISH, Fabbri archive, b. 29.

[33] Masini considered this new tactic a negative development in Malatesta's thought. See: Masini, *Storia degli anarchici italiani nell'epoca degli attentati*, pp. 211–15. See also: Berti, *Errico Malatesta e il movimento anarchico*, pp. 323–31.

[34] 'Agli anarchici di lingua italiana', September 1902, IISH, Luigi Fabbri archive, b. 29.

[35] 'Agli anarchici di lingua italiana', September 1902, IISH, Luigi Fabbri archive, b. 29.

small groups.[36] While the former could induce people to rise up and spark a revolution, only the latter could ensure success.[37]

Malatesta held this position because he assumed that Italy was on the brink of a popular insurrection.[38] Indeed, the wave of general strikes throughout the country in 1902 and the shooting dead of several protesters in the South by the army seemed to confirm in Malatesta's mind that a revolutionary period was approaching.[39] He therefore believed that Giolitti's liberal experiment was about to fail and be replaced with a policy of repression reminiscent of the 1890s. This, according to Giulietti, shows that Malatesta's long absence from Italy meant that he lacked understanding of some of the innovative political and social elements in Giolitti's reformism.[40] *La Rivoluzione Sociale* was intended to argue for Malatesta's new orientation in Italy by taking advantage of the freedom of expression granted in England. Differentiation from reformists, with whom the anarchists often collaborated within workers' associations, therefore became a central theme of the paper. Every past attempt at common action by the anarchists, whether insurrectionary or merely protests against internal exile, had failed. Moreover, relationships with those parties threatened the anarchists' own radical stance with an unnecessary dilution.[41] This fear that contact with socialists could undermine the anarchists' revolutionary purity was explained in a series of articles that strongly criticised the Socialist Party's policies and parliamentarian approach. The decision taken by reformist socialists led by Filippo Turati to lend their support to the Zanardelli-Giolitti cabinet deepened the anarchists' disdain.[42]

Intransigence towards the reformist programme even drove the newspaper to dismiss the Socialist campaigns in the Chamber of Deputies for social reforms such as the legalisation of divorce, or the proposal for an anti-militarist congress to be held in London.[43] According to Virgilio, Malatesta believed

---

[36] 'L'Insurrezione armata', *La Rivoluzione Sociale*, 5 April 1903, no. 9, p. 1.

[37] 'I nostri propositi', *La Rivoluzione Sociale*, 20 February 1903, no. 8, p. 2.

[38] 'Agli anarchici di lingua italiana', September 1902, IISH, Luigi Fabbri archive, b. 29. see also Virgilio's report, 7 and 17 June 1903, ACS, *CPC*, b. 2949, f. (Malatesta Errico).

[39] Peasants were killed at Cassano, Candela, and Giarratana. Between 1901 and 1903 about 30 people, mainly peasants, were killed by the army during demonstrations.

[40] Fabrizio Giulietti, *Storia degli anarchici italiani in età giolittiana* (Milan: Franco Angeli, 2012), p. 21.

[41] 'Noi ed i nostri "affini"', *La Rivoluzione Sociale*, 4 October 1902, no. 1, p. 1.

[42] 'Dopo un Congresso', *La Rivoluzione Sociale*, 4 October 1902, no. 1, p. 1.

[43] See: 'Il Divorzio', *La Rivoluzione Sociale*, 20 February 1903, no. 8, pp. 3–4; 'Il proposto congresso Antimilitarista', *La Rivoluzione Sociale*, 27 January 1903, no. 7, p. 3; E. Malatesta, 'Protesta', *La Rivoluzione Sociale*, 20 February 1903, no. 8, p. 2.

that anarchists' involvement in campaigns for reforms, although seemingly beneficial, was a waste of their energies.[44]

Britain served as an example of the failure of reformism. The description of widespread poverty caused by the economic crisis affecting the United Kingdom was utilised to emphasise the inefficiency of trade unions, charities and political reforms.[45] *La Rivoluzione Sociale* often criticised the British trade unions, which were portrayed as the embodiment of all the negative aspects of reformism. Although born as revolutionary institutions, the trade unions had gradually accepted the role of capitalism. Consequently, they became defenders of corporate interests and incited privileged workers against lower paid immigrant workers.[46]

Moreover, the trade unions developed bureaucratic structures run by a class of well-paid functionaries concerned almost exclusively with their own interests. Malatesta often used British trade unionism to illustrate his criticisms of syndicalism. Indeed, another central focus of *La Rivoluzione Sociale* was the participation of anarchists in workers' associations, thus continuing a theme of *Lo Sciopero Generale*. According to *La Rivoluzione Sociale*, all workers, of whatever political or religious inclinations, should join trade unions; but workers' organisations themselves must remain politically neutral. The newspaper urged anarchist trade union members to preserve their own identities and avoid being absorbed into the union hierarchy by taking positions. At the same time, anarchist members were eager to contrast their policies to socialist attempts to win hegemony inside these organisations and manipulate them for their own political ends. As members, anarchists could strengthen the revolutionary consciousness of organised workers, and persist in their battles against authority, property and religion. Workers' associations were fertile grounds for propaganda aimed at the recruiting of proletariat into the revolutionary movement.[47] Over the following years, the development of the analysis of the relationship between anarchists and labour movement started by Malatesta and *La Rivoluzione Sociale* strongly influenced anarchist participation in revolutionary syndicalism and in the *Unione Sindacale Italiana*.[48]

The last issue of *La Rivoluzione Sociale* appeared in April 1903. Financial difficulties reported in the newspaper in January were, once again, the most likely reason for its demise.

---

[44] Virgilio's report, 7 June 1903, ACS, *CPC*, b. 2949, f. (Malatesta Errico).

[45] 'La società condannata' *La Rivoluzione Sociale*, 20 December 1902, no. 6, p. 1.

[46] See: 'La morte dell'Unionismo classico', *La Rivoluzione Sociale*, 29 December 1902, no. 6, p. 2.; 'La guerra ai lavoratori stranieri', *La Rivoluzione Sociale*, 27 January 1903, no. 7, p. 1.

[47] 'Gli Anarchici nelle Società operaie', *La Rivoluzione Sociale*, 4 October 1902, no. 1, p. 3.

[48] See Levy, 'Currents of Italian Syndicalism' pp. 209–50.

Virgilio reported that Malatesta was disappointed that *La Rivoluzione Sociale* was ineffectual in changing the approach of anarchists in Italy. In April, he reported that Malatesta had said that he was 'tired of the newspaper', and a month later:

> Malatesta [...] would try anything to demonstrate that his purely revolutionary idea must have the upper hand. He says that there is a great disorder of ideas in Italy and this is due to his theories not being properly followed [...] that this program has not been understood.[49]

A subsequent attempt to revive the newspaper did not succeed, primarily for economic reasons but also because the anti-organisationalists were not interested. They published single commemorative issues instead.

The Commune represented the most important event in the anarchist calendar and each year its anniversary was celebrated in their clubs. Moreover, this commemoration was heightened in the London exile community by the presence of several former Communards, among them Louise Michel, the 'Red Virgin', was the most famous. So, in March 1903, Italian anarchists published *La Settimana Sanguinosa*.[50] The promoter of this publication was Adolfo Antonelli, a young anarchist from Rome. Politically active from the age of 17, Antonelli had been a correspondent for various anarchist newspapers in Italy and abroad. He collaborated with *L'Agitazione*, published in Ancona, and *L'Avvenire*, published in Buenos Aires, strongly supporting individualist anarchism in his articles. Arrested at a demonstration of the unemployed in Rome, Antonelli was sentenced to eleven months in prison, so fled Italy. Expelled from France at the end of 1902, he arrived in London in early February 1903.[51] Carlo Frigerio put him up in his home at 12 Dean Street and Malatesta included him in the publishing group of *La Rivoluzione Sociale*. From the very beginning, Antonelli dedicated himself to political activity; as reported by Virgilio: 'He is now the most active propagandist in the Italian quarter and is a regular at the meetings in Berruti's house'.[52]

Most of the articles in praise of the Commune and its martyrs published in the single issue attacked both the parliamentary system and social democracy. The events of the Commune exemplified the risks inherent in a revolution led by 'delegates' and not by the people themselves. From colourful descriptions of 'false shepherds', 'modern rascals of socialism', 'mob of charlatans', to more sober criticisms from Malatesta and Berruti,

---

[49] Virgilio reports, 17 April and 7 June 1903. ACS, *CPC*, b. 2949, f. (Malatesta Errico).

[50] *La Settimana Sanguinosa. 18 March–24 May*, London, 18 March 1903.

[51] See P. Di Paola, 'Antonelli Adolfo' *Dizionario Biografico Degli Anarchici Italiani*, (BFS: Pisa, 2003), pp. 42–43.

[52] Virgilio's report, 17 Marzo 1903. ACS, *CPC*, b. 104, f. (Antonelli Adolfo).

attacks on the socialist democrats dominated *La Settimana Sanguinosa*. The Commune had been a glorious revolutionary experience, the starting point of the social-revolutionary movement. Moreover, some of the conceptions involved in the governing of the Commune were still influential, even in the most unlikely quarters:

> and today, ignorant of continuing the tradition started by the Commune, even the most advanced bourgeois, even the most conservative of English worker, support the municipalisation of public services, the production of basic essentials, school meals – in a word 'municipal socialism'.[53]

However, the Communards had not dared to give political power to the people; they delegated power to an assembly instead. In this way, they perpetuated bourgeois institutions: it was the mistake that caused their downfall. For the publishers of *La Settimana Sanguinosa*, the Commune was an authoritarian parliamentarian government that restricted popular initiative and safeguarded bourgeois privileges. It did not abolish private property. Social reforms either only existed in theory or were ineffective when put into practice. As a consequence, the Paris Commune:

> fell, honoured by the sublime heroism of its supporters, but to the total indifference of the majority that had not seen any considerable difference between the Commune and previous governments.[54]

The duty of the anarchists was therefore to educate and free people from the idea that authority was necessary. Only in this way could the tragedy of the Paris Commune be avoided, a successful revolution be accomplished and new forms of authoritarian control thwarted.[55]

Antonelli sent a few hundred copies of *La Settimana Sanguinosa* to Rome and most likely to other cities in Italy and Europe. *L'Avvenire Sociale* in Messina and *L'Agitazione* in Rome reprinted some of its articles. Antonelli, encouraged by the positive reception of *La Settimana Sanguinosa*, organised the publication of a second issue, *Germinal*, this time for the celebration of May Day.

Compared with *La Settimana Sanguinosa*, *Germinal* had a more markedly individualist and anti-organisationalist flavour. Although the single issue focused principally on the May Day celebrations and the general strike, with criticisms that were rather similar to the traditional reservations the anarchist movement had expressed since the early 1890s when May Day was first celebrated, some of the articles strongly attacked the anarcho-

---

53 W. Tcherkesoff, 'Viva la Comune!', *La Settimana Sanguinosa*, p. 2.
54 Errico Malatesta, 'La Comune di Parigi e gli anarchici', *La Settimana Sanguinosa*, p. 2.
55 C. F. (likely Carlo Frigerio) 'Commemorando', *La Settimana Sanguinosa*, p. 2.

organisationalists, Malatesta in particular. Indeed, in the first half of 1903, Virgilio reported persistent criticisms of Malatesta from the individualists, who considered him to be 'an old man behind in his ideas'.[56]

The articles published in the second part of *Germinal* reflect this campaign against the veteran anarchist. *Germinal* reprinted the content of the polemic between Malatesta and Henry that appeared in the newspaper *L'En Dehors* shortly after Ravachol's execution in August 1892, hoping 'to make those comrades think who were too easily influenced by [...] Malatesta'.[57]

Returning to the anti-organisationalist arguments, passages from an old article published in *L'Agitazione* in which Malatesta had rejected individual acts, were also used to prove that the socialist-anarchist programme had degenerated into authoritarianism.[58] By denying its associates free initiative and by condemning individual acts, the socialist-anarchist party had elaborated a programme and a code of practice that defined right and wrong. That contradicted individual freedom, the fundamental principle of anarchy.

In opposition to Malatesta the article proposed that anarchists could occasionally and temporarily associate together for specific purposes. However, individuals must always maintain their own independence: they could take action according to their own will, and disassociate from others at any moment, or when a common goal was reached.

The article ended by urging the anti-organisationalist anarchists to vent their own individual energies and to depart from antiquated and Jacobin organisations that paralysed the activity of the anarchist movement.[59]

The writing was signed *Due compagni*: probably Margiotti and Pietro Gualducci. No documents exist regarding Margiotti, but Gualducci was well known among the refugees in London. He was arrested and imprisoned on several occasions in Italy – once for merely singing anarchist songs – and in other European countries. In Switzerland, the police suspected him of being an accomplice to Luigi Luccheni, the assassin of the Habsburg Empress, Elizabeth, however Gualducci was discharged for lack of evidence. For seven months in 1897 he served in the Foreign Legion in Algeria. He arrived in London at the beginning of 1902 and immediately joined the 'Bresci' group of anarchist individualists.[60]

Malatesta resented these relentless personal attacks and complained about them in a letter to Corio. He was in a state of deep discouragement and

---

[56] Virgilio's report, 7 June 1903, ACS, *CPC*, b. 2949, f. (Malatesta Errico).

[57] 'Una polemica tra Henry e Malatesta', *Germinal*, p. 4.

[58] Due compagni, 'Anarchia o Partito Socialista Anarchico', *Germinal*, 1 May 1903, pp. 3–4.

[59] Due compagni, 'Anarchia o Partito Socialista Anarchico', *Germinal*, 1 May 1903, pp. 3–4.

[60] Pietro Di Paola, 'Gualducci Pietro', *Dizionario biografico degli anarchici italiani* (BFS, Pisa, 2003), pp. 770–72.

depression and the publication of *Germinal* may have pushed him over the edge. Virgilio reported:

> Malatesta is neurotic. When he faces opposition he goes mad. Sometimes he truly bangs his head against the wall. He did it after the last attacks from 'Germinal', and his fury against Margiotti and Gualducci is boundless.[61]

Nevertheless, the relationship between Antonelli and Malatesta does not seem to have been affected by the publication of *Germinal*. One year later, Antonelli wrote in a letter that Malatesta was his only friend in London.[62] In 1905, after Antonelli's arrest for the publication of *L'Insurrezione*, Malatesta was particularly active in his defence committee.[63]

Germinal, as *La Rivoluzione Sociale* had done, used British trade unions as an example of the worthlessness of workers' organisations. Carlo Berruti advanced several concerns, describing unions as corporate organisations that supported native workers to the detriment of immigrants.[64] In addition and contrary to general belief, trade unions were powerless – as exemplified by the Taff Vale case, in which the House of Lords had ruled that trade unions were liable for the financial losses suffered by employers as a result of strikes. In England, strikes had only been successful when unorganised workers resorted to violence against employers as, for example, during the dockers' and miners' strikes of the 1890s. In all other cases, where the trade unions were in charge, strikes ended in failure. Lastly, the trade unions supported Members of Parliament. For all these reasons, enthusiasm for trade unions among anarchists in Britain and Italy was misguided.[65]

During this period, the Italian anarchists were more involved in collaborative projects with anarchists of other national groups. In December 1904, the *Università Popolare* left its premises in Poland Street in Soho.[66] Two months later, in February 1905, this initiative was extended on a larger scale: the entire international anarchist community was involved. The opening of the *Università Popolare Internazionale* followed a period of

---

[61] Virgilio's report, 11 May 1903. ACS, *CPC*, b. 2949, f. (Malatesta Errico).

[62] Questura di Roma to Minister of Interior, 21 March 1904. ACS, *CPC*, b. 104, f. (Antonelli Adolfo). Their relationship was long-lasting. Antonelli sent financial aid to Malatesta in 1931; two years later, after Malatesta's death, he organised a collection in the United States to support the purchase of a proper grave for the anarchist leader.

[63] Malatesta's letter. Without date or addressee. ACS, *CPC*, b. 2950, f. (Malatesta Errico).

[64] Carlo Berruti arrived in London around 1902. He collaborated to *La Rivoluzione Sociale* and *La Settimana Sanguinosa* signing his articles as 'Bruto'. He died in Turin, killed at his workplace by a fascist squad in December 1922. T. Imperato, 'Berruti Carlo', *Dizionario biografico dell'Anarchismo* (Pisa: BFS, 2003), v.i, p. 153.

[65] Berruti, 'Il movimento operaio in Inghilterra', *Germinal*, 1 May 1903, p. 4.

[66] Mandolesi's report to the Ministry of the Interior, January 1905. ACS, *PS 1905*, b. 22.

intense propaganda in the areas of Soho and Clerkenwell. The programme of the *Università Popolare* was printed in French, the refugees' common language, and widely disseminated. According to the Italian police, the leaflet emphasised the revolutionary character of teaching, thus: 'teaching is not the end, but the means to conduct anarchist propaganda'. The University was therefore seen as a 'revolutionary breeding ground'.[67]

The organisers of the *Université Populaire de Londres*, on the contrary:

> hoped that through the organisation of a library, reading-room, lectures, classes, dramatic representations, concerts, etc., an intellectual and artistic centre may be gradually built up in the foreign quarter of London.[68]

Two classes took place each evening from Tuesday to Friday between 8pm and 10pm. Geometry, English Language, Mathematics, History, Linguistics, Physics, Chemistry, Linear Design and Sociology were the main subjects taught. Lectures were conducted in French, 'but steps are being taken to organise lectures and discussions in German, Italian, Spanish and English'.[69] An 'International Circulating Library' of 1,000 volumes was available at the opening of the *Università Popolare*. The teachers were of different nationalities; the Italian Corio taught design, Bellelli taught history, and Malatesta taught chemistry and physics. A large crowd attended the opening of the *Università Popolare Internazionale* in Euston Road on 25 February 1905; Tárrida del Mármol and Malatesta lectured the audience, then two plays entertained the public. The Italian embassy's informer reported:

> My friend Bologna assured me that the opening of the <u>academy</u> founded by the old mates was brilliant. Outside the door more that 30 plainclothes policemen and 40 in uniform were standing to honour the famous orators! Despite the premises being outside the city centre, the room was crammed with people. All the orators without exception got a lot of applause for the nonsense that they led those unfortunate people to believe.[70]

According to police inspector Mandolesi, Malatesta lectured on anarchism under the pretext of teaching physics and chemistry. The Italian anarchist hoped that the *Università Popolare* could become 'a centre of mutual education that will benefit the workers and show them how progress in science, mechanics and chemistry in particular can be used to shrug off the capitalist yoke'.[71] Moreover, in his classes he lectured on the physical and chemical

---

[67] Mandolesi's report. February 1905. ACS, *PS, 1905*, b. 22.

[68] 'Université Populaire de Londres', leaflet, IISH, Nettlau archive, b. 311.

[69] 'Université Populaire de Londres', leaflet, IISH, Nettlau archive, b. 311.

[70] Soldi's report, 27 February 1905. ACS, *PS 1905*, b. 22.

[71] Mandolesi's monthly report to the Ministry of the Interior, February 1905. ACS, *PS 1905*, b. 22.

reactions caused by explosions. Thus, Mandolesi believed that: 'if he had been able to continue his lectures he would have impudently taught methods for manufacturing bombs'.[72] The *Università Popolare* continued successfully for a few months but the first sign of difficulty, a result of financial problems and dissension between the Italian and the French groups, emerged in the spring of 1905. At the beginning of July, the *Università Popolare* closed, and the anarchists abandoned its premises in Euston Road.[73] Malatesta, Rudolf Rocker and other anarchist leaders were deeply disappointed at the failure of this initiative.

During these same months, the refugees in London were closely following the development of revolutionary events in Russia. On 15 January about 4,000 people attended a meeting held in Whitechapel against the Russo-Japanese War at which the Italian Di Domizio spoke. On the evening of 22 January, 'Bloody Sunday', several Russian, Polish and Italian anarchists – among them Cherkezov, Karaski and Tárrida del Mármol – convened at Malatesta's house to await news from Saint Petersburg. The latest news from Russia was transmitted by telegraph to Charles Malato in Paris and then forwarded by a French journalist (Bonafoux) to Malatesta. At 11pm, Malatesta received a telegramme notifying him that the military were ready to defend the Tsar, and shortly afterwards he was told about the massacre of civilians. Inspector Mandolesi noted with some concern how:

> these events show the ease with which revolutionary leaders understand each other despite the telegraphic censorship when they have something important to do, or when some important event is happening.[74]

A few days later, on 27 January, a large meeting against the massacre was organised in the Wonderland Hall; Malatesta spoke in French and 'he was continuously interrupted by applause and at the end received a standing ovation'.[75] Many other rallies and meetings were organised that year, Malatesta, Bergia and Di Domizio were among the Italian orators. Along with a series of minor meetings that took place in the anarchist clubs, in March a lecture at Wonderland Hall was attended by more than 3,000 people, and another large demonstration was held in November.

Later in 1905 alarm grew over possible terrorist actions organised by the anarchists in London during the visit to England of Alfonso XIII, the king of Spain. On that occasion, a group of anarchists – Antonelli, Corio,

---

[72] Mandolesi's monthly report to the Ministry of the Interior, March–April 1905, ACS, *PS 1905*, b. 22.

[73] Frosali to the Ministry of the Interior, 10 July 1905. ACS, *PS 1905*, b. 22.

[74] Mandolesi's report to the Ministry of the Interior, January 1905. ACS, *PS 1905*, b. 22.

[75] Mandolesi's report to the Ministry of the Interior, January 1905. ACS, *PS 1905*, b. 22.

Defendi, Ferrarone, Mazzotti, and Galassini – published a leaflet against Alfonso XIII and in defence of the failed attempt on his life that had taken place in Paris on 2 June.

> Men ready to action, defensive and offensive, are needed in these times of widespread cowardliness, of disgusting submission, of deceptions, of hypocrisy and crimes! And what most beautiful, most human, most noble action than to free the earth from a little monster that will become more ferocious the longer it will be allowed to grow?[76]

Nonetheless, the police inspector based at the Italian embassy emphasised that there was very little danger of attempts in London against the King of Spain. Indeed, in his opinion, the anarchists believed that such an action would hasten the passage of the Aliens Act. Moreover, they feared a possible violent reaction by the British population and did not intend to jeopardise the freedom they enjoyed in England. However, the publication of the Italian anarchists' leaflet was cause for apprehension in the Italian colony:

> After reading the manifesto published by the anarchists and believing that the anarchists may have plotted and could make an attempt against the King of Spain, many merchants and shopkeepers residing in Soho (French and Italian district) have armed themselves to be ready to defend themselves in case of violent aggression from the Londoners.[77]

The content of the manifesto was also mentioned in the British press: the *Pall Mall Gazette*, *Reynold's Newspaper* and the *Express* argued that the content of the leaflet issued by the *Comitato Internazionale Rivoluzionario* justified the exceptional security measures taken by the police during Alfonso XIII's visit to London. The *Express* used the manifesto to demonstrate the necessity of the Aliens Act. Another event linking the Italian anarchists with the debate about the Aliens Act was the arrest of Antonelli and Barberi for the publication of *L'Insurrezione*.[78]

Antonelli promoted the printing of the single issue *L'Insurrezione* on the fifth anniversary of Bresci's assassination of Umberto I. He broached the idea in April 1905 during a meeting at the *Università Popolare* and faced Malatesta's opposition.[79] Antonelli was able to collect funds from Switzerland, London and Italy with which he paid the printing costs for

---

[76] 'Per un viaggio regale', leaflet. ACS, *PS* 1905, b. 22. According to Frosali the manifesto had been written by Malatesta. Frosali's report to the Ministry of the Interior, 7 June 1905. ACS, *PS 1905*, b. 22.

[77] Frosali's report to the Ministry of the Interior, 7 June 1905, ACS, *PS 1905*, b. 22.

[78] *L'Insurrezione. Numero unico a cura di un gruppa di anarchici*, London, July 1905.

[79] Inspector Mandolesi to the Ministry of the Interior, 'Relazione del movimento dei sovversivi in Londra nei mesi di Marzo e Aprile', London 1905, ACS, *PS*, 1905, b 22.

1,000 copies of the single issue. Antonelli asked for both an article and financial aid from the Italian embassy spy Federico Lauria.[80] *L'Insurrezione* was published on a wave of excitement over the revolutionary events in Russia, particularly the mutiny of the battleship 'Potemkin' and it was a call to anarchists to abandon their endless internal quarrels and theoretical debates and dedicate themselves entirely to revolution. All wings of the anarchist movement should prepare and propagate an armed insurrection, within or outside workers' associations.[81] All the contributors, Crastinus (Corio), Homo (Antonelli), Nerisso (Rissone) and Giacomino Giacomini (Giacinto Ferrarone) repeated insistently the message of immediate action: 'We must cease chattering and embrace the banner on which is written: revolutionaries first, then anarchists.'[82]

Despite the editors' intentions, the impact that single issue had on the anarchist colony in London was exclusively due to the unusual reaction of the local authorities.[83]

On the morning of 29 July 1905, Antonelli collected 1,000 copies of *L'Insurrezione* from his printer and delivered them to Barberi, the owner of a newsagent in Dean Street. Special Branch at Scotland Yard was aware of the publication: indeed, that day they kept Barberi's shop under surveillance from very early in the morning. Once Antonelli had delivered the newspaper, police sergeant Riley purchased some copies of *L'Insurrezione* and later ordered Barberi to refrain from selling them. Barberi did not comply with the injunction. That evening Scotland Yard agents returned to the shop and seized the copies of *L'Insurrezione*. The following day they questioned Antonelli in his home. One week later, on 7 August, Antonelli was arrested in Southampton, where he had apparently gone intending to board a ship and flee abroad. Barberi, although alerted to Antonelli's arrest by a telegram from Enrico Defendi, was not able to escape and was arrested in London. Antonelli was indicted for publishing a scandalous libel which allegedly justified the crimes of assassination and murder and sought 'to encourage certain persons unknown to murder the Sovereigns and rulers of Europe', notably Victor Emmanuel III, King of Italy. Barberi was indicted for aiding and abetting Antonelli.

The article published in *L'Insurrezione* that led to the arrest of the two anarchists was brief:

July 29th, 1900–1905. To Gaetano Bresci, who by the spontaneous sacrifice

[80] Antonelli's letter to Federico Lauria, 14 July 1905. ACS, *PS*, 1905, b. 22.

[81] Quelli dell'Insurrezione, 'L'Insurrezione', *L'Insurrezione*, July 1905, pp. 1–2.

[82] Internationaliste, 'Ai compagni tutti', *L'Insurrezione*, pp. 3–4.

[83] Italian consul to the Ministry of the Interior, 21 August 1905, ACS, *CPC*, b. 154, f. (Antonelli Adolfo).

of his own liberty freed Italy from that crowned monster Umberto I. To Gaetano Bresci, who alone amongst the general cowardice knew how to rise and strike the murderer of Italy's starving. To our heroic companion, barbarously murdered in the prison of St. Stephen by the order of the deformed Emanuele III, we send today – the fifth anniversary of the event – our sincere salutations as fighters with the ardent desire, the firm determination, to follow him as quickly as possible on the way so brightly marked out by him – to rebellion. Hail!![84]

The arrest of Antonelli and Barberi caused intense anxiety in the international anarchist colony. A committee was established:

> to provide adequate means for the defence of Adolf Antonelli and Francesca [*sic*.] Barberi and to protect them against the reactionary Government prosecution [...] and to guard the Right of Asylum which England has always afforded refugees fighting against Tyranny and oppression. We do not believe in any way inciting to assassination, but hold it is the duty of all to guard the freedom of the Press.[85]

William Michael Rossetti, evidently mindful of the importance of the right of asylum for the *Risorgimento* exiles, was part of the multinational Committee which also included J. Tochatti, Cherkezov and Turner.[86] The Italian representatives were Corio, Ferrarone, Di Domizio, Carrara and Zanetti. Malatesta was heavily involved in this committee as well, although he disagreed with Antonelli's individualist views and with the content of *L'Insurrezione*. In a letter he wrote:

> In my opinion, as comrades, we should take an interest in Antonelli and Barberi anyway and the money that will be collected must be used for the defence of the two of them. [...] In such a business, we must bear in mind the interests of propaganda and the liberation of the prisoners at the same time.[87]

An initial meeting attended by Russian, Jewish, German and British anarchists planned a series of concerts to raise funds for the two arrested Italian anarchists. One of the concerts was to be organised by the Italians, another by the British and Jewish groups.[88] *Freedom* published a long list

84 '29 luglio 1900–1905', *L'Insurrezione*, July 1905, p. 5.

85 'Defence Committee for Adolfo Antonelli and Francesco Barberi', IISH, Nettlau archive, b. 3311.

86 Defence Committtee for Adolfo Antonelli and Francesco Barberi, IISH, Nettlau archive, b. 3311. The other members of the committee were: W. Pigott, H. Taylor, F. Ritz, Sam Mainwaring, J. Doody, Silas Ludlam, Morrison Davidson, J. T. Bacon, J. Richmond, Allan A. Durward and Charlotte Roche.

87 Malatesta's letter. Without date or addressee. ACS, *CPC*, b. 2950, f. (Malatesta Errico).

88 Frosali monthly report to the Ministry of the Interior, August 1905. ACS, *PS 1905*, b.

of those who paid a subscription for the two Italian anarchists.[89] The London-based Italian police inspector noted that these initiatives roused the anarchists from a period of lethargy, but despite Malatesta's efforts to turn public opinion in favour of Antonelli and Barberi:

> public opinion is unfavourable, not because they are anarchists – the great English majority neither fears nor listens to those ideas – but because they believe that the accused, as foreigners, took advantage of the freedom of press that English law allows for the expression of all opinions except for incitement to murder.[90]

The trial took place at the Central Criminal Court on 15 September. Inspector-General Baldassarre Ceola of the Department of Public Security came from Rome to testify about the killing of Umberto I by Gaetano Bresci. During the trial, Antonelli was not allowed to read a statement of self-defence in which he accused a fellow anarchist, Bojada, of being the informer who had alerted the English police. W. Thompson, president of the National Democratic League and managing editor of the *Reynold's Newspaper,* came to Antonelli's defence. Antonelli and Barberi's lawyers objected that the words 'sovereigns and rulers' were vague and that 'an allegation of incitement to assassinate an undefined person was not sufficient to support the indictment'. Antonelli's lawyer added that, 'the words complained about did not bear the interpretation put upon them but were merely rhetorical expressions such as were frequently used in Latin countries'.[91] However, after only a few minutes deliberation, the jury found both Antonelli and Barberi guilty. Mr Justice Phillimore, in consideration of Antonelli's youth, sentenced him to ten months' imprisonment with hard labour. Barberi received a sentence of nine months' imprisonment with hard labour. In a letter to the *Daily Chronicle,* the writer H. G. Wells protested against the harshness of the sentence. After serving his prison term, Antonelli moved to the United States; Barberi remained in London.

Catering workers

During the same period, several Italian anarchists were continuing in their attempts to organise the waiters and restaurant workers in the Italian colony. At the end of 1905, an Italian anarchist named Bergia from the northern town of Biella, began a campaign against employment agencies. He opened

---

22. Note dated 25 August 1905, in ACS, *CPC*, b. 320, f. (Barberi Francesco).

[89] A list of the subscriptions in 'Trial of Antonelli and Barberi', *Freedom*, October 1905, p. 32.

[90] Frosali to the Ministry of the Interior, 2 August 1905. ACS, *CPC*, b. 154, f. (Antonelli Adolfo).

[91] 'Central Criminal Court', *The Times*, 16 September 1905, p. 12.

an *ufficio di collocamento gratuito* (free employment agency) in his restaurant at 70 Cleveland Street. In these premises, on 2 December 1905, he organised a meeting for Italian cooks to discuss the constitution of a *Lega di resistenza*. The police inspector reported to the Italian embassy:

> The restaurant that a German opened in 70 Cleveland Street is frequented only by anarchists or by young people about to become anarchist. *La Revue*, which is composed by Bergia, is printed in these premises. In a small room within the same house there is the free employment agency that continues to 'live' thanks to the profits from the restaurant.[92]

The restaurant's address was also used for correspondence by the secretary of the Caterers Employees' Union. Indeed, in order to reach the catering workers Bergia founded, with the English activist M. Clark, the *Revue: International Organ for the Interests of all Employees in Hotels, Restaurants, Boarding-Houses, etc.* The articles in the newspaper were written in English, German and French.[93] The campaign among Italian waiters yielded some results. Inspector Frosali reported that, at a meeting organised at the *German Club* where the French anarchist Gustave Lance spoke about the trade union movement: 'among the audience it was possible to notice many Italian cooks and waiters, attending an anarchist meeting for the first time.[94] Another Italian anarchist involved in the organisation of waiters was Giacinto Ferrarone who, like Bergia, came from the surrounds of Biella, and signed his articles in anarchist newspapers as Giacomino Giacomini.[95] Ferrarone exercised some influence among Italians employed in hotels and restaurants, most of whom were also from Piedmont. For this reason, in April 1905, he was chosen as a speaker at meetings to campaign for the abolition of the employment agencies.[96] Ferrarone joined the socialists but continued his organisational work.[97] He promoted the creation of *sindacati di resistenza* (trade unions) that, in his view, represented workers' real interests.[98]

He was also the tenant of the headquarters of the *Lega di Resistenza dei lavoratori della mensa*, constituted as the *Sezione Italiana della Caterers*

[92] Frosali's monthly report to the Ministry of the Interior, December 1905. ACS, PS 1905, b. 22.

[93] Frosali's monthly report to the Ministry of the Interior, November 1905. ACS, *PS 1905*, b. 22.

[94] Froasali's monthly report, December 1905. ACS, *PS 1905*, b. 22.

[95] Ferrarone's biographical record in: ACS, *CPC*, b. 2029, f. (Ferrarone Giacinto).

[96] Report from the Italian embassy in Paris, 3 April 1905, ACS, *CPC*, b. 2029, f. (Ferrarone Giacinto).

[97] Report from the Italian embassy in Paris, 3 August 1905, and Virgilio's report 10 June 1906, in ACS, *CPC*, b. 2029, f. (Ferrarone Giacinto).

[98] G. Ferrarone, 'Avanti, Lavoratori!', *Revue*, September 1906, p. 48.

Employees' Union, at 55 Frith Street.[99] His career as a labour organiser ended abruptly when he left London at the beginning of August 1907, apparently after stealing funds from the club *Nuovo Sempione* of which he was secretary.[100]

Nevertheless the campaign continued and in 1909 the mobilisation of workers in restaurants and hotels, led mainly by the Socialists, resulted in demonstrations against the 'Truck System', the method used by employers for sharing tips among their employees. Abolition of all Registry Offices and Employment Agencies and a weekly day of rest were the main aims of the protest. In February 1909, the French group and the editors of the *Revue* met at the *International Club* to continue the campaign and plan a demonstration in April. The demonstration took place in Trafalgar Square on Sunday 18 April.

> Sunday 18 big demonstration in Trafalgar Square of cooks, waiters and clerks of restaurants of all nationalities. [...] The procession arrived at Trafalgar Square at 3.30 with band and banners and singing the *Marseillaise*. The majority of the demonstrators were affiliated to the Socialist Party. The Italian Socialists assembled around the banner '*Sindacato fra i lavoratori della mensa*'. The flag was carried by the known Giacomo Quarantini. A Polledro Mario spoke for the Italians ... the same evening Polledro was sacked by the owner of the restaurant Blanchard.[101]

In the same period, Malatesta and the Italian anarchists decided to concentrate their efforts on regular open-air speeches in Clerkenwell at the corners of Saffron Hill and Eyre Street. On several occasions the police prevented Malatesta from giving speeches and forcibly removed him from the area.[102] The Italian police inspector reported that he had been informed by various sources that some Neapolitans were determined to act, maybe with weapons, against the police and whoever else attempted to stop Malatesta from speaking. He informed the local police immediately. A few weeks later, according to the same inspector, Malatesta's efforts began to achieve some results:

> The Italians of the densely populated district begin to take interest in Malatesta's speeches, he deals with issues understandable by everybody and he speaks in Neapolitan dialect. Malatesta is satisfied because, day by

[99] Report from the Italian embassy in Paris, 19 December 1906. ACS, *CPC*, b. 2029, f. (Ferrarone Giacinto).

[100] Virgilio's report, 12 August 1907, ACS, *CPC*, b. 2029, f. (Ferrarone Giacinto).

[101] Frosali's report to Ministry of Interior, April 1909. ACS, *PS 1909*, b. 4, f. 5075/103. Giacomo Quarantini was a member of the anarchist group.

[102] Frosali's monthly report to the Ministry of the Interior, January 1909, ACS, *PS 1909*, b. 4, f. 5075/103.

day, the audience grows and anarchist theories are debated in restaurants, bars and cafés and even the most ignorant and indifferent begin to get interested.[103]

However, in 1909, the anarchists' attention was soon directed to Spain where a popular insurrection took place in July in Catalonia, caused by conscripts being sent to suppress a rebellion in Morocco. In the wake of the riot the authorities arrested the anarchist educationalist Francisco Ferrer, director of the 'Modern School', and charged him with plotting the uprising. Despite massive demonstrations throughout Europe and elsewhere, a military court sentenced Ferrer to death and he was executed on 13 October in the notorious Montjuic fortress.

In the months following the Barcelona rising and Ferrer's arrest many meetings and rallies were organised in London. They were all well attended and many Italian waiters and kitchen boys were present. The Italian anarchists issued a leaflet, *I martiri di Barcellona: Ricordiamoci*, apparently written by Malatesta, which denounced the acts of the Spanish government.

> whether he is an armed rebel that tries the supreme act of liberation or a peaceful thinker, a zealous educator, completely engrossed in his bright dream of peace and love who, like Ferrer, deceived himself that he could lay the foundations for a widespread system of rational education and cover Spain with a network of free schools without fighting tooth and nail to seize them beforehand from the reaction – they are both equally damned to die at executioners' hands according to the government in Madrid and the Roman Church.[104]

On 19 October, a massive demonstration of about 10,000 people organised by the Social Democratic Party, gathered in Trafalgar Square.[105] After the speeches, a procession singing the 'Marseillaise' and 'Keep The Red Flag Flying' proceeded toward Victoria to reach the Spanish Embassy. In Grosvenor Gardens mounted police confronted the protesters and forced them back.[106] The protesters sought to reassemble at Westminster but the police dispersed them. The Italian embassy inspector reported that there were around fifty Italians and included Malatesta, Gualducci, Rossi Giulio, Corio, Spizzuoco, the Defendi family, Corso, Barretta, Beleli [*sic*.], Pesci Giuseppe and some waiters and kitchen-porters.[107]

---

[103] Frosali's monthly report to the Ministry of the Interior, January 1909, ACS, *PS 1909*, b. 4, f. 5075/103.

[104] Gli anarchici, 'Martiri di Barcellona. Ricordiamoci', London, October 1909. Leaflet. In: ACS, *PS 1909*, b. 6, f. 5079.

[105] Demonstrations against Ferrer's execution took place all over the world.

[106] 'The execution of Ferrer, Demonstrations in London', *The Times*, 18 October 1909, p. 8.

[107] Frosali's report to the Ministry of the Interior, 24 October 1909, ACS, *PS 1909*, b. 6, f. 5079.

Two days later, 4,000 people attended a conference at the Memorial Hall, where Kropotkin was among the speakers. Over the following months many meetings were held in the anarchist and socialist clubs in London, raising suspicions of the Italian authorities that the anarchists were plotting to kill a crowned head of Europe as revenge for Ferrer's death. Nothing came of these fears, but in the years before the First World War the anniversary of Ferrer's execution became a day of commemoration for London's refugee community.[108]

Activity up to the First World War

In the years that followed, the activity of the Italian anarchists seems to have remained largely confined to their clubs. The general passivity of the anarchist movement can be gauged by a report published in the *Bulletin de l'Internationale Anarchiste* and in *Freedom* by the Correspondence Bureau. (Both had been organised after the International Anarchist Conference held in Amsterdam in 1907.) The report complained at the lack of response to its appeal for the organisation of a further international anarchist congress.

> Our first appeal published last October for the organisation of the International Congress which should have taken place in the current year, brought only very few answers … If no Congress will be held this year, if comrades do not answer to our repeated appeals for a stronger agitation for the enlargement of the A. I. and for the common and more systematic action of the Anarchists of all countries, the Bureau has no more its raison d'être, and becomes, by the fact of its members' passivity, a platonic organisation, without special ideal, without real value, and consequently non-existent … It is our last appeal … hoping still that you will understand … the absolute necessity of reacting against the apathy which seems to have overtaken all our groups at the present moment.[109]

However events outside the anarchist community served to bring the anarchists back into the public eye. In 1910 and 1911, the 'Houndsditch Robbery' and the 'Siege of Sidney Street' were covered extensively by the press and had serious consequences for the Jewish anarchist movement in

---

[108] In 1910, a meeting was held at the *Communist Club* attended by 250 militants. Among the speakers: Malatesta, Tárrida del Mármol, Rudolf Rocker, and Jack Tanner. Frosali's report to the Ministry of the Interior, 14 October 1910. ACS, *PS 1910*, b. 7.

[109] The Correspondence Bureau, 'The Anarchist International. A Last Appeal', *Freedom*, April 1909, p. 29. This appeal had been previously published in Italian in the *Bulletin de l'Internationale Anarchiste*, March 1909. See also: Le Bureau de Correspondance, 'Pour le Bulletin', *Bulletin de l'Internationale Anarchiste*, October 1909.

London; they also involved Malatesta. For several months in 1910, Malatesta allowed a Latvian refugee, introduced as Muronzeff but whose real name was George Gardstein, to use his workshop. Gardstein was a member of a group of Social Democrat refugees who carried out a botched robbery at a jeweller's shop in Houndsditch. Gardstein built the tools that he needed for the robbery in Malatesta's workshop. Moreover, Malatesta sold another member of the gang the oxygen blowpipe which was used to open the safe. The gang was caught in the act and shot their way out, killing three unarmed policemen and seriously wounding two others. Gardstein was shot by his own friends by accident and died shortly afterwards. A prolonged siege was organised by the Home Secretary, Winston Churchill, which included a detachment of armed soldiers. After a fire in which some of the other gang members probably perished, their mysterious leader, 'Peter the Painter', disappeared.[110]

The police traced Malatesta through the oxygen blowpipe left at the scene of the crime in Houndsditch, and arrested him. However, he was released a few hours later since no evidence could be found of his involvement in the crime. Malatesta claimed several times, in interviews in the days after the robbery, and many years later, that he never had any suspicion of Gardstein's real intentions.

The activities of the Italian anarchists were also revitalised by an anti-militarist campaign opposing the Italian army's invasion of Libya in September 1911.[111] In London, the Italian anarchists organised several meetings. Malatesta spoke at the *Communist Club* on 20 October. The police surrounded the building and many detectives attended the conference. They also reinforced their protection of the Italian embassy. During the conference, Malatesta attacked Giolitti's government and argued against the contention that Italy was bringing civilisation to the Arabs and that most Italians would gain economically from the colony.

> When Vesuvius spews out, the masses take sacred images to stop the lava flow. And we are going to Tripoli to bring civilisation … We shall educate ourselves, and when we are educated and strong we will not oppress anymore, but will find wealth in our own country … I do not hope for a Turkish victory, although it would be a salutary lesson […] but I hope the Arabs will rebel and drive both Turkish and Italians back into the sea.[112]

---

[110] On Houndsditch robbery and the Siege of Sidney Street: Phil Ruff, *Pētera Māldera laiks un dzīve* (*The Life and Times of Peter the Painter*) (Riga: Dienas Gramata, 2012); Donald Rumbelow, *The Houndsditch murders and the siege of Sidney Street* (Stroud: History, 2009).

[111] See Berti, *Errico Malatesta e il movimento anarchico*, pp. 479–520; M. Degli Innocenti, *Il socialismo Italiano e la guerra di Libia* (Rome: Editori Riuniti, 1976).

[112] Frosali's report of Malatesta's meeting to the Ministry of the Interior, 28 October 1911.

Malatesta spoke against the war several other times. After having strongly criticised the Libyan war at a commemoration of the Chicago anarchists ('the Haymarket Martyrs of 1886') on 13 November, he proposed a resolution (passed by those present) calling for the release of anarchist anti-militarist Maria Rygier arrested in Italy. A copy of the resolution was sent to the Italian ambassador.

Another anarchist particularly active in this period was Silvio Corio. Signing his articles as 'Qualunque', he wrote against the war in the left-wing London newspapers the *Star*, *Justice*, the *Daily Herald* and the Italian *Avanti!*, denouncing the futility of the colonial expansion and the massacre of civilians by Italian troops.[113]

> Everybody who was in Tripoli during those two days, 23 and 24 October 1911, knows of blood curdling episodes and particulars. It was, indeed, a veritable manhunt; unarmed women and children were mercilessly shot ... One could see the bodies of dead Arabs, of both sexes and of all ages, who had never been armed, lying about in gardens, on the sands, on doorsteps, next to the oasis where the habitations end.[114]

Gualducci also spoke against the Libyan war.[115] The Italian anarchists in London took part in a demonstration for the release of Augusto Masetti, the soldier who shot at his lieutenant on 30 October 1911, the morning his platoon was due to depart for Libya. They also contributed to fund the publication of the single issue *Pro Masetti*.[116]

The campaign against the imperialist adventure led to the publication of *La guerra tripolina*, which appeared in April 1912 when the war was at its most intense. Malatesta's leading article took on the moral arguments that had been presented to justify the invasion. Firstly, that the Italian people were not conscious of their potential and energy, which was why Italy did not occupy the place it deserved in the world. Secondly, Italy was bringing civilisation to a barbarous country. Finally, the point most stressed by pro-war propaganda was that support for the invasion was a genuine expression of patriotism.[117]

Answering the argument that war and the oppression of the vanquished

---

ACS, *CPC*, b. 2950, f. (Malatesta Errico).

[113] ACS, *CPC*, b. 1474, f. (Corio Silvio).

[114] S. Corio, 'What Our Readers Say. The Tripoli Massacres', the *Daily Herald*, 12 April 1912.

[115] For example, on 21 April he spoke on war and the idea of fatherland at 99 Charlotte Street. *La guerra Tripolina, April 1912, p. 4.*

[116] On Masetti see: Laura De Marco, *Il soldato che disse no alla guerra. Storia dell'anarchico Augusto Masetti (1888–1966)* (Santa Maria Capua Vetere: Spartaco, 2003).

[117] Errico Malatesta, 'La guerra e gli anarchici', *La guerra tripolina*, April 1912, p. 1. This article reappeared several times in other anarchist publications.

served to awaken and develop popular energies, Malatesta sought an alternative for that development in struggles against the adverse forces of nature, in hard scientific research, in helping those left behind, in the conquest for all human beings of more power and comfort.[118]

Moreover, Malatesta argued, war, invasion and robbery did not promote civilisation. On the contrary, by sending its army to Africa Italy not only committed an outrage against Libya but also demeaned itself. Malatesta dealt also with the issue of patriotism, a question of special interest for someone who lived most of his life abroad. Patriotism was a sentiment with a strong appeal for people. The oppressors, claimed Malatesta, knowingly employed it to dampen down class conflict; thus, the call for solidarity of race and nation made the oppressed serve the interests of the oppressors. True patriotism, in Malatesta's opinion, was instead a mixture of positive feelings: attachment to the native village and to the country to which one has the strongest moral ties, memories, affections and intimacies.[119]

However, patriotism had developed when conquerors and oppressors were one and the same; thus often a fight against foreigner invaders meant a fight against oppression. Love of fatherland developed from hatred for foreign oppressors, but this type of patriotism was no longer needed in Italy or elsewhere. The anarchists were Internationalists: their fatherland was the whole world and they did 'abhor war, always fratricidal and always harmful', and wanted 'the liberating social revolution'; they 'deplore fights among peoples and call instead for a fight against the dominant classes'. In the case of a war, however, the anarchists supported people who were fighting for their independence, as they had done during the Boer war. In the case of the invasion of Libya, therefore:

> For the honour of Italy, we hope that the Italian people come to their senses and force a withdrawal from Africa on the government; if not, we hope the Arabs will be able to drive the Italians away.[120]

Corio also advanced his criticisms of the Italian government's reasons for war. The colonial undertaking satisfied the economic interests of a financial élite: namely military suppliers and land speculators. Italian emigration would not find an outlet in Libya. Emigration was caused by poverty and the solution to this problem would be found within Italy. In the meantime the war diverted people's attention from domestic social questions.[121] This campaign against the Libyan expedition had some influence on Corio's

---

[118] Malatesta, 'La Guerra e gli anarchici'.
[119] Malatesta, 'La Guerra e gli anarchici'.
[120] Malatesta, 'La guerra e gli anarchici'.
[121] Silvio Corio, 'La guerricciola dei piccoli italiani', *La guerra tripolina*, April 1912, pp. 2–3.

future activities; over subsequent years, he became deeply involved with his companion Sylvia Pankhurst in the campaigns against the Fascist colonisation of Ethiopia.[122]

La guerra tripolina gives an idea of the difficulties that the anarchists had to face to express their opposition to the war within the Italian colony. In particular, it attacked the pro-war propaganda carried out at the *Club Cooperativo Italiano* by the section of the 'Società Nazionale Italiana Dante Alighieri', which had just been established in London.[123] An 'Open letter to the Italian Ambassador in London', written in response to a speech the ambassador gave at the inaugural-meeting of this Society, is an example:

> Sir, in delivering your speech before a crowded assembly of several hundred Italians from our colony in London, you found a way of singing the praises of the brave military actions of our soldiers who are heroically fighting to conquer Tripolitania and Cyrenaica; and you invited the audience to do the same. Whilst the assembly, overwhelmed and enthralled by the heady words of glory, fatherland, civilising conquests, listened and jubilantly broke out in frenetic acclaim at the eloquent rhetorical speech [...] in a hidden corner of the room a humble worker like me, of low class and without any other authority than knowing himself to be right, quivered with indignation, stifling a shout of protest in his heart.[124]

Criticism was also directed toward another speaker, Antonio Cippico, a professor of Italian Literature at University College and one of the promoters of the London section of the *Dante Alighieri Society*, who gave a lecture supporting the war at the beginning of March.[125]

Anarchists in London were also involved during 1912 in the campaign for the release of Italo-American syndicalists Joseph Ettor and Arturo

---

[122] Corio and Sylvia Pankhurst were deeply involved in supporting Ethiopia before and after the war. From 1936 they published the newspaper *New Times and Ethiopia News*.

[123] The Society was established in Rome in 1889 in order to 'sponsor' Italian language and culture in the lands occupied by Austria. Its purpose 'was not only cultural, but also political and strongly anti-Austrian. The Society did not limit its irredentism to the Trentino and Trieste, but aimed to extend it to every part of the world where Italian emigrants lived'. 'From this point of view, emigration, usually regarded as a negative event because of the loss of vital energies to the fatherland, now acquired a positive aspect as a "pacific" form of expansionism, an "imperialism with clean hands". In particular, the Society was interested in the expansion of *italianità* in the Adriatic (especially in Albania), and in the Mediterranean; in 1908 it founded branches in Tripoli and Cyrenaica. Italian Nationalists promoted similar aims during the years preceding the Great War'. Claudia Baldoli, *Exporting Fascism: Italian Fascists and Britain's Italians in the 1930s* (Oxford-New York: Berg, 2003), p. 8.

[124] Ottavio Valperga, 'Lettera aperta a S.E. il Marchese Francavilla, Regio Ambasciatore d'Italia a Londra', *La guerra tripolina*, April 1912, p. 3.

[125] Natale, 'La Dante Alighieri', *La guerra tripolina*, p. 4.

Giovannitti. The two men were members of the Industrial Workers of the World and leaders of a bitter strike of textile workers in Lawrence, Massachusetts. They were charged as moral accomplices in the murder of Annie LaPezza, a working girl shot by a policeman during an attack on the strikers. Their arrest caused an international outcry. In London, an Ettor-Giovannitti Protest Committee was established on 1 September. The trade unionist Jack Tanner was secretary; Malatesta represented the Italians. Corio wrote a long report about the case in *The Anarchist*.[126] On Sunday 22 September a cosmopolitan crowd attended 'an international protest meeting in Trafalgar Square'.[127] Malatesta, Mann, Tochatti, Rocker and Tanner were among the speakers. Malatesta proposed a boycott of American products. He also spoke against the Libyan war. The Italian police inspector reported that Malatesta:

> All the more pleased that the leaders of the movement were Italian, thus offering a strong contrast to the Italy that murders defenseless Arabs. He became animated when he spoke about the Arabs and the crowd applauded warmly.[128]

At the end of the meeting, the police forbade a collection being made, which led to a minor disturbance.[129] A second rally took place at Clerkenwell Green on 6 October. In front of 300 people Natale Parovich, secretary of the Italian anarchist group, announced that the representatives of the *Società Dante Alighieri* and the president of the *Club Cooperativo* had not answered his invitation to take part in the rally. Moreover, he lamented the poor attendance of Italians at the meeting. Malatesta and Gualducci also spoke.[130]

Above all, the anarchists' attention was drawn to Italy where the revival of the anarchist movement inspired Malatesta to support the funding of a newspaper, an initiative he had been proposing to the Ancona anarchists for a few months. Its publication, Malatesta hoped, would 'stimulate events more important than the newspaper in itself'.[131] In April and May 1913, he discussed the project with Paravich, Corio, Keell, the Defendi family, Calzitta and Tombolesi. Inspector Frosali reported that after an animated

---

[126] Crastinus (Silvio Corio), 'The Ettor-Giovannitti Case', *The Anarchist*, 20 September 1912, p. 2.

[127] 'Our London Letter', *Lichfield Mercury*, 27 September 1912, p. 3.

[128] Frosali's report to the Ministry of the Interior, 27 September 1912. ACS, *PS*, 1912, b. 36, f. k1.

[129] Frosali's report to the Ministry of the Interior, 27 September 1912, ACS, *PS, 1912*, b. 36, f. k1. See also: 'Police Prohibit a Collection', *Daily Mirror*, 23 September 1912.

[130] Frosali's report to the Ministry of the Interior, 12 October 1912, ACS, *PS, 1912*, b. 36, f. k1.

[131] Malatesta to Luigi Fabbri, 7 May 1913, in: Malatesta, *Epistolario 1873–1932*, p. 83.

discussion in which the weaknesses of the anarchist movement were candidly examined, the group agreed to the newspaper as a method to revitalise anarchism in Italy.

> The new newspaper will intensify revolutionary propaganda within socialist trade unions. It will deal with reorganisation and discipline within anarchist ranks to prevent leaving the field clear for the socialist reformists to forbid the use of violence in the case of strikes. It will actively devote itself to preparing the class union to use violence and in case of an uprising ... to acting energetically with the firm resolution of destroying the government.[132]

Funds were collected in London and sent to Ancona. Among the contributors was Emidio Recchioni who, as Malatesta noted, 'is enthusiastic and will be very useful'.[133] Corio was named London correspondent. It was planned for 250 copies to be set aside for distribution in London. The first issue of *Volontà* appeared in Ancona on 8 June 1913. On 29 July Malatesta left London and secretly travelled there, where he played a major part in the 'Red Week' the following June.[134]

---

[132] Frosali's report to Ministry of Interior. 9 May 1913. ACS, *CPC*, b. 2950, f. (Malatesta Errico).

[133] Malatesta to Cesare Agostinelli, 2 April 1913, in: Malatesta, *Epistolario 1873–1932*, p. 82.

[134] In June 1914, as a result of the antimilitarist campaign against the Libyan War, an insurrectionary protest took place in Northern and Central Italy. The insurrection collapsed after one week. See: Luigi Lotti, *La settimana rossa* (Florence: Le Monnier, 1972).

5

The Surveillance of Italian Anarchists in London

The Italian authorities were seriously concerned about the danger represented by anarchists living abroad; they regarded the colonies established outside Italy by the Internationalists as dangerous centres of conspiracy. Since the Italian police could not intervene directly in foreign countries, the prosecution of anarchists fell to the discretion of foreign police forces, but collaboration was often problematic. Therefore, the Italian government attached great importance to its own system of surveillance carried out by an intelligence service largely based on informers and secret agents infiltrating the anarchist groups.[1] Ambassadors and consuls were key elements in establishing the office known as the 'International Police'. In 1888, the consul in Geneva, Giuseppe Basso, writing to the Prime Minister Francesco Crispi, declared himself one of the main founders of this system of international surveillance, a sort of pioneer.[2]

Although the ultimate decision on recruitment belonged to the Ministry of the Interior, consuls and ambassadors enlisted their own informers *in loco*. Moreover, the Minister of the Interior occasionally recruited his own agents without the interference of the ambassadors, who were kept in the dark about their existence.

The Ministry of the Interior administered the espionage budget and decided upon the estimate of expenditure submitted by consuls and ambassadors. To avoid direct involvement by the Italian authorities, anonymous functionaries maintained contacts between the embassies and their informers. The person who for many years received and delivered the reports to the embassy

---

[1] Stefania Ruggeri, 'Fonti per la storia del movimento operaio in Italia presenti nell'Archivio Storico Diplomatico del Ministero degli Affari Esteri. Il fondo "Polizia Internazionale"'. In Fabio Grassi and Gianni Dollo (eds), *Il movimento socialista e popolare in Puglia dalle origini alla costituzione (1874–1946)* (Bari-Lecce: Istituto 'Vito Mario Stampacchia', 1986).

[2] Consul Basso to Crispi, 8 February 1888, Asdmae, *Pol. Int.*, b. 46, f. (1888).

using the alias *Calvo* was Cavalier Manetti, registrar at the embassy. The ambassadors valued the information received from spies and conveyed it to the Foreign Ministry through the *Divisione Prima Affari Politici*, the section in charge of the 'International Police'. Subsequently, the Foreign Ministry passed all relevant information to the Ministry of the Interior or, if criminal acts were suspected, to the foreign governments involved.

Occasionally, more than one secret agent worked at the same time, each without knowledge of the other's existence. This allowed the Italian authorities to compare information acquired by their agents. At the 1881 International Revolutionary Socialist Congress an informer was sent from Marseilles to infiltrate the proceedings, along with the secret agent already present in London. The Ministry of the Interior considered it of the utmost importance to keep the two unaware of one another to cross-check their reports.[3]

However, as underlined by ambassador Tornielli, this practice did have disadvantages: it was highly possible informers would embellish or even invent information for their own gain. Therefore, if more informers worked at the same time, they could easily make an agreement between them to deceive the Italian government.[4]

When more than one agent operated at the same time, a further problem of rivalry could emerge. At the beginning of 1902 when Inspector Prina, who had been sent from Rome, and the informer Calvo, who worked for the embassy, became aware of each other's existence they accused one another of providing inaccurate information, igniting endless and distracting personal disputes.

If the Minister of the Interior judged a police inspector to be inefficient, they would be recalled back to Italy. In 1882, Vice Inspector Amede was recalled from London after the Minister of the Interior and the ambassador seriously suspected that the Internationalists, and Solieri in particular, had discovered Amede's true identity. In their opinion, suspicions were enough to hinder the continuation of his mission.[5]

On that occasion, the Italian ambassador also consulted the inspector of the Central Criminal Police, Charles von Tornow, who was 'unofficially' collaborating with the Italian embassy. In von Tornow's opinion, the Italian vice inspector should be immediately recalled since his remaining in London was worthless for the government and dangerous for him, as he could 'have

[3] Ministry of the Interior to Foreign Ministry, 3 July 1881, Asdmae, *Pol. Int.*, b. 6. D.M. was the code-name of the informer Orlando De Martijs.

[4] Tornielli to Crispi, 19 December 1889, Asdmae, *Serie Politica P*, b. 47.

[5] Italian ambassador to Foreign Minister, 31 May 1882, Asdmae, *Pol. Int.*, b. 4, f. (1882).

been assaulted or stabbed by those sectarians at any time'.[6] It is difficult to establish whether Tornow's judgement was genuinely concerned with Amede's safety, or was merely to facilitate the removal of a rival.

A similar thing happened in 1902 when, following the anarchists' discovery of the informer Gennaro Rubino, Giolitti hastily summoned Inspector Prina back to Italy despite the policeman's remonstrations.[7]

The spies were paid monthly; their wages calculated on a weekly basis and registered as *spese segrete di polizia* (secret expenses). Secret agents and informers signed regular receipts for their payments.

There was probably a distinction between informers and secret agents. In 1905, the embassy recorded on its payroll three informers and one secret agent. The informers, alias *Foster* and *Kite*, received £2 a week. While secret agents provided their information from inside anarchist groups, informers were people who had some contact with them for different reasons. For example, in 1904, the embassy paid one pound sterling a month to Giovanni Ferrari, employee at the 'Istituto di Beneficenza', an organisation to which the anarchists sometimes resorted to receive financial aid, mostly to pay for return voyages to Italy.[8]

Occasionally, especially when the surveillance of the anarchists needed to be more accurate, the Ministry of the Interior resorted to incentive payments. In 1881, the ambassador suggested giving a bonus to 'DM' on the occasion of the International Congress to be held in London.[9] At the end of the month, the Ministry of the Interior granted 'DM' a reward of 150 Italian *lire* for his praiseworthy service.[10]

Spies often claimed refunds to cover unforeseen costs such as subscriptions to anarchist newspapers or contributions to collections for political campaigns. However, the expense that most seriously affected the budget of the spies in London was of a very different nature. In 1881, the consul reported that:

> Malatesta ... as a good socialist, visits De Martijs for supper every day ... considering this unforeseen expense, it may be appropriate to raise De Martijs's wage by 5 shillings a week, and consequently to increase D.M.'s cheque to £2 a week.[11]

The informer Lauria often had guests for lunch at his home as well.

[6] Italian ambassador to Foreign Minister, 23 May 1882, Asdmae, *Pol. Int.*, b. 4.

[7] Inspector Prina to the Italian ambassador, 19 December 1902, ACS, *PS*, 1905, b. 22. Rubino's name is spelled Rubini or Rubino. In all documents concerning his discovery as a spy the name appeared as Rubini, but his real name was Rubino.

[8] Receipt signed by Giuseppe Ferretti, 30 November 1904, ACS, *PS*, 1905, b. 8, f. 70.

[9] Italian ambassador to Foreign Ministry, 13 July 1881, Asdmae, *Pol. Int.*, b. 5, f. (1880–1881).

[10] Ministry of the Interior to Foreign Ministry, 30 July 1881, Asdmae, *Pol. Int.*, b. 6.

[11] Vice Consul Buzzegoli to ambassador Menabrea, 25 June 1881, Asdmae, *AL*, b. 70.

In 1904 he complained that both at Christmas and New Year's Eve 'the brigands forced me to incur debts with the Italian shopkeepers in order to satisfy their hunger'.[12]

Collaboration with the police forces of the host countries greatly affected the efficiency of intelligence. Indeed, for the Italian authorities in London surveillance of the anarchists was more difficult because of the policy adopted by the British police forces. Officially, they did not collaborate in preventive investigations and acted only after a crime was committed. The Foreign Office underlined this point several times during preparative meetings for the international conference against anarchism held in Rome in 1898, and subsequently.[13]

Italian diplomats in London often lamented the lack of collaboration they received from the British police. In 1911, the consul complained to the ambassador about the negative response received from the Metropolitan Police to a request for information: 'to make clear once more the difficulties, unknown in other countries, that the commissionership had to face to accomplish his duties.'[14] The consul wanted to know if an Antonio Polti was in fact the Francesco Polti who had been sentenced to prison for illegal possession of explosives in 1894. The Metropolitan Police replied, 'it would be wholly contrary to the practice of the Metropolitan Police to give any information regarding ex-convicts or others who have been liberated at the expiration of their sentences'.[15] In the consul's opinion this practice meant that, to the British authorities, even the most dangerous criminal after serving his sentence 'has to be considered equal to all other citizens', and thus 'let free to move and to vanish without trace'.[16]

The arrogant attitude often assumed by the British authorities when dealing with surveillance of anarchists also annoyed Italian diplomats. In 1891, Count Tornielli showed Lord Salisbury a ticket for a dance organised at the *Autonomie Club* to raise money for revolutionary propaganda in Italy. Lord Salisbury sarcastically remarked that propaganda that wanted to make a revolution by dancing could not be really considered dangerous.[17] On the other hand, the anarchists employed their own stratagems to avoid police surveillance including the use of secret codes. In 1904, the Ministry of the Interior alerted prefects that the anarchists were using an ingenious code

12 Soldi's report, 9 January 1905, ACS, *PS*, 1905, b. 22.

13 Italian ambassador to Ministry of Foreign Affairs, 6 December 1902, Asdmae, *Serie politica P*, b. 49, f. P 8 Italia.

14 Italian Consul to Italian ambassador, 10 November 1911, Asdmae, *AL*, 1912, b. 305.

15 M. L. Macnaughten to Italian consul, 4 November 1911; Asdmae, *AL*, 1912, b. 305.

16 Consul to ambassador, 10 November 1911; Asdmae, *AL*, 1912, b. 35.

17 Tornielli to Minister of Foreign Affairs, 21 April 1891, Asdmae, *Pol. Int.*, b. 39, f. (1891).

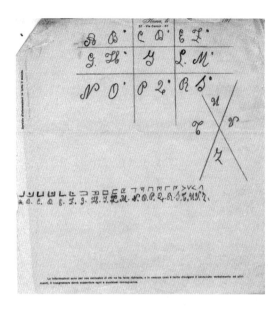

Malatesta's code.
(ACS, PS, 1912. Massime, b. 4, f. 2.)

based on letters and numbers to conceal the content of their correspondence, and provided them with the key to decode anarchist messages. A few years later, Malatesta apparently created a code in which each letter of the alphabet was substituted for by a particular sign.[18]

III. 4. 1. Anarchist 'counterespionage'

The anarchists also had their own systems of 'counterespionage' to uncover government informers. In this regard, the exchange of information among anarchist groups in Italy and abroad was essential. Liaison with anarchists in Turin seems to have been crucial in the unmasking of Inspector Amede.[19] Similarly, in 1881, anarchists in Marseilles warned Malatesta of the real identity of the secret agent Moncada, who had been sent from the city to London to attend the International Social Revolutionary and Anarchist Congress.

In general, the anarchists were extremely suspicious of comrades who did not have visible means of support. In 1881, the spy De Martijs urged the embassy to instruct the Ministry of the Interior to send him two letters from the village of Troja in southern Italy, leaving an interval of ten

[18] Ministry of the Interior 1912, ACS, *PS, Massime*, b. 4, f. 2.
[19] Italian embassy to Ministry of the Interior, 23 May 1882, Asdmae, *Pol. Int.*, b. 4, f. (1882).

days between the two postings. These letters were to demonstrate that De Martijs's relatives assisted him financially.[20] In 1912, in a leaflet distributed to the Italian colony, Malatesta accused Enrico Bellelli of being an informer for the Italian government, and challenged him to openly disclose the nature of his income.

Another way a spy could be exposed was to provide false information only to the person under suspicion and then to check if the information was divulged afterwards. Spies were aware of this danger and when they were aware of being among the few who had knowledge of a certain fact, they warned their controllers of a possible trap.[21]

When the anarchists unmasked a spy, they warned their comrades by publishing notes in their newspapers or, if the case was particularly serious, by printing and circulating special issues. Through *L'Associazione*, Malatesta alerted the anarchist movement about Terzaghi's attempt to infiltrate their groups under the false name of Azzati. In 1896, the London anarchists issued a report on the unmasking of the spy Armande Lapie. Malatesta, Louise Michel and Guerineau contacted him and an open meeting was organised in Grafton Hall to discuss the allegations. Lapie was unable to demonstrate his innocence.[22] In 1902, *La Rivoluzione Sociale* printed a warning against Gennaro Rubino; in 1912, the anarchists in London published the single issue *La Gogna* that reported all events related to the dispute between Malatesta and the spy Ennio Bellelli.[23] Nevertheless, despite these forms of counterespionage, the anarchist movement was generally extremely vulnerable: spies were able to infiltrate quite easily and 'anarchist groups' were 'permeated by police spies'.[24] Indeed, some of them held positions at the highest level: Carlo Terzaghi, the chief spy in the First International, was the founder of the International in Turin.[25] The noted spy Giovanni Domanico played an important role in the development of the International in southern Italy and financed and directed several anarchist newspapers.[26]

It is therefore not surprising that the embassy in London was able to

---

[20] Ambassador Menabrea to Minister of the Interior Mancini, 18 August 1881, Asdmae, *Pol. Int.*, b. 5.

[21] Vice Consul Buzzegoli to Menabrea, 7 March 1880, Asdmae, *AL*, b. 70.

[22] 'Une trahison. Armande Lapie', 8 February 1896, IISH, Nettlau archive, b. 3457.

[23] On Terzaghi see: 'Ultim'ora' and 'Azzati-Terzaghi. Una spia smascherata', in *L'Associazione*, 27 October and 30 November 1889; on Rubino: 'In guardia' in *Lo Sciopero Generale*, 2 June 1902; on Bellelli see: *La Gogna*, July 1912.

[24] Peter Latouche, *Anarchy: An Authentic Exposition of the Methods of Anarchists and the Aims of Anarchism* (London: Everett and Co., 1908), p. 231.

[25] See: Brunello, *Storie di anarchici e di spie*, pp. 27–32.

[26] Natale Musarra, 'Le confidenze di "Francesco" G. Domanico al Conte Codronchi', *Rivista Storica dell'Anarchismo*, III, 1, 1996, pp. 45–92.

obtain information regarding the Internationalists from the very beginning of their settlement in London. Orlando De Martijs was probably the first secret agent who worked for the Italian authorities in surveillance of the Internationalists. He arrived from Naples fleeing arrest after being sentenced for embezzlement.[27] He fitted perfectly into London's community of political refugees; he was part of the steering committees of the *Cercle Italien d' études sociales*[28] and of the *Club international d'études sociales de Londres*.[29] As a delegate to the latter he attended the Social Revolutionary and Anarchist Congress of 1881.[30]

De Martijs, who signed his reports with his initials 'DM', was considered 'extremely useful' by the Minister of the Interior. Moreover, DM was trusted by most of the anarchists in London. The minutes of correspondence between the embassy and the Foreign Ministry are rich with references to letters sent by Cafiero and other anarchists to Malatesta, missives that De Martijs was able to copy and provide to the Italian authorities.[31] Moreover, Malatesta received his mail at De Martijs' address.[32] De Martijs had probably known Malatesta for a long time, since at some point they had lived in the same building in Santa Maria di Capua (Malatesta's home town), near Naples.[33] In 1881, De Martijs was Malatesta's witness for the granting of power of attorney to a solicitor so Malatesta could receive an inheritance from his aunt.[34] Furthermore, a letter Malatesta wrote to De Martijs seems to indicate that he had a close relationship with him.[35] Apparently, De Martijs occasionally fell under suspicion, once in particular because of allegations against him that Domanico, probably to divert suspicion from himself, inserted into a letter to Malatesta. However, it seems that De Martijs always overcame such difficulties.[36] In January 1881, Malatesta offered De Martijs

---

[27] Peter van der Mark, *Revolutie and Reactie*, Ph.D. thesis, Rijksuniversiteit Groningen, 1997, p. 228. De Martjis lived in St Pancreas with his wife Amalia and two children, Luisa and Luigi.

[28] 'Comunications du club', *Le Travail*, 2 May 1880.

[29] 'Communications officielles du Club international d'études sociales de Londres', *Le Travail*, 5 August 1880.

[30] Robin's letter, 'Cercle International d'Etudes Sociales de Londres', 5 June 1881. IIHS, *Brousse archive*.

[31] Unfortunately these copies cannot be found in the archives. The minutes, however, provide highlights of their contents.

[32] Vice consul Buzzegoli to ambassador Menabrea, 8 July 1881, Asdmae, *AL*, b. 70.

[33] DM's report, 9 June 1880, Asdmae, *Pol. Int.*, b. 5, f. (1880–1881).

[34] Malatesta's second witness was Vincenzo Melandri. Vice Consul Buzzegoli to Italian embassy, 24 January 1881, Asdmae, *AL*, b. 70.

[35] Malatesta to De Martijs, Aversa 6 March 1883. ACS, *PS*, 1914, b. 9, f. A8 Martijs (De) Orlando.

[36] Minister of the Interior to Foreign Minister, 17 June 1881 Asdmae, *Pol. Int.*, b. 6.

the money to move to Malta where, in Malatesta's plan, De Martijs would open a tavern and organise the smuggling of weapons to Sicily. The Ministry of the Interior instructed De Martijs to refuse Malatesta's proposal, because it would have been extremely difficult to replace him. In any case, Malatesta did not persevere with the scheme.[37]

De Martijs regularly updated the embassy on Malatesta, Ceccarelli, Solieri and Cafiero. He provided reports on the activities of not only Italian anarchists but also anarchists and revolutionaries from other countries, such as the Russian Hartmann or the Spaniard Figueras. Unfortunately, only a few of his reports have survived in the archives and their contents can be ascertained only through the minutes of correspondence between the embassy and the Foreign Ministry.

De Martijs' collaboration with the embassy in London was terminated at the end of 1886 when his son seriously jeopardised his cover. The two had had a fierce argument, probably over an inheritance; De Martijs' son threatened his father's life and blackmailed him, promising to reveal De Martijs' true identity to the anarchists. Meanwhile, De Martijs experienced serious financial difficulties. The Ministry of the Interior's decision to offer him a more generous form of assistance, 1000 Italian *lire*, indicates how much he was valued,[38] however, the threat represented by his son undermined the effectiveness of De Martijs in London and he was compelled to move to Paris in November 1886.

The Ministry of the Interior agreed with the decision in the hope that it would be temporary.[39] However, De Martijs never returned to England; he lived in France, first in Paris, then in Marseilles, where he continued to spy on the Italian anarchists. No evidence exists as to whether his true identity was ever discovered.[40]

Recruitment and activities of spies

After De Martijs' departure the embassy experienced a number of failures before finding the right person to replace him. These attempts provide a good example of how informers were recruited. Moreover, they also show the direct involvement of a British police inspector.

In April 1888 with the arrival from Paris of Pini and Parmeggiani's

[37] Consul to ambassador, 24 January and 16 February 1881. Asdmae, *AL*, b. 70.

[38] Foreign Ministry to Italian ambassador, 6 September 1886, Asdmae, *Pol. Int.*, b. 39, f. (1886–1887).

[39] Minister Malvano to embassy, 18 November 1886, Asdmae *Pol. Int.*, b. 39, f. (1886–1887).

[40] In 1897 De Martijs was still informing the Italian authorities about the Italian anarchists in Marseilles. De Martijs' report, 20 May 1897, ACS, *CPC*, b. 2477, f. (Goldoni Giorgio).

group the embassy urgently needed an informer. Since it was impossible for De Martijs to return to London because his son still lived in the city, the ambassador asked the Minister of the Interior to make enquiries about a twenty five year old destitute man called Carlo Alberto Rosti,[41] who had pleaded for help to the consul a few months earlier.[42] The following June, the Minister of the Interior authorised Rosti's recruitment with a monthly budget of up to 200 Italian *lire* for payment. However, the new informer – who signed his reports 'Car' – did not have the necessary qualities and, at the end of August 1889, the ambassador Luigi Catalani informed Crispi about the great difficulties he was encountering in finding a new secret agent. He also informed the Ministry of the Interior that George Hepburn Greenham, an inspector at Scotland Yard, had agreed to help the Italian embassy in the search for a valuable spy.[43] The first person Greenham introduced to the Italian ambassador was Leon Beneter, a British citizen of Spanish extraction, who spoke Spanish, French, English and Italian. Inspector Greenham promised the ambassador that he would help Beneter with hints and advice and suggested a payment to the new secret agent of £3 a week, corresponding to 300 Italian *lire* a month.[44] However, on 11 September, the ambassador notified Crispi that 'at the last moment the proposed agent refused to watch the Italian anarchists at any price, frightened by their ferocious nature.'[45]

Inspector Greenham then contacted Antonio Percha, an Albanian owner of an ice-cream shop. Greenham assured the Italian ambassador that he would give Percha direction and suggestions, and also that he would keep an eye on him. At this point the Italian ambassador suggested the Minister of the Interior 'as soon as possible offer Inspector Greenham a watch or some other little object as a gift, to be worth not less than 300 or 400 Italian *lire.*'[46] The Minister of the Interior agreed.[47] Vice Consul Buzzegoli was to be in charge of maintaining contact with the new spy and arranging payment. Buzzegoli was to receive Percha's reports at his personal home address, and forward them directly to the Ministry of the Interior.[48] Nevertheless, at the end of the month, after receiving initial reports from Percha, Catalani and

[41] Ambassador Catalani to Crispi, 7 February 1888; Asdmae, *Pol. Int.*, b. 39, f. (1888).

[42] Rosti to consul Heath, 23 January 1888, Asdmae, *Pol. Int.*, b. 39, f. (1888).

[43] Catalani to Crispi, 27 August 1889; Asdmae, *Pol. Int.*, b. 37, f. (agente segreto Londra).

[44] Catalani to Crispi, 27 August 1889; Asdmae, *Pol. Int.*, b. 37, f. (agente segreto Londra).

[45] Catalani to Crispi, 11 September 1889, Asdmae, *Pol. Int.*, b. 37, f. (agente segreto Londra).

[46] Catalani to Crispi, 12 September 1889, Asdmae, *Pol. Int.*, b. 37, f. (agente segreto Londra).

[47] Ministry of the Interior to Italian ambassador, 17 September 1889, Asdmae, *Pol. Int.*, b. 37, f. (agente segreto Londra).

[48] Ministry of the Interior to Italian ambassador, 17 September 1889, Asdmae, *Pol. Int.*, b. 37, f. (agente segreto Londra).

Greenham shared the opinion that he was unfit for the position due to alleged incompetence and ignorance, and that he should be replaced in the shortest time possible.[49] Writing to the Minister of the Interior, the ambassador dismissed the concern which always arose when a spy had to be discharged that Percha could cause trouble out of revenge. Indeed, Greenham reassured the ambassador that Percha knew he was under surveillance and was aware that, if there was any suspicion of such behaviour, Greenham would have charged him with extortion.

Meanwhile Greenham, on his own initiative, had already contacted Luigi Morio, an Italian sculptor. Morio had lived in London's French and Italian quarters since 1878 and in the past had worked for a police department in the East End. To judge the abilities of the new candidate, Catalani instructed Inspector Greenham to solicit a report from Morio on French and German socialists.[50] After receiving confirmation that Morio knew the Italian anarchist Alessandro Marocco, and before taking a definitive decision, Catalani asked Morio – through Greenham – to scrutinise the activities of Malatesta, Parmeggiani and Marocco. If Morio was employed as a secret agent, the ambassador was determined to involve Inspector Greenham in the matter. Indeed, it was Catalani's intention that Greenham make Morio believe he was working for Scotland Yard, not for the Italian government. Moreover, contact between the embassy and the spy were kept by Greenham and not, as had happened in the past, by vice consul Buzzegoli.[51]

Eventually, Morio was considered suitable for the job and he received the nickname of Marco Lippi. But new difficulties emerged. Since Morio intended to keep his main job and to perform his spying duties only in the evenings, the ambassador proposed a salary of £2 a week. Morio refused to work for less than £3. Catalani, who considered the figure exorbitant, remitted the final decision to Crispi and the Minister of the Interior granted Morio's request.[52] However, on 16 November, Crispi was informed that Morio had refused to work as a secret agent.[53] Despite help received from Inspector Greenham, the embassy in London was once again without an agent to watch the anarchists.

Thus, surveillance on the anarchists operated inefficiently due to lack of informers until the appointment of the new ambassador, Count Tornielli, at

[49] Catalani to Crispi, 30 September 1889, Asdmae, *Pol. Int.*, b. 37, f. (agente segreto Londra).

[50] Catalani to Foreign Ministry, 2 October 1889, Asdmae, *Pol. Int.*, b. 37, f. (agente segreto Londra).

[51] Catalani to Foreing Ministry, 3 October 1889, Asdmae, *Pol. Int.*, b. 37, f. (agente segreto Londra).

[52] Foreign Ministry to Italian embassy, 30 October 1889, Asdmae, *Pol. Int.*, b. 37, f. (agente segreto Londra).

[53] Catalani to Crispi, 16 November 1889, Asdmae, *Pol. Int.*, b. 37, f. (agente segreto Londra).

the end of 1889.[54] Consequently, the reorganisation of the intelligence service was one of Tornielli's first priorities. Following Vice Consul Buzzegoli's suggestion, Tornielli contacted 'a certain Sig. Federico Lauria, singing teacher, aged fifty four, living in London for six years'.[55] The Ministry of the Interior authorised Tornielli to employ Lauria and to pay him £2 a week.[56] But just a couple of weeks after his appointment, Tornielli already wanted to dismiss him and suggested as a substitute a Ministry of the Interior secret agent who was on duty in London at the time. The Minister of the Interior replied to Tornielli's request that, although he did not have any objections to Lauria's dismissal, he could not 'leave the agent in mission there'. In fact, the secret agent in question had already left London to return to his home abroad, from where he provided extremely useful services because of his knowledge of the subversive parties and his personal relationships with their most dangerous affiliates.[57] Lauria was not discharged, and continued to work for the Italian embassy uninterruptedly for fifteen years, until his death in 1907.

Lauria assumed the nickname 'agente Calvo'. Unlike De Martijs' reports, a considerable number of his letters survived. In his reports Lauria referred to himself in the third person, a system commonly adopted by spies, calling himself with self-irony: 'the old man' or 'the little old man'. Lauria's reports were rich in information about the anarchist community in London. Indeed, although he often indulged in not particularly significant details, as a whole his reports, written in a literary style, provide a vivid account of the anarchist colony in London from an informer's point of view.

Lauria was regularly involved in organising anarchist social events. He wrote plays that were performed in the anarchist clubs. In 1893, his comedy *La Congiura, scherzo comico in un atto*, was performed at the *Club Italo-Svizzero* in Clerkenwell Road.[58] In addition, he directed plays written by others, for example by Gori. Although Lauria often overestimated the importance of alleged plots and terrorist projects, some of his information was effective in facilitating the containment of the activities of the Italian anarchists. Indeed, as a result of his reports, the embassy was able to advise the Minister of the Interior about the shipments of anarchist publications to Italy, leading to their seizure at post offices.[59] Moreover, Calvo's reports were

---

[54] Tornielli to Crispi, 19 December 1889, Asdmae, *Serie Politica P*, b. 47.

[55] Tornielli a Crispi, London 3 December 1889, Asdmae, *Serie Politica P*, 1891–1916, f. (ambasciata Londra in partenza 1889).

[56] Ministry of the Interior to Tornielli, 18 December 1889, Asdmae, *Serie politica P*, 1891–1916, f. (ambasciata Londra in partenza 1889).

[57] Minister of the Interior to Tornielli, 9 January 1890, Asdmae, *Pol. Int.*, b. 38, f. (1890).

[58] Leaflet, in ACS, *CPC*, b 1519, f. (Cova Cesare).

[59] The post offices were provided by agents of the Pubblica Sicurezza. Some could even

essential in the arrest of two Italian anarchists. At the beginning of 1892, Calvo alerted the embassy of the anarchist Pietro Bianchi's return to London from America. Bianchi was well-known among the Italian anarchists and an intimate of Parmeggiani's. The previous year he had escaped from the British police and fled to the United States. Thus, the embassy and the consulate were able to entrust the matter to Scotland Yard; Bianchi was arrested and, since he had been found guilty of the manslaughter of his brother in Italy in 1885, Bianchi's extradition was granted,[60] in a rare success for the Italian authorities.[61]

Two years later Lauria facilitated the arrest of another Italian anarchist: Giovanni Fornara, nicknamed 'Piemonte'. Piemonte's capture followed the arrest of another young Italian anarchist, Francesco Polti. On 14 April 1894 Polti was arrested on Clerkenwell Road in possession of a suspect iron cylinder by Inspector John Sweeney of Scotland Yard. A search of Polti's lodgings yielded a large quantity of chemicals and instructions for concocting explosives that Polti sought in vain to pass of as a recipe for cooking '*polenta* pudding'. Polti fingered Fornara as behind the plot to manufacture a bomb. However, the police were not able to find Fornara. During the manhunt, Chief Inspector Melville and his agents searched Lauria's home without realising that he was a police spy. An angered Lauria advised Melville to confirm his identity within the Italian embassy.

On 22 April, at 1.30am, Sergeant Maguire caught Fornara sleeping in a house in Stratford and arrested him. The police located him as a result of information provided by Calvo.

24 Aprile 1894.

I promised to give you an account of the arrest of our learned comrade Piemonte, and I now honour this promise. The police, who failed to arrest Piemonte at the house where he had been residing, did not know what to do next, with the trail gone cold. Mr Melville then visited Lauria's home, on his own, on Saturday, around one o'clock; halfway up the steps, he called 'Madam, madam' in a low feminine voice. Madame Corso came to the doorway and, seeing a man she had not met before, called Lauria and said to him, 'A gentleman is looking for you'. Lauria came out and realised that it was Mr Melville, who was climbing the steps on tiptoe. Lauria said to him: 'Come up, there's nobody here'. Melville entered with perfect manners, and sat down, having first politely shaken Lauria's hand. Melville made the apologies owing to Signor Lauria for the error committed in

recognise the calligraphy of the anarchists. See Brunello, *Storie di anarchici e di spie.*

[60] 'An alleged Italian anarchist in trouble', *Dundee Courier & Argus,* 27 January 1892.

[61] Tornielli to Minister of Foreign Affairs, 8 January and 9 February 1892, Asdmae, *Pol. Int.,* b. 39, f. (1892).

the preceding days, then said to him: 'I spoke to the ambassador and understood everything; all is in order. Everything should now be set up for Piemonte's arrest, and with this in mind I need your full cooperation. London should get rid of these people, who continue to support appalling unrest in this country'. 'That is absolutely right', the intrepid little old man replied, 'I've already done what I could to help you get him, and let's hope that your men don't let him get away like last time. At 13 Back Street, the exact address given by me'. Lauria then said to Melville, 'I sent people to look for Piemonte, without regard to the expense, and I have just learnt that he is in Stratford', giving details of the house, its number and so forth. Melville then asked Lauria for his advice, 'When do you think one might arrest him: tomorrow, Sunday, or Monday, when he will be at work in Crystal Palace?' Lauria replied, 'No, you should go there tonight, Saturday, because on Monday Piemonte could easily hide, or take flight!' Melville then said, 'Along with the men, I'd like to send that inspector you know who speaks French, and who met Piemonte at your house'. With agreement reached, Melville gave his visiting card to Signor Lauria, and on leaving said warmly, 'We'll meet again'. He then went rather cautiously down the steps, on tiptoe, and departed. No other policeman was with him. The arrest operation was straightforward, because when the old man takes matters in hand they can hardly go wrong![62]

Polti and Fornara's arrest and trial resonated in both Italy and the United Kingdom: it was one of the rare cases in which anarchists were arrested because they intended to commit an outrage in England. Fornara stated that, since he did not have the money to take the bomb to France or Italy, he planned to throw it into the Stock Exchange. At the end of the trial he was sentenced to twenty years' penal servitude, Polti to ten.

Polti was released seven years later, but Fornara suffered a different fate. At the end of 1909, his release date approached. Freeing Fornara, who was considered mentally unsound, greatly concerned the British and Italian authorities.[63]

> I think it is out of the question to set Fornara free. He is the subject of interest to so many people on political grounds that if he were at large, either here or in Italy, he would be almost certainly ultimately to get into the hands of anarchist sympathisers. Then not only would his career and 'sufferings' be exploited for political purposes, but he would be very likely to become more or less dangerous again (so far as he was physically capable) when he found himself in anarchist surroundings.[64]

[62]　Calvo's report, 24 April 1894. ACS, *CPC*, b. 4070, f. (Polti Antonio Francesco).

[63]　Italian consul to Ministry of the Interior, ACS, *CPC*, b. 3740, f. (Fornara Giuseppe).

[64]　Report on becoming due for licence, 21 December 1909, NA, HO144/1711/A55860D/14.

The Ministry of the Interior and the Home Office both envisaged solving the problem by having Fornara certified as insane and removing him to a criminal asylum.[65] Only one voice opposed that view.

28.2.10

I do not feel justified in keeping this man in prison after the period has been reached when his licence did not err on the side of leniency. Its full force under that law has now almost spent itself. The fact that if the convict returned to Italy 'his suffering would be exploited by Anarchist Associates' appears to me wholly irrelevant to the question of the rights of the State against him and of his rights against the State. I do not like the suggestion which appears on 1/14, that he can be certified a lunatic as a matter of administrative convenience. I do not misunderstand it in its context, but I cannot recognise it as right. The man being entitled to his discharge, the law cannot hold him under any lien of the original sentence. If, however, he is actually insane at the moment when he would otherwise be discharged, the treatment appropriate to his case must be afforded. An independent examination by two trustworthy medical men, not connected with Government service, should be made on the question of his sanity and fitness to live outside an asylum. By that we must be bound. The rights of a convict against the State must be regarded as at least equal, and often superior, to the rights of the State against the convict.

Sir E. Troup[66]

Just a few days before his release date, Fornara was certified insane and transferred to Broadmoor Criminal Lunatic Asylum. The director of Pankhurst Prison desired that Fornara 'might end his days where he is'; Fornara died at Broadmoor thirty five years later, on 13 July 1941, aged 91.[67]

The Rubino Affair

By 1902 Lauria's reliability as a secret agent was being questioned by Ettore Prina, a police inspector sent on a mission to London to establish his own

---

[65] Report on becoming due for licence, 21 December 1909, NA, HO144/1711/A55860D/14.

[66] Report on becoming due for licence, 21 December 1909, NA, HO144/1711/A55860D/14. Sir E. Troup was Permanent Under-Secretary of State in the Home Office 1908–1922.

[67] In 1907 the Defendi family declared their willingness to provide Fornara with hospitality, one of the preconditions for an earlier release. In 1912 the anarchist David Nicoll contacted the socialist MP Will Crooks to obtain Fornara's release. A detailed reconstruction of the event can be found in: Pietro Di Paola, 'Fornara Giuseppe: Storia di un anarchico italiano a Londra', *Annali di Ca'Foscari*, XXXVIII, 1–2, 1999, pp. 663–80.

intelligence network to run in parallel with that of the embassy.[68] As cover, he was formally in charge of the consulate's conscription office. Prina rented a room in the neighbourhood of the consulate, where he summoned Italian youths eligible for military service. In that way, he was able to mingle with young Italians and to establish a network of informers. Meanwhile, as a precautionary measure, the embassy and the Ministry of the Interior decided to maintain separately the services of Prina and Calvo.[69]

Initially, Prina recruited at least two informers: Gennaro Rubino and Enrico Boiada.[70] He also introduced a systematic photographic record of the anarchists by developing in his lodgings photographs taken by Rubino. Generally, those pictures were taken when the anarchists were eating or relaxing, for example at a restaurant or sharing a bottle of wine. To avoid the possibility that those portrayed could identify where the shots had been taken Prina often confined the developed photographs to the head and shoulders.[71] Prina also supported Rubino's scheme to open a printing company that could both provide a cover for Rubino and follow the anarchists' plans step-by-step by publishing their newspapers and pamphlets. Even more conveniently, the anarchists could use Rubino's print shop to organise conferences and meetings and to give temporary shelter to comrades who were unemployed or passing through. According to Prina, Rubino's project gained the approval of Malatesta, Michel and Kropotkin.[72] But little did the anarchists know that the Italian Ministry of the Interior entirely funded the venture to the tune of £50. Prina reported that Rubino had acquired the press and was about to issue a new journal, *L'emigrato*.[73]

Contrary to their initial decision, the embassy did not maintain the services provided by Calvo and Prina separately. This change of heart turned out to be a mistake. In fact, the two spies began to blame each other in their reports. In Prina's opinion Calvo knew very little about the anarchists' projects and events and his information on single individuals was vague

---

[68] At the end of 1901, according to the spy Virgilio, the anarchists suspected Lauria to be a police informer. They were suspicious of the anarchist Giuseppe Pesci because he associated with him. Virgilio's report, 10 December 1901. ACS, *CPC*, b. 5605, f. (Zucchi Ugo).

[69] Ambassador Pansa to Ministry of the Interior, 30 July 1901, Asdmae, *Pol. Int*, b. 32.

[70] Prina nicknamed Rubino 'Enrico', the other informer was called 'Gallo'.

[71] Prina reported to have the pictures of: Sante Cenci, Pietro Capelli, Carlo Frigerio, Enrico Vincenzo Carrara, Luigi Valsuana, Alfredo Pierconti, Carlo Chignola, Giuseppe Battolla, and Carlo Berrutti. In the same report Prina requested permission to acquire an 'excellent machine' for £6 (150 *lire*). Prina to Ministry of the Interior, 18 October 1902, ACS, *PS*, 1905, b. 22.

[72] Prina's letter, 16 January 1902, ACS, *PS*, 1905, b. 22.

[73] Prina's report to the Ministry of the Interior, 5 July 1902. ACS, *PS*, 1905, b. 22.

and superficial.[74] In a note to the consul, Prina remarked that he had only stopped his confutation of Calvo because the ambassador had ordered it.

Indeed, a few weeks previously, the Ministry of the Interior had informed the embassy that the anarchists suspected Calvo. At that point the ambassador decided to separate 'the two services, avoiding also reciprocal control on the information provided'.[75] Alerted to these suspicions and a possible trap to unmask him, Calvo replied, 'I am not frightened either of being exposed or of possible traps, and I will carry out my duties. If I am unfortunate, I will die a martyr to duty'.[76]

Yet the disputes between Lauria and Prina increased in the aftermath of the subsequent exposure of Rubino. At the beginning of May 1902, documents revealing Rubino's collaboration with the Italian police came into the possession of the anarchists. On 9 May, Malatesta summoned Rubino before a court of honour at the anarchists' club at 55 Charlotte Street. Rubino did not attend the meeting, at which about thirty people were present. Instead, he sent a long letter to Malatesta claiming that his real intention was to double-cross the police inspectors by taking the money without providing them with anything but fabricated information. He insisted on accepting Prina's proposal in order to carry out *ad hoc* counterespionage and discover the identity of other spies. Rubino included three letters received by Inspector Prina to support his version. In these letters, the inspector complained about the unsatisfactory nature of Rubino's spying and warned him to provide useful and trustworthy information if he wanted to continue to support his wife and son. Moreover, in one of them Prina named Calvo explicitly, stating that he had to confront competition from Calvo and that it was his intention to get rid of him. This fact made Lauria furious. Indeed he attended the meeting in which the letters were made public.[77]

Rubino accused other anarchists of being linked with the Italian police.[78] He stated that Malavasi was the person who indirectly gave information to Calvo – an accusation that was actually true.[79] He also named Delboni

---

[74] Prina's report, 18 February 1902, ACS, *PS*, 1905, b. 22.

[75] Pansa to inspector of Ministry of the Interior, 14 February 1902. ACS, *PS*, 1905, b. 22.

[76] Calvo's report, 4 February 1902, ACS, *PS*, 1905, b. 22.

[77] Calvo's report. 15 May 1902. ACS, *PS*, 1905, b. 22.

[78] Virgilio's report, 11 May 1902. Prina's report to Ministry of the Interior, 5 July 1902. ACS, *PS*, 1905, b. 22.

[79] Malavasi was accused of running a brothel and of being involved in the 'white slave trade'. Later, during the *biennio rosso*, he took part in the 'conspiracy of Pietralata' in Rome in 1919 (Marco Rossi, *Arditi, non gendarmi!*, Pisa: BFS, 1997, pp. 77–89) ACS, *CPC*, b. 2954, f. (Malavasi Asdrubale).

and Fumagalli and concluded that the anarchists could not trust Bruto Bertiboni.[80]

As usual when a spy was unmasked, the Italian anarchists issued a leaflet of denunciation, a *diffida*, against Rubino, in which they publicised Prina's address and the name he used as a cover – Piero Marelli.[81] A note was also published in *Lo Sciopero Generale* and other anarchist newspapers in Europe.[82]

The Rubino affair created a climate of suspicion. Malatesta and Pietraroja received more documents from Arturo Tonzi and Bertiboni. Tonzi asserted that he had obtained the papers from consulate employee and that the documents would reveal the identities of the police informers. A restricted number of people had access to them: Malatesta, Pietraroja, Mariani and Bertiboni. Rumours began to circulate: mutual accusations, grudges and uncontrolled suspicions swirled through the anarchist community. A report by Virgilio illustrates the atmosphere:

> Recchioni and Bertiboni go around together frowning. Fumagalli wants to beat up Recchioni, Dall'Acqua wants to beat up Pietraroja and goes round with Jaffei. As you can see, it is a real mess.[83]

Suspicions arose about Spasiano and Ferrini, who had been approached by Rubino to work for his newspaper, and Alfredo Pierconti. Because of the controversies in which they found themselves involved, both Spasiano and Ferrini decided to leave London. According to Calvo, Boiada was also accused of being a spy, which was in fact true.[84]

Meanwhile, all was not well among the authorities. The Italian ambassador was engaged in finding out what papers the anarchists had and how they had been able to obtain them.[85] The consul defended his employees and speculated that the documents could have been taken from Rome, an idea that Giolitti rejected absolutely.[86] Therefore, the ambassador entrusted Inspector Prina with investigation of the matter.[87]

Among the documents – apparently thirty-six photographic reproductions of letters – one signed 'Lari' caused suspicion to fall on the barber, Gaetano

---

[80] Delboni and Fumagalli were named because they had asked for help from the *Beneficenza*.

[81] 'Diffida', London 14 April 1902. ACS, *PS*, 1905, b. 22.

[82] 'In Guardia', *Lo Sciopero Generale*, 2 June 1902.

[83] Virgilio's report, 12 May 1902, ACS, *PS*, 1905, b. 22.

[84] Bojada was effectively Prina's informer as is evident from a letter of Inspector Mandolesi who replaced Prina. 'Bojada jealously keeps all the letters that Prina wrote to him', Mandolesi to Ministry of the Interior, 12 January 1905, ACS, *PS*, 1905, b. 22. Bojada was unmasked by the anarchists in 1904 (see Calvo's report, 18 July 1904, ACS, *PS* 1905, b. 5, f. 10/70).

[85] Pansa to Leonardi, 24 May 1902, ACS, *PS*, 1905, b. 22.

[86] Giolitti to ambassador Pansa, 21 May 1902, ACS, *PS*, 1905, b. 22.

[87] Pansa to Leonardi, 27 May 1902, ACS, *PS*, 1905, b. 22.

Scolari. He was summoned before a court of honour in Charlotte Street on 29 May. To check his handwriting, Pietraroja dictated to Scolari the text of the letter in Malatesta's possession. A particular spelling mistake, present in both letters, aggravated Scolari's position but he strongly denied all allegations against him and favourably impressed part of the audience. At the end of the meeting, it was decided that a graphologist should examine the letter, and a decision was postponed. Over the following days, Scolari continued to defend himself by publishing a leaflet in which he proclaimed his innocence and threatened to take his accusers to court.[88]

The anarchists were also trying to find out the origin of the documents. Indeed, some of them, and in particular those forming the *Bresci* group, began to raise doubts about the authenticity of the papers in Malatesta's possession.[89] They argued that the police could have orchestrated the entire affair and requested Malatesta and the others to reveal who had provided the documents. Moreover, they criticised the fact that these papers were controlled by a small group that formed 'a proscription committee'.[90] This fuelled an already incendiary situation. Tonzi and Bertiboni, who claimed to have received the letters, were unable to explain the origin of the documents and contradicted each other. To complicate the situation further, around the same time Ferrari, an employee of the *'Beneficenza'*, contacted the anarchist Giorgio Giorgi and took him to the consulate where vice consul Righetti proposed he work for the consulate as an informer. Giorgi refused the proposal and spat in Righetti's face.[91]

A number of other meetings of anarchists to clarify the situation ended in quarrels and brawls until Bertiboni's lies were eventually revealed and he moved away from London. Tonzi admitted that he had lied and that the person who gave him the documents was not Ferrari, as he had stated previously, but another man called Galanti. Tonzi also wrote to vice consul Righetti to clear Ferrari of the allegations and advanced the hypothesis that the documents were fabrications.[92] Inspector Prina, who investigated the matter and reconstructed the entire story, confirmed this theory. No papers had been purloined from the consulate; the letters in the anarchists' hands were, in fact, forgeries. The deception was conceived by three individuals:

[88] Gaetano Scolari, 'Sempre protestando' leaflet. ACS, *PS*, 1905, b. 22.

[89] The Bresci group was composed of Corio, Fumagalli, Delbuoni, Perutti, De Maria, Marchi, Gualducci, Barosso, Bianchi, Tosti, Befagnotti and Frigerio.

[90] The group was formed by Malatesta, Recchioni, Mariani, Giulio Rossi, Spodesniac, Enrico Defendi and Pietraroja. Virgilio's report, 4 June 1902, ACS, *PS*, 1905, b. 22.

[91] Vice consul Righetti's letter, 11 October 1902; Pansa to Foreign Minister, 14 October 1902. Asdmae, *Serie Politica P*, b. 49, f. (Inghilterra). Virgilio's report, 17 May 1902, ACS, *PS*, 1905, b. 22.

[92] Tonzi's letter to vice consul Righetti, 10 July 1902. ACS, *PS*, 1905, b. 22.

Galanti, Franchiotti and Bertiboni. The anarchists had expelled Galanti from their circles in 1898 for being a spy. Franchiotti, described as 'a rogue' by Prina, was a former police officer who sought refuge in London to escape a sentence for embezzlement and who had reasons to seek revenge against Rubino. Bertiboni was the most controversial character. Prina did not exclude the possibility that Bertiboni could have been a secret agent.[93] Franchiotti and Galanti produced the forgeries, and Bertiboni, involving Tonzi, delivered them to Pietraroja.

The fact that the ambassador carried out an investigation to discover if and how the documents had been removed from the consulate excludes the possibility that the embassy and the Italian police in London had planned the affair. So it is entirely possible that the entire affair was the result of the spirit of revenge in the three people involved. Yet, Bertiboni's aims remain unclear. Rubino considered Bertiboni a secret agent, and Prina did not entirely exclude that possibility. Apparently, the anarchists believed that Bertiboni worked for the British police. In this case, the fact that the Rubino affair happened just before the coronation of Edward VII could lead to the supposition that the scheme was planned to avoid possible troubles by the anarchists during the celebrations. However, there is no evidence supporting this theory.

The Rubino affair had several consequences. On 1 November 1902, Virgilio reported that Rubino told the anarchist Michele Franchini, who refused to shake hands with him, that 'he [Rubino] had to carry out an act of redemption'.[94] Two weeks later in Brussels Rubino took a shot at the King of Belgium, Leopold II, but missed his target. At his trial, he claimed to have acted on his own initiative and to consider himself an anarchist.[95] He received a life sentence. The police in London felt that Rubino may have made the assassination attempt to prove his good faith to the cause.[96]

In December 1902, Giolitti summoned Prina back to Italy, seconding him to Venice. Prina had compromised the whole intelligence service in London by acting heedlessly and by making public the name of the informer Calvo.[97] Giolitti had reached this decision as early as the end of May. However, at the ambassador's request, Prina remained in London to help organise protection during the visit of the Duke and Duchess D'Aosta

---

[93] Prina's report to Ministry of the Interior, 5 July 1902. ACS, PS, 1905, b. 22.

[94] Virgilio's report, 1 November 1902. ACS, PS, 1905, b. 22.

[95] On Rubino see: Anne Morelli, Rubino, l'anarchiste italien qui tenta d'assassiner Léopold II (Bruxelles: Labor, 2006).

[96] Malatesta commented on Rubino's assassination attempt in: 'Gennaro Rubini', La Rivoluzione Sociale, 1 December 1902, p. 1. Rubino died in prison on 15 March 1918. See also Levy, 'Malatesta in London: the Era of Dynamite', p. 39.

[97] Giolitti to Pansa, 21 May 1902, ACS, PS, 1905, b. 22.

for Edward VII's coronation. Prina seems to have been seriously damaged by the Rubino affair; he pleaded with the consul to intercede on his behalf in order to delay his departure or consign him to another consular office where he could spend the last years of his life 'unknown and forgotten'.[98] Nevertheless, Giolitti ordered Prina to leave London at once.[99]

Lauria was kept on. The ambassador recommended retaining his service because, despite all the limitations, he was cheap and had lasted many years without being discovered.[100] Since the anarchists knew his undercover name, Lauria became secret agent 'Soldi'.[101]

In 1906, Lauria fell seriously ill. Although he could not provide any information because of his illness, the Minister of the Interior decided to continue to pay him in part because he had served zealously for many years, but especially to prevent any possible revelations about the involvement of the embassy with the political police and any consequent scandals'.[102]

On 22 January 1907, Lauria's stepson Marco Corso informed the embassy of Lauria's death and, 'having being his apprentice and *confidente* for more than a year', volunteered to replace him.[103]

The embassy recruited Marco Corso as a secret agent paying him £2.50 a week.[104] Corso assumed the undercover name 'M. Soldi'. However, as noted by the Ministry of the Interior, after Lauria's death the service was less useful.[105]

The Rubino affair affected the anarchists, too. The violent quarrels probably caused the collapse of the newspaper *Lo Sciopero Generale*. Malatesta and Pietraroja were blamed for being easily fooled, and for making allegations against Scolari.[106] According to Virgilio, Pietraroja inferred that Malatesta

[98] Prina's letter, London 19 December 1902. ACS, *PS*, 1905, b. 22.

[99] Prina was replaced by Inspector Paolo Mandolesi. Ministry of the Interior to Italian embassy, 2 January 1903. ACS, *PS*, 1905, b. 22.

[100] Pansa to Leonardi, 24 May 1902, ACS, *PS*, 1905, b. 22.

[101] Pansa to the General Director of PS Leonardi, 16 May 1902, ACS, *PS*, 1905, b. 22.

[102] Italian embassy to Minister of the Interior, 21 December 1906. ACS, *PS*, 1905, b. 5, f. (10/70).

[103] M. Corso to Cavaliere Manetti, 22 January 1907, *ACS, PS*, 1905, b. 5, f. (10/70). Also De Martijs' son asked to be recruited as a secret agent, given the services provided by his father and the fact that he was unemployed. Vincenzo De Martijs's letter, 12 December 1914, ACS, *PS*, 1914, b. 9, f. A8.

[104] Ambassador Pansa to Ministry of the Interior, 6 February 1907, ACS, *PS*, b. 5, f. (10/70).

[105] Minister of Interior to Italian embassy, 4 June 1907, ACS, *PS*, 1905, b. 5, f. (10/70). Many years later, Marco Corso, who was living in poverty, offered his services to the Italian Consulate to work as an informer. The War Office and the Ministry of Interior rejected Corso's offer because there was not record of his previous activity. Italian Foreign Office to Ministry of Interior, 8 May 1930, ACS, *CPC*, b. 1487, f. (Corsi Marco).

[106] A year later Scolari distributed two leaflets in the Italian and the French colonies in which he attacked Pietraroja and Malatesta for the accusations of the previous year.

was weakened by the whole affair. In the same report Virgilio stated that Corio and most of the anarchists thought Malatesta's gullibility made him incapable of leading.[107]

Malatesta's possession of the documents and his accusations against other anarchists deepened the resentment of those who already considered him to be an authoritarian. It is possible that the Rubino and Scolari affairs were among the causes of the heavy depression that affected Malatesta in the winter of 1903.[108]

Rubino's attempt on the life of King Leopold II once more raised the debate among the British authorities about the necessity of effective surveillance of the international anarchist movement. As reported by Melville, Rubino had been watched from the day of his arrival in London in 1898, but the surveillance over him was lighter once he was employed as a spy for the Italian secret police, which had been 'considered a natural guarantee of good faith'.

The Rubino affair reveals much about Metropolitan Police concerns about the activity of foreign political police and secret agents in Britain especially when, as in the case of Inspector Prina, they lacked discretion and caution. On 14 May 1902 (when Rubino had already been unmasked by the anarchists) the Italian embassy sent a memorandum to the Foreign Office offering to collaborate with Scotland Yard in surveillance of anarchists living in London in the run-up to the festivities for the Coronation. The embassy informed the Foreign Office that a 'commissaire' of the Italian police force has been living in London, 'where [...] he has organised a service through which he is already in a position to collect a certain amount of information.' The embassy proposed that 'this "commissaire" might perhaps be put in direct communication with Scotland Yard with a view to a possible exchange of information'.[109] The Foreign Office forwarded the memorandum to the Metropolitan Police Chief Commissioner who replied sharply, rejecting any possible collaboration. Sir E. Bradford underlined that not only 'the presence in London of an Italian Government Agent has been known by the Special Branch [...] from the date of his arrival' but also, referring to the *diffida* against Rubino circulated by the anarchists, 'that there has been no concealment as regards his presence and mode of action is apparent from

'Calendario anarchico 1903 maggio 29' and 'Calendario anarchico 1903 giugno 2', in ACS, *CPC*, b. 3900, f. (Pietraroja Gennaro).

[107] Virgilio's report, 9 July 1902, ACS, *PS*, 1905, b. 22.

[108] Levy, 'Malatesta in Exile', p. 269.

[109] Italian embassy to Foreign Office, 14 May 1902, HO 144/545/A55176/44.

terms of a leaflet which has had a wide circulation. [...] The leaflet [...] mentions the assumed name as well as the real name of the Agent'.[110]

More practical considerations followed. Bradford observed that 'the arrangements made by the Italian Government seriously aggravate the danger they are designed to check'. Indeed, as a result of the alarm created by the discovery of Rubino, precautions had increased among the anarchist circles and the collection of intelligence had become extremely difficult. Moreover, Prina's negligence was likely to foment distrust in those in a position to supply information and to restrain them from doing so out of fear of retaliation. Therefore, according to Bradford, if the establishment of working relations and interchanges of information between the British Police and Italian officers were agreed, 'there would be the gravest risk that the Metropolitan Police would sacrifice one of their most trustworthy sources of obtaining information'.

The Chief Commissioner concluded:

> I beg to be allowed to say in unambiguous language that the assistance we are invited to accept so far from strengthening our powers of control would materially weaken them and might even lead to embarrassing complications.[111]

On account of this feedback, the Foreign Office politely rejected the Italian embassy's offer of collaboration with the assurance that they were aware of the presence of the 'commissaire' in London and would not hesitate to contact him if necessary.

Rubino's assassination attempt demonstrated that the Chief Commissioner's worries were well founded. Disturbing details emerged from the judicial enquiry held in Belgium; it was established that Rubino had used the money obtained from Prina to buy his revolver and ammunition and to pay his way to Brussels. Most irritating for the British authorities was the discovery of Prina's involvement in the purchase of the printing press. The investigation by the British police proved that Prina had secured payment for the press and had met several times at the consulate with the agent of the firm supplying the type. Edward Henry, Bradford's successor as Chief Commissioner, stressed that, if Rubino had not been denounced:

> he would have issued inflammatory pamphlets inciting to crime and through the medium of the post have sent them abroad where their circulation might very reasonably have been objected to by the authorities concerned and representations to this effect would no doubt have been made to our Government, who would have been held responsible for

---

[110] Sir. E. Bradford, Memorandum, 24 May 1902, HO 144/545/A55176.
[111] Sir. E. Bradford, Memorandum, 24 May 1902, HO 144/545/A55176.

providing facilities for the preparations and circulation of printed matter of a character subversive of security and social order.[112]

There were other reasons for concern. The British police believed that Rubino's main motivation for his attempt was his will to rehabilitate himself before his comrades. This was likely to have been the same motivation that drove Angiolillo and Lega in their attempts against the lives of Antonio Canovas and Francesco Crispi.

Henry was concerned that Inspector Mandolesi, who had replaced Prina, was replicating the errors of his predecessor. Indeed, leaflets were circulated warning all anarchists against Beffagnetti for being a police spy in Mandolesi's pay. Consequently, the London police maintained special observation of Beffagnetti as a possible dangerous person. Chief Commissioner Henry concluded his report by underlining his concern that:

> The London police have to deal with Anarchists of whom quite 95 percent are foreigners and if other Governments should follow the example set by the Italian Authorities and locate their agents here, cases corresponding to those of Rubino and Beffagnetti might be of frequent occurrence and the police would have to reckon with men rendered desperate through their relations with the agents of other Government located in our midst.[113]

Virgilio, Belelli and Malatesta

Giolitti was able to follow the developments of the Rubino affair in detail thanks to Virgilio's reports. It was through them that Giolitti found confirmation that, despite his denials, Prina had named Calvo in his letters to Rubino. The embassy and the consulate had no knowledge of Virgilio's presence in London. Virgilio worked in tandem with another spy who was situated in Paris, Enrico Insabato, whose undercover name was 'Dante'.[114] They were both probably sent on missions to the French capital in mid-1900. From Paris they sent a report on the French anarchists Cruisse and Faure, with a long preamble, a model of *captatio benevolentiae*:

> We are here with Dante, united in love for our Italy which we learn to admire more every day, and for which we are convinced that any sacrifice is good. [...] And with the love for Italy we love the men that defend and make it esteemed, and we do not forget you that have directed and lead us so many times to new discoveries and useful works. So, you should have

112 S. E. Henry, 16 March 1903, HO144/545/A55176/51.
113 S. E. Henry, 16 March 1903, HO144/545/A55176/51.
114 See: Berti, *Errico Malatesta e il movimento anarchico*, p. 318.

Errico Malatesta outside Bow Street Police Court, London, 1912.
(IISH BG A59/172)

seen that under the auspices of you and Dad we opened new paths to our explorations.[115]

In Paris, Dante and Virgilio were able to obtain information about the anarchists in London, probably thanks to the letters they received from Corio, with whom they were on close terms. Virgilio not only provided information to the Minister of the Interior, but also suggested a possible plan of action to deepen divisions in the anarchist party.[116]

Virgilio moved to London in 1901. His letters show that he was well placed in the anarchist colony. His reports were of a very different character

[115] Dante and Virgilio's letter, 26 February 1901, ACS, *Carte Giolitti*, b. 2, f. (1).
[116] Virgilio's letter, 25 February 1901, ACS, *Carte Giolitti*, b. 2, f. (1).

than Calvo's. The style was succinct and penetrating. Furthermore, unlike the other informers who worked in London, Virgilio never solicited for money.

Shortly after the appearance of *La Guerra Tripolina*, published by the London anarchists in April 1912 in protest at Italy's invasion of Libya, Enrico Ennio Bellelli, a member of the colony, spread rumours that Malatesta was a Turkish spy. In reply, Malatesta issued a leaflet entitled *Alla Colonia italiana di Londra (Per un fatto personale)* in which he turned attention to the fact that for a long time many in the colony had considered Bellelli to be a spy, although no evidence had been found against him.[117] Malatesta challenged Bellelli to attend a public meeting to explain where his funds came from and prove that he was not an Italian police agent.

The publication of this leaflet heralded one of the most dangerous events to threaten Malatesta's safety during the years of his long exile in London. Initially, Bellelli issued a rebuttal in which he explicitly accused Malatesta of having taken part in the Houndsditch robbery, but he later withdrew the publication,[118] and started proceedings against Malatesta for criminal libel, a clever move that, according to *La Gogna*, the single issue published by the anarchists to expose Bellelli as a spy, was taken after consultation with Inspector Francis Powell of Scotland Yard.

Malatesta's trial took place on 20 May 1912 at the Old Bailey. Bojada, Prina's former informant acted as Bellelli's interpreter. Bellelli declared himself to be a bookseller who had long repudiated anarchist ideas; he denied having accused Malatesta of being a Turkish spy.[119]

In his deposition, Malatesta stated he was an electric engineer, carrying on business as E. Malatesta and Co. at 13 Windmill Street. He had been in England for twelve years and though 'not a professed Anarchist', believed 'in liberty and justice for all'. Malatesta confirmed having been close to Bellelli, having visited him to give Bellelli's children arithmetic lessons. Malatesta added that, in the previous five or six years he had never seen Bellelli sell any books:

> When I say that he is not doing an honest trade as bookseller I mean to imply that he is getting his money as an Italian police spy. When I say he is a liar, I mean it.[120]

Giuseppe Pesci, Giulio Rossi, Alfonso Spizzuoco, Gualducci, Tombolesi, Giorgio Antibando and Enrico Defendi were witnesses for Malatesta and

117 Malatesta, 'Per un fatto personale', 1912. IISH, Nettlau archive, b. 304.
118 *La Gogna*, July 1912, p. 2.
119 Central Criminal Court, Minutes of Evidence: 1911–1912, pp. 209–14. NA, CRIM 10/102.
120 Central Criminal Court, Minutes of Evidence: 1911–1912, pp. 209–14. NA, CRIM 10/102.

all refuted Bellelli's statement. The Common Serjeant refused to accept into evidence Bellelli's rebuttal to Malatesta – which Bellelli denied having written. Spizzuoco and Antibando testified that Bellelli told them Malatesta was a spy for the Turkish government. Defendi, Gualducci, Tombolesi and Rossi denied that Bellelli was a bookseller; all of them admitted to having been Bellelli's friends. Ludovico Brida and Giovanni Moroni, to whom Bellelli claimed to have sold books for a large amount of money, corrected the purchase figure to a few shillings. The Russian anarchist Chaikovsky also testified in Malatesta's favour.

The jury found Malatesta's allegation against Bellelli to be unsubstantiated and found Malatesta guilty of criminal libel. At that point, in a contentious decision, the Common Serjeant allowed Inspector Powell of Special Branch to give evidence following delivery of the verdict.

> Prisoner has been known to the police as an Anarchist of a very dangerous type for a great number of years. He has been imprisoned in his own country and has been expelled from France. He has visited Egypt, Spain, France, Portugal, and, I believe, America, in the interests of Anarchy, and wherever he went there was a great deal of trouble. He is known as the leader of militant Anarchists in this country – in fact, in the world. Many of his former colleagues have passed through this court and had penal servitude for coining. Gardstein, one of the Houndsditch ... had been using prisoner's workshop, or working with him, for 12 months. A tube of oxygen that was used on that occasion was traced to prisoner, who stated that he had sold it to Gardstein. That is all that was known. He has never been in the hands of the police in this country, but on one occasion was fined for assaulting a school teacher who chastised his son at school ... I do not know much in his favour.[121]

Clearly, opinion in the courtroom was swayed by Powell's description of Malatesta as 'an anarchist of a very dangerous type' who had links with forgers and the police murderers of Houndsditch. Powell's pronouncements also prejudiced the sentence handed to Malatesta by the Common Serjeant:

> Three months' imprisonment; recommended for expulsion under the Aliens Act; ordered to pay costs of prosecutions.[122]

---

[121] Malatesta was fined 40 shillings for unjustifiable conduct: 'A boy of the Defendant's was playing in class and laughing loudly. He was called out to receive two strokes on the hand with a cane, but he put his hand in his pocket and refused to hold it out. Complainant tried to flick the boy's hand, and in doing so the cane grazed his cheek. Later in the day the Defendant came, and forcing his way into the school-room struck the Complainant in the face and hit him about the body before all the boys'. 'Police Intelligence', *The Standard*, 10 October 1896.

[122] Central Criminal Court, Minutes of Evidence: 1911–1912, pp. 209–14. NA, CRIM 10/102.

1912

WHY WE DEMAND MALATESTA'S RELEASE

Because the trial ought never to have taken place.

Because the "libel" was a challenge to an accuser to prove his accusation that Errico Malatesta was a Turkish spy.

Because Malatesta proved that the man Bellelli was the aggressor and was the first to circulate a scandalous untruth against him.

Because the alleged "libel" was not malicious and was simply the challenge of an honest man to submit the question to a court of honour.

Because Malatesta produced overwhelming evidence at the trial in contradiction of that given by the prosecutor.

Because the display of bias by the Common Sergeant was so great, both in the conduct of the trial and his summing up.

Because a great quantity of evidence which Malatesta was prepared to produce to prove the truth of his assertion was disallowed by the Common Sergeant.

Because it is in the public interest to *clear up* charges of spying in political and social movements, as so many detestable crimes have been committed by that class of persons in all European countries.

Because statements made by Bellelli as to his opinions, his attainments and his business are alleged to be untrue by many creditable witnesses.

Because the statements made by a political detective in the witness box, after the prosecution and defence were closed, were false, and most reckless assertions were made by him which prejudiced the case against Malatesta.

Because the connection of this political detective with the case has not been fully explained.

Because the appearance of this political detective in the box was totally unjustifiable when no crime against the State or society had been alleged in the charge—which was a personal dispute arising out of the agitation Malatesta carried on against the infamous war in Tripoli.

Because the prosecution and imprisonment of Malatesta appears very like vindictive action on the side of the Italian Government.

Because the conscience of the people of Great Britain and Ireland condemns the Tripolitan outrage perpetrated by the Italian Government, and would honour and not condemn a man who, like Malatesta, opposes it.

Because the political police in this country have for years past worked in collusion with those of continental despotisms, and because the tyrannical treatment of people in other lands is being extended to this country.

Because the cause of Malatesta's imprisonment is *worse* than the case of Miss Malecka, inasmuch Russia makes no pretence to political freedom.

Because it is a double infamy for a judge or police officers to use a man's opinions on public questions against him in what was a private affair.

The recent prosecutions of Tom Mann, Guy Bowman, Fred Crowsley and many others, beside the general effort to curtail the freedom of the people, are indications of a far more dangerous attempt to crush the growing movement of the British workers to secure social redress and emancipation.

Therefore join also in the demand for the release of Frederick Crowsley, condemned to four months imprisonment at Hants Assizes on June 18th, for distributing leaflets appealing to men of the working class in the army not to shoot their brothers, fathers and comrades when on strike against low wages, and bad and tyrannical conditions of employment.

A PROTEST MEETING
WILL BE HELD IN
TRAFALGAR SQUARE
On Sunday, June 30th, at 4 p.m.

Speakers will be announced in the "Daily Herald."

Leaflet issued by the Malatesta's Release committee in 1912.
(IISH, Nettlau archive, b. 304)

The Common Serjeant's decision to brand Malatesta an undesirable alien and recommend him for expulsion at the expiration of his sentence aroused broad indignation. Articles against the punishment appeared in several newspapers, including Conservative ones.[123] Malatesta's sentence was seen as an attack on the tradition of political asylum, an attempt 'to repudiate a principle to which all Liberals and most Conservatives are sincerely devoted'.[124]

[123] Articles were published on the *Manchester Guardian*, the *Nation*, the *Daily Herald*, the *Star*, the *Daily News*, and the *Leader*.

[124] 'The case of Malatesta', *Manchester Guardian*, 25 May 1912, p. 8.

The Russian exile Kropotkin defended Malatesta in a letter to the *Nation* in which he argued that Malatesta's case must be considered in its political aspect. The *challenge*, an appeal to comrades' judgement, such as that addressed to Bellelli by Malatesta, was a defence against the system of agents-provocateurs that had 'lately taken an immense development'. Malatesta's conviction for libel was dangerous because it rendered impossible any appeal to a jury of honour.[125]

A Malatesta Release Committee was immediately established. Initially, Jack Tanner was secretary and treasurer, but he was quickly replaced by Guy Aldred. The committee's official address was Recchioni's shop at 37 Old Compton Street. A protest campaign was launched to oppose the sentence and prevent the deportation order:

> Malatesta is the victim of the despicable international secret police who wish to destroy the RIGHT OF ASYLUM for political refugees which has hitherto been the glory of Britain. Their victory would be our dishonour. If this plot to deliver Malatesta into the hands of the Italian Government were successful, it would also strenghten [*sic.*] the hands of the enemies of freedom in this country.[126]

Over the following weeks the Committee distributed 120,000 leaflets and 100,000 postcards to be sent to the Home Secretary. Rallies were held in Finsbury Park, Peckham Rye and Regent's Park 'for arousing public interest in the dark and low-down tricks of continental political police agents'.[127] A massive meeting was held on 9 June, the day before Malatesta's appeal hearing. According to *The Anarchist* at least 15,000 people joined the demonstration. Four processions with bands and banners convened on Trafalgar Square from Highbury, Mile End, Hammersmith and Harlesden. A large number of trade unions and labour organisations participated: dockers, tailors, gas workers, railwaymen, shop assistants, iron and tin-plate workers, etc. Independent Labour Party and the British Socialist Party banners mingled with those of the anarchist groups. Speakers included James MacDonald, secretary of the London Trades Council, Guy Bowman, editor of *The Syndicalist;* the Italo-Scottish anarchist James Tochatti, Guy Aldred, and Tom Mann.

---

[125] Peter Kropotkin, 'The case of Malatesta', *The Nation*, 8 June 1912, pp. 366–68. In 1908, Kropotkin participated in the jury of honour that dealt with the case of Evno Azef, the chief of the Russian combat organisation of the Social Revolutionaries. See: George Woodcock, Ivan Avakumović, *The Anarchist Prince. A biographical study of Peter Kropotkin* (New York: Schocken, 1971), pp. 371–72.

[126] 'An Appeal to the Men and Women of London', Malatesta Release Committee, IISH, Nettlau archive, b. 304.

[127] 'The Malatesta Release Committee', *The Anarchist*, 7 June 1912, p. 3.

The mobilisation demonstrated the deep esteem in which Malatesta was held, especially among the people of Islington – the area where he lived. Thousands signed the petition in his support.[128]

> Islington knows little and cares less about Malatesta's "philosophical anarchism". It only knows him as one who will give his last copper to the man who needs it, and who for more than twenty years has worked there, teaching useful trade to boys who would have drifted into hooliganism.[129]

The Malatesta campaign stimulated the anarchist movement in London. Corio reported in *La Cronaca Sovversiva* that it had been years since London had seen such anarchist propaganda.[130] Demonstrations were also held in France; the anarchist newspaper *Les Temps Nouveaux* organised a successful meeting in Paris where 'there was an overflow that would have filled the hall twice over'.[131] The main speakers were Charles Malato, M. Yvetot and Dr Pierro. Some £200 was collected for Malatesta. A large open-air meeting also took place in Glasgow on 16 June.

On 10 June, Malatesta's appeal was heard before the Lord Chief Justice, Mr Justice Darling, and Mr Justice Avory. During the hearing Malatesta 'lent his bushy iron grey beard upon his white arm and gazed about the court with keen, penetrating eyes. Throughout the hearing he took apparently a deep interest in the proceeding'.[132] The appeal was rejected. The reasons for refusing the appeal, apart from the legal questions, demonstrated the judges' view of the Italian colony:

> He wrote and published in Italian, the native language of a number of people living together as a colony in this country, among them many anarchists ... it held up Bellilli [*sic*.] to the hatred of this society, a society of a very peculiar character. If a man in such a society was to be convicted of being a police spy ... it followed that that man would be, in a society like that, in a very dangerous position ... The Common Serjeant had made perfectly plain that he did not recommended that Malatesta should be deported as an undesirable alien simply because he was an Anarchist ... His deportation was recommended on the ground that Bel[elli] being an anarchist, and being accused by Malatesta of being an Italian spy, the accusation was a danger to Bel[elli]. It was probable that in consequence of the libel some crime would be committed, and it was not going too far to say that some assassination might take place and that crime would be

128 Levy, 'Malatesta in exile', p. 267.
129 'Malatesta's fate', *The Anarchist*, 31 May 1912, p. 2.
130 Silvio Corio, 'Per Errico Malatesta', *La Cronaca Sovversiva*, 10 August 1912.
131 'The Malatesta case. Protest meeting in Paris', *Manchester Guardian*, 7 June 1912, p. 17.
132 'Malatesta's appeal. Revocation of deportation order refused', *Manchester Guardian*, 11 June 1912, p. 4.

produced in this country. The Court, having taken in consideration all the circumstances, could therefore see no reason for revoking that part of the sentence relating to the deportation of Malatesta.[133]

The *Manchester Guardian* underlined the contradictions in the judges' assessment, and called on the Home Secretary to reverse the decision.[134]

On 18 June Home Secretary Reginald McKenna announced to the House of Commons that he: 'had decided not to make an expulsion order against Malatesta but he saw no reasons to advise the remission of the sentence of imprisonment'.[135] As a result of the pressure of the campaign and the mass demonstrations, Malatesta was allowed to stay in England.

The trial put an end to Bellelli's career as a spy. Malatesta's allegations had been sound: Bellelli was born in the village of Novellara, near Reggio Emilia, on 15 May 1860.[136] The intermediary between Giolitti and Bellelli – and Dante in Paris – was the police superintendent (*questore*) Vincenzo Neri. Neri had much experience in dealing with spies. While still a police inspector in Florence he had approached Domanico, the noted anarchist police spy, and put him in contact with the Ministry of the Interior in 1892.[137] During that period, Bellelli was emerging as one of the leaders of Bologna's anarchist movement. Although possible that he was already a secret agent, it is more probable to surmise that Bellelli's career as a spy began with Neri's appointment in Bologna in April 1896.[138] In September 1897, Bellelli was sentenced to two years' imprisonment for libel, but in May the following year, he was suddenly released, in a decision that completely surprised Bologna's prefect. Bellelli was pardoned as a result of a senator's intervention. It is highly possible that Neri contacted Bellelli while the latter was in prison and organised his release in exchange for his services as a spy. In mid-1900 Bellelli moved to Paris and subsequently expelled in September 1901 when the Tsar visited France.

This example demonstrates the relevance of the international information network among the anarchists. Apparently, serious suspicions against Bellelli were aroused by the solicitations of the anarchist Siegfried Nacht who had applied for a position at the International Institute of Agriculture in Rome. The position had been offered to him on condition that he break all contact

---

[133] 'Malatesta's appeal. Revocation of deportation order refused', *Manchester Guardian*, 11 June 1912, p. 4.

[134] 'Political offenders and their sentences', *Manchester Guardian*, 11 June 1912, p. 6.

[135] *Manchester Guardian*, 18 June 1912, p. 11.

[136] Berti, *Errico Malatesta*, pp. 333–49.

[137] Natale Musarra, 'Le confidenze di "Francesco" G. Domanico', p. 49.

[138] Although he took office only in September of the following year. Bellelli's biographical record 27 June 1894. ACS, *CPC*, b. 440, f. (Bellelli Ennio Enrico).

The spy Bellelli (at the centre standing back)
with Enrico Defendi (standing on the left),
Luigia Defendi (at the centre with the child),
Giulio Rossi (sitting on the right).
(ACS, *CPC*, b. 440, f. Bellelli Ennio)

with the anarchists. From Rome, Nacht sent 45 *lire* to Giovanni Spizzuoco,
Alfonso's brother, to clear an old debt. Some time later, Nacht was questioned
at the Ministry of the Interior about this transfer of funds and was rebuked
for continuing to maintain contact with anarchists. As a result, Nacht urged
his comrades in London to investigate the leak. Spizzuoco claimed the only
person acquainted with the transaction was Bellelli, who had exchanged the
lire for sterling. Moreover, Vezzani reported from Paris that, according to
Bellelli's sister-in-law, Bellelli received monthly registered letters from the
Ministry of the Interior.

After Malatesta's trial, Bellelli returned to Reggio Emilia where he died in
1926. With Bellelli's departure, *Virgilio* disappeared as well. Bellelli was the
person who, for twelve years, had signed his reports with that cover name.
Because of his direct contact with the Ministry of the Interior through Neri,
there are no traces of Virgilio's real identity in the correspondence between
the Ministry and the embassy or the consulate. However, it has been possible
to verify that Bellelli and Virgilio were the same person: in 1901, spy 'X.Y.' in
Paris informed the Italian embassy that Bellelli had put up an anarchist who
had recently arrived from America on his way home to Italy. Two days later,
a note from the Ministry of the Interior informed Neri that 'Virgilio gave

hospitality in Paris to a comrade from America ... it would be of interest to know the identity of that individual'.[139]

Italian anarchists and the British police

The surveillance of foreign political refugees often put British authorities in a quandary. On the one hand, they faced strong pressure from foreign governments that expected co-operation in the surveillance and suppression of anarchism. On the other hand, they had to be loyal to the principles of asylum and individual freedom deeply rooted in British society.[140] This contradiction was evident at the International Conference against Anarchism held in Rome in 1898, when British delegates opposed almost all the proposals advanced by the conference.[141] However, in a standard defence against criticism of Britain's limited co-operation, the former Director of Criminal Investigations at Scotland Yard, Howard Vincent, stated it was,

> in great measure an erroneous idea ... our laws on the subject of Anarchical propaganda are undoubtedly the best in Europe ... our law forbids the advocacy of crime, even if it is to be committed outside the United Kingdom.[142]

In the same interview, Sir Howard rebuffed criticisms that it was impossible for foreign governments to secure the extradition of anarchists from Britain.

Nevertheless, this did not prevent British authorities from acting. The surveillance and containment of the anarchists' activities in Britain was the main duty of Special Branch. Under Inspector William Melville's leadership during the 1890s Special Branch changed 'quite radically ... the Branch appears to have become more dedicated to the suppression of anarchism as a doctrine, as well as its terrorist offshoots, than it had before'.[143] Surveillance of anarchists was carried out within existing law, although 'sometimes that law had to be stretched a little'.[144] The Victorian spirit of liberalism was weakening, and surveillance of foreign refugees could be unscrupulous. The

---

[139] Minister of the Interior to Questore Neri, 18 September 1901, ACS, *CPC*, f. 440 (Bellelli Ennio Enrico).

[140] Bernard Porter, *The Origins of the Vigilant State* (London: Weidenfeld & Nicolson, 1987), pp. 98–114.

[141] On the conference see: Richard Bach Jensen, 'The International Anti-Anarchist Conference of 1898 and the Origins of Interpol', *Journal of Contemporary History*, 16.2 (1981), pp. 323–47.

[142] 'How to deal with anarchists. An interview with Sir Howard Vincent', *Daily Graphic*, 11 August 1900.

[143] Porter, *The Origins*, p. 142.

[144] *Porter, The Origins*, p. 115.

Walsall case, the plot organised by Melville's agent provocateur, Coulon, is the clearest example of such tactics.

Sir Howard made several attempts to keep Malatesta under surveillance, notwithstanding 'official' claims that this was impossible. These attempts went beyond a request to the Italian consulate for permission to arrest the leader of Italian anarchism. In 1882, Sir Howard rented the flat next to Malatesta's lodging in Frith Street in order to spy on the anarchist leader through chinks in the wooden partition wall. Nevertheless, to the disappointment of the Italian ambassador, Malatesta left his lodgings abruptly a couple of days before Vincent's scheme became operational. The police found only cabinet-maker's tools left behind in the abandoned room.[145] Sir Howard had also previously asked the Metropolitan Board of Works to search the lodgings of Malatesta, Cafiero and Ceccarelli, believing them to be handling explosive materials. In this way, Sir Howard intended to be able to examine their papers.[146]

As a general rule, the police in Britain were forbidden to work on political refugee cases directly with foreign police. Co-operation with foreign police forces had to pass through diplomatic channels. Requests for information were made by the Italian embassy to the Foreign Office. For example, following Merlino and Malatesta's arrest in Italy in 1891, the embassy received information on the two anarchists, in particular regarding their last address in London. However, Italian authorities seldom received information directly from the Metropolitan Police.[147]

Nevertheless, there is clear archival evidence that the police in London did freelance work for the Italian authorities. Tornielli was clear in this regard. In 1882, the police officers that arrested the anarchist Pietro Bianchi visited the embassy asking for a financial reward, a common practice. Tornielli proposed a premium of 5 *lire* to be paid in sterling. He also underlined that 'the venality of English policemen must be taken into consideration by those who need them' and suggested funds be allocated to compensate English policemen for significant arrests as an incentive to collaboration, which in the past he considered to be 'lacking and inadequate'.[148]

In 1882 the Inspector of the Central Criminal Police, Charles von Tornow, proposed his offices to the Italian consul for surveillance of Malatesta.

---

[145] Minister of Foreign Affairs to Minister of the Interior, 10 April 1882, Asdmae, *Pol. Int.*, b. 13.

[146] Ambassador Menabrea to Foreign Minister, 1 April 1881, Asdmae, *Pol. Int.*, b. 5, f. (1880–1881).

[147] An exception was the note regarding Malatesta and Consorti's move to Italy with the intent to foment disturbances on the 1 May 1891. Ambassador Tornielli to Minister of Foreign Affairs Rudinì, 29 April 1891, Asdmae, *Pol. Int.*, b. 39, f. (1891).

[148] Tornielli to Foreign Ministry, 20 January 1892, Asdmae, *Pol. Int.*, b. 39, (f. 1892).

He provided the consul with a report from which the latter could judge that Malatesta 'has been followed step by step and he is watched with the greatest attention'. The consul proposed to reward Inspector von Tornow, 'one of the best inspectors in London' and, from time to time, to encourage his zeal with minor amounts of money'.[149] On 1 May 1882 the Minister of the Interior, expressing his great satisfaction, authorised the embassy to award the inspector with £40 and von Tornow spied on Malatesta over subsequent months.[150] The consul put von Tornow in contact with the embassy's secret agent Amede, alias Luigi Bianchi. The consul's enquiry about Amede's discharge shows the strict collaboration established between the inspector and the Italian consulate. Melville's collaboration with the Okhrana, the Russian secret police, few years later, can therefore be placed within a broader pattern of British police behaviour.

Conclusions

A study of the system organised outside Italy to watch the anarchists is essential in understanding the phenomenon of the anarchist diaspora. However, comprehensive research of the intelligence service organised by Italian ambassadors and consuls in countries where anarchist exiles found refuge remains to be carried out. The impact of exile on the development of the anarchist movement in Italy is revealed by the level of efficiency reached in the control and restraint of the activities of anarchist expatriates.

Much of the archival evidence concerning anarchists in London (as well as in other colonies around the world) comes from spies who infiltrated their groups and from police sources. Knowledge of the system through which this information was collected and elaborated is therefore essential, as this documentary evidence raises the pressing question of its historical reliability.[151] Spies were undoubtedly subjected to a *déformation professionnelle*; for an informer 'nothing can be quite what it seems … he will scent daggers – or pretend to scent daggers – where there are kitchen knives and spoons'.[152] Moreover, it is likely that, for their own 'financial convenience', informers tended to exaggerate when they were not completely inventing information, taking advantage of the fact that the Italian authorities overestimated the

---

[149] Italian embassy to Foreign Ministry, 19 April 1882, Asdmae, *Pol. Int.*, b. 4, f. (1882).

[150] Foreign Ministry to the Italian ambassador, 1 May 1882, Asdmae, *Pol. Int.*, b. 4.

[151] Mimmo Franzinelli, 'Sull' uso (critico) delle fonti di polizia', in Voci di Compagni Schede di Questura considerazioni sull'uso delle fonti orali e delle fonti di polizia per la storia dell'anarchismo, *Quaderni del Centro Studi Libertari Archivio Pinelli* (Milan: 2002), pp. 19–30.

[152] Richard C. Cobb, *The Police and the People. French Popular Protest 1789–1820* (Oxford: Clarendon, 1970), p. 7.

real danger represented by anarchists abroad. If spies twisted reality or stressed some aspects rather than others to earn their keep, this tells us what the authorities 'wanted' to hear or know, thus exposing their major fears. So Calvo would emphasise threats to the Italian royal family and plots against the Italian government, reporting outbursts that probably occurred quite frequently in anarchist circles, reserving his most lurid accounts for periods when he was negotiating a 'pay rise'. Nevertheless, due to these informers, the Italian authorities had fairly accurate knowledge of some aspects of anarchist activity and movements in London. Moreover, they were alerted in advance about forthcoming anarchist publications and were able to seize them at the post offices.

The organisation of an intelligence service that monitored the activities of Italian anarchists residing in foreign countries was strictly linked to diplomatic issues. The allegedly inadequate collaboration received from foreign police forces, a point which Italian diplomats frequently complained of, was one of the main reasons for the settlement of the 'International police'. However, the use of informers and spies sometimes had embarrassing consequences: Gennaro Rubino was a case in point for both Italian and British authorities.

On a diplomatic level, differing perceptions of the danger represented by anarchist expatriates often led to disagreements – all of which emerged at the International Anti-anarchist Conference held in Rome in 1898. However, the complaints made by the Italian government that the anarchists in London could carry on their activities almost undisturbed were not true. As the cases of Inspectors von Tornow, George Hepburn Greenham, Howard Vincent, and Inspector Powell show, there was sometimes direct involvement in the surveillance of foreign political refugees by the British police.

6

Politics and Sociability: the Anarchist Clubs

Sociability was a main factor in the birth of socialism in Italy. In Italian villages *osterie* (pubs or taverns) were centres of republican and socialist conspiracies before and after unification; *osterie* opposed the *campanili* (bell towers) as symbols of clericalism and reaction.[1] For Italian exiles in England, that background intersected with the longstanding local tradition of political clubs, and of radical discussion groups in free houses and cafés.[2] The anarchist refugees in England and in other centres of the political diaspora developed – like the *sovversivi* in the United States – 'an extensive and elaborate social infrastructure that contributed to produce a distinctive subculture and community'.[3]

Refugees' living conditions were generally very difficult. In the descriptions and memoirs of their lives in London, it is possible to note similarities, from the depressing weather and the poor quality of the food to the unfriendly temperament of the English people, whom Malatesta described as 'perhaps the most xenophobic in the world'.[4] In this adverse environment, refugees spent their social life with their fellow countrymen and political comrades. For the exiles, as Rudolf Rocker remembered, 'the social life at that period

---

[1] See: Maurizio Ridolfi, *Il circolo virtuoso. Sociabilità democratica, associazionismo e rappresentanza politica nell'Ottocento* (Florence: Centro editoriale toscano, 1992); B. Bottignolo, *Without a Bell Tower. A Study of the Italian Immigrants in South West England* (Rome: Centro Studi Emigrazione, 1985); Ian McCalman, *Radical Underworld: Prophets, Revolutionaries, and Pornographers in London, 1795–1840* (Oxford: Clarendon Press, 1988); David Worrall, *Radical Culture: Discourse, Resistance and Surveillance, 1790–1820* (New York; London: Harvester Wheatsheaf, 1992).

[2] See: S. Shipley, *Club Life and Socialism in Mid Victorian London* (London: Journeyman/London Workshop Centre, 1983).

[3] Bencivenni, *Italian Immigrant Radical Culture*, p. 50.

[4] Errico Malatesta, 'Scarfoglio', *Umanità Nova*, no. 140, 23 September 1920.

depended entirely on the clubs'.[5] Thus, political refugees used to assemble in national and political groups which met in regular restaurants, public houses or clubs. In these centres, they could organise forms of mutual aid and were able to maintain their usual social lives in a foreign context, strengthen the cohesion of the community, and hold their endless political discussions.[6] In the 1870s, when the first groups of Internationalists found refuge in London, numerous small clubs and working class organisations were active around Clerkenwell and cosmopolitan Soho, and these were intertwined with the growing colony of political refugees from all over Europe.[7]

> 'The main artery of the political refugees' quarter in London runs in a straight line from Fitzroy Square, to the base of Ryder's Court, Leicester Square. But there are places of interest in the lateral streets, notably in Old Compton Street. Almost every shop bears a foreign name over the door, and many of the occupants have wonderful stories to relate concerning the adventures and dangers from which they have escaped by establishing themselves in London'.[8]

The major gatherings of Italian refugees took place in Greek Street, which, in the early 1870s, was the site of one of the most famous Italian pubs and meeting point for republican refugees:

> Bendi, the Garibaldian public-house-keeper, [...] had two bars, one for the ordinary English customers, while the other was frequented almost exclusively by foreigners, the great number being Italians. This bar led to a little inner room where private conversation could be held in which Bendi himself often joined, leaving his wife to serve the ordinary customers, with instructions accidentally to drop a pewter pot on the floor if among these she noticed a foreign political spy.[9]

On the corner between Greek Street and Old Compton Street there were:

> two celebrated little hotels. The first, distinguished by a couple of bow windows on the street level, was the Albergo de Venezia. This place used to be frequented by one of Mazzini's confidential secretaries, and for many years was a popular rendezvous for the Italian revolutionists. Many an anathema has been hurled at the Pope and even against the burly head

⁵ Rudolf Rocker, *The London Years* (London: Robert Anscombe, 1956), p. 67.

⁶ Enrico Verdecchia, 'Tedeschi e italiani: rapporti e contrasti tra due comunità nell'esilio londinese', *Bollettino della Domus Mazziniana*, 2, 1996, p. 178.

⁷ On Soho see: J. R. Walkowitz, *Nights Out: Life in Cosmopolitan London* (New Haven, Conn. ; London: Yale University Press, 2012).

⁸ Adolphe Smith, 'Political Refugees', in Sir Walter Besant, *London in the Nineteenth Century* (London: Adam & Charles Black, 1909), p. 404.

⁹ Smith, 'Political Refugees', p. 404.

of Victor Emanuel from this place, and preparations made to support the raids organised by Garibaldi.[10]

This hotel was presumably the *Albergo Bella Venezia* where Italian anarchists used to meet during the 1890s, as was often mentioned by Italian agents in reports to the embassy.

Clubs represented a vital support for refugees who landed in London after long and exhausting journeys, effectively described by Rossetti in the case of a group of Italians:

On entering the office of the *Tocsin* I found that here, too, something unusual was going on. A perfect Babel of voices from the room above greeted my ear, while the printing-room was bedecked with a most unsightly litter of tattered garments of nondescript shape and purpose laid out to dry. I was not surprised at this, however, as I had long grown used to unannounced invasions. [...] But on reaching the composing-room on this particular morning an extraordinary sight presented itself. Accustomed as I was to the unaccustomed, I was scarcely prepared for the wild confusion of the scene. What at first sight appeared to be a surging mass of unwashed and unkempt humanity filled it with their persons, their voices, and their gestures. No number of Englishmen, however considerable, could have created such a din. All present were speaking simultaneously at the top of their voices; greetings and embraces mingled with tales of adventure and woe. The first object which I managed to distinguish was the figure of Giannoli struggling feebly in the embrace of a tall brawny, one-eyed man with thick curling black hair, who appeared to be in a state of demi-déshabille. [...] Bonafede and Gnecco were there; they, too, surrounded by the invading mob, exchanging greetings and experiences. [...] Two cloddish-looking *contadini* stood gazing at him, rapt in awe. [...] The others were quite new to me. They were evidently all of them Italians – some ten or twelve in number – though at the first glance, scattered as they were pell-mell among the printing plant of the overcrowded work-room, they gave an impression of much greater number. They appeared mostly to belong to the working-classes. Their clothes, or what remained of them, were woefully tattered – and they were few and rudimentary indeed, for most of what had been spared by the hazards of travel were drying down below. Their hair was uncut, and beards of several days' growth ornamented their cheeks. Their hats were of incredible size and shape and all the colours of the rainbow seemed to be reproduced in them. Littered around on diverse objects of furniture, they suggested to me a strange growth of fungi.[11]

The Kabv (German Communist Workers' Educational Society) founded

---

[10] Smith, 'Political Refugees', p. 404.

[11] Isabel Meredith, *A Girl Among the Anarchists* (London: Duckworth & Co, 1903), pp. 117–19.

in 1840, contributed to the relief of the French refugees who escaped to England following the fall of the Paris Commune.[12]

In July 1878 the Kabv moved its premises to 6 Rose Street, now Manette Street, in Soho. Apart from German, the Kabv had five other language sections: Italian, French, Polish, Russian and English. The club was flooded by refugees after the passage of the Anti-Socialist Laws in Germany – among them was Johann Most, who moved the printing press of his newspaper *Freiheit* to the club premises.[13] Frank Kitz remembered that, because of the repression:

> Thousands were expatriates, hundreds of families broken up, hundreds imprisoned; [...] a great number sought refuge in London and our club in Rose Street presented at times the appearance of an arrival or departure platform at a station with luggage and cases of prohibited literature and bewildered emigrants going to and fro.[14]

It was at the clubs that refugees received first aid from their comrades, hospitality, some food, and precious advice. These clubs and restaurants organised a network of mutual aid primarily to meet the needs of the poorest, for example providing low-cost dinners as took place from 1846 at the *Hotel des Bons Amis* for French refugees:

> A French dinner soup, two courses, salad, dessert, half a bottle of wine and a demi-tasse of black coffee, could be obtained for the modest sum of eighteen pence all included, and, as the cooking was absolutely French, and hours might elapse without a word of English being heard in the establishment, the exile felt himself at home again, and this without too great a strain upon his slender purse.[15]

Or at Bendi's public house:

> on the first floor there was a large room, and here the Communist Refugees' Society used to meet. This was a non-political association of politicians formed as to help those who in their exiled life had no means of subsistence. The more fortunate refugees, who were able to earn their living, subscribed to help their brothers-in-arms. Sometimes help was obtained from charitable or sympathising outsiders. Many

---

[12] Christine C. Lattek, *Revolutionary Refugees: German Socialism in Britain, 1840–1860* (London: Routledge, 2006), p. 226.

[13] Most was arrested and imprisoned in 1881 for publishing an article applauding the assassination of Tsar Alexander II in the *Freiheit* and for incitement to murder. See: Bernard Porter, 'The *Freiheit* Prosecutions, 1881–1882', *The Historical Journal*, 23, 4, (1980), pp. 833–56.

[14] Frank Kitz, Freedom, 1897, in J. Quail, *The Slow Burning Fuse*, pp. 10–11.

[15] Smith, 'Political Refugees', p. 404.

a despairing communist was saved from literal starvation by the numerous two penny meals which this one donation provided, for this was the society which had organised the refugee's soup-kitchen off Newman Street.[16]

However, as persecution on the continent increased, the consequent overflow of expatriates brought conditions in the clubs to the edge. The French anarchist Malato recalled the efforts that were made at the *Autonomie Club* in order to shelter the wave of refugees escaping from France in 1892:

> They settled down and organised themselves as best they could. The tiny rooms at the club *Autonomie* were transformed into a dormitory, a social kitty was established by and for the most indigent; although it was sustained as much as possible by voluntary donations, it was empty more often than not. The idea was worth something, but life in this small anarchist republic was so harsh that those who composed it had only one desire: to leave.[17]

Clubs were essential instruments of organisation, but they accomplished other functions as well. From the 1870s, anarchist clubs bolstered both the creation of a network between refugees of different nationalities and the establishment of links with British radicalism; they were 'an important feature of the organisation of the party in London'.[18]

By providing the principal meeting points for the Babel of anarchists who lived in the capital, they facilitated socialising between the many different national anarchist groups. In 1891, *Freedom* reported enthusiastically on the outcome of a social evening:

> More than a hundred comrades assembled on the evening of March 28th in the tipper chamber of a City coffee tavern, to enjoy the pleasure of each other's society, to renew old friendships and form new ones, to gain inspiration, in an interchange of opinion and in comradeship, for the work lying before us. A glance round the large room, with its pleasant little tea tables, each brightened by the music of friendly talk, showed Germans and Frenchmen from the Autonomie in conversation with Englishmen from the provinces, Jewish Comrades from Berner Street, laughing and talking with members of the Italian group, the Editor of the Herald of Anarchy in amicable discussion with one of the *Freedom* staff, friends from Hammersmith Socialist Society, the London Socialist League, the

---

16   Smith, 'Political Refugees', p. 405.
17   Malato, *Les Joyeusetés*, pp. 45–46.
18   Ralph Derechef, 'Anarchism in England', in Félix Dubois, *The Anarchist Peril* (London: Unwin, 1894), p. 269.

Individualist Anarchist League, all cordially mingling with Anarchist Communists from every group in London.[19]

The *Autonomie Club* was well known in the 1880s and early 1890s. It was 'a very small place, just two rooms',[20] 'composed of a long and narrow room (hall), a small canteen and two or three tiny rooms on the first floor'.[21] The club, located in Charlotte Street, was founded in 1886 by the German anarchist Peukert after his expulsion from another club in Whitfield Street by Victor Dave, a member of the Socialist League. Later the *Autonomie Club* moved to 6 Windmill Street, off Tottenham Court Road. The *Autonomie* was the key meeting point for the international colony of anarchists in London, although it was frequented by the individualists in particular. Among its regulars were Parmeggiani and the members of *La Libera Iniziativa*. The press and the police believed the *Autonomie* to be the centre of all the anarchist conspiracies and outrages committed in Europe. As Malato pointed out:

> Newspapers on the lookout for sensational information, [...] transformed this modest local [...] into a den of social revolution. Reporters short of copy and happy to take advantage of the terror of the bourgeoisie, claimed that all the deadly resolutions and all the plots fated to explode on the continent were planned there; and that dynamite, chlorate potash, nitro-benzene, the rack-a-rock and the green powder were manufactured there as well.[22]

The *Autonomie* was raided by the police twice: the first time in 1892, during investigations related to the arrest of the Walsall anarchists, the second time two years later, following the explosion that killed the anarchist Martial Bourdin in Greenwich Park in February. Shortly after the raid the premises of the club were mysteriously burned down, signalling the end of the *Autonomie Club*.

Belief that the anarchist clubs in London were hotbeds of international anarchist conspiracies was broadly shared by public opinion, particularly at the end of the nineteenth century. Sernicoli, the police inspector who monitored the Italian anarchist colony in Paris, considered London clubs to be the source of most of the inflammatory publications circulating throughout Europe. From his point of view, meetings at the clubs were used as clearing houses for the promotion of the pet manifestos of anarchists. At these meetings, supporters and the means to publish and distribute political

---

[19] 'Our Social Evening', *Freedom*, V, 53, April 1891.
[20] Rocker, *The London Years*, p. 67.
[21] Malato, *Les Joyeusetés*, pp. 99–100.
[22] Malato, *Les Joyeusetés*, pp. 99–100.

statements throughout Europe and the globe could be found: 'thus, the idea elaborated in a London club, in just a few days circulates throughout all Europe and the World'.[23] Moreover, according to Sernicoli, anarchists from all European countries met in these clubs and debated the most efficient techniques and strategies for committing terrorist outrages. They allegedly discussed:

> If it is preferable to use bombs or daggers, if it is better to murder some peaceful bourgeois in a café or in a restaurant, or to deal the blows against the most prominent men of every country.[24]

In 1892, the magazine *Tit Bits* published the report of a visit supposedly made by one of its contributors to an anarchist headquarters in a London suburb. The article recounted a speech given by an anarchist recently arrived from Paris, who did not look like 'the accepted portrait of a blustering political agitator', exhorting members to commit atrocities and violence. On the contrary, it was possible to perceive from his manners and language that he was a well-educated Frenchman 'accustomed to good society'. In his talk, the speaker stated that:

> the branches of the society in all the principal cities of Europe possessed members residing, either as occupiers or servants of occupiers, near the chief buildings, and they could obtain on immediate notice delicately manufactured instruments which would obliterate from the face of this world the offices of government, as well as their occupants. These machines were made on a most ingenious plan devised by a prominent member, and were so constructed that they could be set to explode at any given time, thus allowing those implicated in the plot to escape from the country.[25]

Allegedly the speech was so absorbing that it produced a 'deadly quiet' amongst the audience – not a whisper or a sound had been heard.

In 1892, the *Morning Post* alarmed its readers about anarchist terrorists from France:

> our country is bombarded by four hundred *desperados*, thieves, forgers and murderers ... These wretches have decided to sneak on any pretext into the houses of the rich in London and the Kingdom and to chloroform them. After making them losing consciousness and applying a gag soaked in this evil material, they will ransack all their properties.[26]

---

23 Ettore Sernicoli, *L'Anarchia e gli Anarchici* (Milan: Treves, 1894), vol. 2, p. 176.

24 Sernicoli, *L'Anarchia e gli Anarchici*, vol. 2, p. 178.

25 'In An Anarchist Club', *Tit Bits*, 7 May 1892, p. 7.

26 Malato, *Les Joyeusetés* , p. 97.

Malato dismissed allegations that clubs were centres of explosives production Ironically, he considered:

> The tragic period being ended ... or interrupted – one never knows what the future holds – I am keen to declare that the only green powder was ever produced there was *la poudre d'escampette* (to take to one's heels).[27]

Clubs were the most visible sign of the colony of foreign anarchist refugees and, for this reason, the easiest source in the construction of the anarchist image. Newspapers and popular magazines nourished the view of anarchist clubs as centres of conspiracy by circulating gloomy descriptions of them. They often pictured entrances to these clubs as narrow, dim passages with security doors and watchmen.

> A ring at the side door of the shop before mentioned secures for anyone admittance into a long passage. The door is opened by means of a wire running from a second door a few yards along this passage. This wire is operated by a swarthy-looking janitor [...] This door-keeper knows by sight all the "admitted" members of the party in London, with not a few of the provincial ones as well, and he would not allow anyone pass the second door if he knew them to be strangers, unless they produce vouchers of their interest in the cause. This second door has rather a deceptive appearance, it does not look formidable, but it is for all that. It is covered with green baize, and has a small slide let into a panel through which the keeper can inspect anyone coming down the passage. The door would take some time to force were the keeper to drop an iron-heathed recess [*sic.*] the iron bar which swings on a pivot ready for emergency.[28]

According to *Tit Bits*, the club was equipped with a second entrance facing onto a back street that allowed members to enter the club unobserved via a labyrinth of quiet streets. The door also served as a means of escape in case of police raids.

Similar lines were written in the description of another alleged visit to an anarchist club in Soho many years later:

> No policeman could protect us where we are going, for it is one of the spots of London where the letter of the law is a dead letter, a spot which the arm of the law does not reach, and which, for obvious reasons, it avoids, as far as possible. We turn here sharply on the left where the houses in the alley-way almost come together. We are in a *cul-de-sac*, but there is a way through the wall at the end via the last house on the left-hand side. Take care that you do not strike that lintel. A few steps, and a door opens before us, our coming is expected. Otherwise we

---

[27] Malato, *Les Joyeusetés*, pp. 99–100.
[28] 'In An Anarchist Club', *Tit Bits*, 7 May 1892, p. 7.

should never have got as far as this, for the people of this part of Soho are as exclusive as any of the West-End "sets". Down this passage. The place is a regular rabbit warren, and dark as a wolf's throat. Now down this flight of steps. What a reek![29]

These and other images such as secret passages, mysterious meetings and passwords were fostered not only by the press but also by a large number of contemporary novels.[30]

Inside the clubs anarchists were thought to reveal their blood lust. At the beginning of the century, shortly after the failed attempt against King Leopold of Belgium by the Italian Gennaro Rubino, *Il Corriere della Sera* published an account of an event held at the Athenaeum Hall in Tottenham Court Road:

The curtain rises on the tiny stage, and the noise from people talking suddenly stops; a woman, unable to hush her crying baby, is forced to leave. The stage-manager [...] announces that an obliging English comrade [...] will play some piano pieces. The young musician steps forward: a black garment hangs straight down from her shoulders, like a priest's robe ... on the left, over her heart, there is a reddish patch. She sits, impassive, and plays various uninspiring pieces. Then, however, this young statue becomes emotional [...]. Her song starts by waxing tender over human suffering, and then scales the heights of hatred. The young woman emphatically promises kisses and happiness to her ideal lover, who will return to her side with pride after fighting society's prevailing injustices. [...] A short, stocky man, in worker's clothes, recites a poetic monologue of his own composition at the top of his voice. Addressed to the judiciary, this defends a worker who, driven by hunger, killed the first person he came across in order to feed his wife and children. At the appropriate moment, the speaker takes a dagger from his belt and forcefully re-enacts the crime, declaring himself ready to do the same again to all wealthy people on this earth. The crime is justified in faltering verses. One after another, in various languages and varying styles, the speakers repeat the same phrases and the same commonplaces. A blonde girl, six or seven years old, is the only one to offer something different. She recites a poem with a resounding line at the end of the chorus:

Onward, with the dagger ever onward!

The first time round, this little thing, pretty as a picture in her white dress with red ribbons, lifts her thin arm to act out the fearsome line. The

---

[29] C. Shaw, 'Among London Anarchists', *Penny Illustrated Paper*, 20 August 1910.
[30] Haia Shpayer-Makov, 'A Traitor to His Class: the Anarchist in British Fiction', *European Studies*, XXVI.3 (1996), pp. 299–325.

"He is not tuneful : but he is fervent ; and his rendering of 'Awake, ye men who toil ! Up, proletariat !' often leaves the piano some distance behind "
AMONG   THE   LONDON   ANARCHISTS :   A   CHANT   OF   LABOUR   ON   SUNDAY   EVENING
DRAWN FROM LIFE BY PAUL RENOUARD

'Among the London anarchists. A chant of Labour on Sunday evening'.
(*The Graphic*, 30 July 1892)

audience erupts. The girl flushes; next time, she tries for a different effect
and has an inspired idea: just as she raises her arm, she stamps her little
foot down. Applause breaks out with such enthusiasm that she rushes off
backstage.[31]

Another quite paradoxical myth about the anarchist clubs circulated at
the beginning of the century. In 1905 Frosali, the Italian embassy police

---

[31] 'Una serata presso gli anarchici', *Il Corriere della Sera*, 21–22 November 1902.

inspector, reported to the Minister of the Interior that, during his visits to England, King Umberto liked visiting London *incognito*. On one of these occasions, the King had called in at two anarchist clubs. Inspector Frosali had picked up this revelation from a short article published in the *Reynold's Newspaper* and carefully clipped a copy of the article to his report 'to avoid speculation that I am providing extravagant information'.[32] The source of this story was supposed to be an Irish anarchist. Three years later, Peter Latouche repeated it:

> The late King Humbert, [...] had on several occasions met and been on friendly terms with members of the violent section of Anarchists when sojourning *incognito* in London. His Majesty spoke English perfectly ... he had an amazing disregard of danger ... It was his delight to roam at will in all parts of our great Metropolis, dressed as an artisan ... In these excursions he was usually accompanied by an Irish gentleman who was at that time attached to the Turkish Embassy. It was impossible to appease his curiosity without a visit to the Anarchist Clubs ... King Humbert, with his Irish guide, visited the *Club Autonomie* on a Sunday evening, and listened to several of the comrades advocating the uprooting of governments, and the hastening on of the millennium of chaos. Here he was introduced to and shook hands with Louise Michel, with whom he had a long, interested and animated conversation [...] His experience of the *Club Autonomie* was uninteresting save for the meeting with Louise Michel, but his visit to the Anarchist Club in the Kingsland Road was exciting enough. While he was present, a "comrade" of the extremist type made a violent speech, advocating the removal of all crowned heads of Europe, and of his own in particular. King Humbert was hailed by the assembled Anarchists as a new "comrade" and as a souvenir of his visit and enthusiasm for the cause he was presented with a cartoon. This was a crude drawing depicting Anarchy freeing the workers, by blowing all the reigning monarchs and presidents in office throughout the world into space. The artist himself made the presentation, and in the handing the King the sheet, he said, pointing to what was intended for the head of the King of Italy detached from the body and flying like a cannon-ball towards the heavens: "*How like you are to that fellow!*". The King, with admirable *sang froid*, admitted the resemblance, and soon after left the club with his Irish guide and the Anarchist artist.[33]

Malatesta, who had been informed about the article in the *Reynold's Newspaper*, discounted these stories as fantasies.

Descriptions from contemporary newspapers and magazines provide specific information about women's participation in the clubs' activities. In

---

[32] Frosali's September report, London, 11 October 1905, *PS*, 1905, b. 22.
[33] Latouche, *Anarchy!* pp. 40–45.

contrast to the information kept in police records, in which women scarcely appeared, these articles make clear that women constituted the majority at the club evenings. However, moralising connotations pervade most of these descriptions. Authors repeatedly deprecated the immoral practices allegedly taking place at the clubs. Sernicoli, for example, quoted one account of an evening organised in an anarchist club that was circulated in French newspapers: 'Little by little the room filled up. Many women, but what kind of women! Shall we say females and let it go at that'.[34]

In his description of the Italian colony, Wilkins briefly mentioned the presence of women at an anarchist club:

Those who enter into the pseudo-club Italo Svizzero in the Italian quarter (where one shelling monthly membership gives the right to bring three women every evening) will quickly notice the total lack of Italian representatives of the weaker sex. English and Irish dancers, servants or mistresses of those vulgar Don Giovanni, bear the honor of dancing.[35]

In 1902, *Il Corriere della Sera* presented its readers with a more folkloric image of anarchist women:

The hall was full. Females were more or less in the majority. There were numerous lower-class women, legitimate wives and unmarried companions, talking about this and that, like neighbours at the market: girls with their hair in a mess, girls with passionate looks, girls with unkempt appearances, who were however not to be confused with the usual streetwalkers scattered around the British Museum area ... A young woman, whose accent and appearance betrayed her as being from the Italian South, was serving drinks, with a nursling in her left arm.[36]

The account given in the *Penny Illustrated Paper* was equally based on stereotypes:

'Bloody scenes are sometimes enacted in these haunts of the underworld, scenes which show how strong is the primitive blood-lust in mankind. It was in a cellar like this that I saw a fight with knives between two women, one an Italian, the other a French-woman, brought about by jealousy'.[37]

Another picturesque account of anarchist women was provided by Latouche: men affected sombrero hats and red neckties, while 'the women usually cut their hair short, wore Trilby hats, short, shabby skirts, red rosettes in mannish coats, and stout, business-like boots'.[38]

---

[34] Sernicoli, *L'Anarchia*, vol. 2, p. 175.
[35] Paulucci di Calboli, *I girovaghi italiani*, p. 175.
[36] 'Una serata presso gli anarchici', *Il Corriere della Sera*, 21–22 November 1902.
[37] C. Shaw, 'Among London Anarchists', *Penny Illustrated Paper*, 20 August 1910.
[38] Latouche, Anarchy! p. 64.

After the funeral of King Umberto I, the front page of the *Pall Mall Gazette* highlighted the supposed sinister significance of women in the anarchist movement:

The task which lies before the police of Europe and America, if Anarchism is to be kept within bounds, presents many and various perplexities. [...] Another factor to be taken into serious consideration is the devotion of women of the movement. A feminine conspirator will always beat a man, if only her enthusiasm can be kept within bounds. It is the Anarchist women who supply their hunted confederates with funds, often by selling the clothes off their own backs, and who smuggled them from under the nose of the police.[39]

Similar descriptions to those in the magazines can be found in spy and police reports. Anarchist women (who generally appear in documents as partners or wives of anarchist militants) are labelled as prostitutes, and anarchist men are often reported to be suffering from syphilis.

Archival sources suggest that there were few politically active women in the anarchist colony. Thus, the peculiarity of being an 'anarchist woman' is obvious in the title chosen by Olivia and Helen Rossetti for her novel: *A Girl Among the Anarchists*. Indeed, the majority of the characters in her book are men. As far as can be discerned, in the Italian colony it seems that the chief anarchist women were the British born Rossetti sisters, who edited *The Torch* in the early 1890s, and Emilia Trunzio, who was married to Giovanni Defendi. Endowed with a strong personality, Trunzio had been Malatesta's lover at one point and had a degree of political influence over the famous anarchist.

Leisure activities

Fermin Rocker remembers how the German anarchist club in Charlotte Street provided a home away from home. 'Not only did it have a hall and a stage with its complement of sets and drops, but at weekends there was nearly always music being played'.[40] In a foreign and uncertain environment, clubs were places where refugees could socialise with compatriots and spend their free time in a friendly atmosphere. According to Rudolf Rocker, up until the First World War, there was very little contact between the foreign colonies and the native English population in London. Indeed, refugees lived their own separate lives, in their own streets, speaking their own languages. Many of the refugees were unable to speak and read more than

---

[39] 'The Common Enemy', *Pall Mall Gazette*, 10 August 1900, p. 1.

[40] Fermin Rocker, *The East End Years. A Stepney Childhood* (London: Freedom Press, 1998), p. 70.

a very few words of English during their sojourns in London. Italians, for example, communicated with other refugees mainly in French, a language most knew. Therefore, 'social life at that period depended entirely on the clubs'.[41] Spies from the Italian embassy often reported on evenings spent by the Italian anarchists drinking and chatting to each other in their clubs, mostly visited at weekends.

> The new Grafton Hall club was the finest meeting place the foreign revolutionaries in London ever had. There was a large room on the ground floor, where the comrades who lived in the neighbourhood came every evening, for company, and for their evening meal. On Saturdays and Sundays it was packed with comrades from other parts of the huge city, who could come only on those days.[42]

Evening festivities were sometimes held at the clubs. At Christmas in 1908 members and their families gathered at the club in Charlotte Street for concert evening. Dinner started at six, vocal and instrumental performances took place at ten, and then dancing lasted from midnight to three in the morning – as reported by police inspector Frosali it was a real bacchanal. On New Year's Eve there was another concert at which the French sang 'La Carmagnole' and the Italians *L'Internazionale*.[43]

Clubs provided different types of recreation. 'The rooms used by the members are comfortably furnished, and all kind of indoor amusements are provided, as well as a good supply of revolutionary periodicals of all nations. Cards and chess are the principal diversions indulged'.[44]

The futurist painter Carlo Carrà, who spent a few months among the anarchists in London, recalled in his memoirs how he used to spend several hours playing *scopone*, a popular Italian card game, against inveterate opponents Recchioni and Bacherini.[45] However, card games were sometimes contentious, since they could degenerate into gambling.

At the *International Club* in Charlotte Street it was possible to play billiards and once a week, a room was used as a gym. The *Grafton Hall Club* was provided 'with a big, bright, comfortable library'.[46]

Generally, concerts, dance evenings and recitals were the main attractions of the *soirées* organised at the clubs; they were political events and entertainment at the same time. Indeed fundraising was usually tied to the

---

[41] Rocker, *The London Years*, p. 68–69.

[42] Rocker, *The London Years*, p. 67.

[43] Frosali's report, December 1908. ACS, *PS*, 1909, b. 4, f. (5075/103).

[44] 'In An Anarchist Club', *Tit Bits*, 7 May 1892, p. 7.

[45] Carlo Carrà, *La mia vita* (Milan: Feltrinelli, 1981), pp. 26–27. Carrà also recalled a forceful argument with Malatesta caused by Carrà's condemnation of Bresci's attempt.

[46] Rocker, *The London Years*, p. 67.

concerts and dances. At the official opening of *L'Università Popolare di Londra* in 1905, after Malatesta's and Tárrida de Mármol's speeches, two comedies – 'the usual of subversive character' – were presented: 'Le gendarmie est sans pitié' by G. Courtelins and 'Le Portefeuille' by Octave Mirabeau.[47] 'Le Portefeuille' had already been staged at a 'Grande Soirée Internationale' in Holborn in conjunction with a meeting given by Malatesta, on 4 July 1903. A few months later, a *Soirée Familiale* was held with musical entertainment.

The newspaper *L'Internazionale* relied on the money collected during these events, of which a detailed report states:

> The rendering of P. Gori's 'Primo Maggio' ['The First of May'], during the evening in aid of our newspaper at the Athenaeum Hall on the 5th of this month, was a great success. One could hardly have wished for a better performance of this sketch. Signorina Annita Scolari made a superb 'people's maiden'. With great grace and feeling, she made the scene flow like an enchantment, holding the public spellbound with the vigour of the inspired lines that Gori gives to the protagonist of his short piece. Signora Cesira played the part of the old mother with surprising naturalness. Comrades Ferraroni, Scolari, and Campagnoli, and also Signor Pifferi, were very good, and deserve a word of praise. The prologue was declaimed by comrade Barberi with self-assurance and feeling, and drew much applause. Well-received talks by comrades H. Tcherkesoff, E. Malatesta, and Tarrida del Marmol preceded the performance. The publicity had been effective and the takings were good.[48]

In March 1901, another *soirée* to raise funds for the newspaper opened with music performed by G. Grossi (tenor) and A. Collo (baritone), accompanied by Professor Salomone at the piano. A presentation of the *Bozzetto Sociale* 'Senza Patria' by Gori and lectures by Michel, Malatesta and Tárrida del Mármol followed. Italians also contributed to the evening with a reading of the poem *L'Infame* by Bruna Magnoni, a monologue by G. Ferrarone, *Il canto del Galeotto,* and opera passages sung by Mr Gemignani. The Italian chorus closed the evening.

In his account of the *soirée*, the secret agent Calvo reported:

> The festival was splendid! The hall was overcrowded. Malatesta filled the public with enthusiasm. In his second speech talking of the young Italians who sell themselves to England, the good comrade used such a great emotive passion that he touched the whole audience. Needless to say that claps and shouts of <u>good</u> and <u>bravo</u> followed each of his sentences and each of his words!!![49]

47 Mandolesi's report, February 1905. ACS, *PS*, 1905, b. 22.
48 Brutus, 'La Nostra Festa', *L'Internazionale*, no. 1, 12 January 1901, p. 2.
49 Calvo's report, 18 March 1901, ACS, *CPC*, b. 1992 f. (Felici Felice).

Beside revolutionary songs, opera was a regular feature of these evenings' programmes. At a grand *soirée*, after a staging of the *vaudeville* 'Mariage par la dynamite' written by Malato, pieces of Italian opera were performed by the professional tenor Ernesto Giaccone, Malatesta's friend.[50]

However, these *soirées* did not always end successfully. Virgilio reported an unforeseen event at a fundraising social evening organised by Arturo Campagnoli:

> At one point someone called Burioli performed a monologue that was against striking. Uproar ensued! There was shouting, screaming, whistling, and arguing. Who knows why the pianist, to distract people, started to play the *Marcia Reale* [National Anthem]: imagine the rumpus!' The following day Malatesta held a lecture and 'having finished, he approached a group that included Arturo Campagnoli, Ferrini, Dalboni, and a Neapolitan called Spasiano, and said: "Well done! With your celebrations based on the *Marcia Reale* and criticising strikes!" Spasiano said: "That's what I was saying. You, Campagnoli, are an idiot!" Campagnoli then gave him a clout, and Spasiano responded by throwing a glass at him.[51]

In 1907, the Italians and the French organised a musical concert to finance *L'Università Popolare*. A crowd of French people attended, but the Italian Ferrarone announced that the artist he had secured could not attend. The crowd booed and went away disappointed. In his apologetic speech to the public, Gustave Lance pointed out that breaking promises was a peculiarity of Italian people, stoking further friction between the two groups.

Generally, the programmes of the evenings were structured in a similar way: speeches or anarchist declarations provided the opening, followed by the reading of novels and poetry, monologues, the playing of revolutionary songs, lectures and eventually dancing. This scheme was very similar to that occurring in other Italian anarchist colonies overseas, for example in Argentina and the United States.[52]

In the 1890s, a 'Social Evening' promoted by an International Anarchist Agitator Group at the *New Cross Inn* in South London opened with a selection

---

[50] Malato, *Les Joyeusetés de l'exil*, pp. 172–74. In 1902, Giaccone performed at the Metropolitan Opera House in New York and at the Boston Opera House.

[51] Virgilio's report, 14 January 1902, ACS, *CPC*, b. 977, f. (Campagnoli Arturo).

[52] José C. Moya, 'Italians in Buenos Aires's Anarchist Movement: Gender Ideology and Women's Participation, 1890–1910' in Donna Gabaccia and Franca Iacovetta (eds), *Women, Gender, and Transnational Lives. Italian Workers of the World* (Toronto-Buffalo-London: University of Toronto Press, 2002), pp. 189–216; Bencivenni, *Italian Immigrant Radical Culture*, pp. 50–65; J. Guglielmo, *Living the Revolution: Italian Women's Resistance and Radicalism in New York City, 1880–1945* (Chapel Hill, N.C.: University of North Carolina Press, 2010), pp. 141–55; T. Goyens, *Beer and Revolution: the German Anarchist Movement in New York City, 1880–1914* (Urbana, Ill.: University of Illinois Press, 2007).

of piano songs, among which the 'Marseillaise' and the 'Carmagnole' were played. Anarchist declarations and speeches followed.[53] At a *soirée* in the Athenaeum Hall, organised by anarchist groups of different nationalities, the evening began with an 'Operatic Melodramatic Burlesque (For the First Time on any Stage)' entitled 'Trafalgar Square'. In this opera, the English anarchist David Nicoll played the character of 'Inspector Bellville', a parody of William Melville, the Chief Inspector of the Special Branch. Italians contributed with a choir of Italian revolutionists. German and British glees and songs were also performed. The *soirée* ended with the 'Marseillaise' and dancing.[54]

A letter from Calvo offers a colourful description of a *soirée* organised at an anarchist club. The main attraction of the evening was a comedy written by Calvo himself in which he also starred. The prompter was Saverio Merlino. The play's plot was based on two anarchists (Don Gregorio and Cicco) who have left Italy to seek refuge in London, and a French woman and exiled Communard (Preziosilla).

13 March 93.

Yesterday, 12 March, at 6 pm in the Club Svizzero Italo [Swiss-Italian Club], the advertised entertainment, aimed at drawing in the simpletons of Eyre Street Hill, took place. Lots of people came. There were no speeches about the sacred cause; Merlino just said a few words to the public, before the show, to let them know that the interests of anarchists include that of entertaining those who come to the meetings, and thus one comrade asks another to come: this to make them understand the rights which are their due as men!!! The little comedy by Lauria met with great enthusiasm! He had given it the title 'A sbalzi' ['In Fits and Starts'], but Merlino didn't like this and wanted to change it to 'La congiura' ['The Conspiracy']! The story: two anarchists, to escape various sentences, flee their native land for a safe place (London) from which to promote their cause. These two gentlemen, to avoid accusations of being ne'er-do-wells, pass themselves off as comedy actors, or tragedians. The less hot-headed comrade has little faith in his companion's plan, and entreats him to rehearse. His fellow anarchist agrees. This leads to a parody of tragic scenes, and other comical events. The two companions, forced into friendship, meet a young woman, who has been thrown out of Paris accused of being a Communard. She agrees to be an actress. Throughout the work there are witticisms and parodies, with the actors insulting each other over their inability to perform: the audience splits its sides laughing, and the comedy finishes to prolonged applause. The greatest applause was owed to little old Lauria

---

[53] International Anarchist Agitator Group, 'Social Evening', IISH, *Nettlau archive*, b. 311.
[54] 'Programme of Concertos', leaflet, 7 October 1899, IISH, *Nettlau archive*, b. 311.

who, being both writer and actor, brought off this triumph! Performers: Lauria, Madame Eugenia, and Pietraroja. Prompter: Merlino! Malatesta and Merlino went to beg the son of Madame Corso to lend his efforts, and those of his (English) friends, in order that musical pieces could be performed in this same club. 4 young men with mandolins and guitars did their duty! ... After the evening, a meeting at Pietraroja's house, at 9.30. Lauria was elected treasurer, and received the few shillings the comrades had scraped together between them.[55]

It is likely that, due to frequent social events in their clubs, the anarchists wrote a great numbers of plays. Unfortunately, apart from those written by 'professional writers' such as Gori, copies have not survived, but from leaflets and spy reports it is possible to know some of their titles. Malatesta's three act drama 'Lo Sciopero' was staged at the Athenaeum Hall in Tottenham Court Road on 21 December 1901.[56] Other dramas included 'Lazzaro il mandriano'[57] and 'La macchia di sangue',[58] and a comedy entitled 'La Vispa Teresa'.[59] Another play was entitled 'I delitti delle comari', a social drama in four acts written by the anarchist sculptor Carlo Magnoni.[60] It was performed at the *Club Cooperativo* in Greek Street in 1915.[61] Two years later, during the Great War, Magnoni presented the drama 'Gli Irredenti' at the same club. The Italian police inspector reported:

> Artists worse than mediocre, dialogue: poor, verbose, often ungrammatical ... In short, a pastiche that has only one merit: to keep alive the sentiments of hate and contempt for the Austrian government ... And an anarchist that carries out such a patriotic act deserves praise.[62]

[55] Calvo's report, 13 March 1893, ACS, *CPC*, b. 1519, f. (Cova Cesare).

[56] It was published in 1933. E. Malatesta, *Lo Sciopero* (Geneva: Edizioni del Risveglio, 1933). Malatesta was always against its publication.

[57] Calvo's report, Campagnoli Arturo, ACS, *CPC*, b. 977, f. (Campagnoli Arturo).

[58] It was performed in Tottenham Court Road in 1899. Calvo's report 23 May 1899, ACS, *CPC*, b. 2949 (Malatesta Errico).

[59] Mandolesi Report, March 1905, ACS, *PS*, 1905, b. 22.

[60] In 1906, according to Inspector Frosali, Magnoni sent a bust representing Sante Caserio (the Italian anarchist who assassinated the President of France, Sadi Carnot) to the 'R. Accademia di Belle Arti di Londra'. The bust was refused. A few years later Magnoni made the ornamental sculptures for Victoria Station and for the harbour in Dover. ACS, *CPC*, b. 2932, f. (Magnoni Carlo). Magnoni was an assistant to the English sculptor Henry Fehr.

[61] Frosali's report to the Minister of the Interior, 3 May 1915. ACS, *CPC*, b. 2932, f. (Magnoni Carlo).

[62] Frosali's report to the Minister of the Interior, 30 July 1917. ACS, *CPC*, b. 2932, f. (Magnoni Carlo).

Ferruccio Mariani, Cesare Cova and Felice Felici sharing
a bottle of wine, 5 November 1908.
(ACS, CPC, b. 1992, f. Felici Felice)

Indeed, a few years later Magnoni used his authorship of the play to prove
his patriotism and loyalty towards Italy and the Fascist regime.[63]

Besides leisure activities, the clubs often organised educational courses.
Tuition in foreign languages was usually a successful initiative. Malatesta,
Tombolesi, Defendi, Quarantini, Di Giulio, Rossetti and Ravaglioli took
courses in German. Malatesta and the Defendi family also attended English
courses. Other subjects were also taught: at the club in Jubilee Street Rocker
lectured on history and sociology, organising weekly visits to the British
Museum, and gave papers on Henrik Ibsen, Richard Wagner, and Edgar
Allan Poe,[64] while the Russian Prokovieff gave lectures on physics and
scientific experiments. At the same club a school of oratory and Sunday
classes for children were organised.

Management of the clubs

The management of clubs was not an easy task. In his memoirs Rudolf
Rocker recalled:

> The club life too had certain unpleasant features, which I discovered later.
> A place like Grafton Hall was expensive to run, and those who were
> responsible for its upkeep could not be selective in their admission of
> members. They also hired the hall to all sorts of bodies; it was not always

---

[63] Magnoni Carlo, ACS, *CPC*, b. 2932, f. (Magnoni Carlo).
[64] 'The Anarchist Leader. Interview with Mr. Rocker', *The Morning Post*, 7 January 1911.

pleasant. Most of the revenue came from the bar, from selling beer, wine and other intoxicants. Most of the people who frequented Grafton Hall were sympathisers with the movement; they had radical ideas, but were not much interested in the movement as such; they contributed to the funds, but only when they were pressed by the comrades. They rarely came to the discussion evenings. We could count on their attendance only when the discussion concerned one of the conflicts that so often occurred in the life of the emigre [*sic.*] population.[65]

The sale of alcoholic drinks was an issue of concern. In 1905, Malatesta, speaking at a discussion at the *German Club*, expressed his disappointment that the managers of anarchist clubs were compelled to sell alcoholic drinks to cover the high cost of rent.[66] According to Malatesta, this was detrimental to propaganda and to political education of the clubs' membership. Although he was not a teetotaller, Malatesta wanted only non-alcoholic drinks sold at the *German Club* and in all anarchist clubs generally.[67] Rocker noticed how the decision not to sell intoxicants at the *Jubilee Street Club* increased participation in the life of club. The *Jubilee Street Club* was opened on 3 February 1906. It was the centre of activity of Jewish anarchists in the East End. It was also widely used by London's other anarchist groups. 'It was a big building, with a large hall, which with the gallery held about 800 people. There were a number of smaller halls and rooms. One hall on the second floor was used as a library and reading room. A smaller building adjoining the Club served as the editorial and printing offices of the "Arbeter Fraint"'.[68] By not selling alcoholic drinks, those who were legally responsible were not compelled to issue membership cards. That allowed everybody to use the library and the reading room or to join the educational classes in English, history and sociology. However, it meant that other sources of revenue needed to be found. One of these was the hiring out of the club's premises to other organisations for their meetings.

Raising funds to support activities was a major problem, and lack of finance was among the main causes of the closure of anarchist clubs. The absence of one central club made it more difficult for the police to monitor the anarchists. At the beginning of 1905, the police inspector at the Italian embassy informed the Ministry of the Interior that an International Anarchist Federation existed in London, though it had not been formalised

[65] Rocker, *The London Years*, p. 69.

[66] The *German Club* was at 107 Hampstead Road and at that time numbered about 74 members.

[67] Frosali's monthly report to the Ministry of the Interior, 11 October 1905. ACS, *PS*, 1905, b. 22.

[68] Rocker, *The London Years*, p. 178.

and still did not have a regular place for its meetings. For this reason, meetings were held in different places: in Poland Street, Brick Lane and Gresse Street, while the decision about the meetings' location depended on unpredictable factors. That caused serious problems for the inspector in organising consistent surveillance of the anarchists.[69] In 1911 his colleague Frosali was requested by the Ministry of the Interior to provide information about the arrival in London of the anarchist Francesco Cini. Once again Frosali was unable to satisfy the request and to justify himself he repeated the same observation made by Inspector Mandolesi in 1905: 'presently the international club does not exist anymore, and the anarchists are scattered around the immense metropolis that has a surface area of 316 square kilometers; consequently the service is difficult, tiring and expensive'.[70]

Other nationalities opened their own clubs, but sometimes these merged in attempts to ease the difficulties of financial management. In 1905 Frosali reported that the Italian anarchists had left their centre at 4 Euston Road, where the *Università Popolare* had been organised, due to lack of funding, and had moved to 2 Dean Street in Soho, merging with the French group. According to Frosali:

> this union proves that a sort of merger is taking place among the anarchists of various nationalities, and this is mainly due to common conditions and needs, because they live in an economically inhospitable foreign country.[71]

This arrangement took place between 1908 and 1909 at the *International Working Men's Society* in 83 Charlotte Street. In April 1909, the club had a membership of 237. National groups held their meetings on different days. The Italian group was supposed to meet every Sunday but, since members were keen to enjoy themselves on that day of the week, meetings were postponed to Tuesdays; the English met on Wednesdays, and the French on Fridays.

In 1909, the *International Working Men's Society* garnered its main income from refreshments, subscriptions, billiards, rent (there were five beds available on the upper floor), and collections during Sunday events. Rent, goods for refreshments, piano and billiard hire, a pianist, heating and lighting represented the most significant expenses. A committee composed of members of various nationalities managed the club. In January 1909 the committee was composed of two Germans, one Jew, one Spaniard, one Frenchman and one Italian – Marco Corso, Lauria's son, who replaced Corio

---

[69] Mandolesi's report to the Ministry of the Interior, 10 February 1905, ACS, *PS*, 1905, b. 22.
[70] Frosali to the Ministry of the Interior, 12 September 1911, ACS, *CPC*, b. 1350, f. (Cini Francesco).
[71] Frosali's report, 7 June 1905, ACS, *PS*, 1905, b. 22.

and whose nomination was unsuccessfully opposed by Malatesta. However, the many attempts to balance the club's books failed and the *International Working Men's Society* closed at the end of 1909 to be later transformed by one of its German members into a restaurant. Most of the Italians then moved to the *Socialist Club*, at number 107 on the same street, since the management of that club had withdrawn its requirement for new members to sign the 'constitution of the Marxist Party'. The club numbered about 500 members, and later changed its name to the *Communist Club*.[72] After the closure of the *International Working Men's Society*, the different groups continued to meet independently from each other in the upper rooms of the building, paying three shillings' rent for each meeting.

Public lectures

Most of the meetings and lectures organised by the anarchists were hosted at the clubs. Alternatively, especially when a large audience was expected, the anarchists hired private halls such as the Athenaeum Hall. In general, the contents of lectures were of three types: historical or commemorative; theoretical, often organised in a debate form with two speakers supporting opposite points of view; and lectures related to major contemporary political events.

Anarchists from different nationalities most often joined together for commemorative events. Celebrations for May Day and commemorations of the Paris Commune were typical of these. Every 18 March, veterans of the Commune relayed their memories; not surprisingly, Louise Michel was a constant figure at these celebrations. Despite the repetitiveness that presumably characterised this particular event, it always maintained its appeal. Still in 1909, 400 people attended the commemoration of the Commune held at the *Jubilee Street Club*, listening to English, Russian, French and Jewish speakers.[73]

Each year the anarchists paid tribute to their 'martyrs', starting with the Chicago martyrs of the 1890s, a celebration that kept its appeal. In 1909 about 250 'subversives' honoured the Chicago martyrs at 165 Jubilee Street; Malatesta, Cherkezov, Rocker, Turner, Leggat and Kaplan gave lectures. Three years later, the meeting for the twenty fifth anniversary of the 'Judicial Murder of the Chicago Anarchists' was planned as a rally to demand the release by the United States government of the anarchists Ettor and Giovanitti.[74] Celebrations were also held to remember Gaetano Bresci.

---

[72] Frosali's report, October 1909, ACS, *PS*, 1909, b. 4, f. 5075/103.

[73] Frosali's report, March 1909, ACS, *PS*, 1909, b. 4, f. (5075/103).

[74] Leaflet *Meeting St Andrew's Hall*, 13 November 1912, ACS, *CPC*, b. 2950, f. (Malatesta Errico).

In 1914, for example, about 120 revolutionaries attended such a commemoration with Pietro Gualducci as the main orator.[75] From 1909 onward, several meetings were held to pay tribute to the Spanish anarchist Francisco Ferrer, executed by the Spanish government. In October 1910 a meeting was held at the *Communist Club* in Soho where Ferrer was remembered in front of more than 250 people by Boulter, Tárrida del Mármol, Aldred, Tanner, Rocker and Malatesta. The latter spoke in French, as he often did.[76]

On other occasions lectures had historical themes. Malatesta spoke on the history of the First International both at the *German Club* and at the club in Charlotte Street, where he recalled the uprising in Ancona of 1898.[77]

Some of the lecturers spoke on much broader topics. In 1909, for instance, at the *International Working Men's Society*, Tárrida del Mármol lectured on 'L'habitabilité des Planètes et avenir du systéme solaire' and, one month later, on a new theory about the creation of the world.[78] Within a series of lectures on neo-Malthusianism, the Spaniard Pedro Vallina gave a conference with slides entitled 'L'anatomie des organes sexuels'. The talk attracted a large audience and was favourably received.[79] In 1901 Malatesta's lecture on 'Sociologia comparata' completely filled two rooms of the club at 104 Wardour Street.[80] In 1913, Malatesta gave a lecture in French on 'Fisica e Metafisica'.[81]

At the *International Working Men's Society*, a meeting point for the anarchist groups in 1908–1909, lectures were organised on a weekly basis; the speakers were usually the leaders of the main anarchist groups. In April and May 1909 the programme of lectures consisted of: W. Wess, 'Anarchist socialism or social democracy: which is nearer the English character?'; Tárrida del Mármol, 'The problem of unemployment'; C. Kean, 'Crime and punishment'; S. Carlyle Potter, 'The crime of government in Barbados and Burma' and Dora Montefiore, 'Why organised democracy must concentrate at the present time on Universal Adult Suffrage'.[82] The Working Men's Society held these meetings also on the first floor of the (still existing) Bath House pub at 96 Dean Street, where Malatesta gave a lecture on the international anarchist movement in February 1908. The premises were also used by the London Anarchist Communist groups for their discussions.[83]

[75] Biographical profile, ACS, *CPC*, b. 2554, f. (Gualducci Pietro).

[76] Frosali's report to the Ministry of the Interior, 14 October 1910, ACS, *PS*, 1910, b. 7.

[77] Frosali's report, February 1909. ACS, *PS*, 1909, b. 4, f. (5075/103).

[78] Leaflet, 6 May 1909, and Frosali's report May 1909. ACS, *PS*, 1909, b. 4, f. (5075/103).

[79] Leaflet, 14 May 1909, and Frosali's report, May 1909. ACS, *PS*, 1909, b. 4, f. (5075/103).

[80] Calvo's report, 29 April 1901, ACS, *CPC*, b. 2949, f. (Malatesta Errico).

[81]Frosali's report, 12 February 1913, ACS, *CPC*, b. 2950, f. (Malatesta Errico).

[82] Leaflet, 'International Working Men's Society', *Course of Lectures*, ACS, *PS*, 1909, b. 4, f. (5075/103).

[83] 'International Working Men Society,' leaflet.1908. IISH, Nettlau archive, b. 3310;

Generally, these speeches attracted between 100 and 200 listeners. At the end of October, for example, about 150 people – half English and half Italian – participated in a 'pro Ferrer' meeting at which Malatesta, Kitz, Turner, Rocker and Cherkezov spoke. However, sometimes speeches did not take place because of the lack of an audience. This happened, for example, at Dora Montefiore's conference. Sometimes meetings reached greater numbers of the public. According to police records, 500 people attended Kropotkin's talk on his memoirs of Spain at the *Workers' Friend Club Institute* at 165 Jubilee Street.[84] Three hundred people assembled at the *Socialist Club* to listen to speeches by Malatesta, Tárrida del Mármol, Rocker and Turner against the Spanish government in September 1909.[85] At a meeting opposing the visit of the Russian Tsar to Britain at which Vera Figner (a Russian *Narodnik* who had spent twenty three years imprisoned in the Schlüsselburg fortress) and Peter Kropotkin were the main orators, a crowd of about 2,000 people attended, while another 500 could not be get into the conference hall.[86]

Theoretical debates were aimed more specifically at ideological discussion. They covered a wide range of topics: individualism, co-operation and anarchy, syndicalism, the general strike, and parliamentary socialism. A typical example was those organised by the *Freedom Group*, to which Merlino contributed in the 1880s. These were directed to 'fellow workers' and 'carried out for the purpose of enlightening you upon all subjects affecting your present condition, and to a means of emancipation from the yoke of capitalism'. The programme for the weekly discussion in April 1890 Kropotkin, 'Why we are communists', T. Pearson, 'Anarchism v. democracy', W. Neilson, 'A worker ideal' and J. Turner, 'Free cooperation'.[87]

In 1906, at the club in 107 Charlotte Street, Malatesta spoke about anarchists' assassination attempts, carefully followed by about 100 'subversives', 'most of whom do not attend the meetings'.[88] In 1911, at the headquarters of the *Gruppo di Studi Sociali* in 6 Meard Street, Malatesta gave a talk on anarchy and syndicalism in front of about fifty anarchists, most of whom were French.[89]

Meetings organised as debates in which two gifted orators, supporting

---

'Lecturers and debates', 1907, leaflet IIHS, Nettlau archive, b. 3295.

[84] Frosali's August monthly report. 4 September 1909. ACS, *PS*, 1909, b. 4, f. (5075/103).

[85] Frosali's monthly report, 19 October 1909, ACS, *PS*, 1909, b. 4, f. (5075/103).

[86] Frosali's report, 31 July 1909, July monthly report, *PS*, 1909, b. 4, f. (5075/103).

[87] 'Freedom Discussion Meetings', Leaflets, April and May 1890, IISH, Nettlau archive, b. 3294.

[88] Frosali's report, 16 July 1906, ACS, *CPC*, b. 2949, f. (Malatesta Errico).

[89] Frosali's report to the Ministry of the Interior, 16 December 1911, ACS, *CPC*, b. 2949, f. (Malatesta Errico). In 1912 the headquarters of the *Gruppo di Studi Sociali* moved to 99 Charlotte Street.

opposite points of view, confronted each other were common. In some cases one of the opponents belonged to the Italian Socialist Party and the debate highlighted ideological differences. At these events discussion turned inevitably to the uses of parliamentary and electoral methods. The debates could rouse the audience, as one member of the Italian Socialist Party, the shoemaker Giuseppe Sinicco who used to attend the debates held at the *Communist Club*, recalled:

> A bigwig came to London: a MP or a famous person. Then everybody attended, not only the socialists or the sympathisers. Often also Malatesta attended and usually there was a debate that generally ended in a brawl or in an exchange of abuse between supporters of the two orators. When the supporters of one clapped, the others shouted and protested.[90]

Malatesta was often the spokesman for the anarchists in debates. Luigi Fabbri remembered that Malatesta 'appeared invincible in the debates, and the opponent seemed to be crushed by his plain dialectic, understandable to everybody, without any literary frills or paradoxes'.[91] In 1913 he debated the French socialist Martin, and during Malatesta's speech, 'The public clapped enthusiastically and Martin could say only few words, repeatedly interrupted by Malatesta and those present, all subversives of different nationalities'.[92] Sometimes debates were not planned in advance, but emerged naturally during public meetings. For example, in 1912 Malatesta strongly attacked the famous French anti-militarist, Gustave Hervé, the main speaker at a rally against the Libyan war at Shoreditch Town Hall. Malatesta spoke in French and was translated into English. A formal debate between the two was held five days later at the *Communist Club*.[93]

Most of the time the debates occurred between two anarchists, rather than against a socialist opponent. For example, Malatesta and Pietraroja argued over 'the anarchists' duty at the present time' in 1902. Malatesta stressed his well-known insistence on organisation. At that debate, 'the very large audience was composed of most known Italians and a great number of rank and file militants, as well as a lot of French, Germans and Russians. For this reason Malatesta spoke also in French'.[94] Malatesta debated with the Spanish anarchist, Tárrida del Mármol, on several occasions, in 1908

[90] G. Sinicco, *Memorie di un calzolaio da Borgognano a Londra* (Udine: Tipografia Pellegrini, 1950), p. 78.

[91] Luigi Fabbri, 'Errico Malatesta', in *Studi Sociali*, 30 September 1932, no. 21, p. 2.

[92] Frosali's report to the Ministry of the Interior, 15 February 1913, ACS, *CPC*, b. 2950, f. (Malatesta Errico).

[93] Frosali to the Ministry of the Interior, 17 December 1912, ACS, *CPC*, b. 2950, f. (Malatesta Errico).

[94] Prina's report, 12 March 1902, ACS, *CPC*, b. 2949, f. (Malatesta Errico).

on the role of science in human civilisation. Tárrida argued that science led necessarily to anarchy. Malatesta, who always opposed belief in the inevitability of anarchism, refused to substitute materialism for God and argued that, although science could help humanity, it would not necessarily bring about an anarchist society. In March 1913, at a club in Manette Street, Malatesta debated with Tárrida on 'La Metafisica contro le scienze naturali'.[95]

The anarchist clubs in London brought together different traditions of sociability and, to some extent, different traditions melded together. In these centres, the cosmopolitan anarchist community in London developed a distinctive radical subculture: here the anarchists performed comedies, plays, and songs. Clubs served not only propaganda and recreational purposes but also reinforced identity, a sense of belonging and solidarity among the refugees. Music and theatre played a great part in all this. Theatre in particular was an important feature, not only as a propaganda tool but also as a way to reinforce bonds between refugees through the complex process of staging, rehearsing and acting. It is significant that the anarchist Pacini in 1901 was the president of the *Filodrammatica* in London. Moreover, it was at these performances that the oftentimes hidden presence of women in the anarchist movement emerges. Music and songs were both powerful instruments of propaganda and a reinforcement of identity; repertoires often mixed political and popular chants, ranging from the 'International', 'Carmagnole' and revolutionary choruses, to opera pieces such as *Carmen*, *Cavalleria Rusticana*, or popular songs like 'Funiculà' and 'O Sole Mio.'

This cultural production developed *in loco*, but it was also nurtured in Italy and other centres of the anarchist diaspora; for example Gori sent the scripts of his plays to be performed in London, and the collection of revolutionary songs *Canzoniere dei ribelli* was usually on sale alongside other political pamphlets. In London, Sante Ferrini published 2,000 copies of a short novel entitled *Canagliate!* that was sold in London and sent to Milan, Rome, Mantua, Leghorn and Naples.[96] Recreational activities in the London anarchist clubs followed a pattern common to those organised in the centres for political exiles in other parts of Europe and overseas, with the staging of a wide variety of material such as songs, poems and monologues, and the concluding dancing session and singing of the 'International' or the 'Carmagnole'.[97] Also in common with other centres of the anarchist diaspora, and with the labour movement more generally, was the

---

[95] Frosali's report, 28 March 1913, ACS, *CPC*, b. 2950, f. (Malatesta Errico).

[96] Inspector Prina to the Minister of the Interior, 6 March 1902 and Virgilio's report, 11 March 1902. ACS, *CPC*, b. 2639, f. (Ferrini Sante). Sante Ferrini, *Canagliate* (London: Tipografia Internazionale, 1901), with introduction by Silvio Corio. A copy of the novel in ACS, *CPC*, b. 2044, f. (Ferrini Sante).

[97] Bencivenni, *Italian immigrant radical culture*, pp. 102–3.

establishment of educational circles for the schooling of the working class. Libraries, sometime of noteworthy dimension and quality, were often among facilities provided by the clubs. As they did for radicals in the United States, elsewhere these libraries 'represented as enormous source of information, knowledge, and, often, political conversion'.[98]

In the case of the Italians, it appears that the clubs also served the broader community. Indeed, the fact that the anarchists influenced the social life of youth in the colony through their clubs was a cause of great concern for the Italian authorities in London. In 1903, the vice-consul denounced the bad habits of youth who 'spend their time in immoral locations that, to save appearances, call themselves clubs.' The consul wished instead for the opening of an Italian recreational centre where unoccupied young people 'could meet and spend the time in pleasant, moral and instructive occupations'. The establishment of this centre was necessary, he felt, not only for moral but especially for political reasons, because: 'popularisers of subversive theories, the anarchists in particular, found in those clubs fertile ground to disseminate the evil seed of their iniquitous propaganda. The damage of this daily work of moral demolition among our youth is immense'.[99]

However, the clubs also revealed the limits of refugees' political action in their host country. The frequency with which they closed, for financial reasons in the majority of the cases but sometimes as a result of internal ideological dissent, is a sign of the inability of refugees to pursue consistent political action. Moreover, as Rocker recognised, although the clubs were an essential element in the social lives of exiles, 'it was clear to me that in that way one never came out from a specific circle. One always saw the same faces and listened to the same speeches. It could not have been otherwise, because a movement of migrants can never have an influence on the conditions of the host country, particularly in England, and therefore it is destined to incest'.[100]

Nevertheless, the clubs became a conduit between host country, home country and the wider world, and played a significant role in the dissemination of anarchist ideas and forms of organisation. They provided a home from home: havens for refugees who often felt shut out from English life or were homesick. Thus, the clubs were at the heart of the experience of anarchist exiles in London before their world was shattered by the outbreak of the Great War.

[98]   Bencivenni, *Italian immigrant radical culture*, p. 54.

[99]   P. F. Righetti, 'La colonia italiana di Londra', in *Ministero degli Affari Esteri, Emigrazione e colonie – Rapporti di RR agenti diplomatici e consolari*, 1903.

[100]   Rudolf Rocker, En La Burrasca, (Años de destierro) (Buenos Aires: Editorial Tupac, 1949) p. 80.

7

The First World War: the Crisis of the London Anarchist Community

After Malatesta's escape from Ancona, the Italian police frantically sought him for fomenting riots during the Red Week in June 1914. Malatesta safely returned to London on 28 June 1914. The same day, in Sarajevo, the Serb nationalist Gavrilo Princip killed the Archduke Franz Ferdinand, heir to the throne of Austria-Hungary. The generalised response among people was a failure to foresee the devastating consequences of that event, and the anarchists did not differ. Like the socialists, in the days following the assassination, 'after the first shock, they turned to the more pressing and interesting problems of domestic politics and scandals'.[1] Thus, the Italian anarchists in London focused their attention on the aborted opportunity for revolutionary outbreak in Italy and on Malatesta's adventurous escape.

Just a few days after Malatesta's return to England, the correspondent for *Giornale d'Italia* arranged a meeting with the Italian anarchist leader. In his interview, there was no mention of the assassination in Sarajevo or any allusion to the possibility of war in Europe.[2] Three days later, Malatesta and Rocker spoke at a conference organised by the Federation of Jewish Anarchists in the East End. Rocker remembered how 'Malatesta referred in his speech to what had happened at Sarajevo, saying he feared there would be very serious consequences. But he did not think there would be war'.[3] The same month, Malatesta contributed an article to *Freedom* giving an account of the events of the Red Week, without any comment about the international political situation. Malatesta concluded his article optimistically:

These events have proved that the mass of people hate the present order; that the workers are disposed to make use of all opportunities to

---

[1] James Joll, *The Second International 1889–1914* (London-Boston: Routledge & Kegan Paul, 1974), p. 161.

[2] 1 July 1914, *Giornale d'Italia*, interview with Malatesta.

[3] Rocker, *The London Years*, p. 240.

overthrow the Government; and that when the fight is directed against the common enemy – this is to say the Government and the bourgeoisie – all are brothers, though the names of Socialist, Anarchist, Syndicalist, or Republican may seem to divide them.[4]

Yet, in the following months, Malatesta's expectations crumbled: nationalist and militarist sentiments spread throughout Europe; harsh disagreements divided socialist, anarchist, syndicalist and republican parties against one another and affected militants belonging to the same political groups. The ideals of international unity and the solidarity of the working class were shattered. The belief that the war could be stopped by a general strike and by international workers' solidarity proved to be an illusion. Recchioni mentioned the anarchists' disappointment 'on seeing how easily the masses were persuaded to answer the call to arms made by the various Governments. A.[narchists] had in fact been dreaming that their propaganda of so many years must have taught the working classes not to place themselves in the hands of the State, at least to the extent of being pushed into a war against one another'.[5]

An irreparable schism

The outbreak of the First World War caused an irreparable schism in the international anarchist community. Different positions over the war ended friendships and comradeship that had linked militants for many years and that formed the bases of the exile network.

Many of the protagonists in this harsh dispute on the position anarchists should take on the Great War lived in the exile community in London, including Kropotkin and Malatesta who became the chief adversaries in the debate. Emma Goldman remembered how in the United States 'rumours had been filtering through from England that Peter had declared himself in favour of the war. We ridiculed the idea ... but presently we were informed that Kropotkin had taken sides with the Allies'. Kropotkin's declaration in favour of the war 'was a staggering blow to our movement, and especially to those of us who knew and loved Peter'.[6]

The support that the most emblematic figure of anarchism gave to the Entente had a profound impact on both pro-war and anti-war factions. Pasquale Binazzi wrote in a letter to Malatesta:

I was saddened by comrade Kropotkin's attitude, an attitude that has been

---

[4] E. Malatesta, 'The General Strike and the Insurrection in Italy', *Freedom*, July 1914.

[5] E. Recchioni, 'Between Ourselves', *Freedom*, September 1915.

[6] Emma Goldman, *Living My Life* (New York: Dover Publications, 1970), vol. II, p. 564.

exploited very cunningly by the opportunists, the militarists and the ... heroes of De Ambris's sort.[7]

Signs of Kropotkin's sympathy for the French Third Republic had emerged in earlier years. In 1913 Luigi Bertoni, after a long discussion with Kropotkin in Geneva, was disconcerted by the nationalist tinge of Kropotkin's praise for the French Revolution, and revealed his doubts to Malatesta. Indeed, Kropotkin's deep interest in the French Revolution had converted his love for France 'into a kind of adoptive patriotism'.[8] Kropotkin regarded the Third Republic as one of the most advanced governments in Europe and never hid his sympathies for it. In 1906, he affirmed that in case of an attack on France, socialists 'should not stand aside and see the republic defeated by a reactionary monarchist power'.[9] At the same time, Kropotkin shared the anti-German feelings which were traditionally present in Russian radical circles and had influenced revolutionaries such as Herzen and Bakunin. Eventually, Kropotkin's aversion to the German State extended into hostility toward the German population, which he considered to be as belligerent and imperialist as its government. Therefore, following the invasion of Belgium, Kropotkin supported the pro-war view of the conflict as a war to defend democracy against barbarism and imperialism. Malatesta, during his debate with Kropotkin and the Italian interventionist factions (Italy did not enter the war until 1915), acknowledged that it had been a mistake to underestimate Kropotkin's Franco-Russian patriotism and not to anticipate the consequences of his anti-German bias.[10] In the summer of 1914 Thomas Keell, the editor of *Freedom*, met Kropotkin in a café on Oxford Street. Kropotkin 'was sketching on paper the military situation in France [...] He spoke of German militarism and its barbarity in Belgium, and the duty of the Allies to throw the enemy back over their own frontiers'.[11] Indeed, as the war continued Kropotkin assumed a more militarist position, forgetting his 'past advocacy of a popular rising to expel the invaders'.[12] His feelings remained confined to anarchist inner circles until October 1914, when *Freedom* published 'A Letter on the Present War' – an open letter to the Swedish professor G. Steffen – in which Kropotkin publicly declared his support for the Entente.

I consider that the duty of everyone who cherishes the ideals of human

---

[7] Pasquale Binazzi's letter to Malatesta, 14 December 1914, ACS, *CPC*, b. 2950, f. (Malatesta Errico).

[8] G. Woodcock, I. Avakumović, *The Anarchist Prince*, p. 374.

[9] Woodcock, *The Anarchist Prince*, p. 375.

[10] E. Malatesta, 'Anti-Militarism. Was it Properly Understood?' *Freedom*, December 1914.

[11] J. Quail, *The Slow Burning Fuse*, p. 288.

[12] G. Woodcock, I. Avakumović, *The Anarchist Prince*, p. 379.

progress, and especially those that were inscribed by the European proletarians on the banner of the International Working Men's Association, is to do everything in one's power, according to one's capacities, to crush down the invasion of the Germans into western Europe.[13]

Kropotkin believed the roots of the conflict lay in the outcome of the war between Germany and France in 1870–1871 and the annexation of Alsace and Lorraine by the German Empire. From that date, Germany had been a standing menace in Europe. All European countries were compelled to maintain large armies to protect themselves from the threat of Prussian imperialism. Moreover, Kropotkin argued, for almost half a century Germany had paralysed European progress: socialists in Belgium, France and Switzerland were conscious that, if an internal social struggle began in their countries, a German invasion would immediately follow. Should Germany win the war, Europe would be plunged into an era of general reaction and backwardness. Kropotkin concluded his article by criticising pacifism and anti-militarist propaganda:

It is certain that the present war will be a great lesson to all nations. It will have taught them that war cannot be combated by pacifist dreams and all sorts of nonsense about war being so murderous now that it will be impossible in the future. Nor can it be combated by that sort of antimilitarist propaganda which has been carried on till now ... The German invasion *must* be repulsed – no matter how difficult this may be. All efforts must be directed that way.[14]

The article caused turmoil among anarchists of all nationalities and enflamed the debate about the war. The subsequent issue of *Freedom* was entirely dedicated to this dispute, and several articles appeared in response to Kropotkin's. Malatesta, who was linked to Kropotkin by many years of warm friendship, firmly stated his opposition in the article 'Anarchists Have Forgotten their Principles'.[15] The Italian argued that the only acceptable war for the anarchists was the fight of the oppressed against the oppressors. To speak of 'Germany' and 'France' as homogeneous ethnographic units, each having its proper interests and mission was misleading; this was possible only in the case of those countries in which the working class lacked political and social consciousness. The duty of all anarchists was to awaken awareness in the conflict of interest between dominators and dominated, to develop solidarity among workers across the frontiers, to organise class struggle in

[13] P. Kropotkin, 'A Letter on the Present War', *Freedom*, October 1914, pp. 76–77.

[14] P. Kropotkin, 'A Letter on the Present War', *Freedom*, October 1914, pp. 76–77.

[15] Errico Malatesta, 'Anarchists Have Forgotten their Principles', *Freedom*, November 1914, pp. 85–86.

each country, and to weaken the State and the capitalist class. The disillusion caused by widespread nationalism was not a reason for abandoning anti-war propaganda but for intensifying it. If the anarchists found it impossible to act, as was likely during the war, then they should avoid giving any voluntary help to the cause of their class enemies; they had to 'stand aside to save at least their principles – which means to save the future' and 'to keep outside every kind of compromise with the Governments and the governing classes'. Indeed, for Malatesta, there was no difference between the governments engaged in the war. Whichever side won the war, it would mean either the triumph of militarism and reaction, or a 'Russo-English knouto [*sic.*] capitalist domination in Europe and in Asia'. Malatesta only wished for Germany's defeat because he believed that revolution was more likely in a vanquished Germany. However, in his opinion:

> It is most probable that there will be no definitive victory on either side. After a long war, an enormous loss of life and wealth, both sides being exhausted, some kind of peace will be patched up, leaving all questions open, thus preparing for a new war more murderous than the present.[16]

Among the other articles on this issue, one by Cherkezov appeared in the November issue of *Freedom*. Cherkezov was a close friend of Malatesta's, but supported Kropotkin's point of view, and was even more uncompromising. In a letter to Jean Grave he wrote that, 'The Germans must be defeated, annihilated, humiliated'.[17] In his article, Cherkezov argued that the war was mainly due to the machinations and lust for power of the ruling classes of Germany and Russia, both of whom were composed of powerful castes of aristocrats and the military. However, the wars fought against Turkey in the nineteenth century by the despotic Russian government were inspired by the aim of liberating Slavic and Balkan nations, and as a result Bulgaria, Serbia, Romania and Greece had achieved their independence. Germany, by contrast, had never helped small nations to attain their independence but also had always expanded its territories through wars and annexations. The invasion of Belgium was a prologue to the tragedy awaiting 'France, the country of the great Revolution, the initiator of the revolutionary wave through Europe in 1848, of the Commune in 1871, the mother of Socialism, Anarchism, and Revolutionary Syndicalism'. Therefore, according to Cherkezov, 'all honest people' of any political or social conviction, all 'friends of social emanci-

---

[16] Errico Malatesta, 'Anarchists Have Forgotten their Principles', *Freedom*, November 1914, pp. 85–86.

[17] J. Maitron, *Le mouvement anarchiste en France. De 1914 à nos jours* (Paris: Maspero, 1983) vol. 2, p. 22.

pation and lovers of justice', should support France and Belgium in their fight against Germany.[18]

Rocker remembered a meeting at the headquarters of *Freedom* in which Malatesta and Cherkezov bitterly confronted each other:

> The discussion was a heated one. Tcherkesov shared Kropotkin's attitude. He went even further than Kropotkin. He said that if Germany won the war the entire free development of Europe would be ended. The Labour movement would be dead. It would start a long period of reaction throughout Europe which would destroy all the achievements of the past hundred years. He was therefore convinced that we must take our stand with the Allies. It was our duty as revolutionaries to prevent the victory of the Prussian militarism. Malatesta couldn't contain himself. He kept angrily interrupting Tcherkesov, who had been his intimate friend for many years. He said this war like every other war was being fought for the interests of the ruling classes, not of the nations. It would be different if the workers of France and Britain had fought for their countries, and had won, to introduce a new social order. Then it would be right to fight to repel a foreign invasion. But now it was different, and whichever side the workers fought on they were only cannon-fodder.[19]

The French anarchist Grave contributed to the debate in *Freedom*, arguing that recent events had proved the impossibility of stopping the war by starting a revolution. He shared the opinion that Germany's victory would mean the end of freedom and all struggles for social emancipation. From his point of view, the military defence of the State did not necessarily mean safeguarding the interests of the 'class-oppressors', but was a defence of the wealth and rights that workers had been able to gain in their struggle for social emancipation. In contrast to Kropotkin, Grave, although supporting the war, carefully distinguished the responsibilities of the German ruling class in endorsing Prussian militarism from those of the German population. The aim of the war was to destroy the menace of Prussian militarism, not Germany. For this reason, after the Entente's victory, Grave believed that Germany should not be punished by the request for war reparations.

In the correspondence section, *Freedom* published a sarcastic letter by Scottish anarchist Robert Selkirk who attacked Kropotkin's analysis of the causes of the outbreak of the war, and criticised the decision to publish Kropotkin's article, warning the editor that 'A large number of our comrades are sliding down the declivity of militarism, and we should be careful that

---

[18] W. Tcherkesoff, 'The War, Its Causes, and German Responsibility', *Freedom*, November 1914, p. 86.

[19] Rocker, *The London Years*, pp. 247–48.

we do not in any way increase the number'.[20] Apparently Kropotkin was highly annoyed by the content of that letter.

The debate in *Freedom* also involved the issue of anti-militarism. Kropotkin urged the anarchists to revise their concept of anti-militarism; in particular, they should reconsider the view that the general strike could be a means to prevent the war.

> A general strike, to be efficacious, must be entered upon by the *two* nations going to fight. But in case of a Franco-German war there was not the slightest chance of this being the case. The German Social Democrats would not think, even for a single moment, of *not* joining the mobilisation; and in such a condition, even one single day of war-strike in France would mean the loss of a province, the gift of a hundred thousand men to the Germans, and the addition of a thousand million francs to the indemnity. No sensible man in France would join the strike. So it happened in reality.[21]

Kropotkin reached the conclusion that the conduct of anti-militarist propaganda needed to be reviewed. He believed anti-militarism had to be based on the assumption that, if it failed, anti-militarists would give their full support to the countries that suffered from invasion by the aggressors. Otherwise their inaction would mean giving tacit support to the invaders: 'They help them to make slaves of the conquered populations; they aid them to become still stronger and thus to be a still stronger obstacle to the Social Revolution in the future'. Kropotkin concluded that, 'in a war of invasion everyone is bound to take sides against the invaders'.[22] Malatesta replied to Kropotkin's article, pointing out his bitterness in having to oppose 'an old and beloved friend like Kropotkin who has done so much for the cause of Anarchism', but stating that Kropotkin seemed to have forgotten the class struggle, the necessity of economic emancipation, and all other anarchist teachings. According to Kropotkin, the national question had to be solved before the social question. The idea that anti-militarists had to take sides in defence of the country that was going to be invaded meant 'that Kropotkin's 'anti-militarism' ought always to obey the orders of his Government. What remains after that of anti-militarism, and, indeed, of Anarchism?'[23]

When the November issue of *Freedom* was published, Kropotkin and Cherkezov clashed with its editor, Keell, who strongly opposed the war.

---

[20] R. Selkirk, 'Correspondence', *Freedom*, November 1914.

[21] P. Kropotkin, 'Anti-Militarism. Was it Properly Understood?' *Freedom*, November 1914, p. 82–83.

[22] P. Kropotkin, 'Anti-Militarism. Was it Properly Understood?' *Freedom*, November 1914, p. 82–83.

[23] E. Malatesta, 'Anti-Militarism Was it Properly Understood?' *Freedom*, December 1914.

In the same issue that carried Kropotkin's letter, Keell had expressed a completely divergent point of view:

> The more I study the evidence, the more certain I am that the growing commercial as well military power of Germany was a challenge to Britain and the Allied Powers, and the supremacy of one or the other is the sole point at issue. And the workers are slaughtering each other to decide it. They will gain nothing by this war; whatever the result may be, they must lose.[24]

In a meeting in Brighton, Kropotkin pressured Keell to resign: *Freedom*, he said, should shut down. Keell refused and continued to publish the newspaper, which became a mouthpiece of the anti-war group. Kropotkin and Keell never met again.

Many years later Malatesta recalled the sorrow caused by his clash with Kropotkin:

> He seemed to forget that he was an Internationalist, a socialist and an anarchist; he forgot what he himself had written only a short time before … and began expressing admiration for the worst Allied statesmen and Generals, and at the same time treated as cowards the anarchists who refused to join the Union Sacré [sic.], regretting that his age and his poor health prevented him from taking up a rifle and marching against the Germans. It was impossible therefore to see eye to eye: for me he was a truly pathological case. All the same it was one of the saddest, most painful moments of my life (and, I dare to suggest, for him too) when, after a more than acrimonious discussion, we parted like adversaries, almost as enemies.[25]

Due to different stands on the conflict, a planned international meeting of anarchists due to be held in London at the end of August 1914 was cancelled.[26]

Only a minority of anarchists in Britain and the wider anarchist movement adhered to Kropotkin's position. However, several high-profile figures with international reputations took his side. Many of them had been Malatesta's closest friends. These included Cherkezov, who testified in Malatesta's favour during his trial in 1912; Jean Grave, the editor of *Les Temps Nouveaux*, the most important French anarchist newspaper; Charles Malato, the

[24] T. H. Keell, 'Have the Leopards Changed their Spots?' *Freedom*, October 1914, p. 78.

[25] E. Malatesta, 'Pietro Kropotkin. Ricordi e critiche di un vecchio amico', *Studi Sociali*, 15 April 1931. Translated in: R. Vernon (ed.), *Errico Malatesta. His Life and Ideas* (London: Freedom Press, 1965), p. 260.

[26] Frosali's report to Ministry of the Interior, 18 August 1914. ACS, *PS*, 1914, b. 34. On the preparation of the congress see: *Bulletin du Congrès Anarchiste International, nn. 1 and 2*, May and July 1914, ACS, *PS*, 1914, b. 34.

well-known anarchist writer with whom Malatesta went to Belgium in the hope of fomenting a possible insurrection during the general strike of 1893; the Swiss anarchist James Guillaume, militant of the First International who had edited Bakunin's writings, and Amilcare Cipriani, Garibaldian and hero of the Paris Commune. In his memoirs, Grave advanced a generational explanation for the division over the war:

> we can say that, as a whole, supporters of the Union Sacrée were closer in age and ideological affiliation to the Paris Commune and the anti-authoritarian First International than those who opposed the war. These two facts resulted in an opposition on principle against a Germany considered to be dictatorial and Marxist.[27]

The Italian interventionists took immediate advantage of the pro-war positions of Kropotkin and the others, claiming that the entire anarchist movement supported the conflict. The censorship introduced during the war made it difficult for the anti-war anarchists to counter these misleading statements. With this aim, in March 1915, *Freedom* published an 'International Anarchist Manifesto on the War'.[28] Among the signatories were the Italians Calzitta, Malatesta, Natale Parovich, Recchioni, Bertoni and Frigerio. Emma Goldman, Alexander Berkman, Ferdinand Domela Nieuwenhuis and Alexander Shapiro also signed the manifesto. The manifesto stated the impossibility of distinguishing between offensive and defensive war; all countries had prepared themselves for the conflict by strengthening their armies and armaments for almost fifty years. It was therefore 'foolish and childish to seek to fix the responsibility on this or that Government'. At the same time, the manifesto rejected the assertion that supporting the war meant defending civilisation. None of the belligerents was entitled to invoke civilisation or 'to declare itself in a state of legitimate defence'; neither the militarist German State, nor repressive Russia, nor Great Britain with its colonial Empire, nor France with its 'bloody conquests in Tonkin, Madagascar, Morocco'. The real cause of war rested solely 'in the existence of the State, which is the political form of privilege'.

> The role of the Anarchists in the present tragedy, whatever may be the place or the situation in which they find themselves is to continue to proclaim that there is but one war of liberation: that which in all countries is waged by the oppressed against the oppressor, by the exploited against the exploiters.[29]

A year later the schism between pro and anti-war anarchists became

---

[27] Jean Grave, *Quarante ans de propagande anarchiste* (Paris: Flammarion, 1973), p. 546.

[28] 'International Anarchist Manifesto on the War', *Freedom*, March 1915.

[29] 'International Anarchist Manifesto on the War', *Freedom*, March 1915

unbridgeable. At the beginning of 1916, when rumours began to circulate that Germany intended to campaign for peace with territorial annexations, Grave and Kropotkin promoted the publication of a manifesto urging the continuation of the war. It appeared in February 1916 in *La Bataille Syndicaliste* and was signed by fifteen anarchists; however Grave affirmed in his memoirs that, after the publication, they received more than 100 signatures, half of them from Italy.[30] The *Manifesto of Sixteen* claimed that the minimal conditions for starting a peace process did not exist, and that the war must continue until Germany's defeat and retreat to its original boundaries.

> To speak of peace at this moment is precisely to play the game of the German Ministerial Party, of Prince Bülow and his agents. For our part, we refuse absolutely to share the illusions of our comrades concerning the peaceful disposition of those who direct the destinies of Germany. [...] If the German workers began to understand the situation as we understand it, [...] and if they could make themselves heard by their government, there could be common ground for beginning discussions about peace. But then they should declare that they absolutely refuse to make annexations, or to approve them; that they renounce the claim to collect "contributions" from the invaded nations, that they recognise the duty of the German state to repair, as much as possible, the material damage caused by its invasion of neighbouring states, and that they do not purport to impose conditions of economic subjection, under the name of commercial treaties. Sadly, we do not see, so far, symptoms of an awakening, in this sense, of the German people. That is why we anti-militarist, enemies of war, passionate partisans of peace and the fraternity of people, take the side of resistance, and have not considered our duty to separate our lot from the rest of population.[31]

Malatesta replied with an article in *Freedom*, significantly entitled 'Pro-Government Anarchists'. He wrote:

> in the problematical hope of crushing Prussian Militarism, they have renounced all the spirit and all the traditions of Liberty; they have Prussianised England and France; they have submitted themselves to Tsarism; they have restored the prestige of the tottering throne of Italy. Can Anarchists accept this state of things for a single moment without renouncing all right [*sic*] to call themselves Anarchists?[32]

Malatesta did not believe the defeat of Prussian militarism was possible. In his opinion, even with the defeat of Germany, militarism was going to

---

[30] Jean Grave, *Quarante ans de propagande anarchiste*, p. 547.

[31] The manifesto of the sixteen was published in *La Bataille*, 14 March 1916. Translation in http://libertarian-labyrinth.blogspot.co.uk/2011/05/manifesto-of-sixteen-1916.html

[32] E. Malatesta, 'Pro-Government Anarchists', *Freedom*, April 1916.

become a permanent feature in post-war Europe. Indeed, nothing could prevent Germany from preparing its revenge or could avoid other countries from keeping themselves ready for further conflict. Then the 'self-styled Anarchists' who were presently supporting the war would become again 'at the first threat of war, recruiting-sergeants for the Governments'. The war could be stopped only by revolution or the threat of it. Therefore, the anarchists should avoid every compromise and devote themselves 'to deepen the chasm between capitalists and wage-slaves, between rulers and ruled'. For Malatesta even foreign occupation, if it led to revolt, was preferable to meekly bearing domestic oppression, 'almost gratefully accepted in the belief that by this means we are preserved from a greater evil'. He concluded:

> It seems to me that it is criminal to do anything that tends to prolong the war, that slaughters men, destroys wealth, and hinders all resumption of the struggle for emancipation.[33]

Malatesta reiterated these views at public meetings. At the end of January 1916 he lectured on 'War and working class conditions after the war.' A couple of months later, he and Carlo Frigerio attacked Kropotkin and the Manifesto of Sixteen at a meeting at March House at which Malatesta spoke in English.[34]

The London Italian anarchist community during the First World War

The war also divided the colony of Italian anarchists in London. Corio initially stood with the pro-war factions and did not sign the International Manifesto against the war. On 2 February 1915, he published an article entitled 'Parlando con Hyndman' in Mussolini's interventionist newspaper, *Il Popolo d'Italia*, in which he stated that the war was necessary to weaken German militarism. His article caused deep resentment among the anti-war anarchists, in particular Malatesta and Recchioni. Corio later changed his mind; in April 1916 at a private lecture with fifty anarchists of different nationalities present, he gave a long speech against the war.[35] Other anarchists in London became and remained interventionist. Thus Carlo Magnoni, in a letter written to his brother many years later, recalled how he became a nationalist at the outbreak of the First World War and how

---

[33] E. Malatesta, 'Pro-Government Anarchists', *Freedom*, April 1916.

[34] Inspector Frosali to Ministry of Interior, 11 April 1916, ACS, *CPC*, b. 2950 (f. Malatesta Errico).

[35] 'Conference', Ministry of the Interior note, 2 June 1916. ACS, *CPC*, b. 1474, f. (Corio Silvio).

his drama *Gli Irredenti*, played at the *Club Cooperativo* in 1917, had aroused patriotic enthusiasm among the public.[36] *Londra-Roma* reviewed the play:

> *Irridenti* turns up in our Colony at the right time to accompany the hopes, aspirations, and the passion of our compatriots, so they will be unanimous when facing the war saboteurs who attempt to lead the people astray by whatever means and to hide the truth by disseminating false or exaggerated ideas, by anticipating a future afflicted by starvation and discord.[37]

Within a few weeks of the beginning of the conflict, most opposition to the war had already disappeared in Britain. The Parliamentary Labour Party and the trade unions ended their opposition and urged workers not to strike during the war. Pro-war and patriotic, indeed jingoist, feelings dominated British society, especially in the first years of the war. These sentiments were carefully nurtured by an intense and unprecedented propaganda campaign organised by the British government. Anti-war groups could do little to contest the posters, parades, pamphlets, films and martial music which bombarded the eyes and ears of the British populace.[38] Moreover, 'the opposition to the anti-war agitators by patriots was constant ... Meetings were attacked with monotonous regularity, sometimes platforms were smashed, sometimes the speakers were violently handled. Meetings were banned by the police and free-speech fights were fought'.[39] This outburst of patriotism was followed by a wave of xenophobia: the war was perceived not only as a national but also a 'racial' struggle. Germanophobia pervaded British society; several anti-German riots took place and mobs looted and destroyed German shops and businesses, particularly after the sinking of the passenger ship *Lusitania* in 1915. However, 'the line between anti-German sentiment and hatred of all foreigners was easily erased. Mobs who began by destroying German shops often ended up looting businesses owned by Italians and Russians (British allies), or attacking blacks and Chinese'.[40] In October 1914, with the enforcement of the Alien Restriction Act, freedom of movement for aliens was limited – they could not move more than five miles from their homes – and all resident aliens were required to register with the police. Sending letters abroad was prohibited. In the summer of 1914 the army organised a postal censorship bureau to monitor the correspondence of foreign nationals and suspicious persons. Initially intended for preventing leakage of intelligence and espionage, it was soon utilised to police the mail

---

[36] Carlo Magnoni's letter, 30 January 1934, ACS, *CPC*, b. 2932, f. (Magnoni Carlo).

[37] 'Arte e Artisti, Gli Irredenti', *Londra-Roma*, in ACS, *CPC*, b. 2932, f. (Magnoni Carlo).

[38] G. Robb, *British Culture and the First World War* (Basingstoke: Palgrave, 2002), pp. 96–128.

[39] Quail, *The Slow Burning Fuse*, p. 290.

[40] Robb, *British Culture*, p. 9.

of dissenters and dissenting organisations.[41] Subsequently, the government assumed the power to close down restaurants and bars regularly frequented by aliens. While the war continued, war regulations were applied without distinguishing between aliens from allied or enemy countries.[42]

In autumn 1914 unnaturalised Germans, Austrians and Hungarians were interned or repatriated; in September 10,500 enemy aliens were held in internment camps. Many German and Jewish anarchists were arrested – including Rudolf Rocker who was arrested by special order of the War Office because of his anti-militarist propaganda.[43] In October 1914, the British police raided the German Anarchist Club in Charlotte Street, arrested all the German anarchists and interned them at the Olympia camp.[44] This atmosphere was aggravated by the spread of spy-fever: 'anything German and anyone thought to have the least sympathy for Germans became the target for bitter personal attacks'.[45]

In this climate, anyone opposed to the war was immediately labelled as pro-German. The political activities of dissenting groups were heavily restricted by emergency legislation, in particular by the Defence of the Realm Act. The D.O.R.A. was initially intended 'to prevent persons communicating with the enemy or obtaining information for that purpose or any purpose calculated to jeopardise the success of the operations of any of His Majesty's forces or to assist the enemy',[46] but was increasingly used to silence dissent. Moreover, in 1915, attempts by either word or deed to obstruct recruiting became an offence. After the introduction of conscription in 1916, those who refused to register were immediately arrested. These laws hit the anarchist camp: Guy Aldred, editor of the *Spur* newspaper, was imprisoned in 1916 for refusing to register for conscription. Thomas Keell and Lilian Wolfe were tried and sentenced to three and two months' imprisonment respectively for distributing leaflets opposing recruitment. The police raided the *Freedom* offices on several occasions. The *Labour Leader* offices were also raided in summer 1915. In July 1916, *Freedom*'s press was seized and the newspaper was only printed due to help from the Independent Labour Party.

---

[41] The mail of leading dissenters was examined on a systematic basis by the end of 1915. On the control of dissent see: B. Millman, *Managing Domestic Dissent in First World War Britain* (London-Portland: Frank Cass, 2000).

[42] G. J. De Groot, *Blighty. British Society in the Era of the Great War* (London-New York: Longman, 1996), pp. 140–60.

[43] On Rocker's internment see P. Di Paola (ed.), R. Rocker, *Sindrome da filo spinato* (Caserta: Edizioni Spartaco, 2004).

[44] Frosali's report to the Ministry of the Interior, 28 October 1914. ACS, *PS*, 1914, b. 34.

[45] D. French, 'Spy Fever in Britain, 1900–1915', *Historical Journal*, 21, (1978), p. 364.

[46] Arthur Marwick, *The Deluge* (London: Macmillan, 1991), pp. 76–77.

The *Voice of Labour* ceased publication in August 1916 as a result of the arrests of many contributors under the Military Service Act.

Censorship was directed against all journals and newspapers and 'was carried out by the Admiralty and the War Office acting independently, with the result that newspapers had practically no war news at all'.[47] As a result of the lack of information, the Italian anarchists in London found themselves almost completely cut off from the rest of Europe. When Italy joined the war in May 1915 Malatesta admitted that:

> We do not know, for want of reliable information, the present situation in Italy, and what are the true factors that have determined so quick a change in her attitude.[48]

Lack of communication with the United Kingdom also created difficulties for the anarchist movement in Italy. In the summer of 1914, anarchists in Italy hardly received any news from Malatesta. This was due both to family reasons and censorship. Emilia Defendi fell seriously ill soon after Malatesta's return to London. Consequently, for months Malatesta spent every night looking after her. A short time later Enrico Defendi, who was probably Malatesta's son, died of tuberculosis in hospital on 8 November 1916. Emilia Defendi died in March 1919.[49]

In September 1915, the British police intercepted a letter directed to, or sent by, Malatesta. In this correspondence Bertoni, who was in Geneva, proposed that Malatesta launch a campaign against the war which would be financed by a wealthy Indian man. Malatesta, before beginning this enterprise, requested guarantees that the money did not come from Germany. British police summoned Malatesta 'for some clarifications, and to advise him to be quiet'.[50] In 1917, Malatesta wrote: 'I am as in prison. All my mail is apparently intercepted'.[51] During the first period of the war Malatesta's silence was misinterpreted by interventionists as a signal of his support for the war, a position that the anarchist leader was compelled to refute in a letter to the newspaper *L'Università Popolare* published in Milan.

The Italian anarchists in London concentrated their propaganda on the colony, aiming in particular at youths who had to register for conscription with the Italian embassy. The anarchists probably took advantage of the

---

[47] Marwick, *The Deluge*, pp. 76–77.

[48] E. Malatesta, 'Italy also', *Freedom*, June 1915, pp. 45–46.

[49] See ACS, *CPC*, b. 1653, f. (Defendi Enrico) and b. 5234, f. (Trunzio Emilia in Defendi).

[50] Frosali's report to Ministry of Interior, 24 September 1915, ACS, *CPC*, b. 2950, f. (Malatesta Errico).

[51] However, according to police sources, Malatesta was in continuous correspondence with Luigi Fabbri. Santi Fedele, *Una breve illusione. Gli anarchici e la Russia Sovietica 1917–1939* (Milan: Franco Angeli, 1996), p. 12.

traditional reluctance of Italians in Britain to register their newborn boys with the General Consulate in order to avoid the call-up.[52]

Indeed, Italians in the colony did not appear particularly eager to join the war, especially in the initial eight months of the conflict. When Garibaldi's son, General Ricciotti Garibaldi, visited London in February 1915 to recruit soldiers for his legion in France 'he was greeted with enthusiasm by his compatriots' but apparently did not succeed 'in recruiting Italian (or other) volunteers'.[53]

A few weeks after Italy entered the conflict, Frosali, the police inspector at the Italian embassy, reported that the anarchists had begun a campaign of propaganda to prevent conscripts from presenting themselves for the call-up.[54] The same month he communicated that many young men within the Italian colony had not reported for the required medical examination. He underlined that, 'this deplorable fact is mostly due to the active and seditious propaganda carried out daily by the anarchists Emidio Recchioni, Enrico Defendi, Vittorio Calzitta and others'.[55] In September 1915, the Italian consulate published in *Londra-Roma* a warning to those who had not responded to the call-up threatening to declare them deserters.[56] In January 1918, inspector Frosali requested that the Ministry of the Interior be provided with the names of twenty people, 'without doubt members of subversive parties' who Gualducci had recommended to the socialist deputy Dino Rondani to obtain their exemption from military service.[57]

The consulate informed the English authorities about the anti-war Italian anarchists in London for possible prosecution, although it wanted to avoid their expulsion to Italy. Thus, for example, in summer 1915, Italian authorities reported Calzitta, Gualducci and Recchioni for 'persuading Italian reservists not to join the colours', but at the same time withdrew a previous request for expulsion of the three. The Home Office complied with the Italians' requests, as shown in correspondence between the War Office and the Home Office:

> My dear Pedder, referring to your letter of the 10th instant about three Italian anarchists Recchioni, Calzitta and Gualducci, it seems to me that

[52] Lucio Sponza, *Divided Loyalties. Italians in Britain during the Second World War* (Bern: Peter Lang 2000), p. 21.

[53] Sponza, *Didived Loyalities*, p. 21.

[54] Inspector Frosali to Ministry of the Interior, 12 June 1915, ACS, *CPC*, b. 4260, f. (Recchioni Emidio).

[55] Inspector Frosali's letter, 4 June 1915, NA, HO/ 144/18949.

[56] Between 1915 and 1918 around 8.500 Italians returned to Italy to join the Army. Sponza, *Divided Loyalties*, p. 22.

[57] Inspector Frosali to Ministry of the Interior, 15 January 1918, ACS, *CPC*, b. 2554, f. (Gualducci Pietro).

in view of the decision of the Home Secretary that it is not proposed to make Deportation orders, the only possible course is to apply regulation 30 of the Alien Restriction Order and place these men under as many restrictions as possible with a view of checking their anti-recruiting tendencies.[58]

Inspector Frosali reported many times on similar events, but always stressed the necessity of avoiding deportation. At the beginning of 1918 he reported that:

On 30 December 1917 [Gualducci] went to the Società Operaia Italiana at 10 Laystalle [sic.] Street. [...] to spread defeatist propaganda [...] He is one of the leading minds of the anarchist movement. Good speaker, convinced Germanophile, he must be kept under careful surveillance. Repatriation would be of great detriment to our country. For my part, I would suggest that military authorities invite him to desist from his propaganda and if caught red-handed he should be taken to court for trial and possible sentence. Yet, I repeat that expulsion from the United Kingdom should be avoided.[59]

Frosali advanced similar advice in the case of Cesare Cova:

He often visits the small restaurant 'Restighino' where he spreads a terrible and evil defeatist propaganda, besides prophesying the forthcoming revolution in Italy [...] I am against Cova's expulsion from the United Kingdom for reasons easy to understand. It would be opportune, however, to call him to order and, just in case, to bring him in front of a magistrate for the subsequent sentence without expulsion.[60]

Some restrictions were applied to Italians involved in the anti-war campaign. Gualducci saw his passport application rejected, since the authorities believed that he could easily foment disorder in Italy.[61] Local authorities also put pressure on the anti-war activists. In May 1915 Silvio Corio gave a speech about Italy and the war, in which he stated that it was unlikely that Italy would join the conflict. The following day a detective from Scotland Yard went to his house and told him:

You can talk about anarchy as much as you like, but do not interfere with

[58] W. Kell (War Office) to John Pedder (Home Office), 19 July 1915, NA, HO 144/18949.

[59] Frosali's report to Ministry of the Interior, 13 January 1918, ACS, CPC, b. 2554, f. (Gualducci Pietro).

[60] Inspector Frosali to Ministry of the Interior, 13 January 1918, ACS, CPC, b.1519, f. (Cova Cesare).

[61] Inspector Frosali to Ministry of the Interior, 23 July 1917, ACS, CPC, b. 2554, f. (Gualducci Pietro).

war, because we do not want trouble, especially from foreigners. Be quiet, it is better for you.[62]

At the end of 1915, the Italian police inspector in London reported that Parovich Natale lectured against the war every Tuesday at March House in Mecklemburg Street.[63] A few months later, the inspector informed the British authorities that Parovich persisted in speaking against the war to his friends in a café in Oxford Street. Parovich, who was born in Pola and was therefore considered an Austrian subject, was interned as an enemy alien in Stramford in the summer of 1916.[64]

In December 1917, Recchioni was summoned by the police and the military authorities and informed that they intended to expel him for having sent some money abroad. Recchioni avoided deportation, stating that he used the money to buy products for his trade.[65]

In 1917, the outbreak of revolution in Russia ignited new enthusiasm among the exile colony in London and aroused great expectations among the anarchists, even if they soon became disenchanted by the Bolsheviks' rise to power.[66] Apparently, Malatesta was attracted to the events and tried to travel to Russia, but 'the British government forbade his departure on the grounds that he was an Italian citizen and only Russian expatriates were allowed to return'.[67]

According to the Italian police, Malatesta received large funds by Bolsheviks Georgij Čičerin and Maksim Litvinov in order to support the cause of the Russian revolution in Europe.[68] In 1918 Malatesta, together with Sylvia Pankhurst, Harry Pollit and Jack Tanner, was a member of the *Hands Off Russia* committee which opposed British intervention against the revolution.[69]

---

[62] Inspector Frosali to Ministry of the Interior, 3 May 1915, ACS, *CPC*, b. 1474, f. (Corio Silvio).

[63] Inspector Frosali to Ministry of the Interior, 18 December 1915, ACS, *CPC*, b. 3745, f. (Parovich Natale).

[64] Inspector Frosali to Ministry of the Interior, 5 August 1916, ACS, *CPC*, b. 3745, f. (Parovich Natale).

[65] Inspector Frosali to Ministry of the Interior, 13 December 1917, ACS, *CPC*, b. 4260, f. (Recchioni Emidio).

[66] Despite enthusiasm for the revolution and the fall of the provisional government, the anarchists were critical and suspicious of the establishment of a 'revolutionary government'. The repression of Russian anarchists in Petrograd and Moscow by the Bolsheviks in April 1918 confirmed their fears. See: Fedele, *Una breve illusione*.

[67] M. Graur, *An 'Anarchist Rabbi': The Life and Teachings of Rudolf Rocker* (New York: St Martin's Press, 1997), p. 129.

[68] Berti, *Errico Malatesta e il movimento anarchico*, p. 633.

[69] Berti, *Errico Malatesta e il movimento anarchico*, p. 633.

Many Russians left London at the outbreak of the revolution. Indeed, 'the whole radical community was in a state of euphoria, and many of Rocker's friends flocked back to Russia to take part in the making of a new society', Alexander Shapiro among them. When Kropotkin received news of the February revolution, he decided to return to Russia with his wife 'to place ourselves at the service of popular revolution'.[70] In the summer of 1917, they reached Petrograd where a crowd of 60,000 people welcomed them. Cherkezov also returned to Russia in this period.

These departures of Russian militants contributed to the progressive dismemberment of the colony of anarchist refugees during the war. Indeed, 'like the fault in a geological fold, the war years constituted a spectacular break' in the history of the anarchist community in London. According to Meltzer, the British anarchist movement had shrunk: 'post war slumps had hit the movement and a surprising number had emigrated.' Most of the anarchist leaders around whom the various nationally-based anarchist communities had formed departed. Malatesta's efforts were solely directed at finding a way of returning to Italy. The German movement 'with individual exceptions' largely disappeared. Most of the French, instead, became 'completely integrated with the English speaking movement'. The Yiddish-speaking anarchist movement in the East End of London vanished, 'due partly to the disintegration of working class Jewry, certainly to the disappearance of Yiddish as a language, and partly to emigration.' Many of the top activists in this movement, already weakened by Rocker's internment, were either deported to their countries of origin or left voluntarily.[71] The anarchist colony had collapsed. Moreover, in the post-war period governments around the world tightened restrictions on migration and increased the surveillance of foreign radicals.[72] Thus, the anarchists who remained in Britain found that the conflict had been 'a shaking up of references such that everything seems to start again from square one, consigning old, "pre-war" references and arrangements to the museum.'[73]

London was no longer one of the major centres of international revolutionary politics in Europe.

[70] G. Woodcock, I. Avakumović, *The Anarchist Prince*, p. 392.

[71] A. Meltzer, *The Anarchists in London, 1935–1955* (Orkney Islands: Sanday, 1976), p. 8.

[72] See: Gabaccia, *Italy's Many Diasporas*, p. 131.

[73] D. Colson, *Anarcho-syndicalisme et communisme*, Saint Etienne 1920–1925 (Saint Etienne: Université de Saint Etienne/Centre d'Etudes Foréziennes/Atelier de Création Libertaire, 1986). Quoted in: D. Berry, *A History of the French Anarchist Movement 1917–1945* (Westport Connecticut-London: Greenwood Press, 2002) p. 21.

Conclusions

In August 1900, a few days after Bresci's killing of King Umberto, former director of Criminal Investigations at Scotland Yard Howard Vincent was interviewed by the *Daily Graphic* and rebutted criticism of Britain for giving refuge to foreign revolutionaries. Vincent turned the criticism on his accusers, claiming that other governments were opportunistic: 'The way in which foreign countries dump their objectionable characters down upon our coasts is most unfair. They are sending them every day'. Vincent considered this practice 'very convenient to them', and believed it would not stop 'as long as we keep our door open'. He considered that foreign governments 'were not greatly distressed at the inconvenience caused to the British government' and supported the idea of an international agreement to limit the use of expulsion. As he stated in the interview: 'Let each nation look after its own criminals and semi-criminals'.[1]

Some of Vincent's remarks were well founded. On the one hand, the British policy of free asylum allowed anarchists from all over Europe to conduct a relatively free life in Britain; on the other hand, the concerns of foreign governments about alleged conspiracies organised by the anarchists in London mostly were proved to be groundless. Scotland Yard kept foreign anarchists under continuous surveillance, by shadowing them and by gathering information through informers. Moreover, when the British authorities believed that a dangerous action was being organised, they broke with their traditional discretion and passed information to the foreign government involved, as happened in 1891 on the occasion of May Day, when Scotland Yard alerted the Italian embassy about Malatesta's disappearance from London. Another question was that of the services provided 'privately'

---

[1] 'How to deal with anarchists. An interview with Sir Howard Vincent', *Daily Graphic*, 11 August 1900.

on occasion by agents of Scotland Yard, with payment, to the Italian embassy – and almost certainly to all other foreign embassies.

Vincent had good reasons for underlining the convenience for foreign governments in having revolutionary leaders living abroad and therefore not having to deal with their presence in their homelands. During the First World War, the Italian embassy asked the British authorities to stop the expulsion of Italian anarchists active in anti-war propaganda. The impediments faced by Malatesta on his return to Italy are a good example of this policy. In 1916 Malatesta put in a request to the Italian consulate in London for a passport. However, his request was rejected with all kinds of excuses for several years, forcing Malatesta to find other ways to leave the country. Malatesta recalled:

> I tried every possible way to be arrested and returned to Italy by breaking English laws. But the English policemen were saying to me: "You know what? There is no point in making us run after you. We could arrest you. But we will not do it, because if we do, we have to send you to Italy; and the Italian government thinks that it is better if you stay in England".[2]

There were many demonstrations in Italy demanding Malatesta's return, mainly organised by the anarchist-led trade union *Unione Sindacale Italiana*. In November 1919 Malatesta's passport was eventually issued, yet his difficulties did not end there. The Italian authorities pressurised other governments to stop the Italian anarchist; the French government did not allow him to cross French borders and the British authorities impeded his attempts to travel by sea.

Malatesta secretly boarded a Greek ship and was smuggled to Italy at the end of 1919 with the assistance of Captain Giulietti, head of the Seamen's Federation union. He disembarked at the southern city of Taranto on Christmas Eve. From there, he reached Genoa where he was welcomed by tens of thousands of workers.[3] Malatesta never returned to Britain. His departure signalled the end of London's role as one of the most important centres of the transnational anarchist movement.

Many aspects need to be taken under consideration in evaluating London's part in the Italian anarchist diaspora.

It is difficult to establish with precision the number of Italian anarchists who settled in London. During this research around 300 names emerged from police and spy reports, private letters and newspapers published in

[2] Errico Malatesta, *Autobiografia mai scritta. Ricordi (1853–1932)*, edited by Piero Brunello and Pietro Di Paola (Santa Maria Capua Vetere: Spartaco, 2003), pp. 185–86.

[3] See: Levy, 'Charisma and Social Movements'; Paolo Finzi, *La nota persona. Errico Malatesta in Italia. Dicembre 1919–Luglio 1920* (Ragusa: La Fiaccola, 1990).

London (taking into consideration contributors, members of the editorial board and subscribers). It is possible that some of the people listed in the documents were not 'active militants' but 'sympathisers' or, if named by spies, neither of the two. Moreover, for the period around 1881, some of the people mentioned may have been republicans and not Internationalists. In general refugees lived with their wives and children. In most cases, according to the census records, their children were born in London.

Although the Italian anarchists often changed jobs, the data collected shows that a high percentage of them (perhaps one third) were artisans and craftsmen: tailors, shoemakers, barbers, hatters, decorators and carpenters. In most cases they had practised the same occupations in Italy. Another significant section of the anarchist community worked in the catering trade as dishwashers, waiters or cooks and some opened their own restaurants. A number of anarchists were active in trade, especially food products and produce and a good number of their wives worked as tailors or dressmakers.

Most of the Italian anarchists in London came from the Italian regions where the presence of anarchist groups was most prominent.[4] Most arrived from Tuscany, the Romagna, Piedmont and the Marche. Smaller numbers came from Campania, Veneto, Lombardy and Lazio. Their regions of origin were therefore different from those of Italian economic migrants who came from poor areas, notably from Lucca, Parma, Liri and the Como valleys.[5] However, like the economic migrants, political refugees followed a system of chain migration, indeed many militants came from the same town.[6]

We can speculate that in the 1880s and 1890s the number of Italian anarchists in London amounted to a few hundred. However, the number was subject to significant changes: the Congress of 1881 certainly attracted a considerable number of activists; persecution against anarchists in Italy in the 1890s led to a huge wave of emigration to London. The last chapter of Malato's book *Les joyeusetés de l'exil* gives us indirect proof of the importance of this phenomenon. Malato ended his publication with a 'handbook' for the refugees who escaped to London. He provided timetables of ships from France to England and of rail services, addresses of anarchist clubs, and an English phrasebook. There was probably a high degree of mobility for activists in this period. From the beginning of 1900 militants were probably settling in London more permanently, although the community's mobility

---

[4] See Carl Levy, 'Italian Anarchism 1870–1926', in *For Anarchism. History, Theory and Practice,* edited by David Goodway (London-New York: Routledge, 1989), p. 31.

[5] Sponza, *Italian Immigrants,* p. 35.

[6] On the mechanism of chain migration of Italians to England see Terri Colpi, *The Italian Factor. The Italian Community in Great Britain* (Edinburgh-London: Mainstream, 1991), pp. 19, 33–34.

remained high. In 1905, 1,000 copies of the newspaper *L'Insurrezione* were printed, though these were also intended to be distributed abroad. A more precise indication is provided by the meeting to organise publication of *Volontà* in 1914 at which 200 copies were requested for distribution in London. Based on numbers mentioned in documents between 1901 and 1909 it is possible to argue that there was a core of about fifty to eighty Italian activists in London from the beginning of the century up to the First World War.

There are questions about the anarchists' capability to recruit new militants among the Italian community. In 1881, at the beginning of the settlement of Italian Internationalists in the British capital, the number of Italian-born people living in London amounted to about 3,500. In 1891, the figure rose to more than 5,000 and in 1901 to almost 11,000. During the following decade the colony was subject to a period of stagnation due to both socio-economic changes in the areas of emigrants' provenance and the introduction of the Aliens Act.[7] The Italian anarchists made several attempts to organise hotel and restaurant employees, but were never able to establish long-lasting organisations. The fact that the hotel trades and catering were 'so fragmented in small units and so often temporary and seasonal' represented a major obstacle.[8] Secondly, many of the anti-organisationalist and individualist anarchists had little or no time for trade unions. Moreover, these attempts were affected by the high turnover of anarchist activists in London. Political and personal arguments also limited the effectiveness of refugees' actions. Some of these quarrels were concocted by spies to create an atmosphere of mistrust, but others were caused by political and ideological differences that divided the whole anarchist movement to varying degrees. The dispute between the anti-organisationalist members of *L'Anonimato*, led by Parmeggiani, and the organisational followers of Malatesta affected activity in the 1890s. Although Parmeggiani eventually moved to France, many of his followers remained in London and stoked feelings of resentment among the anarchists. Personal disputes were a feature of the anarchists' everyday lives. In 1911, Cova and Recchioni were opponents in a dispute concerning an alleged affair between Recchioni and Cova's daughter. The controversy ended in court where Cova was convicted of libel.[9] Both Calvo and Virgilio referred frequently to quarrels that were probably exacerbated due to the close-knit nature of the anarchist colony and which on occasion

---

[7] See Sponza, *Italian Immigrants*, p. 13. According to Sponza's table, Italian-born people living in London in 1901 amounted to 10,889, and in 1911 to 11,668.

[8] Sponza, *Italian Immigrants*, p. 260.

[9] Frosali's report to Ministry of the Interior, 21 November 1911, ACS, *CPC*, b. 1519, f. (Cova Cesare).

ended in physical fights. At the beginning of the 1900s Malatesta, certainly the anarchist most endowed with organisational skills, was heavily criticised by his companions and the recriminations that followed the Scolari affair after the unmasking of Rubino in 1902 undermined his leadership in London for a considerable time. All these aspects contributed to the fact that the anarchists achieved few tangible results for all their political actions within the Italian colony. Several police reports indicated that members of the colony, especially young people, participated in anarchists' initiatives. However, in the collection of records of subversive militants kept at the National Archive in Rome (*CPC*), the number of files on individuals who converted to anarchism while in London is negligible, though this could be also due to police methods used for collecting and preserving information. Nevertheless, it must also be noted that the majority of militants named in the course of research, for example from the lists of subscriptions to newspapers, were already members of the anarchist movement before travelling to England.

This connected with the fact that the anarchists were chiefly interested in events back in Italy and their main aim was a revolution there, although it was frustrating to follow these events from afar. Their activity focused essentially on general issues and particularly on Italian political events; they never published a newspaper specifically devoted to issues concerning the Italian community in London. Their aim was to smuggle their publications back to Italy or to circulate them to other anarchist colonies around the world. On several occasions the Italian anarchists in London sought to publish their own newspapers. However, these publications shared the same destiny of those published in Italy. In the majority of cases, they were short-lived, mainly for financial reasons. To overcome financial problems the anarchists published single issues on special occasions, such as the celebration of the First of May or the commemoration of the Paris Commune. A further difficulty was to find the availability of a printer. In general, the printer of the majority of Italian anarchists' publications in London was Giuseppe Pesci, alias Bologna.[10] The Italian anarchists sold their newspapers in shops owned by militants or by sympathisers. Alternatively, they distributed them inside their clubs. The distribution to other countries, and to Italy particularly, was a more difficult task. The anarchists used to send the newspapers by mail, wrapped up with 'unsuspected bourgeois' newspapers in order to disguise them. However, the police were often able to seize them in the post offices thanks to forewarnings from spies and informers. Moreover, the circulation of these publications in Italy was necessarily restricted to militants. The

---

[10] The real name of Giuseppe Pesci was Zucchi Ugo. He moved to London at the beginning of 1890s to avoid military service. ACS, *CPC* 5605, f. (Zucchi Ugo).

Italian anarchists in London often did not publish any newspapers for years due to periods of organisational weakness or because the colony's denizens preferred to concentrate their efforts on other activities. Nevertheless, some of the newspapers published by the Italian anarchists in London were of high significance in the history of the anarchist diaspora.

Although short-lived, these newspapers were significant in the ideological and tactical orientation of the Italian anarchist movement in periods of political difficulties and uncertainty. They played an essential role, not only in maintaining contacts between expatriates and anarchist groups in Italy and the rest of the world, but also in the transmission of a revolutionary culture.

The fact that Italian anarchist exiles' political horizons remained predominantly focused on events in Italy illustrates the retention of practical and conceptual nationalist frameworks, and underlines the complexity of the dichotomy between the 'national' and the 'international' character of the anarchist diaspora. As the German exile Rudolf Rocker commented, 'a movement of migrants can never have an influence on the conditions of the host country, particularly in England, and therefore it is destined to incest'.[11] The anarchist refugees in London maintained a strong national structure; the divisions of spaces and times in the management of the clubs were clear signs of this; groups and meetings were organised according to national affiliation. This characteristic places under discussion the 'internationalism' of the anarchist movement and, at the same time, emphasises the need for a translocal approach in the study of the anarchist diaspora. More detailed studies on other nodes of anarchist exile, especially in North and South America, will allow for an evaluation of the extent to which this was a common feature of the anarchist diaspora, and to expand other aspects emerging from the research, primarily the production of a subversive, radical culture and the use of a common 'symbolic' language.

Though national structure was maintained, Italian anarchists joined fellow anarchist refugees from other parts of Europe, and personal friendships were cemented in the many clubs established in London, especially in Soho, Fitzrovia and the East End. Clubs were also centres of a radical culture that was transmitted through the other nodes of the anarchist diaspora. If the clubs did not necessarily always lead to the greater politicisation of members of the Italian colony, they 'became an important social component of the colony's life'.[12] Within the confines of their circles debates and discussions organised by the anarchists did encourage an exchange of opinion among

11 Rudolf Rocker, *En La Burrasca (Años de destierro)* (Buenos Aires: Editorial Tupac, 1949), p. 80.

12 Sponza, *Italian Immigrants*, p. 270.

members of the anarchist colony and the development of ideological and political viewpoints. Anarchists of different nationalities joined together to organise political campaigns like the demonstrations in support of Francisco Ferrer, for the Russian revolution in 1905, for the liberation of Ettor and Giovannitti in 1912, or the mobilisation to prevent Malatesta's expulsion in the same year. Moreover, anarchist groups from different nationalities organised common political initiatives on the occasion of May Day or 18 March, the anniversary of the Paris Commune. These ritual celebrations reinforced identity and cohesion, and were key in the construction of an imagined community that bound together not only the refugees in London, but the whole transnational anarchist movement. An investigation of the ways in which this counterculture was produced and transmitted between the international anarchist centres will provide a relevant contribution to the understanding of the anarchist diaspora.

Since Italy remained often the main political focus of the anarchist exiles, local and national studies are also necessary to evaluate the impact of the anarchist exile back home; for example by considering the extent of anarchist involvement in labour disputes and syndicalist organisations, which was strongly promoted from London through *L'Anarchia* and *Lo Sciopero Generale*.

The web of personal relations established at the centre of the anarchist diaspora, especially among the anarchist elite, was another crucial aspect of the international anarchist exile. The study of the colonies as a whole does not permit analysis of all facets of these interrelations. Most militants spent very specific periods of time in London, but the relationships they built were maintained afterwards and mutual influences continued over time. Individual and collective biographies, a genre that has experienced a resurgent interest in recent years, are also a good way to illuminate this aspect of the transnational anarchist movement.[13] Turcato's and Levy's biographies on Malatesta provide a valuable contribution in this regard.[14] As far as the Italian colony in London is concerned, at least other two figures deserve specific studies: Silvio Corio and Emidio Recchioni. Corio for his relations with Sylvia Pankhurst and their contacts with the Bolsheviks in London and in the Third International; Emidio Recchioni, for his conspiratorial life both in Italy and in England, and also for his connections with the anti-Fascist migration in France in the late 1920s and early 1930s.

---

[13] See: Benedict Anderson, *Under Three Flags: Anarchism and the Anti-colonial Imagination* (London: Verso, 2005). On Italian anti-Fascist exile: Patrizia Gabrielli, *Col freddo nel cuore. Uomini e donne nell'emigrazione antifascista* (Rome: Donzelli, 2004).

[14] Davide Turcato, *Making Sense of Anarchism: Errico Malatesta's Experiments with Revolution, 1889–1900* (Basingstoke: Palgrave Macmillan, 2012); Carl Levy, *The Rooted Cosmopolitan: Errico Malatesta and Italian Anarchists in Exile, forthcoming.*

The First World War had enormous consequences for the anarchist community in London. Many personal relationships broke down when the anarchist movement was devastated by the outbreak of the conflict. As elsewhere in Europe, disagreements between pro- and anti-war anarchists lacerated the London exile community, and the war destroyed the international framework of solidarity and the web of personal relationships that had been the backbone of the experience of exile before 1914.

In December 1919, when Malatesta did finally return to Italy, the Italian movement in London lost its most charismatic leader. However, some other influential anarchist activists remained in Britain: Corio, Recchioni, Gualducci, Francesco Galasso and Vittorio Taborelli.[15] From the early 1920s, this small group opposed the transformation of the Italian community into a 'Little Fascist Italy' which the *Fasci* Abroad were trying to create.[16] Between 1922 and 1924, Galasso, Gualducci and Taborelli managed to publish *Il Comento*, the only anti-Fascist newspaper to appear in the Italian colony. However, in the 1930s, the Fascists took almost complete control of the community, and opposition to Fascism found expression only outside the colony. Corio and his companion Sylvia Pankhurst published the newspaper *New Times and Ethiopia News*, which denounced Fascist activities in Ethiopia and opposed Mussolini's regime until the end of the Second World War. The newspaper sold an average of 10,000 copies an issue, reaching at times a peak of 40,000. Recchioni, instead, took a more individual and conspiratorial approach. His shop *The King Bomba* in Soho became a centre of anti-Fascist activity. Recchioni's son, Vernon Richards, recalled how the Fascists often damaged the shop's windows. In 1931, in the anarchist newspaper *L'Adunata dei Refrattari* published in the United States, Recchioni launched a public subscription to raise money for whoever would devote himself to the mission of killing Mussolini; he opened the subscription with a donation of $1,000. Recchioni was involved in Michele Schirru and Angelo Sbardellotto's failed attempts to kill Mussolini and in many others alleged plots.[17]

The outbreak of the Second World War completely changed the relationship between the Italian colony and its host country.[18] The anarchists opposed the war. Among them, symbolically representing a link with the

[15] On the anti-Fascist activity in London see: Bernabei, *Esuli ed emigrati italiani nel Regno Unito, 1920–1940* (Milan: Mursia, 1997). See also the entries by P. Di Paola: Corio Silvio; Gualducci Pietro; Recchioni Emidio, in Antonioli, Berti, Fedele, Iuso (eds), *Dizionario Biografico*.

[16] On the activity of Fasci Abroad in Britain see: Claudia Baldoli, *Exporting Fascism. Italian Fascists and Britain's Italians in the 1930s* (Oxford-New York: Berg, 2003).

[17] E. Recchioni, 'Per la nostra guerra', *L'Adunata dei Refrattari*, 4 April 1931.

[18] On the impact of the Second World War on Britain's Italian community see: Sponza, *Divided Loyalties*.

past, were Recchioni's son, Vernon Richards – future editor of *Freedom* – and Marie Louise Berneri, daughter of the Italian anarchist Camillo Berneri.

The experience of this second generation of refugees is emblematic of the relevance of the international anarchist diaspora. In contrast with the previous generation, these Italians merged with the British anarchist movement. Without Richards, the British anarchist movement 'would have been not different, but inexistent',[19] while 'Marie Louise Berneri's personality and spirit infused every activity undertaken by Freedom Press' from the time of her arrival to England in 1937 until her premature death in 1949.[20] With the help of Galasso, Thomas Keel, Emma Goldman and Camillo Berneri from France, Richards published the newspaper *Spain and the World* in 1936 and, from 1939, *War Commentary*. Gathered around these newspapers were the militants who would contribute to blowing new life into the British anarchist movement after the war.

But that is another story.

---

[19] Philip Sansom, 'Freedom Press and the anarchist movement in the 50s and 60s', in *Freedom: A hundred years* (London: Freedom Press, 1986), p. 35.

[20] Marie Louise Berneri Memorial Committee, *Marie Louise Berneri 1918–1949: A Tribute* (London, 1950).

Biographies

Agresti, Antonio (1864–1926)

Agresti became a political militant in Florence. In 1884 he was sentenced to imprisonment for publishing a seditious manifesto and escaped to France. He returned to Italy in 1889 and resumed his political activities. In 1891 he returned to France from where, after an expulsion decree, he moved to London where he contributed to the newspaper *The Torch*. In London he married Olivia Rossetti. In 1895 he travelled to the USA where he contributed to the newspaper *La Questione Sociale*. In 1897 he returned to Italy, first to Florence and then to Rome, withdrawing from militancy and devoting himself to journalism.

In 1914 he supported Italy's intervention into the war. After the conflict he worked for a conservative newspaper and was a Fascist sympathiser. He died in Rome in 1926.

Antonelli, Adolfo (1883–?)

Antonelli was born in Rome. Employed in a post office, he was sentenced to six months' imprisonment in 1901 for revealing the seizure of a pamphlet by the police. In 1902 he was arrested and sentenced to several months' imprisonment for fomenting disorder. He escaped to France and was expelled from the country. Antonelli reached London at the end of 1903 where he worked as a stonemason. He was considered one of the most active propagandisers in the Italian colony. He promoted the publication of the single issues *La Settimana Sanguinosa* and *Germinal*. The latter was strongly anti-organisationalist and harshly criticised Malatesta's ideas. In 1905 Antonelli published the single issue *L'Insurrezione*. On account of a short article in Bresci's memory, Antonelli was charged and sentenced to ten months' hard labour for incitement to murder. In 1906 he moved to the USA with his companion

Delfina Burzio. In San Francisco he published the newspaper *Nihil* in 1909. In 1937 he was identified as an active anti-fascist. The date of his death is unknown.

Bellelli, Ennio Enrico (Virgilio) (1860–1926)

Bellelli attended university in Bologna and apparently was taught by Carducci. In Bologna he knew the poets Severino Ferrari and Giovanni Pascoli and published some poems of his own. He was also involved with Guido Podrecca in the publication of the satirical newspaper *Bononia ridet*. In 1886 he worked as a clerk in a law chamber. In 1891 he edited the newspaper *L'Orizzonte* in Reggio Emilia. During this time he became active in the anarchist movement and collaborated on various newspapers. In 1896 Bellelli authored an April Fool's joke, writing a poem in Carducci's name praising the colonial war in Abyssinia that was published by several newspapers. In 1897, Bellelli was arrested and imprisoned for libelling a lawyer. He was released thanks to the good offices of a Senator. However, he was imprisoned again for a few months in 1898. It was probably during his imprisonment in Bologna that Bellelli began his collaboration with the Italian police. In 1900 he went to Paris where he spent time with another informer, Enrico Insabato (Dante). In 1901 Bellelli was expelled from France and went to London where he reported on the activities of the Italian anarchists for eleven years. Bellelli was married to Ida Emiliani. They had four daughters and two sons. In 1907 he was in Amsterdam when the International Anarchist Congress took place. In London he claimed to work as a bookseller. Apparently, he had a rich collection of books in Bologna. In 1912 Bellelli was unmasked as an informer and he returned to Reggio Emilia. During the war Bellelli was forced to sell his book collection. In the post war years Bellelli found himself in poor health and financial hardship. His son Ferruccio bore the weight of the maintenance of the family.

Calzitta, Antonio (Parussolo Angelo 1874–?)

For many years the Italian authorities were unable to identify Calzitta's real identity.

In London he sold citrus fruit wholesale in Greek Street. According to Virgilio, Calzitta escaped from home when very young because his stepmother ill-treated him. He worked in Dusseldorf as a servant to a family from Naples. After his marriage he moved to Canada and New York for two years where he lived in poverty. Around 1906 he moved to London where, with Recchioni's financial help, he opened his shop. He was on very close terms with Malatesta and the Defendi family, Enrico Defendi in particular.

Calzitta was active in the anarchist colony and financially helped several comrades, including Malatesta. In the 1920s and 1930s he participated in the activities of the Italian anti-Fascists in London. In 1939 he was still considered a dangerous anti-Fascist.

Cafiero, Carlo (1846–1892)

A leading figure in the Italian anarchist movement. Cafiero promoted the establishment of the International Working Men's Association in Italy after meeting Marx and Engels in London. In 1872 he broke with them and sided with Bakunin in the struggle for control of the First International. In 1873 he bought a piece of land near Lugano where he built a house to provide hospitality for Bakunin and other refugees. Cafiero took part in the insurrectionary attempts in Bologna in 1874 and Benevento in 1877. In 1879 he published the Compendium of Marx's Capital. Due to repression in Italy Cafiero, settled first in France and then in Lugano, where he wrote the essays *Revolution* and *Anarchy and Communism*. In 1880–1881 he attended the International Congress in London during which the first symptoms of his mental illness emerged. In 1882 he was arrested in Milan and attempted suicide in prison. In 1883 he was admitted to a mental asylum.

Cini, Francesco (1857–1943)

Until 1889 Cini was active in anarchist circles in Italy and in Egypt. To escape imprisonment he took refuge in Switzerland where he was involved in the organisation of the Congress of Capolago in 1891. Extradited by the Swiss authorities, he served one year's imprisonment in Italy. In 1894 he moved to London where he collaborated on the single issue *L'Anarchia*. He moved back to Egypt in 1898 where he continued his political activities. He returned to his native Livorno in the 1930s.

Cipriani, Amilcare (1844–1918)

Cipriani participated in the expedition of the Thousand with Garibaldi in 1860. He took part in other struggles for national independence in Greece and Crete. He fought in the Paris Commune in 1871. Sentenced to death, his punishment was commuted to exile for life in New Caledonia. After eight years he returned to Paris as a result of an amnesty. In 1881 Cipriani was arrested in Rimini and sentenced to twenty five years' imprisonment. Socialists, republicans and anarchists campaigned for his freedom and obtained his release in 1888. In 1891 he attended the Capolago congress. In 1897 he participated in the Greek-Turkish war and was wounded in one leg. He returned to France and lived in Paris. In 1914 he supported the war against Germany and Austria.

Corio, Silvio (1875–1954)

Corio became a militant at an early age and frequented socialist and anarchist circles in Turin. In 1897, during his national service, he was punished for propagandising subversive ideas. After his discharge, he moved to Paris where he was suspected of being involved in the killing of King Umberto. In 1901 Corio was expelled from France and took refuge in London. He actively participated in all the initiatives of the anarchist colony, contributing to several newspapers using the pen name 'Crastinus'. He was the editor of the newspaper *L'Internazionale, Lo Sciopero Generale* and *La Rivoluzione Sociale*. In 1902 Corio was among the founders of L'Università Popolare and in 1909 was the secretary of the International Club in Charlotte Street. In 1907 he participated in the international Congress in Amsterdam. From 1911, with the Italian invasion of Libya, anti-colonial activities became a central focus of his militancy. In 1911 he was active in the Malatesta Release Committee. In 1914 he initially supported the war, but then changed his position and engaged in anti-militarist propaganda. In 1917 he came into contact with Sylvia Pankhurst and became deeply involved in the publication of her newspaper *Workers' Dreadnought*. Corio became Pankhurst's companion. In 1927 the couple had a child, Richard Keir Pethick, who took Pankhurst's surname. In the 1920s Corio promoted the anti-Fascist newspaper *Il Comento*. Later, Corio was involved in the publication of *Spain and the World* with Vernon Richards, Emma Goldman, Francesco Galasso and Marie Louise Berneri. After the Fascist invasion of Ethiopia, Corio and Pankhurst published *New Times and Ethiopia News* which had a circulation of 40,000 copies at its peak. Corio was also involved in helping Italian anti-Fascists interned as enemy aliens during the war. After the conflict he carried on his pro-Ethiopia activities.

Defendi, Eugenio Giovanni (1849–1925); Defendi, Enrico (1883–1916)

Giovanni Defendi was sentenced to eight years in prison for his participation in the Paris Commune. In 1880 he moved to London where he became Emilia Trunzio's companion. He managed a grocer's shop. Defendi and Trunzio had six children, though some of them may have been Malatesa's children. Malatesta lived almost constantly with the couple during his exile in London. Enrico Defendi (1883–1919) was probably Malatesta's son. In 1883, when Malatesta went to Ancona to edit *L'Agitazione*, he took the fourteen year old Enrico Defendi with him. Enrico worked as errand boy for the newspaper. In 1898, after the suppression of the Ancona uprising, Enrico Defendi was sentenced to six months in prison. He returned to London after serving his sentence. Enrico Defendi remained active in the anarchist colony until his death from tuberculosis in 1916.

Fornara, Giuseppe (1850–1941)

Nicknamed Piemonte, Fornara arrived in London around 1890. He frequented the *Autonomie Club* and was a member of the group *L'Anonimato*. He was on friendly terms with Louise Michel. Arrested in 1894 for possession of explosive materials, he was sentenced to twenty years in prison. The British and Italian authorities prevented his release by certifying him as insane. He died in Broadmoor Criminal Asylum in 1945.

Frigerio, Carlo (1878–1966)

As a teenager, Frigerio attended conferences organised by socialists and anarchists in Milan. Expelled from Italy in 1898 he lived in Berne then moved to London in 1901 where he joined Malatesta's group and contributed to Italian anarchist publications. In 1905 he moved to Paris but was subsequently expelled. In 1907 he attended the International Anarchist Congress in Amsterdam. In 1908 he returned to Geneva where he was on the editorial committee of the newspaper *Il Risveglio*. His knowledge of four languages enabled him to maintain contact with many European anarchists. In 1910 he moved to Paris and in 1914 to London where he remained until 1919. In 1915 Frigerio was among the subscribers of the manifesto against the war. After the war he returned to Italy where he contributed to the newspapers *Umanità Nova* and *Pensiero e Volontà*. With the advent of Fascism, after a period in hiding, he returned to Geneva where he continued his anti-Fascist activities and his collaboration with *Il Risveglio*. After the war Frigerio helped to establish the *Centre Internationale de Recherches sur l'anarchisme*.

Ginnasi, Francesco (1859–1943)

A doctor, Ginnasi was the son of a Count. He met the Internationalists in Naples where he went to study. He was one of the organisers of the insurrectional attempt in Benevento in 1877. In 1878 he moved to Switzerland where he lived with Malatesta before being expelled. In 1881 he moved to London where he stayed for a brief period. In 1884 he obtained a degree in medicine in New York. He returned to Italy in 1919.

Gori, Pietro (1865–1911)

Lawyer and poet, Gori defended anarchists at many trials (including Paolo Schicchi, C. di Sciullo, Luigi Galleani and Sante Caserio). He is the most famous anarchist author of theatrical plays and a composer of anarchist songs and poems. He graduated in law in 1889. An active propagandist in Tuscany, in 1891 Gori took part in the foundation congress of the Anarchist Socialist Party at Capolago. In 1894 he was implicated in Caserio's assassination of the French President Carnot was forced to take refuge in Switzerland. However, harassment continued. Gori escaped an attempt on his life when two gun shots were fired at him. In January 1895, Swiss authorities arrested and expelled him and other anarchist refugees. While in prison Gori composed 'Farewell to Lugano'. From Switzerland he moved to London. After a few months he moved to the United States where he undertook a long propaganda tour. In Paterson he first staged his play, *First of May*. As a trade union delegate he attended the international socialist labour congress in London (27 July–1 August 1896). While in London he fell seriously ill. On return to Italy, he resumed his political and professional activities. However, in 1898 he was forced again to take the path of exile and moved to South America. In Argentina he engaged in a variety of political and editorial activities. Gori was among the promoters of the anarcho-syndicalist FORA (Argentine Regional Workers' Federation). He conducted a propaganda tour in Uruguay, Chile and Patagonia. In 1901 he explored the sources of the Panama River. Following an amnesty he returned to Italy in 1902 and he published the newspaper *Il Pensiero* with Luigi Fabbri. In 1906 his fragile health collapsed and he retired to the island of Elba. He died in 1911.

Gualducci, Pietro (1871–?)

Gualducci received his first sentence of one month in prison for singing a revolutionary song in 1893. He received another sentence of three months for use of force against a public official during a demonstration in 1894. Enlisted in the Cavalry, Gualducci was sent to a penal colony because of his subversive ideas. In 1897 he joined the Foreign Legion and spent eight months in Algeria. After returning to Italy he moved to Switzerland where he was arrested in 1898 on suspicion of being an accomplice to the assassi-nation of the Empress of Austria. Deported to Italy he was arrested and sentenced to three months' imprisonment for praising anarchy in a tavern. To avoid further persecution Gualducci took refuge in France in 1899 from where he reached London in 1900. In London he worked as a carpenter and waiter and participated in all the initiatives of the anarchist colony. He assumed an anti-organisational stand. In the 1920s he was a well-known figure among Italian anti-Fascists in London. He collaborated on the newspapers *Il Comento* and *New Times and Ethiopia News*. In the 1930s Gualducci published single issues (also in English), denouncing the crimes of the Fascist regime to the British public.

Malatesta, Errico (1853–1932).

Malatesta was one of the leading figures of the Italian and international anarchist movement for around sixty years. He was the author of anarchist propaganda pamphlets that have been translated into many different languages, of which *Anarchy, Between Peasants*, and *At the Café* are among the most famous. Malatesta was one of the founders of the Italian Federation of the International Working Men's Association (First International) in 1872. In the same year he attended the Congress of St Imier which established the international anarchist movement. He played a central role in two insurrectionary attempts in South and Central Italy in 1874 and 1877. Between 1878 and 1919 Malatesta spent most of his life in exile. He travelled to Egypt, South and North America, France and Britain. During those years, his visits to Italy were mostly aimed at organising revolutionary attempts. Malatesta published several influential anarchist newspapers: *La Questione Sociale*, *L'Associazione, L'Agitazione, L' Anarchia*, and *Volontà*. In 1920 after returning to Italy, Malatesta edited *Umanità Nova*, the first anarchist daily newspaper. The paper's offices were destroyed by Fascists at the end of 1922. Under the regime Malatesta was kept under house arrest in Rome and was subject to constant surveillance. He died after a short illness in 1932.

Merlino, Francesco Saverio (Naples 1856–1930).

Lawyer and theorist of libertarian socialism, Merlino defended the anarchists at many trials. His militancy began in Naples in 1879. In 1881 he attended the international anarchist congress in London. In 1883 he was sentenced to four years' imprisonment for conspiring against the State and fled to London. During his exile Merlino devoted himself to intellectual and theoretical studies that led him to the development of the idea of libertarian socialism. In 1890 he published a critical analysis of Italian society (*L'Italia com'è*). In the 1890s Merlino opposed the terrorist tendencies of the anarchist movement. In 1896 he engaged in a public polemic with Malatesta, who opposed Merlino's views on the necessity of participating in parliamentary elections. In 1900, despite having left the anarchist movement, Merlino defended Gaetano Bresci, the anarchist who killed King Umberto. (Turati, the leader of the Italian Socialist Party, refused to defend him.) After the war Merlino reestablished his contacts with the anarchist movement. With the advent of Fascism he retired to private life. He died in Rome.

Pacini, Isaia (1856–1922)

Pacini moved to Lugano in 1884 to avoid fifteen months' imprisonment, and he opened a tailor's shop. Active in the anarchist groups of that area he was one of the organisers of the anarchist congress at Capolago. He became a reference point for anarchists who escaped from Italy to Switzerland. Expelled from Lugano in 1895 he moved to London where he contributed to the single issue *L'Anarchia*. He continued to work as a tailor. In 1911 he moved to Paris with his wife and five children. He returned to Italy in 1919.

Parmeggiani, Luigi (1858–1945).

Parmeggiani was a rather controversial character. In the 1880s in Paris he established several anarchist groups along with Vittorio Pini which promoted and practised expropriation as a revolutionary means. Parmeggiani was sentenced to thirty years' imprisonment for his involvement in the attempt on the lives of the socialist Celso Ceretti and Camillo Prampolini in 1889. Parmeggiani took refuge in London where he became leader of the anti-organisational group *L'Anonimato /La Libera Iniziativa* that opposed Malatesta and Merlino's attempts to organise the anarchist movement. At the same time, under the name of Louis Mercy, Parmeggiani was known as a successful art dealer both in London and Paris. He moved to the French capital to manage his antique shop at the end of the 1890s. In 1905 he sued an inspector of Scotland Yard for libel for describing him as an anarchist in his memoirs. In 1924 he returned to his native town of Reggio Emilia. In 1932 he donated his whole collection to the city council in exchange for an annual subsidy. His collection is held at the Museo-Galleria Parmeggiani.

Petraroja, Gennaro (1860–1937).

Petraroja migrated to France in 1886, and was arrested and expelled in 1890. After six months' imprisonment in Naples in 1892, he escaped to London where he was actively involved in the anarchist colony. He returned to Naples in 1907 where he was arrested several times because of his militancy. From 1919 Petraroja was involved in trade union activities. In 1926, under the Fascist regime, Petraroja was sent into exile for one year on the islands of Favignana and Lipari. In 1936 he was admitted to a mental ayslum where he died the following year.

Recchioni, Emidio (1864–1934)

Recchioni became a militant in Ancona. Employed by a rail company, he was able to facilitate contact between the region's anarchist groups. In 1894 he was arrested on suspicion of complicity in Paolo Lega's attempt on the life of Prime Minister Crispi. Acquitted, he was subsequently placed under house arrest in 1895 and again in 1897. After his release in 1899, Recchioni moved to London where he actively participated in the initiatives of the anarchist colony. In 1909 he bought and successfully managed a delicatessen shop (the King Bomba) in Soho. He used part of the revenue to finance many anarchist enterprises and newspapers and to help comrades in hardship. He provided the anarchist historian Max Nettlau with a monthly subsidy. Recchioni contributed to several anarchist newspapers under the pen-name 'Nemo'. In the 1920s and 1930s he was a leading figure among Italian anti-Fascists in London, maintaining contact with anti-Fascist exiles in France. Recchioni was involved in organising the attempts against Mussolini by Michele Schirru (1931) and Giovanni Sbardellotto (1932). He died after a long illness in 1934.

Solieri Vito (1857–1923)

Employed as a barber. In 1874 when he was seventeen years old Solieri participated in the insurrectionary attempt in Bologna. He was acquitted after spending almost two years in preventive detention. To avoid military service he escaped to Switzerland where he joined Malatesta and Cafiero. He was expelled from Switzerland in 1879 and went to join the international colony of anarchists in London. He strongly criticised Andrea Costa's turn towards parliamentarism. In 1887 he moved to the United States.

Tombolesi Romeo (1869–1921)

Worked as a tailor. Active in Ancona in the 1890s. In 1894 Tombolesi was sentenced to a prison term of two years and seven months by default as a member of a subversive association.

He took refuge in France and moved to London in 1901. Tombolesi contributed to the newspaper *La Rivoluzione Sociale*. He participated in the constitution of the Università Popolare and in following years was involved in the activities of the political refugee colony. In 1918 he suffered an apoplectic attack and returned to Italy.

Bibliography

Agosti, Aldo, Gian Mario Bravo, and Patrizia Audenino, *Storia del movimento operaio, del socialismo e delle lotte sociali in Piemonte*, vol. 2, 'L'età giolittiana, la guerra e il dopoguerra: saggi' (Bari: De Donato, 1979).

Alvarez Junco, Jose, *The Emergence of Mass Politics in Spain: Populist Demagoguery and Republican Culture, 1890–1910* (Brighton; Portland [Or.]: Sussex Academic Press, 2002).

Anderson, Benedict, *Under Three Flags: Anarchism and the Anti-colonial Imagination* (London: Verso, 2005).

Antonioli, Maurizio, *Il sindacalismo italiano. Dalle origini al fascismo, studi e ricerche* (Pisa: BFS, 1997).

Antonioli, Maurizio, Berti Giampietro, Fedele Santi, Iuso Pasquale (eds), *Dizionario biografico degli anarchici italiani* (Pisa: BFS, 2003).

Antonioli, Maurizio and Pier Carlo Masini, *Il sol dell'avvenire: l'anarchismo in Italia dalle origini alla prima guerra mondiale* (Pisa: BFS, 1999).

Arcangeli, Stefano, *Errico Malatesta e il comunismo anarchico italiano*, 2nd edition (Milan: Jaca Book, 1974).

Audenino, Patrizia, *Cinquant'anni di stampa operaia: dall'Unità alla guerra di Libia* (Parma: Guanda, 1976).

Baldoli, Claudia, *Exporting Fascism: Italian Fascists and Britain's Italians in the 1930s* (Oxford: Berg, 2003).

Bantman C., *The French Anarchists in London, 1880-1914. Exile and Transnationalism in the First Globalization* (Liverpool: Liverpool University Press, 2013).

Bantman, Constance, 'Internationalism without an International? Cross-Channel Anarchist Networks, 1880–1914' in *Revue Belge de Philologie et d'histoire*, vol. 84, no. 4 (2006), pp. 961–81.

Bartoloni, Valerio, *I fatti delle Tremiti: una rivolta di coatti anarchici nell'Italia umbertina* (Foggia: Bastogi, 1996).

Bencivenni, Marcella, *Italian Immigrant Radical Culture: The Idealism of the*

Sovversivi in the United States, 1890-1940 (New York: New York University Press, 2011).

Bernabei, Alfio, *Esuli ed emigrati italiani nel Regno Unito, 1920-1940* (Milan: Mursia, 1997).

Berry, David, and Constance Bantman (eds), *New Perspectives on Anarchism, Labour and Syndicalism: the Individual, the National and the Transnational* (Newcastle: Cambridge Scholars, 2010).

Berti, Giampietro D., *Francesco Saverio Merlino: dall'anarchismo socialista al socialismo liberale (1856-1930)*, (Milan: F. Angeli, 1993).

Berti, Giampietro D., *Errico Malatesta e il movimento anarchico italiano e internazionale: 1872–1932* (Milan: F. Angeli, 2003).

Bettini, Leonardo, *Bibliografia dell'anarchismo / vol.1, tomo 2, periodici e numeri unici anarchici in lingua italiana pubblicati all'estero (1872-1971)* (Florence: Crescita politica editrice, 1976).

Binaghi, Maurizio, *Addio Lugano bella: gli esuli politici nella Svizzera italiana di fine Ottocento: 1866-1895* (Locarno [CH]: A. Dadò, 2002).

Blair, Claude, and Marian Campbell, *Louis Marcy: oggetti d'arte della Galleria Parmeggiani di Reggio Emilia*, Cataloghi dei Musei civici di Reggio Emilia (Turin; London: U. Allemandi, 2008).

Boldetti, Ambra, 'La repressione in Italia: il caso del 1894' in *Rivista di storia contemporanea*, vol. 6, no. 4 (1977), pp. 481–515.

Borghi, Armando, *Errico Malatesta* (Milan: Istituto Editoriale Italiano, 1947).

Borghi, Armando, *Mezzo secolo di anarchia 1898–1945* (Naples: E.S.I., 1954).

Bottignolo, Bruno, *Without a Bell Tower: a Study of the Italian Immigrants in South West England* (Rome: Centro Studi Emigrazione, 1985).

Bottinelli, Giampiero, *Luigi Bertoni, la coerenza di un anarchico* (Lugano: La baronata, 1997).

Briguglio, Letterio, *Il partito operaio e gli anarchici* (Rome: Edizioni di Storia e Letteratura, 1969).

Broggini, Romano, 'Un gruppo internazionalista dissidente: la sezione del Ceresio', in *Anarchismo e socialismo in Italia (1872–1892)*, edited by Liliano Faenza (Rome: Editori Riuniti, 1973), pp. 187–208.

Brunello, Piero, *Storie di anarchici e di spie* (Rome: Donzelli Editore, 2009).

Burton, June K, *Essays in European History: Selected from the Annual Meetings of the Southern Historical Association, 1986-1987* (Lanham: University Press of America, 1989).

Butterworth, Alex, *The world that never was: a true story of dreamers, schemers, anarchists and secret agents* (London: Vintage, 2011).

Cafiero, Carlo, *La rivoluzione per la rivoluzione*, edited by Gianni Bosio (Milan: Edizioni del Gallo, 1968).

Campolonghi, Luigi, *Amilcare Cipriani: memorie raccolte da Luigi Campolonghi* (Milan: Società editoriale Italiana, 1912).

Carlo Carrà, *La mia vita* (Milan: Feltrinelli, 1981).

Carlson, Andrew, *Anarchism in Germany* (Metuchen: The Scarecrow Press, 1972).

Castronovo, Valerio, *La stampa italiana dall'unità al fascismo, etc.* (Bari: Laterza, 1970).

Cham, Caroline, *Kropotkin and the Rise of Revolutionary Anarchism 1872-1886* (Cambridge: Cambridge University Press, 1989).

Chesterton, G. K., *The Man Who Was Thursday* (Harmondsworth, Middlesex: Penguin Books Ltd, 1975).

Cipriani, Amilcare *Bresci e Savoia. Il regicidio* (Paterson: Libreria Sociologica, 1900).

Civolani, Emilia, 'La partecipazione di emigrati italiani alla Comune di Parigi' in *Movimento operaio e socialista*, vol. 2, no. 21 (1979), pp. 151–83.

Cobb, Richard Charles, *The Police and the People: French Popular Protest, 1789-1820* (Oxford: Clarendon, 1970).

Collyer, Michael, 'Secret agents: Anarchists, Islamists, and Responses to Politically Active Refugees in London', *Ethnic and Racial Studies*, 28.2 (2005), pp. 278–303.

Colpi, Terri, *The Italian Factor: The Italian Community in Great Britain* (Edinburgh; London: Mainstream, 1991).

Damiani, Franco, *Bakunin nell'Italia post-unitaria, 1864-1867: anticlericalismo, democrazia, questione operaia e contadina negli anni del soggiorno italiano di Bakunin* (Milan: Jaca Book, 1977).

Darlington, Ralph, *Syndicalism and the Transition to Communism: an International Comparative Analysis* (Aldershot: Ashgate, 2008).

Davis, John A., *Conflict and Control: Law and Order in nineteenth-century Italy* (Basingstoke: Macmillan Education, 1988).

De Groot, Gerard J., *Blighty: British Society in the Era of the Great War* (London: Longman, 1996).

De Marco, Laura, *Il soldato che disse no alla guerra: storia dell'anarchico Augusto Masetti (1888–1966)*, Il risveglio (Santa Maria Capua Vetere [Caserta]: Spartaco, 2003).

De Vito, Christian, ed., *Global Labour History* (Verona: Ombre Corte, 2012).

Degl'Innocenti, Maurizio, *Il socialismo italiano e la guerra di Libia* (Rome: Editori Riuniti,1976).

Degl'Innocenti, Maurizio, ed., *L'esilio nella storia contemporanea* (Manduria: Pietro Lacaita editore, 1992).

Della Peruta, Franco, 'Il socialismo italiano dal 1875 al 1882' in *Annali dell' Istituto Gian Giacomo Feltrinelli*, vol. 1 (1958), pp. 15–58.

Della Peruta, Franco, *Mazzini e i rivoluzionari italiani, 1830–1845* (Milan: Feltrinelli, 1974).

Derechef, Ralph, 'Anarchism in England' in *The Anarchist Peril*, edited by Félix Dubois (London: T. Fisher Unwin, 1894), pp. 262–84.

Diemoz, Erika, *A Morte il tiranno. Anarchia e violenza da Crispi a Mussolini* (Turin: Einaudi, 2011).

Di Paola, Pietro, 'La più forte e qualificata concentrazione di anarchici di tutte le nazionalità. Pietro Gori a Londra' in Antonioli, Bertolucci, Giulianelli (eds), *Nostra Patria è il mondo intero. Pietro Gori nel movimento operaio e libertario italiano e internazionale* (Pisa: BFS, 2012).

Di Paola, Pietro, 'Club anarchici di Londra: sociabilità, politica, cultura', in *Società e Storia*, no. 108, 2005, pp. 133–55.

Di Paola, Pietro, 'Giuseppe Farnara. Storia di un anarchico italiano a Londra', in *Annali dell'Università di Ca' Foscari*, vol. 38, nos 1–2 (1999), pp. 663–80.

Di Paola, Pietro, 'The Spies Who Came in from the Heat: the International Surveillance of the Anarchists in London' in *European History Quarterly*, vol. 37, no. 2 (April 2007), pp. 189–215.

Emiliani, Vittorio, *Gli anarchici* (Milan: Bompiani, 1973).

Emiliani, Vittorio, *Libertari di Romagna. Vite di Costa, Cipriani, Borghi* (Ravenna: Longo Angelo Editore, 1995).

Fabbri, Luigi, *Malatesta: l'uomo e il pensiero* (Naples: Edizioni RL, 1951).

Fabbri, Luce, *Luigi Fabbri: storia di un'uomo libero* (Pisa: BFS, 1996).

Faenza, Liliano, *Anarchismo e socialismo in Italia, 1872–1892: atti del Convegno di studi Marxisti e 'Riministi', Rimini, 19–21 ottobre 1972*, Biblioteca del movimento operaio italiano (Rome: Editori Riuniti, 1973).

Fedele, Santi, *Una breve illusione: gli anarchici italiani e la Russia sovietica, 1917–1939* (Milan: Franco Angeli, 1996).

Fedeli, Ugo, *Luigi Galleani: quarant'anni di lotte rivoluzionarie 1891–1931* (Cesena: Edizioni L'Antistato, 1956).

Fedeli, Ugo, *Giuseppe Ciancabilla* (Imola: Galeati, 1965).

Felici, Isabelle, *La Cecilia histoire d'une communauté anarchiste et de son fondateur Giovanni Rossi*, Collection Commune mémoire (Lyon: Atelier de création libertaire, 2001).

Felici, Isabelle, *Poésie d'un rebelle: poète, anarchiste, émigré: 1876–1953* (Lyon: Atelier de creation libertaire, 2009).

Finzi, Paolo, *La nota persona. Errico Malatesta in Italia. Dicembre 1919-Luglio 1920* (Ragusa: La Fiaccola, 1990).

Fishman, W. J., *East End Jewish Radicals 1875–1914* (Nottingham: Five Leaves, 2004).

Flor O'Squarr, Charles Marie, *Les Coulisses de l'Anarchie* (Paris, 1892).

Fozzi, Daniela, *Tra prevenzione e repressione: il domicilio coatto nell'Italia liberale* (Rome: Carocci, 2010).

Franzinelli, Mimmo. 'Sull'uso (critico) delle fonti di polizia' in *Voci di compagni, schede di questura* (Milan: Quaderni del Centro Studi Libertari Archivio Pinelli, 2002).

Freedom Press, *Freedom: A Hundred Years* (London: Freedom Press, 1986).

Freitag, Sabine, *Exiles from European revolutions: refugees in mid-Victorian England* (New York; Oxford: Berghahn Books, 2003).

French, D., 'Spy Fever in Britain, 1900–1915' *Historical Journal*, vol. 21 (1978).

Furiozzi, Gian Biagio, 'Sindacalisti rivoluzionari e anarchici', *Ricerche Storiche*, 2–3 (1982), pp. 495–512.

Gabaccia, Donna, *Italy's Many Diasporas* (London: UCL Press, 2000).

Gabaccia, Donna, 'Class, Exile and Nationalism at Home and Abroad: the Italian Risorgimento' in *Italian Workers of the World: Labor Migration and the Formation of Multiethnic States* (Urbana: University of Illinois Press, 2001).

Gabaccia, Donna, *Militants and Migrants: Rural Sicilians Become American Workers* (New Brunswick: Rutgers University Press, 1988).

Gabaccia, Donna and Franca Iacovetta, *Women, gender and transnational lives: Italian workers of the world* (Toronto: University of Toronto Press, 2002).

Gabaccia, Donna and Fraser M. Ottanelli, *Italian Workers of the World: Labor Migration and the Formation of Multiethnic States* (Urbana: University of Illinois Press, 2001).

Gainer, Bernard, *The Alien Invasion: the Origins of the Aliens Act of 1905* (London: Heinemann Educational, 1972).

Galante Garrone, Alessandro, 'L'emigrazione politica italiana del Risorgimento' in *Rassegna Storica del Risorgimento*, vol. 41 (1954), pp. 223–42.

Galzerano, Giuseppe, *Gaetano Bresci: la vita, l'attentato, il processo e la morte del regicida anarchico* (Salerno: Galzerano, 1988).

Garrard, John Adrian, *The English and Immigration, 1880–1910* (London; New York; Toronto: Oxford University Press, 1971).

Gelvin, James, 'Al-Qaeda and Anarchism: A Historian's Reply to Terrorology', *Terrorism and Political Violence*, 20.4 (2008).

Giulietti, Fabrizio, *Storia degli anarchici italiani in età giolittiana* (Milan: Franco Angeli, 2012).

Goldman, Emma, *Living My Life, Volume 2* (New York: Dover, 1970).

Goldstein, Robert J., *Political Repression in 19th Century Europe* (London: Croom Helm, 1983).

Goodway, David (ed.), *For Anarchism. History, Theory and Practice* (London; New York: Routledge, 1989).

Gori, Pietro, *Pagine di Vagabondaggio* (Milan: Editrice moderna, 1948).

Gori, Pietro, *La Miseria e i delitti* (edited by M. Antonioli and F. Bertolucci) (Pisa: BFS, 2011).

Gosi, Rosellina, *Il socialismo utopistico: Giovanni Rossi e la colonia anarchica Cecilia* (Milan: Moizzi, 1977).

Goyens, Tom, *Beer and Revolution: the German Anarchist Movement in New York City, 1880–1914* (Urbana: University of Illinois Press, 2007).

Graur, M., *An Anarchist Rabbi: The Life and teachings of Rudolf Rocker* (New York: St. Martin's Press, 1997).

Grave, Jean, *Quarante ans de propagande anarchiste* (Paris: Flammarion, 1973).

Guglielmo, Jennifer, *Living the revolution: Italian women's resistance and radicalism in New York City, 1880–1945* (Chapel Hill, N.C.: University of North Carolina Press, 2010).

Gundle, Stephen, and Lucia Rinaldi, *Assassinations and murder in modern Italy: transformations in society and culture* (Basingstoke: Palgrave Macmillan, 2007).

Halevy, Elie, and E. I. Watkin, *A History of the English People in the Nineteenth Century: Vol. 5. Imperialism and the Rise of Labour.* (London: Benn, 1951).

Hamon, Augustin, *Le Socialisme et le congrès de Londres, étude historique* (Paris: P.-V. Stock, 1897).

Haupt, George 'Il ruolo degli emigrati e dei rifugiati nella diffusione delle idee socialiste all'epoca della Seconda Internazionale', in *Anna Kuliscioff e l'età del Riformismo* (Rome: Mondo Operaio, Edizioni Avanti!, 1978), pp. 59–68.

Hirsch, Steven, and Lucien van der Walt, *Anarchism and Syndicalism in the Colonial and Postcolonial World, 1870–1940: the Praxis of National Liberation, Internationalism, and Social Revolution* (Leiden; Boston: Brill, 2010).

Hostetter, Richard, *The Italian Socialist Movement. Origins (1860–1882)* (Princeton van Nostrand, 1958).

International Workingmen's, Association, *The General Council of the First International, 1864–1866(–1871–1872)* vol. 5 (Foreign Languages Publishing House: Moscow, 1963).

Isabella, Maurizio, 'Italian Exiles and British Politics' in *Exiles From European Revolutions*, edited by Sabine Freitag (Oxford; New York: Berghahn Books, 2003), pp. 59–87.

Isabella, Maurizio, *Risorgimento in exile: Italian émigrés and the liberal international in the post-Napoleonic era* (Oxford: Oxford University Press, 2009).

Jensen, Richard Bach, 'The International Anti-Anarchist Conference of 1898 and the Origins of Interpol', *Journal of Contemporary History*, vol. 16, no. 2 (1981), pp. 323–47.

Jensen, Richard Bach, 'Italy's Peculiar Institution: Internal Police Exile, 1861–1914', in *Essays in European History: Selected from the Annual Meetings of the Southern Historical Association, 1986–1987*, edited by J. K. Burton (Lanham: University Press of America, 1989), pp. 99–114.

Jensen, Richard Bach, 'Daggers, Rifles and Dynamite: Anarchist Terrorism in Nineteenth Century Europe', *Terrorism and Political Violence*, 16. 1. (2004).

Joll, James, *The Second International, 1889–1914* (London & Boston: Routledge & Kegan Paul, 1974).

Joll, James, *The anarchists*, 2nd ed. (London: Methuen, 1979).

Jones, Mark, Paul Craddock, and Nicholas Barker, *Fake? The Art of Deception* (London: British Museum Publications Ltd, 1990).

Khuri-Makdisi, Ilham, *The Eastern Mediterranean and the Making of Global Radicalism, 1860–1914* (Berkeley, CA; London: University of California Press, 2010).

Knepper, Paul, 'The other invisible hand: Jews and anarchists in London before the First World War' in *Jewish History*, vol. 22, no. 3 (2008), pp. 295–315.

Kropotkin, Petr Alekseevich, *Memoirs of a revolutionist* (Boston and New York: Houghton, Mifflin and Company, 1899).

Latouche, Peter, *Anarchy: An authentic exposition of the methods of anarchists and the aims of anarchism* (London: Everett &Co., 1908).

Lattek, Christine, *Revolutionary Refugees: German Socialism in Britain, 1840–1860* (London: Routledge, 2006).

Levy, Carl, 'Malatesta in London: the Era of Dynamite' in *A Century of Italian Emigration to Britain 1880–1980s. Five essays*, edited by Lucio Sponza and A. Tosi, supplement to *The Italianist* (1993).

Levy, Carl, 'Currents of Italian Syndicalism before 1926' in *International Review of Social History*, vol. 45, no. 2 (2000), pp. 209–50.

Levy, Carl, 'Social Histories of Anarchism' in *Journal for the Study of Radicalism*, vol. 4, no. 2 (2010), pp. 1–44.

Levy, Carl, 'Anarchism and Cosmopolitanism' in *Journal of Political Ideologies*, vol. 16, no. 3 (2011), pp. 265–78.

Levy, Carl, 'Malatesta in Exile' in *Annali della Fondazione Luigi Einaudi*, vol. 15 (1981), pp. 245–80.

Levy, Carl, 'Charisma and Social Movements: Errico Malatesta and Italian Anarchism' in *Modern Italy*, vol. 3, no. 2 (1988), pp. 205–17.

Levy, Carl, 'The Anarchist Assassin and Italian History, 1870s to 1930s' in *Assassinations and Murder in Modern Italy: Transformations in Society and Culture*, edited by Stephen Gundle and Lucia Rinaldi (Basingstoke: Palgrave Macmillan, 2007), pp. 207–22.

Linden, Marcel van der, and Wayne Thorpe, *Revolutionary syndicalism: an international perspective* (Aldershot: Scolar, 1990).

Lodolini, Elio, 'L'esilio in Brasile dei detenuti politici romani 1837' in *Rassegna Storica del Risorgimento*, vol. 65, no. 1 (1978), pp. 132–74.

Lodolini, Elio, 'Deportazione negli Stati Uniti d'America di detenuti politici dello Stato pontificio' in *Rassegna Storica del Risorgimento*, vol. 88, no. 2 (2001), pp. 323–54.

Lollini, Vittorio, *L'ammonizione e il domicilio coatto* (Bologna: Fratelli Treves, 1882).

Lombroso, Cesare, *Gli Anarchici. Seconda edizione con aggiunte* (Turin: Fratelli Brocca, 1895).

Lorenzo, Anselmo, *El proletariado militante* (Mexico: ed. Vertice, 1926).

Lotti, Luigi, *La settimana rossa; con documenti inediti* (Florence: F. Le Monnier, 1965).

Maitron, Jean, *Ravachol et les anarchistes* (Paris: René Julliard, 1964).

Majetti, Raffaele, *L'Anarchia e le leggi che la reprimono in Italia* (Caserta: Tip. Elzeviriano Domenico Fabiano, 1894).

Malatesta, Errico, and Rosaria Bertolucci, *Epistolario lettere edite e inedite*

1873–1932, edited by Centro studi sociali Avenza (Carrara: Centro studi sociali, 1984).

Malatesta, Errico, edited by Piero Brunello and Pietro Di Paola, *Autobiografia mai scritta: ricordi (1853–1932)* (Santa Maria Capua Vetere (Caserta): Spartaco, 2003).

Malatesta, Errico, and Gino Cerrito, *Scritti scelti* (Rome, 1970).

Malatesta, Errico, and Vernon Richards, *Errico Malatesta, His Life & Ideas* (London: Freedom Press, 1965).

Malato, Charles, *De la Commune a l'Anarchie* (Paris, 1894).

Malato, Charles, *Les Joyeusetés de l'exil* (Paris, 1897).

Marie Louise Berneri Memorial Committee, *Marie Louise Berneri 1918-1949: a Tribute* (London, 1950).

Martinez, P., 'A Police Spy and the Exiled Communards, 1871–1873 in *English Historical Review*, vol. 97, no. 382 (1982), pp. 99–112.

Martinez, P. K., 'Paris Communard refugee in Britain, 1871–1880' (Ph.D. thesis, University of Sussex, 1981).

Marwick, Arthur, *The Deluge: British Society and the First World War* (Basingstoke: Macmillan Education, 1991).

Masini, Pier Carlo, *Gli internazionalisti: la banda del Mate, 1876–1878* (Milan: Avanti, 1958).

Masini, Pier Carlo, 'La Prima Internazionale in Italia. Problemi di una revisione storiografica' in *Il Movimento operaio e socialista. Bilancio storiografico e problemi storici. Convegno di Firenze. 18–20 gennaio 1963* (Milan: Edizioni del Gallo, 1965), pp. 85–142.

Masini, Pier Carlo, *Storia degli anarchici italiani: da Bakunin a Malatesta (1862–1892)* (Milan: Rizzoli, 1969).

Masini, Pier Carlo, *Cafiero* (Milan: Rizzoli, 1974).

Masini, Pier Carlo, *Storia degli anarchici italiani nell'epoca degli attentati* (Milan: Rizzoli, 1981).

McCalman, Iain, *Radical Underworld: Prophets, Revolutionaries and Pornographers in London, 1795–1840* (Oxford: Clarendon Press, 1988).

Meredith, Isabel pseud., Agresti Olivia Rossetti, and Helen Rossetti, *A Girl Among the Anarchists* (London: Duckworth and Co., 1903).

Merlino, Francesco Saverio, *Nécessité et bases d'une entente*, Propagande Socialiste-Anarchiste-Révolutionnaire, no. 1 (Bruxelles: imprint A. Longfils, 1892).

Merlino, Francesco Saverio, Aldo Venturini and Pier Carlo Masini, *Concezione critica del socialismo libertario* (Florence, 1957).

Merriman, John M., *The Dynamite Club: How a Bombing in* fin-de-siècle *Paris Ignited the Age of Modern Terror* (London: JR Books, 2009).

Millman, Brock, *Managing Domestic Dissent in First World War Britain* (London: Frank Cass, 2000).

Moisio, Francesco, *Anarchici a Venezia* (Venice: La Tipografica, 1989).

Morelli, Anne, *Rubino l'anarchiste italien qui tenta d'assassiner Léopold II* (Bruxelles: Labor, 2006).

Most, Johann Joseph, *Memoiren, Erlebtes, Erforschtes und Erdachtes* (New York: the Author, 1903).

Moya, Jose, 'Anarchism', in *The Palgrave Dictionary of Transnational History*, (Basingstoke: Palgrave,2009).

Musarra, Natale, 'Le confidenze di "Francesco" G. Domanico al Conte Codronchi' in *Rivista Storica dell'Anarchismo*, vol. 3, no. 1 (1996), pp. 45–92.

Nejrotti, Marietta, 'Zanardelli Tito' in *Il movimento operaio italiano: Dizionario biografico, 1853–1943* edited by Andreucci and Detti (Rome: Editori Riuniti, 1975–1979), pp. 271–2.

Nejrotti, Marietta, 'La stampa operaia e socialista 1848–1914' in *Storia del movimento operaio e del socialismo e delle lotte sociali in Piemonte*, edited by Aldo Agosti and Gian Mario Bravo (Bari: De Donato, 1979), pp. 375–445.

Nettlau, Max, 'Ein verschollener Nachklang der Internationale: The International Labour Union (London 1877–1878)' in *Archiv für die Geschite des Sozialismus und der Arbeiter bewagung Neunter Jaughang*, edited by Carl Grünberg (1921).

Nettlau, Max, *Errico Malatesta, vita e pensieri* (New York: Casa editrice Il Martello, 1922).

Nettlau, Max, *Bakunin e l'Internazionale in Italia, dal 1864 al 1872* (Geneva: Edizioni de 'Il Risveglio', 1928).

Nettlau, Max, *Saverio Merlino* (Montevideo: Edizioni Studi Sociali, 1948).

Nettlau, Max, *La Première Internationale en Espagne (1868–1888)* (Dordrecht: D. Reide, 1969).

Nettlau, Max, *Die erste Blütezeit der Anarchie, 1886–1894*, Geschichte der Anarchie/Max Nettlau (Vaduz: Topos, 1981).

Nicoll, David, *The Walsall Anarchists. Trapped by the police. Innocent men in penal servitude, etc.* (London, 1895).

Oliver, Hermia, *The International Anarchist Movement in Late Victorian London* (London: Croom Helm, 1983).

Ortalli, Massimo, *Gaetano Bresci. Tessitore, Anarchico e uccisore di re* (Rome: Nova Delphi, 2011).

Ovida, 'The legislation of fear' in *Fortnightly Review*, vol. 56 (1894), pp. 552–61.

Parmeggiani Luigi, *Ricordi e Riflessioni* (Paris: 1914).

Paulucci Di Calboli, Raniero Marquis, *I girovaghi italiani in Inghilterra ed i suonatori ambulanti, etc.* (Città di Castello, 1893).

Pernicone, Nunzio, *Italian anarchism, 1864–1892* (Princeton, N.J.; Chichester: Princeton University Press, 1993).

Pernicone, Nunzio, *Carlo Tresca: Portrait of a Rebel* (Basingstoke: Palgrave Macmillan, 2005).

Porter, Bernard, *The Refugee Question in Mid-Victorian Politics* (Cambridge: Cambridge University Press, 1979).

Porter, Bernard, 'The Freiheit Prosecutions, 1881–1882' in *The Historical Journal*, vol. 23, no. 4 (1980), pp. 833–56.

Porter, Bernard, *The Origins of the Vigilant State: the London Metropolitan Police Special Branch before the First World War* (London: Weidenfeld and Nicolson, 1987).

Prato, Giuseppe, 'Gli italiani in Inghilterra' in *La Riforma Sociale*, vol. 7, no. 10 (1899).

Quail, John, *The Slow Burning Fuse* (London: Paladin, 1978).

Radnoti, Sandor, *The fake: forgery and its place in art* (Lanham; Oxford: Rowman & Littlefield Publishers, 1999).

Ridolfi, Maurizio, *Il circolo virtuoso sociabilità democratica, associazionismo e rappresentanza politica nell'Ottocento* (Florence: Centro editoriale toscano, 1990).

Rinaldo, Fanesi Pietro, 'Le vie dell'esilio. Emigranti marchigiani tra discriminazione e disagio sociale dalla fine dell'Ottocento al 1939' in *Le Marche Fuori dalle Marche* (Ancina: Sori Ercole, 1998), pp. 476–506.

Robb, George, *British Culture and the First World War* (Basingstoke: Palgrave, 2002).

Rocker, Fermin, *East End Years. A Stepney Childhood* (London: Freedom Press, 1998).

Rocker, Rudolf, *En la burrasca* (Buenos Aires: Editorial Tupac, 1949).

Rocker, Rudolf, *The London Years* (Edinburgh: AK Press, 2005).

Rocker, Rudolf, *Sindrome da filo spinato. Rapporto di un tedesco internato a Londra (1914–1918)*, edited by Pietro Di Paola (Caserta: Spartaco, 2006).

Rodrigues, Edgar, *Os anarquistas: trabalhadores italianos no Brasil*, 1st ed. (São Paulo, SP: Global Editora, 1984).

Rosselli, Nello, *Mazzini e Bakunin: dodici anni di movimento operaio in Italia, 1860–1872*, 4th ed. (Turin: Giulio Einaudi, 1973).

Ruff, Phil, *Pētera Māldera laiks un dzīve (The Life and Times of Peter the Painter)* (Riga: Dienas Gramata, 2012).

Ruggeri, Stefania, 'L'emigrazione politica attraverso le carte della polizia internazionale conservate presso l'Archivio Storico Diplomatico del Ministero degli Affari Esteri' in *Varese: emigrazione e territorio: tra bisogno e ideale. Convegno internazionale. Varese 18–20 maggio 1994*, edited by Carlo Brusa and Robertino Ghiringhelli (Varese: Edizioni Latina, 1994).

Rumbelow, Donald, *The Houndsditch murders and the siege of Sidney Street* (Stroud: History, 2009).

Sacchetti, Giorgio, 'Controllo sociale e domicilio coatto nell'Italia crispina' in *Rivista storica dell'anarchismo*, vol. 3, no. 1 (1996), pp. 93–104.

Sanborn, Alvan Francis, illustrated by Vaughan Trowbridge, *Paris and the social revolution, a study of the revolutionary elements in the various classes of Parisian society* (Boston: Small Maynard and Co., 1905).

Santarelli, Enzo, *Il socialismo anarchico in Italia* (Milan: Feltrinelli Editore, 1973).

Saville, John, '1848 – Britain and Europe' in *Exile from European Revolutions. Refugees in Mid-Victorian England*, edited by Sabine Freitag (New York; Oxford: Berghn Books, 2003), pp. 19–31.

Senese, Donald J., *S.M. Stepniak-Kravchinskii, the London Years* (Newtonville, MA: Oriental Research Partners, 1987).

Sernicoli, Ettore, *L'Anarchia e gli Anarchici, etc. (Gli attentati contro Sovrani, Principi ... Note cronologiche, etc.)* (Milan, 1894).

Shipley, S., *Club Life and Socialism in Mid Victorian London* (London: Journeyman/London Workshop Centre, 1983).

Shpayer-Makov, Haia, 'A Traitor to His Class: the Anarchist in British Fiction' in *European Studies*, vol. 26, no. 3 (1996), pp. 229–325.

Shpayer-Makov, Haia, *The ascent of the detective: police sleuths in Victorian and Edwardian England* (Oxford: Oxford University Press, 2011).

Sinicco, Giuseppe, *Memorie di un calzolaio da Borgognano a Londra* (Udine: Tipografia Pellegrini, 1950).

Smith, Adolphe, 'Political Refugees' in Sir Besant, Walter, *London in the Nineteenth Century* (London: Adam & Charles Black, 1909), pp. 399–406.

Sponza, Lucio, *Italian Immigrants in Nineteenth-century Britain: Realities and Images* (Leicester: Leicester University Press, 1988).

Sponza, Lucio, *Divided Loyalties: Italians in Britain During the Second World War* (Bern; New York: P. Lang, 2000).

Sweeney, John, *At Scotland Yard* (London: Grant Richards, 1904).

Toda, Misato, *Errico Malatesta da Mazzini a Bakunin: la sua formazione giovanile nell'ambiente napoletano (1868-1873)* (Naples: Guida, 1988).

Tolstoi, Leone, *Per l'Uccisione di Re Umberto* (Chieti: Centro Stud Libertari Camillo Di Sciullo, 2003).

Trautmann, Frederic, *The voice of terror: a biography of Johann Most* (Westport, CT; London: Greenwood Press, 1980).

Turcato, Davide, 'Italian Anarchism as a Transnational Movement 1885–1915' in *International Review of Social History*, vol. 52 (2005), pp. 407–44.

Turcato, Davide, *Making Sense of Anarchism. Errico Malatesta's Experiments with Revolution, 1889–1900* (London: Palgrave Macmillan, 2012).

Twattle-Basket, Todeas pseud. Tommaso De Angelis, *Note di Cronaca, ossia i giornali, gli istituti e gli uomini illustri italiani a Londra durante l'era Vittoriana (1837–1897)* (Bergamo: Fratelli Bolis, 1897).

Valiani, Leo, 'Dalla Prima alla Seconda Internazionale (1872–1889)' in *Movimento Operaio*, vol. 6, no. 2 (1954), pp. 177–247.

Van der Mark, Peter, 'Revolutie and Reactie' (Ph.D. thesis, Rijksuniversiteit Groningen, 1997).

Venturi, Franco, 'L'Italia fuori d'Italia' in *Storia d' Italia. Dal primo settecento all'Unità* (Turin: Einaudi, 1973).

Verdecchia, Enrico, 'Tedeschi e italiani: rapporti e contrasti in due comunità nell'esilio londinese' in *Bollettino della Domus Mazziniana*, no. 2 (1996), pp. 177–89.

Verdecchia, Enrico, *Londra dei cospiratori* (Milan: Tropea, 2010).

Vincent, K. Steven, *Between Marxism and Anarchism: Benoit Malon and French Reformist Socialism* (Berkeley; Oxford: University of California Press, 1992).

Vuilleumier, Marc, 'Paul Brousse et son passage de l'anarchisme au socialisme' in *Cahiers Vilfredo Pareto*, vol. 3, nos 7/8 (1965).

Walkowitz, Judith R., *Nights out: life in cosmopolitan London* (New Haven, CT; London: Yale University Press, 2012).

White, Arnold, *The destitute alien in Great Britain* [S.l.] (London: Swan Sonnenschein and Co., 1892).

Wilkins, W. H., 'The Italian Factor' in *The Destitute Alien in Great Britain*, edited by Arnold White (London: Swan Sonnenschein and Co., 1892), pp. 146–67.

Woodcock, George and Avakumovic, Ivan, *The Anarchist Prince. A biographical Study of Peter Kropotkin* (New York: Schocken, 1971).

Worrall, David, *Radical Culture: Discourse, Resistance and Surveillance, 1790–1820* (New York; London: Harvester Wheatsheaf, 1992).

Zanardelli, Tito, *Della utilità e dello scopo di un Circolo italiano di Studj Sociali a Londra* (London: Biblioteca del circolo di studi sociali, 1879).

Index